# First and Second Language Phonology

# First and Second Language Phonology

*Edited by:*
**Mehmet Yavaş**

**SINGULAR PUBLISHING GROUP, INC.**
San Diego, California

**Singular Publishing Group, Inc.**
4284 41st Street
San Diego, California 92105-1197

**©1994 by Singular Publishing Group, Inc.**

Typeset in 10/12 Stempel Schneidler by So Cal Graphics
Printed in the United States of America by McNaughton & Gunn

**Library of Congress Cataloging-in-Publication Data**
First and second language phonology / editor, Mehmet Yavaş.
     p.    cm.
  Includes bibliographical references and index.
  ISBN 1-56593-167-X
  1. Language acquisition.  2. Grammar, Comparative and general—
Phonology.  3. Interlanguage (Language learning)  4. Second language
acquisition.   I. Yavaş, Mehmet S.
  P118.F545   1993
  401'.93—dc20
                                                 93-26874
                                                    CIP

# Contents

# List of Contributors

**Barbara Bernhardt, Ph.D.**
School of Audiology and Speech
  Sciences
University of British Columbia
Vancouver, B.C., Canada

**Robert S. Carlisle, Ph.D.**
Department of English
California State University,
  Bakersfield
Bakersfield, California

**Stephen B. Chin, Ph.D.**
Department of Psychology
Indiana University
Bloomington, Indiana

**Shula Chiat, Ph.D.**
Department of Clinical
  Communication Studies
City University
London, England

**Daniel A. Dinnsen, Ph.D.**
Department of Linguistics
Indiana University
Bloomington, Indiana

**Fred R. Eckman, Ph.D.**
University of Wisconsin—
  Milwaukee
Milwaukee, Wisconsin

**Gregory K. Iverson, Ph.D.**
University of Wisconsin—
  Milwaukee
Milwaukee, Wisconsin

**Roy C. Major, Ph.D.**
Department of English
Arizona State University
Tempe, Arizona

**Lorraine McCune, Ph.D.**
Department of Educational
  Psychology
Rutgers University
New Brunswick, New Jersey

**Lise Menn, Ph.D.**
Department of Linguistics
University of Colorado
Boulder, Colorado

**D. Kimbrough Oller, Ph.D.**
Departments of Psychology,
  Pediatrics, and
  Otolaryngology
University of Miami
Miami, Florida

**Mark S. Patkowski, Ph.D.**
Brooklyn College
City University of New York

**David Snow, Ph.D.**
Child Language Laboratory
University of Arizona
Tucson, Arizona

**Michele L. Steffens, M.S.**
Department of Psychology
University of Miami
Miami, Florida

**Joseph Paul Stemberger, Ph.D.**
Department of Communicative
    Disorders
University of Minnesota
Minneapolis, Minnesota

**Carol Stoel-Gammon, Ph.D.**
Department of Speech and
    Hearing Sciences
University of Washington
Seattle, Washington

**Shelley L. Velleman, Ph.D.**
Bay State Medical Center
Springfield, Massachusetts

**Marilyn May Vihman, Ph.D.**
Department of Special
    Education

Southeastern Louisiana
    University
Hammond, Louisiana

**Steven H. Weinberger, Ph.D.**
Department of English
George Mason University
Fairfax, Virginia

**Henning Wode, Ph.D.**
English Department
University of Kiel
Kiel, Germany

**Mehmet Yavaş, Ph.D.**
Department of English
Florida International
    University
Miami, Florida

# Preface

In phonology courses, students from linguistics, applied linguistics, education, and communication disorders frequently inquire about a good reader on first and second language phonology. Early on students seem to discover the relevance of phonological acquisition to discussions in phonology and look for a more elaborate, detailed examination of issues in the acquisition of first language (normal and disordered), and second language that goes beyond a few references in their phonology texts. This book hopes to respond to this need by bringing workers in first and second language phonology together to present current thinking on various aspects of phonological acquisition. By dealing with a wide range of issues in different populations, it is hoped that this volume will help lead the students of the disciplines mentioned above to a fuller understanding of phonological acquisition.

Needless to say, a volume such as this cannot cover all the relevant issues in the entire field of phonological acquisition. I am aware of the omission of a number of topics which might have been included. Yet, their inclusion would have made this project a much bigger one than I originally planned.

The reader will notice also that there are several unresolved issues in phonological acquisition requiring further investigation. Consequently, we have more questions than answers on several issues where our understanding is limited. Opinions expressed in this volume are not attempts to give definitive answers to the questions posed, but rather should be treated as ideas to stimulate further discussion.

# Acknowledgments

I would like to express my gratitude to the authors who participated in this project. Their enthusiastic response with original contributions made it possible for me to set the goals of this volume. I am deeply grateful for their cooperation.

# Introduction

Historically, there has been very little contact between the phonologists and the researchers of first language (L1) phonology and those of second language (L2) phonology. One of the main reasons for this stems from the view that L1 phonology is a legitimate area of inquiry with implications and insights for phonological theory, whereas L2 phonology has not had the same status. Interlanguage phonology has been trivialized and considered of little interest or importance, because the difficulties encountered by L2 learners were thought to be due to native language interference and that contrastive analysis could account for them. As such, interlanguage phonology has had no relevance to theory, nor anything to offer to L1 phonology. Moreover, the reluctance of L1 researchers and theorists to look at L2 phonology has been partly due to the belief that the concerns of the latter were basically pedagogical, directed toward classroom practice.

These attitudes have resulted in a closer relationship and greater mutual exchange between phonological theory and L1 phonology than between phonological theory and L2 phonology. Theoretical models have been utilized more frequently in studies of phonologies of L1 than L2. Likewise, theories have paid more attention to the phonology of L1 than L2.

The recognition of L2 phonology as relevant to phonological acquisition and phonological theory recently has found more enthusiasts. This change of attitude has occurred because we have developed a different view concerning the nature of the learner's language and the role of contrastive analysis. Although contrastive analysis is still regarded as rather successful in accounting for several aspects of L2 phonology (especially in the early stages of development), during the last two decades, it has become apparent, that many learner errors cannot be explained with reference to the learner's native language. Studies of several aspects of interlanguage phonologies have revealed universal tendencies (Anderson, 1987; Benson, 1988; Broselow & Finer, 1991; Carlisle, 1988; Eckman, 1981, 1985, 1987, 1991; Hodne, 1985; Tropf, 1987). Thus, it has become apparent that studies of L2 phonology, like studies on L1 phonology, can make contributions to the study of universals.

Once the importance of L2 phonology to phonological acquisition is recognized, very little effort is needed to convince anyone that L1 and L2 phonologies have a lot to offer to one another; hence, students of the two areas need to pay close attention to each other's work. The goal of this book is to bring workers in the areas of L1 and L2 phonology together to represent current thinking on several aspects of L1 and L2 phonology. The intention in doing so is to demonstrate that each field can benefit from the other, as findings in each contribute to our understanding of the constraints involved in phonological acquisition.

Of course, L2 learners, unlike first language acquirers, are confronted with the interaction of two (or more) systems; and consequently, some of their difficulties are due to their native languages. But even then, the acquisition of L2 is significant because it can give us insights into the native language and, as such, might be very important for the theory. For example, as Broselow (1988) showed, errors stemming from L1 interference can lead us to a certain analysis of L1 which is otherwise not available. Vogel (1991) illustrated that L1 transferred phonological behavior in L2 could "answer questions as to what the domain of application of a particular phonological rule is and how to define a given prosodic constituent when the crucial information is absent in L1" (p. 63). Thus, besides providing valid data in the study of universals, L2 phonology also can offer crucial information to phonology in elucidating the analysis of L1.

The areas of first and second language phonology, together with phonology of language change, loan phonology, and sociophonological variation, constitute important testing grounds for theoretical positions. In other words, it is not just that these fields should follow and utilize advances in theory, but that theory should be tested against the data in these applied areas. In reality, however, the relationship has almost always worked in such a way that applied fields paid much more attention to theory than vice versa.

The field of phonology has changed significantly during the last two decades. Post SPE (*The Sound Pattern of English*, Chomsky and Halle, 1968) tendencies in phonology have included a greater role and better treatment for syllable, stress, and many other prosodic phenomena. These have been dealt with in a much more principled way by metrical, autosegmental, and lexical phonological models. These advances have not just been accepted at the theoretical research level but have been made accessible through basic introductory books such as Durand (1990), Giegerich (1992), Goldsmith (1990), Hogg and McCully (1987), Katamba (1989), Kaye (1989), Nespor and Vogel (1986), along with somewhat more advanced but quite comprehensive texts (Goldsmith, 1990; Nespor & Vogel 1986). Consequently, many students of applied as well as theoretical linguistics have become familiar with these developments through their introductory courses in phonology, and studies utilizing newer frameworks in applied phonology have flourished. It should be pointed out, however, that the influence of advances in phonology has been reflected in a greater proportion in L1 phonology than L2 phonology. The chapters in this book also reveal this difference. This is due to the longer tradition of exchange between the theory and L1 studies mentioned earlier. The picture is changing, however (see the section on nonlinear phonology in Chapter 8), and the decade of the '90s promises greater utilization of recent developments in L2 phonology.

This book is divided into two parts. Part I examines several aspects of L1 phonology in relation to different levels of development (from babble to early word combinations). It will be obvious to the reader that there is considerable heterogeneity in these chapters in terms of emphases, implications, and conclusions. Menn's preface, Perspective on Research in First Language Developmental Phonology, is aimed at providing the necessary background to facilitate the interpretation of these divergent accounts and point out some other relevant issues. Although written for Part I, First Language Phonology, some of the points she raises are equally valid for the interpretation of the claims made in L2 phonologies.

The first two chapters deal with very early periods of development. In Chapter 1, Vihman, Velleman, and McCune, looking at the transition from babble to early words, examine the emergence of phonological systematicity and relate this phenomenon to other cognitive processes. They stress the importance of "referential" or "context-free use of words," as these imply a "categorical change" in the use of language and represent the moment where systematicity is attributable to the child's underlying form.

After discussing the notions of "mental representation" and "internal representation," the authors argue that both the psychological mental representation and the linguistic internal representation emerge at the same point in the child's cognitive development.

On the issues of the emergence of a phonological internal representation, Vihman et al. argue for the need of a hierarchical model of phonological structure that can adequately represent levels of word and syllable, and in their view, a connectionist model of cognitive functioning is the most viable option. To support their claims, Vihman et al. give a detailed analysis of development of two children. From the evidence they gather, the authors claim that the temporal correspondence between the onset of phonological systematicity and cognitive advances suggests that the emergence of phonological systematicity is rooted in a more general process of cognitive development.

In Chapter 2, Oller and Steffens focus on an earlier period, in phonological development, babbling, and propose that research on infant and young child speech has been hampered by the emphasis on the phonetic transcription of the specific segments of sounds rather than on the developmental stages of speech in the first year. They assert that the use of phonetic transcription to represent the vocalizations of infants is insufficient because this approach presupposes segmental specificity. The authors state that the infraphonology of the system during the first year reveals a unidimensional "syllabic layer" as opposed to a multi-tiered arrangement of syllable and segment. Although Oller and Steffens allow that a child may very well produce segmental vocalizations, they deny that the child has any command of a system with multiple layers because the small inventory of syllables means the system is simple, not complex. The authors point out that just because a child produces a "variety" of segments and syllables does not mean that the child uses this inventory of speech sound contrastively. They claim that there is growing evidence that no distinct segmental level of representation exists during the first year and the true appearance of segments does not occur before the second year.

The following two chapters deal with issues in developmentally higher stages of early words and early word combinations. Stoel-Gammon and Stemberger (Chapter 3) look at the question of whether there are any general biases across children in patterns of consonant harmony. The authors propose an account of this phenomenon based on the notion of phonological underspecification (Kiparsky, 1985) which suggests that it is easier to convert an unspecified segment to a specified one than the reverse because the latter would require the insertion of one feature and the deletion of another. They predict that the different characterizations of these changes will affect the types of harmony that occur in child speech and will determine what assimilates to what. The addition of a feature to an underspecified phoneme is a natural event, but the deletion of features is not a natural operation. The authors hypothesize that assimilation of specified segments to underspecified ones will be relatively uncommon (i.e., assimilatory processes will show a bias toward replacing underspecified elements with specified ones).

Their hypothesis found strong support on the basis of data from 51 children: Underspecified phonemes assimilate to specified phonemes, on the whole. The authors also consider their results in terms of three alternative explanations—order of acquisition, frequency, and regressive overgeneralization—and reiterate that none of these offer a principled account of consonant harmony like underspecification.

The development of phrase-final prosodic patterns in early child language is the topic of Snow and Stoel-Gammon's Chapter 4. The authors discuss two models of the relationship between intonation and timing. One of them, the Association model, claims that final lengthening is directly associated with changes in fundamental frequency, and thus, the speed at which fundamental frequency of the voice can change is limited. The association model implies that lengthening is a secondary automatic effect of intonation, which also means that final lengthening and intonation are acquired at the same time. Thus, lengthening is not learned, it is directly linked to intonation.

The other model, the Dissociation model, claims that final lengthening and intonation are acquired independently. The authors set out to find out which of these two models could account for the data from children, and examined the speech samples of three children. The results support the hypothesis that young children develop the skills that control intonation earlier than speech timing skills. The data also suggest that children acquire prosodic features first in the context of falling intonation contours and then in rising contours.

The remaining three chapters in Part I are devoted to disordered phonology. Two of these, Chiat and Dinnsen and Chin, deal with the phonology of early words in disordered populations.

In Chapter 5, Chiat addresses phonological impairment from the point of view of the psycholinguistic processing involved in speech production, exploring evidence for the point at which impairment occurs. Although studies done on children's phonological impairment through clinical observation have claimed that input is not the problem and that impairment is caused by output disorders, Chiat states that phonological impairment and delay are caused by disorders that occur somewhere from the input moment to the output processing. More specifically, the problem must be located in lexical retrieval and subsequent stages of output planning.

The author argues that the pattern of errors found in the production data of children with speech disorders also can play an important role in determining the level of processing that is impaired. An analysis of phonological impairment in terms of stages of processing has resulted in a proliferation of stages of output planning and a dispersion of problems across these stages. Chiat claims that, instead of positing problems across stages, there needs to be a model in which problems are interpreted within a single stage. This, she states, would lead to what she calls a "connectionist approach," which consists of nodes which are interconnected within a complex network, not by stages. The strength (i.e., the proximity and weight) of the connections will determine the relationships between different features and between different levels of information and be responsible for the child's phonological impairment.

The correctness of children's underlying forms in disordered phonologies is the topic of Dinnsen and Chin (Chapter 6). The authors note that clinical research and practice on children's phonological disorders have been dominated for years by "the relational perspective" which assumes that the child's underlying representations of words are correct and that a set of processes convert the underlying forms into the child's surface errors. On the other hand, "the Indiana perspective," advocated by Dinnsen and Chin, proposes an independent account and analyzes disordered systems independently of the target system. That is, the child's system is based on facts evident only in that child's speech, and abstractions that are allowed in the relational account are not permissible in the independent account. The resulting crucial question is the correctness of the child's underlying form, because incorrect underlying forms may be responsible for the disorder. Analyzing data from 40 phonologically disordered children independently of the target system, the authors found that a significant proportion of each child's phonology was constituted by "incorrect" underlying representation. Dinnsen and Chin introduce a measure (percent correct underlying representation) that quantitatively expresses the relative proportions of correct/incorrect underlying representation in any given child's system.

In the last chapter in Part I (Chapter 7), Bernhardt focuses on the contributions of recent developments, more specifically nonlinear phonological theories, in the field of phonological disorders. Previous treatments such as phonological processes and standard generative phonology consider syllable/word structure constraints linearly. Modern nonlinear theories have elements which are hierarchically organized and consist of sets of universal principles/conventions. The purpose of the chapter is to show how nonlinear models can predict the observations on syllable/word structure and its interaction with segments, by its emphasis on multi-tiered representation, and suggest directions for intervention based on the analyses. CV tier, onset-rhyme, and moraic models are considered for the analysis of disordered data.

The section on L2 opens with Wode's preface, First and Second Language Phonology: Looking Ahead. Touching on several issues such as speech perception and phonological processes that would enhance our understanding of L2 phonology, Wode stresses the need for a theory of developmental phonology.

The chapters in Part II represent a more homogeneous picture. Although Major presents a general overview and Patkowski offers an in-depth look at the critical age factor in L2 phonology, the majority of the chapters are concerned with the universal factors that have been found to influence the acquisition of interlanguage phonologies.

In, Chapter 8, Major looks at the literature on the development of L2 phonology. The themes that are covered include age, personality, transfer and contrastive analysis, phonological similarity, markedness, universal developmental factors, style, perception, production, underlying representation, attrition, and nonlinear phonology. Pointing out the evolution in interlanguage phonology studies where there is increasing concerns over universal factors rather than native language transfer, Major emphasizes the lack of bidirectionality of exchange between L2 phonology research and linguistic theory. In other words, whereas current interlanguage phonology studies employ linguistic theory, linguistics has been indifferent to L2 research. He ends the chapter with a plea for a change of this attitude.

The age factor in interlanguage learning is the topic of Patkowski's detailed account in Chapter 9. Reviewing the current literature on the subject, Patkowski concludes that the existence of a sensitive period for the acquisition of second language phonology is strongly supported and suggests that, rather than questioning the existence of the observed phenomenon, we should channel our efforts to explaining it. The chapter concludes with the implications of this phenomenon for language instruction in the classroom.

The common theme of the remaining four chapters in Part II relates to the importance of factors related to the markedness that are effective in shaping interlanguage phonology. Although these chapters have linguistically oriented goals, they certainly are not devoid of pedagogical concerns.

In Chapter 10 Carlisle's theme is the account of variability in interlanguage phonology via internal linguistic constraints, markedness, and environment. One of the well known findings of researchers in L2 phonology is that the learners' phonology is variable. In other words, the same structures can have different surface realizations. Most studies that have dealt with variability were concerned with external constraints such as style, the interpersonal relationship of the speaker and hearer, the length of residency in the L2 speech community, and the context of speech. Carlisle offers explanations for variability through markedness and environment to complete the picture. In doing so, he looks at studies dealing with universal preference for the CV syllable, the markedness of onsets and codas by length, marked onsets and codas of equal length, markedness distinctions between onsets and codas, and final obstruent devoicing. Finally, he examines the interaction between markedness relationships and environments and suggests that environment is a more powerful constraint than markedness. He stresses the need for more studies regarding interaction between markedness and environment in interlanguage phonology.

The following two chapters consider some of the issues mentioned by Carlisle in greater depth. Eckman and Iverson (Chapter 11) investigate the pronunciation difficulties of English as a second language (ESL) learners regarding the coda consonants in English. Their purpose is to demonstrate that theoretical approaches to second language acquisition which assign a significant role to universals in explaining L2 syntax can also be extended to the study of L2 phonology. The authors postulate that pronunciation difficulties of ESL learners can be explained not only in terms of the differences between L1 and L2, but also with respect to the general principles of markedness. Certain L2 syllable codas and their relative sonority-sensitivity are analyzed. The authors conclude that relatively marked coda obstruents of English are more troublesome for the subjects than the coda sonorants and that this was independent of the L1 structure. The authors offer the results of their study that analyzed single-segment codas in the interlanguage of six adult subjects (two speakers each of Korean, Cantonese, and Japanese) learning English which supported their hypothesis.

In Chapter 12 Yavaş takes up the question of final devoicing in interlanguages. Reviewing the studies done on devoicing of final stops (and in some cases obstruents in general) in L2 as well as L1 phonology, he emphasizes the universal aspects of the phenomenon. He attempts to show that certain phonetic environments are crucial for the relative ease/difficulty of the target final voiced stops and suggests that the discoveries of the parameters that are responsible for patterned behavior of the learners could be exploited in the pedagogical context. The chapter is concluded with thoughts on future research on the topic.

In Chapter 13, Weinberger's aim is to show that two independent types of linguistic knowledge (phonetic knowledge and functional knowledge) are involved in phonological development and that they interact in interesting ways and can explain the differences we find between first and second language learners.

Challenging the traditional account, which considers first language patterns as relevant to language universals, but reduces second language patterns to transfer, Weinberger shows that universal grammar is also available to second language learners. Examining syllable structure processes, the author notes different realizations for the same target by first and second language learners, namely, deletion and epenthesis, respectively. The tendency for epenthesis by adult second language learners is explained on the basis of the universally established recoverability principle, which is visible in languages in general. Weinberger proposes that the recoverability principle matures according to some pre-set schedule and is not available to children at early stages in phonological development. Thus, they choose deletion. Weinberger also explains certain behaviors in disordered language in terms of their phonetic knowledge and the principle of recoverability.

By dealing with several aspects of phonological acquisition in different populations, this book hopes to encourage L1 and L2 researchers to look more carefully at one another's work and derive implications for their respective fields. The main motivation for this should come from the fact that not only L1 phonology but also several aspects of L2 phonology are governed by universal principles. Consequently, the findings on either side could have important implications for the other. These are easily seen in several chapters on L2. Besides explicit comparisons and evaluations, such as the one given by Weinberger, other chapters— Carlisle, Yavaş, Eckman and Iverson—offer opportunities that can be carried over to the L1 context. Although not attempted, implications also can be derived in the other direction if we consider the findings of several chapters on L1 dealing with underspecification, nonlinear models for syllable and word structure, erroneous underlying forms, and so on.

It is my hope that this book will encourage further investigation and exchange in L1 and L2 phonologies and that they in turn, as a united front, will be used as evidence for distinguishing between phonological theories.

## REFERENCES

Anderson, J. (1987). The markedness differential hypothesis and syllable structure difficulty. In G. Ioup & S Weinberger (Eds.), *Interlanguage phonology: The acquisition of a second language sound system* (pp. 279–291). Cambridge, MA: Newbury House.

Benson, B. (1988). Universal preference for the open syllable as an independent process in interlanguage phonology. *Language Learning, 38*, 221–242.

Broselow, E. (1988). Metrical phonology and the acquisition of a second language. In S. Flynn & W. O'Neil (Eds.), *Linguistic theory in second language acquisition.* Dordrecht, The Netherlands: Kluwer.

Broselow, E., & Finer, D. (1991). Parameter setting in second language phonology and syntax. *Second Language Research, 7*, 35–59.

Carlisle, R. (1988). The effect of markedness on epenthesis in Spanish/English interlanguage phonology. *Issues and Developments in English and Applied Linguistics, 3*, 15–23.

Chomsky, N., & Halle, M. (1968). *The sound pattern of English.* New York: Harper & Row.

Durand, J. 1990) *Generative and nonlinear phonology.* London: Longman.

Eckman, F. R. (1981). On the naturalness of interlanguage phonological rules. *Language Learning, 31*, 195–216.

Eckman, F. R. (1985). Some theoretical and pedagogical implications of the markedness differential hypothesis. *Studies in Second Language Acquisition, 7*, 289–307.

Eckman, F. R. (1987). The reduction of word final consonant clusters in interlanguage. In A. James & J. Leather (Eds.), *Sound patterns in second language acquisition* (pp. 143–162). Dordrecht, The Netherlands: Foris.

Eckman, F. R. (1991). The structural conformity hypothesis and the acquisition of consonant clusters in the interlanguage of ESL learners. *Studies in Second Language Acquisition, 13*, 23–41.

Hodne, B. (1985). Yet another look at interlanguage phonology: The modification of English syllable structure by native speakers of Polish. *Language Learning, 35*, 404–422.

Hogg, R., & McCully, C. B. (1987). *Metrical phonology: A coursebook.* New York: Cambridge University Press.

Giegerich, H. (1992). *English phonology.* New York: Cambridge University Press.

Goldsmith, J. (1990). *Autosegmental and metrical phonology.* Cambridge, MA: Basil Blackwell.

Katamba, F. (1989). *An introduction to phonology.* London: Longman.

Kaye, J. (1989). *Phonology: A cognitive view.* Hillsdale, NJ: Lawrence Erlbaum.

Kiparsky, P. (1985). Some consequences of lexical phonology. *Phonology yearbook* (pp. 83–138). New York: Cambridge University Press.

Nespor, M., & Vogel, I. (1986). *Prosodic phonology.* Dordrecht, The Netherlands: Foris Publications.

Tropf, H. (1987). Sonority as a variability factor in second language phonology. In A. James & J. Leather (Eds.), *Sound patterns in second language acquisition* (pp. 173–191). Dordrecht, The Netherlands: Foris.

Vogel, I. (1991). Prosodic phonology: Second language acquisition data as evidence in theoretical phonology. In T. Huebner & C. Ferguson, (Eds.), *Crosscurrents in second language acquisition and linguistic theories* (pp. 47–65). Amsterdam: John Benjamins.

# PART I

*First Language Phonology*

# INTRODUCTION

## Perspective on Research in First Language Developmental Phonology

LISE MENN, Ph.D.

This introduction to the chapters on the acquisition of first language phonology attempts to provide background material for readers who are relatively new to this research area. Here are some things you might bear in mind as you begin to assimilate the rich body of information and insight contained in these chapters. My perspective is, of course, shaped by my own research experience, which is in normal phonological development rather than developmental disorders, and with case studies rather than group studies.

First, empirically based research claims are influenced by the personal experience of the authors. We put the most trust in what we have worked on directly: Paraphrasing a Japanese saying, the carrot-digger points the way with a carrot.[1] The chapters on first language (L1) are concerned with production or the relation of production to perception. In terms of

---

[1] A daikon, in the original, which is a well-known haiku by Basho. Thanks to Bill Bright for the source information and other editorial suggestions.

developmental level, they go from babble (Oller & Steffens) through the transition from babble to early words (Vihman, Velleman, & McCune), through early words (Dinnsen & Chin; Stoel-Gammon & Stemberger) and up to early word combinations (Snow & Stoel-Gammon). Two of the papers deal with the phonology of early words in language-delayed/disordered populations (Chiat, Dinnsen & Chin). In addition, Barnhardt offers a tutorial on recent developments in phonological theory. The reader, in deciding how to reconcile or contrast discrepant accounts, terminologies, or emphases, needs to take into account what each author's subject population and research methods have been: case study, small-group, or large-group; cross-sectional or longitudinal; instrumental or transcriptional.

One specific case in the present book is terminological: the meaning of the notion of "underlying form." Dinnsen and his co-authors have consistently used this term for what I used to call an output lexical entry; that is, the child's stored information about how a word is to be pronounced, which—as Chiat shows—may be quite a bit less accurate than the child's knowledge of what a word sounds like. More usual linguistic usage for the term "underlying form" involves recognition knowledge of input words in some way. In standard linguistic usage (and in "one-lexicon" models generally) the "underlying form" (that is, the phonological form of the mental lexical entry) is an abstract representation adequate for handling both recognition and production phenomena. Some developmentalists (myself included) depart from this standard usage in a different way: They claim that important distinctions need to be made between the representation used for recognition and the representation used for production. A strong form of this view is found in "two-lexicon" models. Since such models claim that no single representation is adequate, discussions in this framework must always specify whether the input/recognition lexical entry or the output/production lexical entry is being referred to. Therefore, they rarely use the phrase "underlying form," as it is ambiguous in the "two-lexicon" context.

A second key to understanding these chapters is this: The empirical research approach to an organism with largely unknown mechanisms—sometimes called a black box approach—is to observe the input and the output systematically, and then try to construct an account of what sort of mechanism could produce the observed effects. Typically, neither the input nor the output data are complete; furthermore, several different models of the hidden mechanism are equally compatible with the data that are available, each accounting for some areas more adequately than others.

A third key to understanding, related to both of the above, is to remember that we tend to build our theories on our clearest cases, because they are the ones from which we can make strong arguments.

Most children probably fit many theories or models; therefore, they don't do anything "worth writing about." Model building must, of course, be able to deal with the clear cases; yet a good model must also explain why the clear cases are rare. Hence, both case studies and group studies should be brought to bear on the evaluation of a model.[2]

A fourth key is to keep in mind that the history of developmental phonology of the second year of life is largely a dialectic between phonological theory and child language data. On the one hand, innovations in phonological theory have shaped our ideas of which phenomena are significant, and have provided us with basic analytical tools, such as the notions of "underlying form" and "phonological rule." On the other hand, we have uncovered many phenomena in L1 acquisition that are at best marginal in adult phonology—consonant harmony and the gap between input and output capabilities being two prime examples. As adult-based L1 phonology does not need to make any provision for the unskilled speaker, it is not surprising that we have needed to add or elaborate such constructs on our own. Second language (L2) phonological theory has developed more recently, and its history shows a similar pattern for the same reasons.

This dialectic continues with the successful adaptation of many aspects of newer formal mechanisms from phonological theory: autosegmental phonology, feature geometry, and metrical theory. Note that Barnhardt's tutorial introduction to these approaches as they are used for normal adult language stays within a linguistic framework. In particular, the "explanation" for a general characteristic or universal is that it is present in Universal Grammar (UG). The reader should note the contrast between this purely linguistic type of explanation and the type used in the psycholinguistic framework of Vihman et al.; the latter treats the general properties of children's language as consequences of the way in which processing and storage mechanisms work. The psycholinguistic approach feels more concrete and testable; however, until we have independent evidence as to the workings of psycholinguistic mechanisms, we cannot prove it to be superior. And indeed, uninterpreted models can also give testable and useful predictions.

I personally, however, am most comfortable with adaptations/applications of phonological theory that attempt or invite psycholinguistic interpretation of the theoretical notations, as in Stoel-Gammon and Stemberger's detailed application of underspecification theory to the well-known child phonology phenomenon of consonant harmony. Much progress, I think, will be made by taking the frameworks presented by

[2] Thanks to Carol Stoel-Gammon for bringing up the points in this paragraph.

Barnhardt and working out in detail how they may be able to organize particular phenomena of normal and disordered language acquisition. Autosegmental phonology has been applied in this way almost since its inception (e.g., Menn 1978, Spencer 1986); metrical phonology and feature geometry offer new invitations.

A preference for an interpreted or psycholinguistic approach to phonological development does not necessarily imply a preference for the "environmental" side of another dialectic in our field, namely the well-recognized tension between those who think that innate factors are more important/interesting and those who think environmental factors are of equal or greater importance. Many psycholinguists who emphasize innate factors (e.g., Locke, Kent; see their contributions to Ferguson, Menn, & Stoel-Gammon 1992) are thinking not of universal abstract linguistic parameters, but of anatomical constraints on articulators or of relatively peripheral neural control factors.

The recent history of normal L1 developmental phonology has two other Big Stories which are relatively mature: the nature of the (partial) loss of the ability to perceive phonetic contrasts which are not phonemic in the ambient language (treated elswhere; see papers in Ferguson et al. 1992 and deBoysson-Bardies, de Schonen, Jusczyk, MacNeilage, & Morton 1993), and the continuity of the transition from babble to speech, dealt with both in the cited references and in this book by Vihman and her co-workers, as well as by Snow and Stoel-Gammon.

Progress is also to be made by re-examining established findings and trying to elaborate the mechanisms that might underlie them. For example, given that mappings from adult model to child word are often— but not always—captured by writing rules, why should this be the case? Here, L1 developmental phonology has a new story, still in the promissory stage. This is the attempt to apply connectionist models of learning, extended to developmental disorders by Chiat's chapter. Such models look like they may be able to deal with recognized inadequacies in the "box-and-arrow" L1 developmental models of the last 15 years. Rules, as taken from phonological theory, have in fact proven inadequate to deal with apparent direct interactions among words and other "unruly" phenomena. Similarly, underlying forms, long taken to refer either to stable auditory representations or to stable articulatory representations, now seem to involve aspects of both the input and the output modality (see Chiat, Chapter 5; Menn & Matthei, 1992; Stemberger 1992).

Unfortunately, connectionist models require sophisticated computer implementation for testing, and this has been carried out only for limited cases (e.g., Lindblom 1992). In the meantime, for everyday descriptive purposes, we must rely on the more familiar notions, keeping their limitations in mind.

Rigorous testing of developmental models in L1 or L2 requires fine-grained data collection and microanalysis: Are changes smooth or saltatory, or sometimes one and sometimes the other? When there is regression, under what conditions does it occur? An interesting controversy appears to be shaping up. Its resolution will require a lot of data and probably some new theory. Oller and Steffens, working with instrumental analyses, have found considerable mutual interaction (coarticulation) between consonants and vowels in early speech, although their data do not support the stronger position taken by MacNeilage and Davis (1990). On the other hand, Macken (1992), working with transcribed data, has noted the relative independence of consonants and vowels, and thence the utility of the notion of "planar segregation," that is, the separate representation of consonants and vowels in underlying form. Reconciliation of these positions, although it may come partly in terms of differences due to the child's level of development, will require a model in which consonants and vowels can be both separate and interacting.

A final word, on a point made explicit by Oller and Steffens (see Chapter 2) but applicable everywhere: Just because an analyst makes use of a construct—segment, rule, feature, rime, or whatever—does not mean that a corresponding reality exists in the child. As literate adults, we hear—or at least think—in terms of features bundled into segments, but the validity of imputing segments to the child must be demonstrated. The most egregious examples of failing to distinguish between terms of analysis and the child's knowledge were probably in the early literature about child phonology rules. To avoid giving any names, I will take a hypothetical and simplified example. Suppose a child has learned to produce /s/ correctly as needed by the target word, but still uses stops to replace all affricates and fricatives other than [s] . There is no easy way to express the set of phones "all affricates and fricatives other than [s]" in most feature systems, so a long list of features and combinations of features is needed to describe this child's pattern—the reader may take a favorite system and work it out. Any formal rule for the pattern described thus appears to call for the child to "know" the features that distinguish /s/ from /f/, /ʃ/, /θ/, and all the other fricatives and affricates. But we have no evidence for anything of the kind. All we know is that she can recognize /s/ and produce it, and that she knows further that /s/ is different from the rest of the friction sounds. She may have no idea of the nature of this difference—that is, of the information expressed by such labels as "grooved," [+distributed], "interdental," "labiodental," [−anterior], [+strident], or "alveopalatal," even though some such terms will be needed to express formally the facts that /s/ is used correctly while /f/ is replaced by [p], /ʃ/ and /θ/ by [t], all of the voiced non-labial fricatives and affricates by /d/, and so on.

My parting advice to readers—and thanks to those who have felt like bearing with me so long!—is to consider these fine contributions in the light of all the resources you can bring to bear on them; work through them not just to see what they say, but to see why they say it, what else might be said, and where the story might go from here. Enjoy!

# REFERENCES

Boysson-Bardies, B. de, Vihman, M. M., Roug-Hellichius, L., Durand, C., Landberg, I., & Arao, F. (1992). Material evidence of infant selection from target language: A cross-linguistic phonetic study. In C. A. Ferguson, L. Menn, & C. Stoel-Gammon (Eds.), *Phonological development: Models, research, implications* (pp. 369–392). Timonium, MD: York Press.

de Boysson-Bardies, B., Scania de Schonen, S., Juszcyk, P., MacNeilage, P., & Morton, J. (Eds.). (1993). *Developmental neurocognition: Speech and face processing in the first year of life.* Dordrecht: Kluwer.

Ferguson, C. A., Menn, L., & Stoel-Gammon, C. (Eds.). (1992). *Phonological development: Models, research, implications* (pp. 249–269). Timonium, MD: York Press.

Lindblom, Björn. (1992). Phonological units as adaptive emergents of lexical development. In C. A. Ferguson, L. Menn, & C. Stoel-Gammon (Eds.), *Phonological development: Models, research, implications* (pp. 131–163). Timonium, MD: York Press.

Macken, M. A. (1992). Where's phonology? In C. A. Ferguson, L. Menn, & C. Stoel-Gammon (Eds.), *Phonological development: Models, research, implications.* (pp. 249–269). Timonium, MD: York Press.

MacNeilage, P. F., & Davis, B. (1990). Acquisition of speech production: Frames, then content. In M. Jeannerod (Ed.), *Attention and performance XIII.* Hillsdale, NJ: Lawrence Erlbaum.

Menn, L. (1978). Phonological units in beginning speech. In A. Bell & J. B. Hooper, (Eds.), *Syllables & segments* (pp. 157–172). Amsterdam: North Holland.

Menn, L., & Matthei, E. (1992). The "two-lexicon" model of child phonology: Looking back, looking ahead. In C. A. Ferguson, L. Menn, & C. Stoel-Gammon (Eds.), *Phonological development: Models, research, implications* (pp. 211–247). Timonium, MD: York Press.

Spencer, A. (1986). Towards a theory of phonological development. *Lingua, 68,* 3–38.

Stemberger, J. P. (1992). A connectionist view of child phonology: Phonological processes without phonological processing. In C. A. Ferguson, L. Menn, & C. Stoel-Gammon (Eds.), *Phonological development: Models, research, implications* (pp. 165–189). Timonium, MD: York Press.

# CHAPTER     1

*How Abstract is Child Phonology? Toward an Integration of Linguistic and Psychological Approaches*

MARILYN MAY VIHMAN, PH.D., SHELLEY L. VELLEMAN, PH.D., AND LORRAINE McCUNE, PH.D.

Our goal in this paper is to explore the emergence of phonological systematicity within a psychological framework. We begin by reviewing earlier work which traces the initial phonological system back to its origins in babble and proposes a model of the interaction of perception and production in emergent vocal organization. Our account of the origins of system attempts to suggest answers to the question: How can an initial system be constructed? That is, how does the child move from the production of unrelated vocal forms (sometimes known as item-based phonology; see Menn, 1983; Waterson, 1971) to an idiosyncratic holistic system (word-based phonology; see Ferguson & Farwell, 1975)? We will consider a number of issues concerning representation, focusing on these questions: Can the categorical change in language use, from contextually embedded word production to symbolic reference, be related to some underlying qualitative change in mental representation? How does the linguistic notion of internal representation relate to the psychological notion of mental representation? Finally, we explore the issues that arise in attempting to model the onset of phonological systematicity, such as: When are we justified in imputing a phonological internal representation to the child? That is, what is the evidence from the child's observable behavior (word production shapes) that a formal system of interrelated representations has begun to cohere? How much structure should be specified in such internal representations? Or what counts as sufficient evidence for positing contrasting levels or units in the child's emerging system? And what is the status of extra-systemic elements, either in the early period, when a small repertoire of vocal production patterns are used in response to specific familiar eliciting situations, or in the later period, when a phonological system appears to underlie the child's productions?

To develop a sufficiently general basis for examining these issues we present microanalyses of the early phonological development of two children who differ in overall strategy as well as in units of organization and in the articulatory basis for their first word productions. This allows us to illustrate some of the ways in which individual children follow distinct paths in phonological and lexical development, and also to place linguistic advances within a larger psychological framework.

## ORIGINS OF SYSTEM

The first adult-like syllable production (canonical or reduplicative babbling) emerges in normal infants within a narrow temporal frame (6–10 months) and evinces strong neuromotor constraints. A small consonantal repertoire usually is reported, reflecting simple ballistic movements (stops and nasals account for most true-consonant-like productions); the syllable nucleus is restricted largely to low- to mid-central or front vowels, resulting from relatively wide jaw opening with neutral tongue placement (Davis & MacNeilage, 1990; Kent, 1992; MacNeilage & Davis, 1990). By 10 months individual differences in production are apparent as infants explore their vocal resources, developing "vocal motor schemes" (McCune & Vihman, 1987), or preferred production patterns, which reflect both sensitivity to adult language phonetic tendencies and emergent vocal control.

As the child develops articulatory control and familiarity, through self-monitoring, with the sound as well as the feel of well-practiced phonetic gestures, some routinely used sound patterns of the adult language become perceptually salient through their resemblance to the child's own often repeated vocal motor schemes. When the child reproduces such vocal patterns in situationally appropriate contexts, caretakers may identify them as first words. We interpret such early words as the products of a tight developmental interaction. They reflect an interindividual construction process based on the child's evolving vocal capacities and parental attunement to child vocal production and to the focus of child attention. The child's vocal capacities themselves globally echo dominant patterns of the ambient language and, in turn, serve as a filter for the child's more detailed (production-driven) auditory processing of that language.

Figure 1–1 (adapted from Vihman, 1993a) displays the model of the interaction between perception and production which we assume gives rise to the first phonological system. A certain number of adult words are made salient by virtue of prosodic heightening (the combination of pitch change, increased amplitude, and increased duration which enters into word or phrasal accenting in most languages and is usually emphasized further in caretaker talk; see Ferguson, 1964; Fernald, 1984, 1991; Garnica, 1977), frequent occurrence in isolation or in sentence-final position (Aslin, 1993; Goldfield, 1993), and the inherent interest of the situation of use to a particular child (Lewis, 1936; Ferguson, 1978). These words are taken to provide the child, over the first several months of life, with an aural impression of ambient speech patterns.

Attention to the sound patterns made prominent by these three factors can be assumed to play an important role in channeling the child's prelinguistic vocalizations toward the phonetic characteristics of the ambient language; these salient words and phrases must make up the global auditory impression which is reflected in the babbling of infants on the threshold of speech (Boysson-Bardies, Hallé, Sagart, & Durand, 1989; Boysson-Bardies & Vihman, 1991). Visual effects also play a role in shaping the child's prelinguistic vocalizations. For example, the visual image of jaw opening and closing is a likely component in the sudden emergence of the first canonical syllable production, which is sometimes observed to occur silently before it is accompanied by vocalization (Roug, Landberg, & Lundberg, 1989). Similarly, the characteristic facial set of adult caretakers could explain early ambient language effects on the use of vowel space (Boysson-Bardies et al., 1989).[1] Finally, the predominance of labials in the early words of sighted children (Locke, 1983; Vihman, Macken, Miller, Simmons, & Miller, 1985), especially the hearing-impaired (Stoel-Gammon & Otomo, 1986) but apparently not

---

[1] For a discussion of "why faces are special to infants," and a possible connection between early enactive imitation and social identity, see Meltzoff and Moore (1993).

the blind (Mulford, 1988), may be ascribed to the facilitative effect of the visual cue afforded by lip closure.[2]

These global ambient language influences on babbling are expressed in Figure 1–1 by the dotted line linking auditory and visual effects and vocal exploration; the interaction of the two may be taken to guide the construction of individual vocal motor schemes, consistent "motor acts performed intentionally and . . . capable of variation and combination to form larger units" which evolve in the course of babbling (McCune & Vihman, 1987, p. 72). The vocal motor schemes are different for each child, regardless of ambient language, but nevertheless are shaped by that language.

The placement of a "perceptuo-motor link" at the center of Figure 1–1 expresses the view that many of the characteristics of the child's earliest words which have been established over the past two decades—their relative accuracy along with their apparent "selectivity" with regard to adult models (Ferguson & Farwell, 1975), their lack of interrelationship or "piecemeal" quality (Macken & Ferguson, 1983)—are most readily understood if we assume that once a child has begun to repeat a few vocal patterns with some regularity or apparently at will, that is, once some vocal motor schemes have developed, these patterns add to the salience of certain adult words that are, besides, prosodically highlighted, frequent, and inherently interesting to the child.

More specifically, adult words that (more or less) match some pattern which the child has come to produce with facility eventually will be attempted by the child, in appropriate (remembered) context. This can be taken to be the characteristic route by which the first words are uttered by children and identified by caretakers, often before the child has progressed cognitively to the point of making adult-like general or symbolic reference to classes of objects and events (Bates, Benigni, Bretherton, Camaioni, & Volterra, 1979; Vihman & McCune, in press). That is, when a familiar situation arises in which a particular word or phrase—*allgone, byebye, duckie, no*—tends to be repeatedly expressed by adults, if one of those words also happens to be "close enough" to a vocal pattern the child has come to know through self-monitoring and can now make at will, the child is likely to be "reminded" of that matching pattern (Rovee-Collier, Sullivan, Enright, Lucas, & Fagen, 1980), resulting in what adults identify as first (context-limited) word production.

The arrow at the bottom of Figure 1–1 represents the route from phonetically salient adult words, in combination with the development of one or more vocal motor schemes, to word production patterns, or production formulae that allow the child to make rapid lexical progress by simplifying the number of options available when a word is uttered

---

[2] Labials were nearly 10% more common in early words than in contemporaneous babble in the four languages investigated by Boysson-Bardies and Vihman (1991).

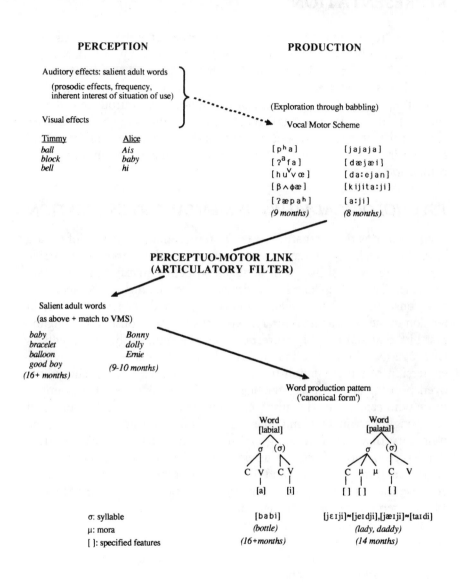

**Figure 1–1.** Model of the interaction of perception and production.

(Kiparsky & Menn, 1977; Menn, 1983). It is this last step with which we will primarily be concerned here, a step that constitutes the bridge from phonetics into phonology.

# REPRESENTATION

The term "representation" is widely and somewhat ambiguously used in scientific fields, including linguistics and psychology. To clarify the issues raised in this chapter, in which the term "representation," is applied in several senses, we first will address controversy regarding mental representation in the field of psychology and introduce evidence for relations between mental representation and language. We then consider the systematically ambiguous meaning of "internal representation," as used in the field of linguistics, to prevent misunderstanding of the comparable usage here.

## *PSYCHOLOGICAL VIEWS OF MENTAL REPRESENTATION*

Two basic positions regarding mental representation in the infant are current in psychology today: (1) It is present from birth and demonstrable early in life, with subsequent changes reflecting maturation of innate capacities (Leslie, 1987); and (2) it develops over the first two years of life as a consequence of the organization of motor and behavioral actions in relation to the developing central nervous system, with onset following the first birthday and roughly corresponding to significant developments in language (McCune-Nicolich, 1981b). Investigations of the behavioral expression of representation from these disparate viewpoints show little overlap in the tasks used or the ages of the subjects tested. For example, those who espouse the innatist view study infants in the early months of life, using differential looking time or the infant's tendency to continue the trajectory of visual following when an object disappears from view (Baillargeon, 1987). Studies deriving from the developmental position begin after 6 months of age and utilize motor responses to phenomena of absence, such as object search (Ramsay & Campos, 1978; Uzgiris & Hunt, 1975) or representational play (McCune, 1993; Nicolich, 1977).

Sartre's (1966) contrast of perceptual versus "imaginal" or representational experience suggested that the early phenomena are best understood as PERCEPTUAL PROCESSING OF PRESENT REALITY, which may include memory of the immediate past and expectancy regarding the immediate future. According to Sartre, perceptual processing draws continually from the sensory present, in which the contents of consciousness can be specified in relation to phenomena observable in the environment. In contrast, imaginal (or mental) representation may use a perceived event as a starting point (e.g., a portrait of a friend), but the resulting experience is an instance of "pure consciousness," an internal contentful state that is not directed at perceived reality.

If we take perceptual processing to be infants' original tendency, the developmental course of the ability to relate the present to the absent and the past to the present provides an index to the emergence of a capacity for mental representation. Memory research spanning the age range of 8 weeks to 6 months by Rovee-Collier and her colleagues (e.g., Rovee-Collier et al., 1980) have provided the strongest indicator of both the strengths and the limitations of infants' capacity to retrieve past experience. In these studies, infants learn to set a mobile in motion by kicking the leg attached to the mobile by a ribbon. After several training sessions it is possible to test both immediate and long-term retention (up to weeks and months). The results clearly indicate that even 8-week-olds are capable of "retention." However, the degree of dependence of this effect on exact replication of the training context, the limitations on the length of the retention period, and the relative power of cuing to "reinstate" the memories each show strong developmental trends. Furthermore, the behavioral expression of memory in this task is itself a motor response (foot kick) that occurs in the context of perceptual recognition. These studies demonstrate the strengths of perceptual motor processes for learning and memory. The fact that at 6 months of age infants succeed at this paradigm but fail to search for and retrieve small hidden objects suggests that a qualitatively different type of processing may characterize memory that depends upon contextual reinstatement (here termed PERCEPTUALLY DEPENDENT MEMORY) as opposed to memory that is able to function in the presence of confusing contextual cues (here termed mental representation). We use the term *mental representation* to refer to a contentful mental state distinguished from perception by its capacity to reference absent and past realities.

## MENTAL REPRESENTATION AND LANGUAGE

Piaget (1962) suggested that the infant's ability to retrieve an object placed in the experimenter's hand or a container and then released beneath a cloth outside the infant's view indicates an initial capacity for mental representation (Stage 6 of Object Permanence). Given the nature of language as "symbolic" or "representational," it was at first assumed that development in understanding of object permanence would correlate with language development. In fact, children in the early stages of language acquisition are capable of solving the Stage 6 task. However, the number of object permanence test items passed in Stage 6 shows no continued correlation with advances in language (Bates et al., 1979; McCune-Nicolich, 1981). The lack of correlation can be attributed to the fact that entry into Stage 6 constitutes a culminating milestone in the concept of object permanence but marks only the onset of language use.

Representational play, which begins only toward the end of the sensorimotor period, does show reliable relationships with later language milestones (Bates et al., 1979; McCune, 1993; McCune-Nicolich & Bruskin, 1981). The transition to representational play, in which the child first demonstrates knowledge of the function of small replicas (toy cups and saucers, tiny cars and trucks) and later indicates awareness of the "pretend" nature of such acts by vocal elaborations and coy smiles, corresponds to the production of early nonreferential (CONTEXT-LIMITED) words in precocious talkers, whereas REFERENTIAL words are likely to be noted at the transition to play in which two or more acts are combined. We interpret the temporal correspondence between this combinatorial play and referential language use as following from the more differentiated character of mental representation, which allows an event to be portrayed with a variety of gestures and objects and vocal forms to be produced outside of their original context in relation to a variety of new situations. For example, *doggie*, learned with reference to the family pet, is now produced in relation to the neighbor's dog and to pictures of dogs as well. It should be noted that close play-language "correspondences" characterize early talkers, whereas studies have indicated that later talkers may show the play milestone well before the corresponding language is observed. McCune (1992) demonstrated that lack of available vocal motor schemes accounted for the time lags between representational and language milestones for some subjects.

## INTERNAL REPRESENTATION IN PHONOLOGY

In child phonology the term *internal representation* is intended to characterize underlying aspects of the child's understanding and production of speech. Diagrammatic descriptive models typically are used to characterize the structure imputed to the child's system. The child's internal representation and the linguist's description thereof are sometimes assumed to be isomorphic. When the linguist claims psychological reality for internal representation, that reality can best be considered roughly equivalent to the psychologist's term "mental representation," which is a form of mental processing, or a contentful state of the organism. The linguist's model attempts to describe the organization or complexity of the relations among elements imputed to the child's system as evidenced by systematic relations among the utterances produced. The model is, therefore, a characterization of information about the child's system as we know it, whereas the child's internal representation is a system of unknown parameters capable of generating the utterances appropriately described by the model (cf. Van Gulick, 1982).

Internal representation generally is taken to refer to a form of mental "storage" (e.g., Locke, 1988; Menn & Matthei, 1992). For example, Locke (1988) argued that "we cannot know whether a phonology is needed until it is determined that a discrepancy exists between stored and produced patterns. Nor can we propose explicit phonological rules until we have inferred the phonetic structure of internal representations" (p. 4). Developmental approaches to internal representation are rare (but see Velleman, 1992; Waterson, 1981); to our knowledge, there has been no previous effort to explicitly relate the linguist's "internal representation" to the psychologist's "mental representation."

In our view, the production of context-limited words, which have been observed to occur prior to the onset of combinatorial representational play (McCune, 1992), is in some ways comparable to the perceptually dependent memories of the Rovee-Collier experiments. A specific familiar event evokes an intentional state and associated vocalizations (Bloom, 1991). There is minimal differentiation among such components as speaker, hearer, physical context, and vocal motor action (Werner & Kaplan, 1963). Such production requires the availability of one or more vocal motor schemes, but not a word production pattern generalized across a variety of word types.

Somewhat later, a new capacity for mental representation allows the elements of the speech situation to be differentiated, yet integrated. An unfamiliar event might now evoke the word associated with a related event. A given event might be referenced by one of several words. The child experiences an increasing range of potential representational meanings, whereas vocal motor skill may remain limited. Vocal expression thus comes to rely on the word production patterns which now evolve, made possible by the increased capacity for separating word form from situation of use and for the internal experience of relationships between linguistic elements, which facilitates the juxtaposition of one or more vocal motor schemes and a range of phonetically related adult words.

Storage need not be postulated at either of these developmental time points. Whereas in the earlier period a familiar context may provide sufficient perceptual support to elicit instantiation of the one vocal motor scheme associated with the situation, in the later period instantiation of a variety of situationally appropriate adult-based forms is possible, given adequate articulatory capacity. Furthermore, once the child's vocal forms are no longer embedded in a particular situation of use, they can be compared or "superposed" (as in connectionist models, such as Stemberger, 1992) as a basis for the development of a generalized word production pattern. We believe that this is the basis for the beginnings of phonological systematization, which we find to emerge at about the same time as the first referential or generalized use of words. At this point, something more abstract than a vocal motor scheme operating in combination with perceptual attention to particular auditory patterns has materialized. This is a phonological mental representation which may become instantiated when reference to the corresponding object or event is contemplated.

# MODELING THE CHILD'S SYSTEM

There is a wealth of persuasive evidence regarding the importance of the word and syllable levels in child phonology, particularly in the early period (Chiat, 1979; Ferguson & Farwell, 1975; Kent & Bauer, 1985; Macken, 1979; Vihman, 1992). A hierarchical model of phonological structure is needed to capture this important aspect of children's systems. It appears to us that the most viable option currently available is nonlinear phonology.

Several phonologists have suggested nonlinear models of early child words, especially for the frequently observed patterns of harmony and reduplication. The task has been approached in a variety of theoretical frameworks, including prosodic (Waterson, 1971), parametrical (Fikkert, 1991; Lleó, 1992), connectionist (Berg, 1992; Menn & Matthei, 1992), and cognitivist (Menn, 1978; Velleman, 1992). All of these approaches seek to account for the fact that the child's phonology is simpler than the adult's, at least at the output level. However, depending on the child and/or the model, "simple" may have many different meanings; these will be reviewed briefly.

A child system may be simpler in its hierarchical structure, lacking whole levels of representation (e.g., the skeletal or segmental tier). Menn and Matthei (1992), for example, suggested within a connectionist framework that priming-type interactions among similar articulatory patterns (words) may induce the beginnings of autosegmental structure "potentially . . . without segmentation below the word level" (p. 243). Velleman (1992) suggested that the phonological representations of children with highly restrictive, often babble-based "word recipes" may have lexical representations with almost no structure at all (e.g., word-level representation only), relying on their existing articulatory patterns to provide whatever redundant phonetic detail is required to flesh out productions.[3]

The child's representation also may be simpler within a given level. For example, early syllable constituents may be nonbranching (Fee, 1991; Fikkert, 1991; Lleó, 1992; Ohala, 1991; Velleman, 1992). That is, only CV syllables may be possible at first. If no branches are available at the word level (i.e., if all words are monosyllabic), then "word" and "syllable" are synonymous and no lexical distinction need be made.

The child's system may be less integrated, with consonant and vowel effects occurring independently due to planar segregation (Fikkert, 1991; Lleó, 1992; McDonough & Myers, 1991; Macken, 1993; Velleman, 1992),

---

[3] On the other hand, Goad (1992) argues on the basis of feature geometry that the segment must be a primitive.

in which consonants and vowels occur on separate phonological tiers. Such segregation was originally proposed for Semitic languages in which morphological templates require either consonants or vowels, for other types of templatic morphology in which linear order of consonants and vowels is redundant, and for languages with very simple CV phonotactic structures (Lleó, 1992; McCarthy, 1989). Planar segregation in child phonology allows vowels to be transparent to consonant harmony, and vice versa, and accounts for the increased frequency of such harmony processes in early phonologies. It also provides a model of C/V metathesis that is consistent with principles of adult phonology: If consonants and vowels are on separate tiers, then they may appear to switch places without violating constraints against crossing association lines.

Children's lexical feature specifications may be minimal as well. Such "underspecification" is identified in child phonologies when elements of surface form are completely predictable. This may stem from pervasive harmony patterns, in which the degree of feature spreading is so great that the positions receiving harmony are thought to be vulnerable to spreading due to the lack of any feature specification of their own. For example, if a child demonstrates regressive and progressive harmony affecting target coronals (or dento-alveolars) whenever a labial or dorsal (velar) consonant occurs anywhere in the word, then we assume that [coronal] is not underlyingly specified. Redundancy, or predictability in surface features, also may stem from phonetic or phonotactic restrictions. For example, if all consonants in a child's system are stops, then [–continuant] is predictable and need not be lexically marked.

Features also may be specified but lexically unordered where their order is predictable. This lack of lexical ordering is manifested in apparent C/C or V/V metathesis in children (e.g., Virve's productions of [asi] for /isa/ "father" and [amɨ] for /ɛma/ "mother," described in Vihman, 1976) and in redundantly ordered complex clusters in some adult phonologies. (See Velleman, 1992, for further discussion.)

Sometimes an unspecified feature also will serve as a default feature value, to be filled in at the surface level whenever the corresponding C or V slot remains otherwise unspecified (Fikkert, 1991: Lleó, 1992; Velleman, 1992). Although coronal has been proposed by some as both a default and a lexically unspecified feature for adult languages (Stemberger & Stoel-Gammon, 1991), a child's unspecified features need not necessarily be defaults (Lleó, 1992). Either spreading of a harmonic feature or the lack of any surface realization ("omission") may be the fate of such unspecified elements.

Although some features may not need specification, feature specifications that are necessary may encompass a broader domain than in adult phonology, applying to an entire mora, syllable, word, or even phrase (Iverson & Wheeler, 1987; Velleman, 1992). The eventual "trickle-down" of such features to the segmental level has been referred to as "deautosegmentalization" (Goldsmith, 1979; Spencer, 1986). Similarly, rules or processes may show a greater breadth of application. For example, spreading of a particular feature may affect all possible recipient segments in either direction ("right" or "left") over a large domain, such as an entire phrase (Lleó, 1992).

Whether these options are available to all children, specified by innate parameters, determined by some characteristics of the language to which the child is exposed, "chosen" by the child based on idiosyncratic perceptual, physiological, or cognitive biases, or some combination of the above is an open and widely debated question. In any case, the course of phonological development includes the addition of complexity to any or all of these aspects of the representation.

We prefer to attribute the minimal possible structure and the fewest possible rules to the child at any given point in development and will attempt to demonstrate that a nonlinear model can be constructed to account for developmental increments of phonological complexity, attributing complexity to representations rather than rules and adding rather than changing structure over time. Given our assumptions about the origins of early words in production and perception and about the relation of emergent phonological systems to the child's evolving representational capacity, we see no need to posit specifically linguistic innate structures (contra, e.g., Macken, 1992).

## IDENTIFYING THE ONSET OF SYSTEM

Although the emergence of phonological system is clear, even dramatic, in most of the children we have observed, bits of the system typically are already apparent (at least in retrospect) before they come together sufficiently to lead to a sudden flourishing of diverse lexical items. The system itself coheres gradually, over time, but when a critical point is reached (either cognitively or phonologically; it may be impossible to decide which is determinative), the system seems suddenly to have power enough to strongly affect lexical choice and production and to assimilate adult words that do not provide an obvious fit with the child's template. Close analysis of the phonological progress of two children, reported below, will demonstrate that the onset of system can be recognized not only in the interesting cases of distortion of adult models (regression in accuracy) in child word production, but also in the spurt in acquisition of words that fit the template.

## EXTRA-SYSTEMIC ELEMENTS

Adult phonological systems include marginal elements, especially in words which are salient because they are exotic (ZsaZsa), humorous (schmaltzy), chic (au jus, karaoke), or newsworthy (détente, Sri Lanka, Schwartzkopf). Similarly, the child's production may include a small set of extra-systemic words, recognizable by their inconsistency with the majority of the child's forms. Children sometimes produce surprisingly accurate renditions of difficult words before a system has coalesced (e.g., Hildegard Leopold's famous production of pretty). Such "progressive idioms" may be regularized when the child's phonological system has become established, or they may persist as extra-systemic elements. Later, extra-systemic words may reflect aspects of the adult shape as perceived by the child as well as aspects of the child's existing template, and so include both systemic and extra-systemic elements.

Words that are partially or wholly extra-systemic can be expected to be shorter-lived than other forms. The child's system, by definition, is more consistent and persistent than other aspects of production and tends to dominate lexical production and to dictate selection, once it is in place. However, extra-systemic items may serve as precursors or even triggers for change in the child's system; the system may accommodate to them some time after they first appear as marginal elements.

# TWO PHONOLOGICAL PROFILES

In a paper that focused on syllable production, Vihman (1992) presented sketchy profiles of the initial steps in lexical development of two children as well as the syllables they "practiced" at 9–11 months. One of these children seemed to base his early phonology on the syllable. The other child seemed instead to operate with a phonetic gesture involving tongue fronting and raising, or palatal articulation; the syllable did not play an important role for her. In this chapter we consider the phonetic and phonological development of the same children in finer detail, attempting to trace the interaction of perceptual biases, vocal motor schemes, and representational capacity in the formation of phonological systems.

## TIMMY: THE SYLLABLE PATTERN

Timmy provides an example of a child who progressed phonetically rather slowly and apparently effortfully. His words and babble forms were unusually difficult to distinguish for several months (Vihman et al.,

1985). His first 6 months of word production were based largely on phonetic variants of a single syllable shape, <Ca>, with a gradual increase in the consonantal choices available. Nevertheless, it is possible to distinguish an early, presystematic period (9–13 months) and a later, system-based period (from 14 or 15 months on).

At 9 months Timmy already responds with <ba> to adult monosyllabic /b/ words (*ball, block*); by 10 months he produces <ba> spontaneously in situations associated with those words (at 10 and 11 months <ba> is also produced in imitation of *basket, bell, boat, book, button* and spontaneously for *box*; by 15 months *bird, brush, bunny, baa(-baa)* are produced as <ba>).[4] From 11 months on Timmy responds to /k/ words (*kitty, quack-quack, car, duck, key*) with <ka(ka)>.[5] The word-length distinction (between monosyllabic /b/ words and disyllabic /k/ words) derives from the models, but is maintained somewhat inconsistently, particularly after the first month of use for each word.[6] There is little evidence of a phonological system operating here. Instead, Timmy draws on one of the articulatorily simplest syllables, [ba] (Davis & MacNeilage, 1990; Vihman, 1992), when he is "reminded" to produce his matching vocal motor scheme by situations in which a familiar auditory pattern is commonly produced by adults (in relation to some of his favorite toys, balls, blocks, bells). Similarly, he produces his second vocal motor scheme, <ka(ka)>, in situations associated with stop-initial word forms other than /b/ (*car, kitty, Teddy*, later also a deictic form which begins as a response to *Great Gable*, referring to a frequently identified drawing of a mountain; Vihman & Miller, 1988).

It is only at 14 months that we see the extension of this pattern, first to a single word, *eye*, assimilated to Timmy's pattern as [ja], then (at 15 months) to words that elicit a range of different consonants: [ßa] for words characterized by labiality and continuant friction, first *Ruth*, with its

---

[4] The notation < > will be used in referring to the word shapes used by this child, to cover a fairly wide range of phonetic variants. The initial stop, whether labial or dorsal, is produced at first with the full continuum of voice onset time possibilities, from fully voiced to voiceless aspirated. The nuclear vowel may also be voiceless, although only after voiceless onset consonant. The initial syllable may be preceded by a short "support" or "onset" syllable, typically a low vowel or schwa; the low vowels range from front to back.

[5] The asymmetry in Timmy's selection, resulting in a first lexicon of /b/- and /k/-words, fits within the reported universals governing stop systems: Where one or two gaps are found in a voiced and voiceless series, it is voiceless /p/ and/or voiced /g/ that are most likely to be missing (Gamkrelidze, 1975).

[6] The adult models for the most frequently occurring <ka(ka)> words provide both one- and two-syllable target forms (*cat/kitty* and *quack[-quack]*). Monosyllabic *car* seldom elicits a disyllabic response, whereas most tokens of *baa(baa)* are iterated as <baba> when the word is first produced at 15 months.

rounded initial approximant and final fricative, later *fire, flies, flowers,* and *plum* [cf. Waterson, 1971][7]; [ɟa] for *light,* where the palatal place appears to derive from the nuclear diphthong while the stop articulation derives from the final consonant; [na] for *nose* and later *Nana;* and [ja] for *ear, hair* as well as *eye*—these latter perhaps best glossed, together with the probable phonological model *eye,* as "response to questions about my body."

At 15 months, furthermore, Timmy for the first time produces two forms outside his vocal motor scheme, both involving special sounds or sound effects in the adult models: *hiss* is reproduced as [ʂ], while the word *moo,* produced by adults with a long, low-pitched vowel, is reproduced as [m̩ʊ:] and the related form [ʔm̩mʌ] is used to imitate the phonetically similar words *moon* and *mushrooms.* A week later *moo* and *moon* have both been incorporated into Timmy's system as <ma> (with phonetic variants such as [ʔm̩mã~ʔm̩:mʌ]; extra-systemic vowel length, which derives from adult modeling of "moooo," is incorporated into variants of both words).

Let us assume that an internal representation begins to take shape at 14 months, when Timmy first extends the two related vocal motor schemes, <ba> and <ka(ka)>, to a third word type, <ja>. Until now vocal production in appropriate situational context has involved a choice of two vocal motor schemes, labial and not labial (see Figure 1–2 and Table 1–1). Now a palatal choice is added to the repertoire of lexical possibilities, but there is little else that is not redundant in Timmy's forms. The vowel [a] is predictable as the only consistent vowel; the variations in production are wholly unsystematic. "Labial" is Timmy's default consonantal feature value and thus need not be represented lexically. The word is still equivalent to the syllable and the syllable to the sequence C + a. Thus, there is only one autosegmental level (W, "the prosodic word") and only two lexically represented feature geometry options. Only one consonant type may occur within a word, so we assume that consonant features mark the entire word, not the individual consonants. Indeed, there is no evidence that individual consonants play a role in Timmy's phonology at this point.

Because of the extreme simplicity of Timmy's system, we have no need to posit phonological rules such as spreading to account for the harmony in his productions. Similarly, the issue of planar segregation is moot; there is no possible interference between vowel and consonant tiers because there is no need for a vowel tier. In addition, because the adult model provides information about iteration, which occurs as an expression of attention (affecting new words only), we assume that it is

---

[7] The syllable [βa] was an occasional phonetic variant for <ba> from 11 months on; now it is drawn on for a newly emergent contrast and takes its place in the lexical/phonological system.

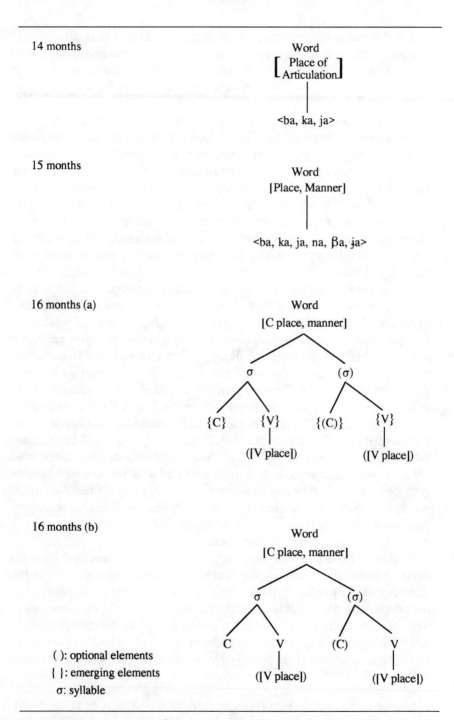

**Figure 1–2.** Development of a lexical representation.

not represented lexically. In short, Timmy has added one more syllable to his repertoire, suggesting emergent systematicity (see Table 1–1). But his vocal motor schemes, together with the information about number of syllables provided by the adult model, continue to suffice to account for almost everything about his word production.

With the expansion of available word (or syllable) shapes at 15 months, Timmy adds manner specifications to his representation, further elaborating feature geometry, since the first contrasts at a given place of articulation now emerge: stop-initial <ba> contrasts with fricative-initial <ßa> and glide-initial <ja> contrasts with stop-initial <ɟa>. Within the same month, a stop:nasal contrast also appears, as *moo* and *moon* enter the system as <ma> (as evidenced by the loss of accuracy in vowel production). Consonantal feature geometry is the only lexical element exhibiting change; the rest of the system remains as before. Nevertheless, the multiple lexical expression of both place and manner contrast seems sufficient to suggest that a phonological system is now minimally established.

At 16 months Timmy's word production reflects a number of systematic advances as well as some continuing extra-systemic experimentation. Because syllables within a word may now contrast, the representation must include a separate syllable level. Iteration itself has now entered the system as a separate lexical possibility: <ba> *block/peg, boat* contrasts with <baba> *baby, bracelet*. This is further evidence of lexical status for the syllable. In addition, a vowel contrast is now available, although the new vowel, [i], occurs in only one monosyllable ([di] "the letter D") and as second vowel in a sequence <a...i>, where it contrasts with the iterated sequence <a...a> (<baba> *baby, bracelet* vs. disyllabic <bai> *balloon, boy, please*; <kai> *car*; <kaki> *cookie*; and the restructured <ai> *eye* as well as <aija> *hiya*). Since default [a] is no longer the only vowel and its distribution is not completely predictable, the lexical representation must now explicitly include [i]. This is the first sign of emerging skeletal (C-V) and segmental levels of representation.

Until now, the formal problem of representing consonantal harmony across intervening vowels did not arise, as no lexical vowel specification was necessary ([a] was redundant). Now this issue comes to the fore: If vowels and consonants share feature specifications, as proposed by some phonologists (e.g., Sagey, 1986), then we have to explain why, for example, the feature [dorsal], which we have placed at the word level and which is meant to "trickle down" and create harmonic [k]s in <kaki>, does not also affect the two vowels in this word. There are three plausible solutions: (1) assume that consonants and vowels do not share feature specifications; (2) assume that consonant features are now also represented at the segmental level and that the high frequency of harmony in Timmy's system is a remnant of his previous word-level consonant feature

**Table 1-1.** Development of a child's lexical representation (Timmy)

| | | Portions Provided by | | | | |
| | | Motor Control | Perception | Lexicon (Phonological Representation) | | |
| Age (in months) | Word Forms | Vocal Motor Scheme | Adult Model | Feature Geometry | Autosegments | Skeleton |
|---|---|---|---|---|---|---|
| 10 | <ba> | Ca syllable | | | | |
| 11–13 | <ba>, <ka> | [a], +/−labial open syllables | iteration | | | |
| 14 | <ba>, <ka>, <ja> | [a], labial default open syllables | iteration | {3-way place contrast} | {W} | |
| 15a | <ba>, <ka>, <ja> | [a], labial default open syllables | iteration [u], [ʃ] | C place and manner | W | |
| 15b | <na>, <ʃa>, <ʤa> as above + <ma> | [a], labial default open syllables | iteration | C place and manner | W | |
| 16a | $C_1V_1(C_2)(V_2)$: $C_1$ = above+[t, s] $C_2 = C_1$ or labial V = [a, i] | [a] default open syllables C order if $C_2 \neq C_1$ V order if $V_1 \neq V_2$: [a]1st | [u] | C place and manner: 2 features, unordered or 1 feature per word [a] unspecified [[i] specified at segmental level] | W, σ | {CV(C)(V)} |
| 16b | [a, i, u] Vowel sequence no longer predictable | [a] default open syllables C order if $C_2 \neq C_1$ | | C place and manner: 2 Features, unordered or 1 feature per word [a] unspecified [i,u] specified at segmental level | W, σ | CV (C)(V) |

*Note:* { } = emergent element/level; W = word ("prosodic word"); σ ≠ syllable; a = earlier in month; b = later in month.

specification; or (3) propose that Timmy's consonants and vowels are on separate tiers ("planar segregation"), an interpretation that is compatible with his simple word shapes but one to which we had no need to appeal previously. Without taking a stand on the issue of vowel versus consonant features, we assume the last of these options, as it attributes the least possible lexical structure to Timmy's phonological system.[8]

Similarly, the possibility of paradigmatic consonantal contrast in place has now been extended to allow syntagmatic contrast within a word: <nama> *Simon*, <gaba> *goodbye*. Again sequence is predictable: [labial] always occupies second position in noniterative words. Because the consonants within a disyllable are always either identical or ordered in a predictable way, we assume that consonant features remain autosegmental. Labial can no longer be specified as a default, but must be represented in its own right. The word is marked either for one feature (or set of features) which, in production, spreads to all closants or for two features (or sets of features) which are lexically unordered. Output rules will specify the ordering.

The place feature [coronal], first introduced in nasal <n> at 15 months, now occurs in stop <t> followed by either <a> (*daddy* <tata>) or <i> (*D* <di>). The feature also occurs in the fricative-initial syllable <sa>, used to assimilate the word *fish* to Timmy's system. Thus, previously extra-systemic [s] now has been incorporated. The vowel [u] remains extra-systemic, occurring only in a variant of onomatopoeic *toot*.

Three unusually difficult words show continued phonetic (extra-systemic) exploration: *helicopter* is produced as <ga(li)ga>: [əgaga~ʌgʌlɪga~gʌlɪgʌlɪgæ]; attempts at *tape-recorder* show the same range of variation. The word *light*, represented as <ja> at 15 months, now reflects Timmy's new attention to the initial /l/. It can be represented as <aija>, like *hiya*, but shows considerably more variation, the medial consonant being produced as a voiced or voiceless palatal glide, voiced or voiceless palatal fricative, voiced alveolar fricative, or even voiced dorsal fricative or sequence dorsal + [l]. Finally, we represent the name *Simon* as <nama>, but the variation here is also considerable, suggesting some child attention to the discrepancy between adult model and his own word shape. The vowels range over front and back low variants as well as palatal on- and off-glides ([næɪmæ], [nɪʌmɪnɪʌmɪnɪʌme]) and the consonantal sequences [m...m] and [m...n] occur alongside the system-based sequence <n...m> (4 tokens out of 6).

---

[8] There are reasonable phonetic arguments both for and against positing different feature representations for consonants and vowels. Timmy's data do not provide strong phonological evidence either way, whereas Alice's data show the palatalizing influence of vowels on consonants as well as some apparent fronting and backing influence on vowel choice from neighboring consonants (see "Alice: The palatal pattern," below).

In summary, Timmy's representation now includes a syllabic as well as a word level, and both vowel and consonant features now are represented. Because vowels show some autonomy, they must be individually specified, although <a> remains the default vowel. For this reason we are forced to posit a skeletal tier for Timmy at this point. By definition, this tier must include both vowel ([+syllabic]) and consonant ([−syllabic]) slots. Vowels are individually specified and therefore can be considered to be the first genuine segments in Timmy's system. Consonant slots remain unspecified, because order of occurrence of features remains predictable (represented at word level). Planar segregation prevents these autosegmental consonant feature specifications from affecting vowels as well.

In a later 16-month session, the combinatorial potential of the system is unleashed (see Table 1–2). Whereas <i> earlier combined only with <t> or, in second syllable, <k> or <l>, it now occurs in monosyllabic <bi> *bee*, <ki> *key*, and disyllabic <mami> *mummy*, <nimi> *Simon* as well as <kaki> *coffee*, <kuki> *computer*, and <kibi> *good boy*. The previously extra-systemic vowel <u> has entered the system, occurring in monosyllables <tu> *Drew, juice, toe*, <mu> *moo, moon* (tokens of both words still marked by extra-systemic lengthening and low pitch) as well as disyllabic <kuki> *computer*, <kaku> *bicycle*. In addition, sequences of <a...i>, <a...u>, and <u...i> are permitted as well as <k...b> and <n...m>.

In addition, the child produces an unusual contrast of <ba'bi> *bottle* but <ba'bu> *bubble*.[9] The second syllables, <bi> versus <bu>, appear to carry the medial [d] : [b] contrast of the model into the vowel of the child's production as "nonlabial" [i] versus "labial" [u], suggesting attention to the adult contrast as well as continuing constraints on possible within-word syllable sequences. Since no instances of the sequence labial...nonlabial have yet appeared (cf. *Simon* <nimi>, *money* "coin" <mami>), the expected "solution"—*<badi> vs. <babu>—is not available. Furthermore, word forms combining both consonant and vowel contrast do not yet occur either (*good boy*, for example, might otherwise be produced as *<kubi> or *<kuba>).

On the word level we now have multiple examples of mono- versus disyllabic forms, corresponding in each case to one versus more syllables in the model (monosyllabic *ball, boat, bee, car, key, Drew, juice, toe, moo(n)*, and *neck/sun*—both produced as <na>—versus disyllabic *balloon, bottle, bubble, coffee, good boy, money, quack-quack* and *Simon*, but also *computer* and *bicycle*). However, sequences of [−low]...[+low] and of [+labial]...[−labial] are still excluded. Consonants have yet to be completely

---

[9] The intention of maintaining contrast seems clear, given the consistent effortful extra stress on the [i] of <babi> *bottle* (all four tokens) as well as on the final vowel of all 27 uses of <babu> *bubble* (produced as the child attempts to catch the bubbles his mother is blowing), phonetically a front rounded [y] in this form only.

**Table 1–2.** Inventory of a child's syllables (Timmy)

| Age (in months) | Consonant at syllable onset | | | | | | | | | |
|---|---|---|---|---|---|---|---|---|---|---|
| | \<b\> | \<t\> | \<k\> | \<ß\> | \<s\> | \<ɟ\> | \<m\> | \<n\> | \<j\> | \<w\> |
| 9 | ba | | | | | | | | | |
| 10 | ba | | | | | | | | | |
| 11 | ba | | ka | | | | | | | |
| 12 | ba | | ka | | | | | | | |
| 13 | ba | | ka | | | | | | | |
| 14 | ba | | ka | | | | | | ja | |
| 15a | ba | | ka | ßa | | ɟa | | na | ja | |
| 15b | ba | | ka | ßa | | ɟa | ma | na | ja | |
| 16a | ba | ta | ka | ßa | sa | ɟa | ma | na | ja | |
| | | ti | ki | | | | | | | |
| 16b | ba | ta | ka | ßa | sa | ɟa | ma | na | ja | (wa) |
| | bi | ti | ki | | | | mi | ni | | |
| | bu | tu | ku | | (dzu) | | mu | | | |

*Note:* a = earlier in month, b = later in month.

released from the restrictions of harmony and predictable order to become segments in their own right.

Voicing of obstruents is only partially consistent and never contrastive. All tokens of \<b\> and \<ß\> syllables are voiced; similarly \<da\>, \<di\>, and \<du\> are voiced, regardless of the model (including *toe* and *toot(-toot)*). However, the dorsal words vary, with [k] for the old word *quack-quack*; [g] for such new words as *bicycle, coffee,* and *key*; and variation between [k] and [g] for *car. Computer* is imitated as [kugɪ]. On the other hand, [g] is produced consistently in continuing use of the protoword \<ga\> (originally *Great Gable*) and in the new (proto-)word *golly-goo* (as Timmy's mother dubbed it), which originated as *helicopter* but is now used for Humpty-Dumpty, pictures of elephants and squirrels, and elsewhere. A new, highly variable word is *lizard*, reported by the mother as *zazoo*, but occurring in the session (in repeated reference to pictures of a large caterpillar) as iterated \<jai\> or \<wa\> and, once only, [əja:dʒu] ("zazoo").

We have followed Timmy's emergent phonology from his first pair of undifferentiated <ba> words to a fairly well developed system including extensive feature geometry and autosegmental levels of representation with word, syllable, and segmental units. We have seen how he gradually added first consonant, then vowel features to his lexical representations. And we have seen how the emergence of feature contrast, first in vowels, then in consonants, was followed by a combinatorial explosion, reflecting the logic of the underlying system very much as outlined in Lindblom (1992).

## ALICE: THE PALATAL PATTERN

Alice's phonological development illustrates the emergence of a far more complex initial structure. Alice appears to organize her phonology on two independent planes at once. At the autosegmental level, she gradually works her mastery of the motoric control needed to produce a palatal glide, [j], into a word-based palatal melody. The melody may be seen to evolve gradually out of the words which Alice "selects" or attempts to produce, words that naturally accommodate her preferred phonetic gesture, [j] (e.g., *hi, baby* at 10 months). At first the melody is applied inconsistently in production, to whole words (*no* [njæ]: 9 mos., *bottle* [böjö]: 11 mos.), then to both words and syllables (*dolly* [dali:], *elephant* [ʔɛni ʔaɪ]: 13 mos.). At each of these levels Alice explores a variety of options. We identify the beginnings of a phonological system at 14 months, when a single relatively consistent word production pattern begins to be applied to a range of different words. Some examples:

> *baby* [beːbi]      *blanket* [bæɲi]
>
> *bottle* [baɖi]      *mommy* [maːɲi]
>
> *Bonnie* [baɲi]

The pattern found in these productions is related to the form of the adult models, but cannot derive from them alone; it fits closely with *baby* and *Bonnie*, but distorts *blanket* and *mommy*.

Figure 1–3 tracks over time the emergence and decline of the various elements which participate in the formation of the system in evidence at 14 months. Three patterns are isolated and identified in the order from most to least complex or inclusive (beginning with the bottom-most panel): <$C_0VCi$>, or polysyllabic word shapes including a final [i] (e.g., *baby, Bonnie, mommy*); <Vi>, or monosyllabic word shapes including a front rising diphthong (e.g., *hi, Ais*—the child's nickname, which rhymes

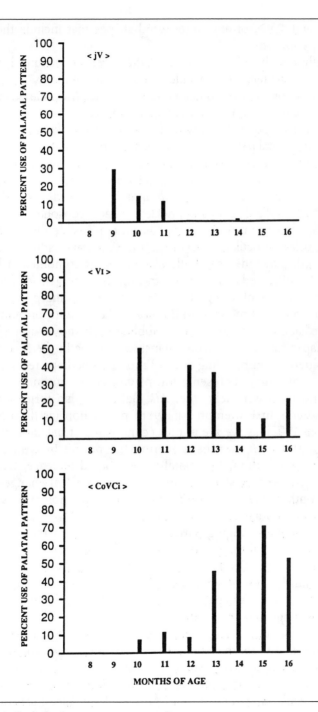

**Figure 1–3.** Palatal pattern use in words.

with *haze*); and <jV>, or any other word shapes that include the glide yod ([j]: e.g., *yumyum*).

At 8 months only babble was produced; there were no identifiable words. Babble vocalizations tended to include yod to an uncommonly great extent (24% vs. a mean of 6% for 9 other American infants; McCune & Vihman, 1987). At 9 months three words were identified, realized in 7 tokens. The <jV> pattern is incorporated into two of these tokens: *hello/hi[ya]* [hije], *no* [n:jæ]. No other palatal pattern is used in words in this month.

At 10 months we see the first and strikingly high use of the <Vi> pattern in words, accounting for 50% of all word tokens. Two likely adult sources of this pattern for Alice are *hi* and *baby*, words she produces "accurately," with syllable count and nuclear-syllable consonant and vowel matching the adult form. Both words constitute plausible models for the shaping of a palatal articulatory gesture in the direction of adult speech.

Figure 1–4 displays the use of all palatal patterns combined in babble as compared with words to facilitate tracing the emergence of a word schema out of the babble repertoire. Here we see a sharp increase in word production at 10 months (to 20 word tokens), with proportionate increase in palatal pattern use, while babbling itself shows little change. Babbling shapes foreshadow word shapes, as we see in the first "wave" of palatal patterning in babbling at 8–12 months—perhaps reflecting the child's global auditory representation of words like *mommy, daddy, baby, hi*, and her own nickname, *Ais*. Babbling also reflects newly emergent patterns first attempted in word production (as illustrated in Elbers & Ton, 1985), as we see in the second wave of palatal patterning in babbling, at 13–16 months, covering the period in which word production shows a dramatic palatal-pattern-based increase. Only the emerging lexicon shows sharp or apparently categorical changes from month to month, however, reflecting the ongoing phonological work of construction and reorganization or systematization.

Looking over the changing patterns in Figure 1–3 in the remaining months, we see that all three patterns are used in at least 10% of Alice's word tokens at 11 months. From 12 months on (when word production drops temporarily), the <jV> pattern is replaced by the other more differentiated patterns. Two patterns compete at 13 months, the <C₀VCi> pattern dominating from 14 months on.

Whereas one or at most two different palatal patterns had been used in earlier months, at 14 months a full range of possibilities is explored, with some words varying across subpatterns. For example, tokens of *daddy* vary between the fairly accurate [tædi], a <Vi> form [taɪdi], and a more fully palatal [jæɪji]. Similarly, the word *hi*, a staple of Alice's lexicon for 5 months, now receives experimental shaping into [ha:ji]. It is worth noting that at 14 months, when the majority of her productions (42 tokens) are

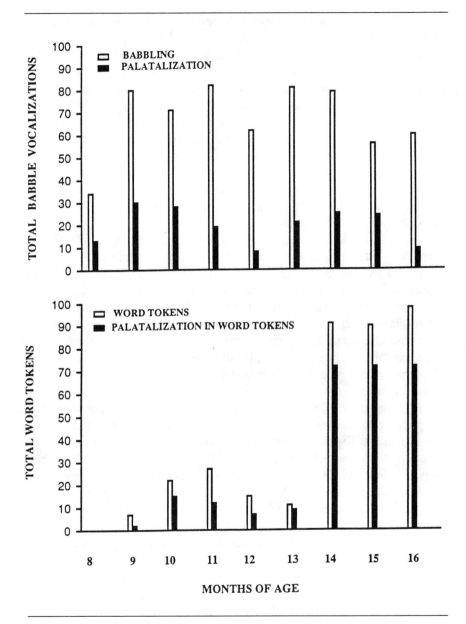

**Figure 1–4.** Raw frequency of vocalizations and palatal pattern use.

disyllabic [i]-final word shapes, almost all of these are in relatively good conformity with the adult model; similarly, the diphthongal production of words such as *bye* and *eye* (also '*kay* and *nigh'-nigh'* at 15 months) owes as much to the model and the child's evident experience of a match as to assimilatory or creative reconstruction by the child.

Until now Alice's words seem to have been selected, at least in part, on the basis of the increased salience of palatals. However, her palatalization pattern has appeared to exist in some sense separate from its manifestation in any particular word, because it is imposed inconsistently on various portions of different words, even within the same recording session, and its effects vary from one token to the next, even of the same word. Palatalization appears to have the status of an autosegmental melody for Alice, independent of the segments on which it operates. Furthermore, this palatal melody can be seen as a direct outgrowth of the phonetic gesture [j] which marked Alice's vocal production at 8–10 months.

We propose that the vocal motor scheme which is first manifest as [j] is gradually shaped into the more extensive and flexible palatal melody expressed in both mono- and disyllabic words from 14 months on. Until a range of different words are produced in a phonologically consistent way, we have vocal production under the dual influence of the infant's own previous vocalizations and prior experience of adult vocalizations, each embedded in a familiar situation of use. Once a stable word production pattern is established, we can infer the existence of phonological system. This system is emergent at 14 months, as Alice experiments with different palatal patterns for "old," previously palatalized word shapes.

At 15 months Alice's palatal pattern is no longer independent of the underlying word shapes; it has begun to shape them. Words now begin to change in a way that cannot be accounted for by the shape of the adult model. A number of the relatively accurate earlier shapes have been replaced by disyllabic [i]-final renditions that also incorporate yod, which had been submerged earlier in the more abstract realization of palatal articulation affecting different parts of the word—vowel nucleus ([Vi]), palatalized stop or nasal ([ɖ], [ɳ]), and final [i]. Now we see a resurgence of intervocalic yod in forms such as *blanket* [baji] and *dolly* and *daddy* [daji]. The manifestation of palatalization has become systematic, reminiscent of the spread of tones in tone languages or of nasalization in a language like Guarani. This is the sign of an active phonological system exerting an influence on production patterns, where earlier those patterns merely reflected various possible interactions between Alice's well-developed motoric capacity and her auditory experience of the adult language.

A clear picture of Alice's phonological system now emerges. Palatalization is redundant everywhere except in word onsets. Medial consonant features nevertheless will be specified in most words, as they may emerge in any one of three ways: intact, palatalized, or replaced by Alice's default, [j]. First-syllable vowels must be specified, because these are not predictable. However, each initial syllable must include two morae, the first of which will be specified whereas the second will be either filled by the default palatalization or left unrealized. Production factors may determine which of the consonantal and vocalic options occurs as the output form. Alice seems to allot motoric attention to the onset of a word pattern and then, in the remainder, allow her default palatal to fill in wherever attention or articulatory agility fails. In some cases (e.g., *lady* at 16 months) even the initial consonant is lexically unrealized at times, and is therefore supplied with the default [j]. Vowels in second syllables remain unspecified as they are redundantly palatal, with one or two extra-systemic exceptions (e.g., one production of *blanket* as [bɛpoʊ], *hammer* as [həv:a]).

These aspects of Alice's system provide an interesting contrast to Timmy's. Her motor skills are more developed than his, as reflected in far greater phonotactic and phonetic variety. She is willing to experiment (at 14 months) with various ways to integrate her palatalization pattern into her phonological system. Like Timmy, she is able to underspecify some elements in her lexical representation because she has a preexisting well-practiced motor pattern which will fill in for them. However, she shows greater variability in use of her pattern; production variables as well as lexical organization influence the extent to which it is used for any given word token. Whereas the concept of planar segregation can serve to simplify our model of Timmy's phonology, it cannot account for Alice's system. The primary reason it cannot is that our autosegmental representation of Alice's pattern must include branching within the syllable, with two morae available for her frequent diphthongs and occasional CVC forms (e.g., *clean* [kin]). In the absence of a simple CVCV phonotactic pattern, the relative order of consonants and vowels is not predictable, and planar segregation is ruled out. It is in any case unnecessary here, because the palatal melody affects consonants and vowels alike.

Let us now consider the last month for which phonological data are available, 16 months. Alice's polysyllables have begun to return to the balance reflected at 14 months; there are no new examples of "regression" affecting formerly "correct" forms, although experimentation continues in words which are difficult for the child, such as *mommy*, now sometimes produced with medial [m], sometimes with [ŋ], and *lady*, in which the initial lateral and the medial stop are both subject to replacement by yod in variant tokens. The word that gives Alice the most trouble is *elephant*. The toy set which engaged Alice at each recording session included a Jack-in-the-box elephant. In a classic illustration of a child valiantly attempting a situationally salient word with an alien phonological shape, Alice progressed from [ʔeː], [ʔaɪ] or [ʔɛni] at 13 months, to [ʔaɪnjə], [ʔaijʌ] or [ʔæɪjɨ] at 16 months—still far from the model, yet hardly "random" productions. In fact, it seems clear that Alice is guided here, as elsewhere, by the interacting effects of her emergent range of available word production routines and her auditory impression or perceptual experience of the adult word—for the exact nature of which we have no independent information.

There is yet another "categorical" advance in phonological organization to be observed, however. Throughout the period studied the few forms that show no palatal patterning typically are monosyllables; longer forms that fail to match the full $<C_oVCi>$ pattern generally incorporate some individual element of palatality, as in the *elephant* tokens noted above. At 16 months, nonpalatal word shapes are exclusively monosyllables. However, these nonpalatal patterns now have begun to receive phonological attention, and two new patterns can be discerned: (1) monosyllables with a low back vowel nucleus and (2) monosyllables with nuclear [i]. For (1), models appear to include *down, man, (grand)pa,* and *up,* all produced relatively accurately. Other words are assimilated to this pattern: *duck* [tæʔ] and even *milk* [m:æ] (perhaps assimilated to the "back" [a/æ] pattern instead of the expected [i] pattern due to the influence of postvocalic velarized [ɬ]. The second pattern constitutes a new departure for Alice's palatal gesture: The preceding consonant typically is palatalized, and even the word *shoe* ([çi]) is assimilated to it (here it is the initial consonant that appears to dictate the choice of the front-vowel pattern).

Thus, we are proposing partial lexical representations for Alice which may include specifications at the word or syllable level. In addition, we propose that unspecified vowel slots are redundantly filled in with a palatal feature specification on output, and that the same palatal feature specification may variably affect other portions of the word, depending in part on production variables.

In a sense, the groundwork for a syllable versus word-level phonological distinction was already laid at 13 months, when Alice's phonetic-level palatal pattern, based on a prior vocal motor scheme, was first optionally applied to either one or both syllables in disyllabic words, demonstrating emergent control of units smaller than the word. At 14 months we see the first consistent treatment of a range of different words; we date the internalization of a schematic phonological pattern or system to this month. Before that, there is no reason to claim that a phonological system is operational, because the only evident influences on her productions remain the motoric preference for palatalization and its apparent perceptual salience (based on word selection for production). It is only at 14 months, when Alice begins restructuring words from previously more adult-like shapes into forms that fit a consistent pattern of her own, that these influences can no longer provide an adequate account of her developing phonology. At this point, the convergence of preferred motoric organization and specific auditory bias is represented in an internal system independent of particular word forms; at 15 months this system has begun to actively assimilate both old and new word forms.

## DISCUSSION

Now that we have considered Timmy and Alice's development in detail, we can return to Figure 1–1. We notice that the production patterns governing the children's early words are surprisingly similar (see also Molly in Vihman & Velleman, 1989: [kak:ɪ] *clock, glasses*; [ɪn:i] *Nicky*). Simple CV(CV) word shapes persist in both lexicons. Both children have "discovered" segments, but have retained some word-level feature specifications. When Timmy's default labial occurs only once in a word, it is in medial position. Alice's consonants continue to be subject to palatalization at the segmental, syllabic, or word level, as we see in her variable productions of *lady* and *daddy*. When her phonetic default consonant, palatal yod, occurs only once in a word, however, it too is medial.

We take the preferred or default consonant types to be overlearned motorically, given their roots in babble and their overgeneralized use in words. Although Timmy and Alice arrive at their word production patterns in different ways, it is striking that, in both cases, the default consonant finds a slot in the second syllable. This can be accounted for in formal terms by directional association: Lexically specified consonant features are first associated with the initial ("left-most") consonant slot, whereas the medial consonant is assigned what is left, a default, or nothing. Phonetically speaking, the child can be seen here to devote the most motoric attention to word-initial position, producing the most challenging or less familiar elements in that position and relying on more automatic production options (harmony, default, or omission) for medial consonants (cf. Branigan, 1976: Contrasts should occur first in the "most favorable environment for their unaffected production . . . Consonants in initial position . . . receive the first neural commands and therefore [should] be least influenced by preceding positions of the articulators" [p. 129]). The production pattern described in Vihman & Velleman (1989) also fits this account, as does the [l]-default pattern described for a French child in Vihman (1993b).

Timmy and Alice enter into adult-like vocal production with different phonetic resources. The adult words that appear to be most salient to them, based on the relative accuracy and frequency of their early production attempts, are correspondingly different. What they share in the early months of word production is the apparent reliance, for imitation or spontaneous word production in restricted contexts, on a small number of well-practiced ("preferred") phonetic patterns or vocal motor schemes, identifiable in context as modeled on similarly patterned, apparently "preselected" or "matching" adult words.

Following the first few months of word production (six months for Timmy, five for Alice), there is a sharp change in production (best seen in Table 1–2 for Timmy, at 15 months, and in Figure 1–4 for Alice, at 14 months). Now a generalized word production pattern has emerged, and a wider range of word shapes begins to be attempted, expanding the phonological repertoire ("accommodation," in Piaget's terms) but also adapting adult models to fit the child's pattern ("assimilation"). At this point, it is hard to deny the psychological reality of a shift to a rudimentary phonological system. This system is built around the pre-existing vocal motor schemes and the adult models by which those early vocal patterns were shaped, and is thus "continuous" with prelinguistic vocal production. However, the system has a logic and a dynamic of its own. Once the system has evolved, integrating the child's vocal resources and activating a particular pattern of interconnections among potential phonetic gestures, new words are more readily admitted to the child's active lexicon, and production accuracy decreases while "boldness" or departures from a set pattern increase (see Lewis, 1936, Fig. 1; Leonard, Schwartz, Folger, & Wilcox, 1978; Schwartz & Leonard, 1982).

## CONCLUSION

We have suggested that the advent of phonological systematicity is rooted in cognitive advances. Increases in representational capacity have been found to be identifiable in the nonverbal domain through the more flexible use of symbols in combinatorial play (McCune, 1993). This results in a more differentiated experience of the situation, of the events and objects of interest and the accompanying vocal forms, and also in greater "processing space" with which the child may compare and contrast his or her own vocal patterns and those of adults. The change in representational capacity affects the use of words, which now refer to a range of instances or tokens for a single "name" or word type, including relational words whose appropriate use presupposes awareness of alternative potential states (e.g., *allgone, more* imply a mental comparison of presence vs. absence: McCune-Nicolich, 1981a). The relatively rapid increase in vocabulary often observed at this point in the child's development may reflect new understanding of the function of language, but also may result from a new capacity for phonological internal representation, which simplifies word production by creating a small set of routines to be followed, requiring perceptual and motoric attention only to selected aspects of the target word.

The connectionist model of cognitive functioning recently has been invoked in a number of studies as a promising way to model children's phonological production (Berg, 1992; Menn & Matthei, 1992; Menn, Markey, Mozer & Lewis, 1993; Stemberger, 1992). We view such models as particularly apt for the early period we have described here, in which the child's vocal exploration through babbling results in the laying down of preferred neural pathways (with motor connections activating auditory connections as a result of self-monitoring), thereby "setting" connection strengths that will influence phonetic patterning at least for the first several months of word production. Connectionist models also are helpful in conceptualizing or accounting for the interaction between extra-systemic and systemic elements and the high variability associated with production shortly before a new pattern becomes established as part of the system (cf. Thelen, 1989 and Vihman & Velleman, 1989; Figs. 1–4).

We argue, however, that "something changes" at the point we have identified as the beginnings of phonological system. Underlying the change is cognitive advance. The effect on language is a qualitative, categorical change in function (generalized or referential word use) as well as form (the emergence of a generalized word production pattern). Whereas the combined effects of vocal motor scheme and auditorily salient patterns were sufficient to account for the individual vocal shapes of early, context-limited words, an internal representation—minimally modeled with a subset of the phonological structures characteristic of the adult lexicon, including autosegmental levels, consonant and vowel contrasts, feature specifications—must be invoked to account for the regularities found in the word production patterns characteristic of the more advanced stage of context-flexible word use. Once a rudimentary phonological system has begun to cohere, systemic pressure takes its place alongside production capacity (range of vocal motor schemes) and the influence of the adult model (auditory salience) as a primary factor shaping not only vocal production but all subsequent phonological development.

# REFERENCES

Aslin, R. (1993). Segmentation of fluent speech into words: Learning models and the role of maternal input. In B. de Boysson-Bardies, S. de Schonen, P. Jusczyk, P. MacNeilage, & J. Morton (Eds.), *Changes in speech and face processing in infancy: A glimpse at developmental mechanisms of cognition* (pp. 305–315). Dordrecht: Kluwer.

Baillargeon, R. (1987). Object permanence in 3¹/₂ and 4¹/₂ month old infants. *Developmental Psychology, 23*, 655–664.

Bates, E., Benigni, L., Bretherton, I., Camaioni, L., & Volterra, V. (1979). *The emergence of symbols.* New York: Academic Press.

Berg, T. (1992). Phonological harmony as a processing problem. *Journal of Child Language, 19*, 225–257.

Bloom, L. (1991). Representation and expression. In N. Krasnegor, D. Rumbaugh, R. Scheifelbusch, & M. Studdert-Kennedy (Eds.), *Biological and behavioral determinants of language development* (pp. 117–140). Hillsdale, NJ: Lawrence Erlbaum.

Boysson-Bardies, B. de, Hallé, P., Sagart, L., & Durand, C. (1989). A crosslinguistic investigation of vowel formants in babbling. *Journal of Child Language, 16*, 1–17.

Boysson-Bardies, B. de, & Vihman, M. M. (1991). Adaptation to language: Evidence from babbling and first words in four languages. *Language, 67*, 297–319.

Branigan, G. (1976). Syllabic structure and the acquisition of consonants: The great conspiracy in word formation. *Journal of Psycholinguistic Research, 5*, 117–133.

Chiat, S. (1979). The role of the word in phonological development. *Linguistics, 17*, 591–610.

Davis, B. L., & MacNeilage, P. F. (1990). Acquisition of correct vowel production: A quantitative case study. *Journal of Speech and Hearing Research, 33*, 16–27.

Elbers, L., & Ton, J. (1985). Play pen monologues: The interplay of words and babbles in the first words period. *Journal of Child Language, 12*, 551–565.

Fee, E. J. (1991, October). *Prosodic morphology in first language acquisition.* Paper presented at the Boston University Conference on Language Development, Boston, MA.

Ferguson, C. A. (1964). Baby talk in six languages. *American Anthropologist, 66* (6, Part 2), 103–114.

Ferguson, C. A. (1978). Learning to pronounce: The earliest stages of phonological development in the child. In F. D. Minifie & L. L. Lloyd (Eds.), *Communicative and cognitive abilities—Early behavioral assessment* (pp. 273–297). Baltimore: University Park Press.

Ferguson, C. A., & Farwell, C. B. (1975). Words and sounds in early language acquisition. *Language, 51*, 419–439.

Fernald, A. (1984). The perceptual and affective salience of mothers' speech to infants. In L. Feagans, C. Garvey, & R. Golinkoff (Eds.), *The origins and growth of communication* (pp. 5–29). Norwood, NJ: Ablex.

Fernald, A. (1991). Prosody in speech to children: Prelinguistic and linguistic functions. In R. Vasta (Ed.), *Annals of child development*, (Vol. 8, pp. 43–80). London: Jessica Kingsley.

Fikkert, P. (1991, October). *Well-formedness conditions in child phonology: A look at metathesis.* Paper presented at Crossing Boundaries: Formal and Functional Determinants of Language Acquisition, Tübingen, Germany.

Gamkrelidze, T. V. (1975). On the correlation of stops and fricatives in a phonological system. *Lingua, 35*, 231–261.

Garnica, O. K. (1977). Some prosodic and paralinguistic features of speech to young children. In C. E. Snow & C. A. Ferguson (Eds.), *Talking to children: Language input and acquisition.* Cambridge: Cambridge University Press.

Goad, H. (1992, January). *Learnability and inventory specific underspecification.* Paper presented at the meeting of the Linguistic Society of America, Philadelphia.

Goldfield, B. (1993). Noun bias in maternal speech to one-year-olds. *Journal of Child Language, 20*, 35–99.

Goldsmith, J. A. (1979). The aims of autosegmental phonology. In D.A. Dinnsen (Ed.), *Current approaches to phonological theory* (pp. 202–222). Bloomington: Indiana University Press.

Goldsmith, J. A. (1990). *Autosegmental and metrical phonology.* Oxford: Blackwell.

Iverson, G., & Wheeler, D. (1987). Hierarchical structures in child phonology. *Lingua, 73*, 243–257.

Kent, R. D. (1992). The biology of phonological development. In C. A. Ferguson, L. Menn, & C. Stoel-Gammon (Eds.), *Phonological development: Models, research, implications* (pp. 65–90). Parkton, MD: York Press.

Kent, R. D., & Bauer, H. R. (1985). Vocalizations of one year olds. *Journal of Child Language, 12*, 491–526.

Kiparsky, P., & Menn, L. (1977). On the acquisition of phonology. In J. Macnamara (Ed.), *Language learning and thought* (pp. 47–78). New York: Academic Press.

Leslie, A. M. (1987). Pretense and representation: The origins of "theory of mind." *Psychological Review, 4*, 412–426.

Leonard, L. B., Schwartz, R. G., Folger, M. K., & Wilcox, M. J. (1978). Some aspects of child phonology in imitative and spontaneous speech. *Journal of Child Language, 5*, 403-415.

Lewis, M. M. (1936). *Infant speech: A study of the beginnings of language.* New York: Harcourt Brace.

Lindblom, B. (1992). Phonological units as adaptive emergents of lexical development. In C. A. Ferguson, L. Menn, & C. StoelGammon (Eds.), *Phonological development: Models, research, implications* (pp. 131–163). Parkton, MD: York Press.

Lleó, C. (1992). *A parametrical view of harmony and reduplication processes in child phonology.* Manuscript submitted for publication.

Locke, J. L. (1983). *Phonological acquisition and change.* New York: Academic Press.

Locke, J. L. (1988). The sound shape of early lexical representations. In M. D. Smith & J. L. Locke (Eds.), *The emergent lexicon* (pp. 3–22). New York: Academic Press.

Macken, M. A. (1979). Developmental reorganization of phonology: A hierarchy of basic units of acquisition. *Lingua, 49*, 11–49.

Macken, M. A. (1992). Where's phonology? In C. A. Ferguson, L. Menn, & C. Stoel-Gammon (Eds.), *Phonological development: Models, research, implications* (pp. 249–269). Parkton, MD: York Press.

Macken, M. A. (1993). Developmental changes in the acquisition of phonology. In B. de Boysson-Bardies, S. de Schonen, P. Jusczyk, P. MacNeilage, & J. Morton (Eds.), *Changes in speech and face processing in infancy: A glimpse at developmental mechanisms of cognition* (pp. 435–449). Dordrecht: Kluwer.

Macken, M. A., & Ferguson, C. A. (1983). Cognitive aspects of phonological development: Model, evidence and issues. In K.E. Nelson (Ed.), *Children's language* (Vol. 4, pp. 256–282). Hillsdale, NJ: Lawrence Erlbaum.

MacNeilage, P. F., & Davis, B. L. (1990). Acquisition of speech production: Frames, then content. In M. Jeannerod (Ed.), *Attention and performance XIII: Motor representation and control* (pp. 453–476). Hillsdale, NJ: Lawrence Erlbaum.

McCarthy, J. (1989). Linear order in phonological representation. *Linguistic Inquiry, 20*, 71–99.

McCune, L. (1992). First words. In C. A. Ferguson, L. Menn, & C. Stoel-Gammon (Eds.),

*Phonological development: Models, research, implications* (pp. 313–336). Parkton, MD: York Press.

McCune, L. (1993). *A normative study of representational play at the transition to language.* Manuscript submitted for publication.

McCune, L., & Vihman, M. M. (1987). Vocal motor schemes. *Papers and Reports on Child Language Development, 26,* 72–79.

McCune-Nicolich, L. (1981a). The cognitive bases of relational words in the single word period. *Journal of Child Language, 8,* 15–34.

McCune-Nicolich, L. (1981b). Toward symbolic functioning. *Child Development, 52,* 785–797.

McCune-Nicolich, L., & Bruskin, C. (1981). Combinatorial competency in symbolic play and language. In K. Rubin (Ed.), *The play of children: Current theory and research* (pp. 5–22). Basil, Switzerland: Karger.

McDonough, J., & Myers, S. (1991). *Consonant harmony and planar segregation in child language.* Unpublished manuscript, U.C.L.A. and University of Texas at Austin.

Meltzoff, A., & Moore, M. K. (1993). Why faces are special to infants—On connecting the attraction of faces and infants' ability for imitation and cross-modal processing. In B. de Boysson-Bardies, S. de Schonen, P. Jusczyk, P. MacNeilage, & J. Morton (Eds.), *Changes in speech and face processing in infancy: A glimpse at developmental mechanisms of cognition* (pp. 211–225). Dordrecht: Kluwer.

Menn, L. (1978). Phonological units in beginning speech. In A. Bell & J. B. Hooper (Eds.), *Syllables and segments* (pp. 157–171). Amsterdam: North-Holland.

Menn, L. (1983). Development of articulatory, phonetic, and phonological capabilities. In B. Butterworth (Ed.), *Language production* (Vol. 2, pp. 3–50). London: Academic Press.

Menn, L., Markey, K., Mozer, M., & Lewis, C. (1993). Connectionist modeling and the microstructure of phonological development: A progress report. In B. de Boysson-Bardies, S. de Schonen, P. Jusczyk, P. MacNeilage, & J. Morton (Eds.), *Changes in speech and face processing in infancy: A glimpse at developmental mechanisms of cognition* (pp. 421–433). Dordrecht: Kluwer.

Menn, L., & Matthei, E. (1992). The "two-lexicon" account of child phonology: Looking back, looking ahead. In C. A. Ferguson, L. Menn, & C. Stoel-Gammon (Eds.), *Phonological development: Models, research, implications* (pp. 211–247). Parkton, MD: York Press.

Mulford, R. (1988). First words of the blind child. In M. D. Smith & J. L. Locke (Eds.), *The emergent lexicon: The child's development of a linguistic vocabulary* (pp. 293–338). New York: Academic Press.

Nicolich, L. McC. (1977). Beyond sensorimotor intelligence: Assessment of symbolic maturity through analysis of pretend play. *Merrill-Palmer Quarterly, 23,* 89–101.

Ohala, D. (1991). *A unified theory of final consonant deletion in early child speech.* Unpublished manuscript, University of Arizona.

Papousek, M., Papousek, H., & Bornstein, M. H. (1985). The naturalistic vocal environment of young infants: On the significance of homogeneity and variability in parental speech. In T. M. Field & N. A. Fox (Eds.), *Social perception in infants.* Norwood, NJ: Ablex.

Piaget, J. (1962). *Play, dreams and imitation in childhood.* New York: W. W. Norton.

Ramsay, D., & Campos, J. (1978). The onset of representation and entry into stage 6 of object permanence development. *Developmental Psychology, 52,* 785–797.

Roug, L., Landberg, I., & Lundberg, L. -J. (1989). Phonetic development in early infancy: A study of four Swedish children during the first eighteen months of life. *Journal of Child Language, 16*, 19–40.

Rovee-Collier, C., Sullivan, M. W., Enright, M., Lucas, D., & Fagen, J. W. (1980). Reactivation of infant memory. *Science, 208*, 1159–1162.

Sagey, E. (1986). *The representation of features and relations in nonlinear phonology.* Unpublished doctoral dissertation, Massachusetts Institute of Technology, Cambridge, MA.

Sartre, J -P. (1966). *The psychology of imagination.* (B. Frechtman, Trans.) New York: Washington Square Press. (Original work published in 1948.)

Schwartz, R. G., & Leonard, L. B. (1982). Do children pick and choose? An examination of phonological selection and avoidance in early lexical acquisition. *Journal of Child Language, 9*, 319–336.

Spencer, A. (1986). Towards a theory of phonological development. *Lingua, 68*, 3–38.

Stemberger, J. P. (1992). A connectionist view of child phonology: Phonological processing without phonological processes. In C. A. Ferguson, L. Menn, & C. Stoel-Gammon (Eds.), *Phonological development: Models, research, implications* (pp. 165–189). Parkton, MD: York Press.

Stemberger, J. P., & Stoel-Gammon, C. (1991). The underspecification of coronals: Evidence from language acquisition and performance errors. In C. Paradis & J. -F. Prunet (Eds.), *Phonetics and phonology, Vol. 3. The special status of coronals* (pp. 181–199). New York: Academic Press.

Stoel-Gammon, C., & Otomo, K. (1986). Babbling development of hearing impaired and normally hearing subjects. *Journal of Speech and Hearing Disorders, 51*, 33–41.

Thelen, E. (1989). Self-organization in developmental processes: Can systems approaches work? In M. R. Gunnar & E. Thelen (Eds.), *Systems and development: The Minnesota Symposia on Child Psychology* (Vol. 22, pp. 77–117). Hillsdale, NJ: Lawrence Erlbaum.

Uzgiris, I., & Hunt, J. (1975). *Assessment in infancy: Ordinal scales of psychological development.* Champaign: University of Illinois Press.

Van Gulick, R. (1982). Mental representation: A functionalist view. *Pacific Philosophical Quarterly, 63*, 3–20.

Velleman, S. L. (1992, January). *A nonlinear model of early harmony and metathesis.* Paper presented at the meeting of the Linguistic Society of America. Philadelphia, PA.

Vihman, M. M. (1976). From pre-speech to speech: On early phonology. *Papers and Reports on Child Language Development, 3*, 51–94.

Vihman, M. M. (1992). Early syllables and the construction of phonology. In C. A. Ferguson, L. Menn & C. Stoel-Gammon (Eds.), *Phonological development: Models, research, implications* (pp. 393–422). Parkton, MD: York Press.

Vihman, M. M. (1993a). The construction of a phonological system. In B. de Boysson-Bardies, S. de Schonen, P. Jusczyk, P. MacNeilage, & J. Morton (Eds.), *Changes in speech and face processing in infancy: A glimpse at developmental mechanisms of cognition* (pp. 411–419). Dordrecht: Kluwer.

Vihman, M. M. (1993b). Variable paths to early word production. *Journal of Phonetics, 21*, 61–82.

Vihman, M. M., Macken, M. A., Miller, R., Simmons, H., & Miller, J. (1985). From babbling to speech: A re-assessment of the continuity issue. *Language, 61*, 397–445.

Vihman, M. M., & McCune, L. (in press). When is a word a word? *Journal of Child Language.*

Vihman, M. M., & Miller, R. (1988). Words and babble at the threshold of lexical acquisition. In M. D. Smith & J. L. Locke (Eds.), *The emergent lexicon* (pp. 151–183). New York: Academic Press.

Vihman, M. M., & Velleman, S. L. (1989). Phonological reorganization: A case study. *Language and Speech, 32,* 149–170.

Waterson, N. (1971). Child phonology. *Journal of Linguistics, 7,* 179–211.

Waterson, N. (1981). A tentative developmental model of phonological representation. In T. Myers, J. Laver, & J. Anderson (Eds.), *The cognitive representation of speech* (pp. 323–333). Amsterdam: North-Holland.

Werner, H., & Kaplan, B. (1963). *Symbol formation.* New York: John Wiley. (Reprinted, 1984. Hillsdale, NJ: Lawrence Erlbaum.)

# CHAPTER 2

## Syllables and Segments in Infant Vocalizations and Young Child Speech

D. K. OLLER, Ph.D.
MICHELE L. STEFFENS, M.S.

The study of infant vocalizations and young child speech has been conducted largely through phonetic transcription and subsequent phonological analysis. This approach appears to have born fruit in a number of domains, providing the basis for insightful analysis of speech errors of young children (Ingram, 1974; Smith, 1973; Vihman, 1978) and laying the groundwork for illustrations of the relationship between babbling and speech (Cruttenden, 1970; Menyuk, 1968; Oller, Wieman, Doyle, & Ross, 1975). Yet however useful the transcriptional method has been in demonstrating the existence of systematic correspondences between child speech and its adult targets, it is in fact uncertain that infants and young children actually command a system of speech segments, not even the one implied by the transcriptions of the child's own utterances.

How could this be? If the child makes systematic errors, in which particular adult segments appear regularly to be replaced by other segments, how could the child not be in command of some rudimentary segment system in production, and given the rule-governed nature of the correspondences between child and adult forms, how could the child not be in command of an even richer segment system in perception? Although the predominant frameworks of research presuppose segmentalization, questions regarding the validity of segmental assumptions have pre-occupied child phonologists since the beginning of the modern era of study. Ferguson and Farwell (1975) expressed doubt regarding the segmentalization of young child speech inventories and suggested that children seemed to begin the process of speech acquisition operating at a level of word units, without segmental organization. Their reasoning assumed that only at a later point would the child diversify the analysis of speech units to establish a syllabic, and a segmental system. Waterson (1971) also argued that young children had only global sound categories that lacked segmental specificity.

Recent studies of infant vocal development offer additional reason to doubt the early emergence of segmentalization in young child speech. Investigators evaluating stages of vocal development in the first year of life have recently gravitated away from the segmental transcriptional approach in favor of description of infrastructural (or "infraphonological") properties of speech systems (Holmgren, Lindblom, Aurelius, Jalling, & Zetterström, 1986; Oller, 1980; Stark, 1980). Such descriptions take note of the extent to which infant utterances conform to prototypical patterns of speech units in natural languages—for example, the phonatory characteristic of prototypical (or canonical) units in languages, called "normal phonation," is produced without dysphonation (as in crying), hyperphonation (as in screaming), or tense/creaky voice (as in growling). In assessment of early infant sounds the appearance of normal phonation in the first month of life is thus taken to have potential significance in laying a groundwork for speech. In the second to third month of life, infraphonological description focuses on the appearance of articulated vocal acts (yielding potential consonant-like elements of "gooing") accompanied by normal phonation. This development is also taken to indicate the emergence of a fundamental requirement of speech, namely the ability to adjust the vocal tract position while vocalizing. In the fourth to fifth month, infraphonological description focuses on the infant's exploitation of the resonance capabilities of the vocal tract in producing normal phonation with a variety of supraglottal postures corresponding to distinct vowel qualities, on the production of a wide range of pitches and amplitudes, and on the production of sequences of consonant-like elements and vowel-like elements (although at this age the sequences usually are not yet well-timed, see Oller, 1981). These developments also show the infant controlling the infraphonological necessities of speech systems to an increasing extent, even though the bulk of sounds produced during this period could not serve as well-formed "words" in natural languages. One more step is necessary for the vocalizations to be identifiable as representative of prototypical speech-like units. By the middle of the first year, most children take that step with the production of well-timed sequences of articulation between consonant-like closures of the supraglottal tract and vowel-like postures. At this point "canonical" syllables are a part of the controlled repertoire of infant sounds, and parents often mistake the infant babbling for attempted speech.

Infraphonological descriptions do not begin with the assumption that the infant possesses a rich knowledge (tacit or otherwise) of speech from birth, but rather assume that in the course of the first years of life, an increasingly abundant system unfolds, at each stage manifesting more elaborately the infrastructural components of speech systems. Parents recognize this progress, and when new infraphonological features come into the child's repertoire, the parents tend to make adjustments in their own speech to the child. In particular with the onset of the canonical stage, parents tend to begin speaking to the child as if the child's utterances were meaningful (Papoušek, 1992). This attribution of meaning to the child may begin as a "mistake" by the parent, but it appears to help mold infant speech-like utterances into meaningful usage.

Thus, when infants begin to produce reduplicated canonical babbling, commonly characterized by sequences such as "dada" or "baba," they have reached a significant stage, because the utterances they produce by that time are capable of functioning as well-formed exemplars of words in any language that might have lexical items with such forms. This is reflected in the fact that languages all over the world tend to have a repertoire of nursery terms that have precisely the form of the early reduplicated sequences of infants (Jakobson, 1962), forms that themselves tend to be relatively universal.

Infraphonological description provides a direct account of the emergence of the ability to produce sounds that can function as speech units, but it does so without a necessarily segmental description. It notes the appearance of underpinnings and frameworks for speech, but does not depend on the characterization of infant achievements in terms of concrete phonetic or phonological segments. One does not need to resort to transcription of the infant sounds to characterize the gains made across the first months of life, because the infraphonological framework offers deeper (or perhaps more primitive) categories of description that provide a more accurate description of the actual progress of the child.

The steps of the process of unfolding infraphonological abilities provide a basis for the recognition of the developmental progression, and by virtue of the description's accuracy in focusing on the actual steps of gain, the framework facilitates the diagnosis of emerging disorders. For instance, it has been shown beyond doubt that deaf and hearing infants differ dramatically in the occurrence of stages of infraphonological development. The differences between deaf and hearing infants in onset of well-formed syllables are so great that they could provide the basis for a screening evaluation for severe and profound hearing losses (Kent, Osberger, Netsell, & Hustedde, 1987; Oller & Eilers, 1988; Oller, Eilers, Bull, & Carney, 1985; Stoel-Gammon & Otomo, 1986). Even though the differences in vocal development between deaf and hearing infants are extremely clear, they were unnoticed prior to the development of the infraphonological framework. For example, using a segmental transcription of the vocalizations of deaf and hearing infants, Mavilya (1969) provided results suggesting that deaf and hearing infants babbled alike in most of the first year of life. The difficulty with the conclusion was, of course, that the segmental description provided no basis for a distinction between canonical and precanonical vocalizations, and consequently, the salient distinction of deaf and hearing babbling was simply inaccessible to the study. Additional recent research also has indicated that Down syndrome infants show notable aberrations in infraphonological development (Lynch, Oller, Lewis, & Steffens, 1991), and there is reason to believe that autistic children are delayed in onset of canonical babbling in ways that resemble those of infants with hearing impairment (Oller, 1992).

It is of particular interest in the context of this chapter that canonical infant syllable sequences *do* appear to be segmentally "transcribable," because they seem to conform to the infraphonological principles of syllable formation. Yet the fact that adult listeners can impose a segmental transcription on infant utterances does not necessarily imply that the infants command the entirety of the structure assumed by the transcription. It seems likely that infants merely command the syllable structures, but have little if any awareness of segmental substructures.

There are reasons to suspect that for many months after the onset of the canonical stage (which occurs between 5–8 months in most cases), the infant functions primarily at a syllabic, but not a segmental, level in vocal production. Although the mature system of phonology is multilayered (syllables, segments, features), the infant system *appears* to consist of a single syllabic layer. In part we are lead to this suspicion because the inventory of syllable types in infants *appears* (and we emphasize "appears" because empirical verification is difficult) to be very small. The small size implies simplicity because only in a system with a large number of contrasting units is it important to structure the transmission system with multiple layers (syllables, segments, features) such as occur in mature natural languages. The advantages of multilayered structures in complex systems of speech is seen in the self-organization of neural networks trained to recognize speech (Gasser, 1992). A proposed advantage of the multilayered structuring for humans is that it may facilitate the mental storage of a lexicon of contrasting units that are virtually unlimited in number, but coded in terms of a relatively small set of contrastive transmission units. English has 40 or so phonemic segments in terms of which its entire lexicon can be characterized. This may provide a much simpler categorization than would be required if syllabic units were used as primary lexical units, since in English there are hundreds of syllable types.

The claim that development of a large lexicon ultimately may impose a requirement of segmentalization has been proposed by a number of authors. For example, it has been noted, based on Templin's (1957) vocabulary acquisition data, that a median child acquires about 20 words per day, between the ages of six and eight. In referring to this amazing feat, Studdert-Kennedy (1983) emphasized that the principle of "phonemic coding" is necessary for such acquisition to be possible, and he noted that other animal communication systems do not possess this key feature. He argued that "recurrent patterns of sound and gesture crystallize into phonemic control units." Lindblom (1992) contended that the process of change from presegmental to segmental inventory should be viewed as one of self-organization in response to the interaction of biological tendencies of the human organism and the linguistic inputs that are presented to it. The segmental system consists, then, of a set of "emergents," crystallized naturally and rather automatically from the process of human interaction. This view, compatible with our own theoretical preferences, is a functionalist one that can be contrasted with a more formalistic approach wherein it is assumed the primary units of linguistic function are deep biological givens.

It is also worth emphasizing that the functionalist approach makes no claim that the change from presegmental to segmental coding need be sudden. On the contrary, the emergence of segments is viewed as a process motivated by simplification that may be introduced gradually across the lexicon (Lindblom, 1992).

To monitor the process of change, it will be necessary to track infant lexicons longitudinally or, for prelinguistic infants, to track prelexical inventories of repeatable utterances. In listening to early infant inventories of vocalization, canonical syllables are perhaps the most auditorily salient unit of function that is compatible with the ultimate development of a lexicon. In focusing on such syllables we are in good company. Not only have infant vocal development theories tended to focus on them, but so have efforts to model the perceptual and articulatory factors that guide the selection pattern of languages for particular sound types. Lindblom, MacNeilage, and Studdert-Kennedy (1983) demonstrated that CV syllables operationalized as "holistic formant trajectories" are naturally organized in accord with perceptual and production constraints into groupings that reflect the most commonly occurring syllables (as well as segment types) in languages. These very commonly occurring syllables tend to be the very types that appear to predominate in prespeech.

However, the empirical evaluation of the size of an infant's production inventory is fraught with difficulties in the context of the issue of segmentalization. If we transcribe the utterances and count the different syllables that are indicated in the transcriptions, we are trapped in our own segmental web, imposing our perceptual categories (whether from a specific language or from an IPA-like system of potential phones) on the child's productions. Such an imposition may be misleading because the infant may have different intentions. A key challenge to the future study of child phonology is to establish workable and well-motivated criteria by which to assess the infant's contrastive system of potential speech sounds

After the onset of meaningful speech, we have at least a limited basis on which to assess contrastivity in terms of function. But even then, it is difficult to determine an optimal procedure for counting the number of elements in the child's phonetic (or potential phonetic) repertoire.

Consider, for example, the utterances listed in line 1 of the LIPP (Logical International Phonetic Programs, described in Oller, 1991) transcript provided as Figure 2–1. Each utterance here is separated by the # sign. Note that this 1-year-old child, who was followed in a diary study by a linguist parent, produced many sequences, mostly monosyllabic, that possessed a generally similar form—the tonic syllable was always initiated with a labial obstruent, and the tonic vowel was always mid or low. Yet, there are many different forms (listed in an order that corresponds roughly to the observed frequency of occurrence for each form), suggesting in the transcriptions presented that the child may have commanded a large inventory of segments and syllables. Yet the variability of production may have been accidental. Could it be that all the utterances had the same target, and that the variations of pronunciation result from a combination of child error in pronunciation and adult error in transcription? Such questions would be hard to answer in the absence of external evidence on context of production.

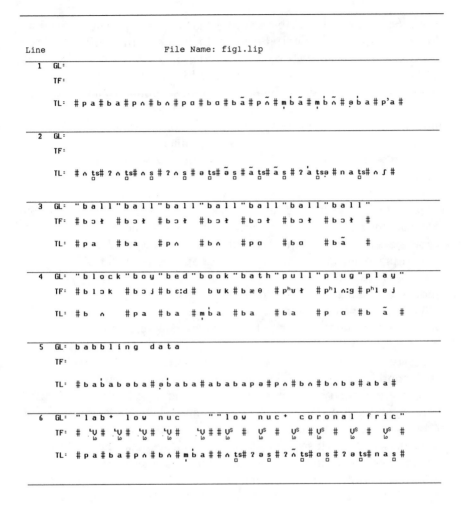

**Figure 2–1.** LIPP transcriptions of utterances of two children at 12 and 16 months of age.

Consider also the utterances indicated in line 2 of Figure 2–1, based on utterances of another 1-year-old. Again the variable productions could be read as indicating a large syllable and segment inventory, yet it seems possible that all the utterances resulted from a single intent on the part of the infant.

By 16 months of age, many of the utterances of the first infant were clearly attempts to produce the word *ball* as indicated in line 3. The variability of these pronunciations was, however, not obviously less than that occurring when the child attempted to produce a variety of additional forms that were monosyllabic with a labial stop as the first segment as shown in line 4. The variability of pronunciations thus was not apparently associated with contrastive intentions on the child's part, at least not in the perceptions of parents and friends of the child. Common babbling forms of the same child a few months before meaningful speech (indicated in line 5) provide an indication that both the phonetic character and the tendencies toward variability of pronunciation seen in early meaningful speech had been present much earlier.

Similarly, the second child (the one in line 2) was believed by parents and friends (both linguistically sophisticated and not) to have a single intended form that simply resulted in variable pronunciation. It should be noted that only the linguistically sophisticated observers of these children took particular notice of the phonetic variations in these forms—on the whole, after a brief familiarity with either child, adults tended to conclude that the pragmatic intents of the children's speech acts were fairly simple. The adults seemed to categorize the infant utterances very broadly and ignore much of the phonetic variation that occurred.

As a result of such observations, we have come to feel uncomfortable with segmental transcriptions of very young children if the fine distinctions implied by the transcriptions are used as a basis for assigning an inventory to the child. In the two cases just mentioned, neither child had a rich contrastive system of speech communication—even at 16 months of age the first child had only six or seven different syllable types (which were used homonomously to denote many lexical items), and the second child had only the syllabic form indicated above. So for the items listed in Figure 2–1, it seems reasonable to suggest that there was really just one target form involved for each child, and that they were syllabic in nature. Line 6 of the transcript provides an indication of a nonsegmental transcription proposal for the intended forms. For the first child, the GL (gloss) row refers to a labial, low nucleus, designated on the TF (target form) row by an underspecified vowel with a labial onset feature (indicated by the diacritic L) and a low vowel quality feature (indicated by the diacritic LO). Consistent with the variable pronunciations indicated in the child's data, this underspecified syllable is manifest in the varying forms provided on the TL (transcriptional) row. For the second child, the deep form is assumed to be a low nucleus with a coronal friction offset, designated on the TF row by an underspecified vowel with a low quality feature and a frication offset (indicated by the subscript S). Again, consistent with the data, the underspecified target corresponds to variable forms on the TL row.

The notational conventions suggested here are consistent with the attempt to reduce the extent to which our transcription conventions imply segmentalization. By designating a syllable nucleus with onset and offset features indicated by diacritics, we intend to make explicit the suspicion that the child's syllables are more like rhythmic chunks with specifiable onset and offset characteristics than sequences of segmental elements. Although it may be useful to continue to perform transcription of child forms to obtain a view of the variability adults can hear in the child utterances (and, consequently, an appreciation for the potential contrasts of the child utterances), it seems more consistent with the functional child system to invoke an underspecified notation such as the one suggested here.

In the past months we have embarked on a broad study of the development of syllables and segments in child phonology based on a longitudinal investigation of infant vocal development and young child speech. In the attempt to prepare a framework for evaluation of the early words of children in the study, and to acquire pilot data, we assessed the speech of three children at 10, 12, 16, 20, and 24 months of age, and at 10, 12, and 16 months for an additional child. A summary is provided in Figure 2–2 (lines 1–4) of the apparent contrastive inventories of syllables with a consonant-like onset in the four children at 10 months (a few syllables with vowel only onset apparently were also present, but were difficult to evaluate and have thus been ignored in the present description). Note that the inventories ranged in size from 3 to 8 syllables. By 24 months of age, the inventories ranged in size from 6 to 12 syllables, indicating some growth in contrastive units. At the same time, it is interesting to note that the inventories even at 24 months are actually a minute fraction of the syllable inventories that are manipulated by mature speakers of English.

The syllabic evaluations performed in this study are based on an intuitive approach to transcription, wherein the observer is required to make a determination not just about what auditory distinctions can be made among the various forms, but also about the functions of utterances, and the contexts in which particular forms appear to occur repeatedly. To the extent that auditorily variable (though grossly similar) forms are used similarly, the transcriber is encouraged to denote them similarly. In this approach, contrasting pronunciation is not assumed to represent contrastive intent unless there is concrete reason to attribute such intent to the child based on situational data. This approach to description is not without precedent in child language research, but ironically it has not been common in child phonology. To find studies of early speech that imply or directly indicate underspecified phonetic forms, it is most beneficial to evaluate the early literature on childhood semantics and the onset of referential communication (e.g., Dore,

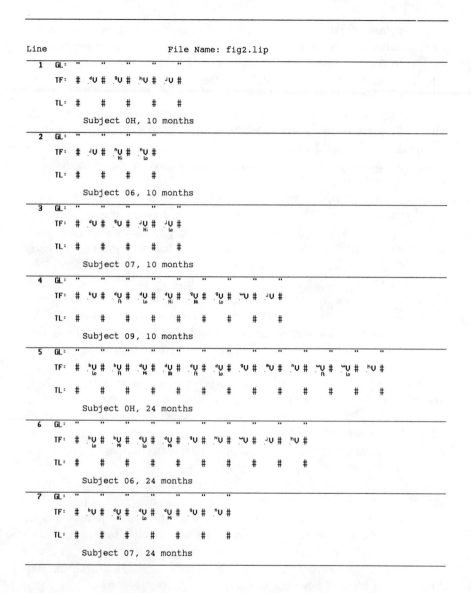

**Figure 2–2.** LIPP transcription of contrastive syllable inventories in four children at 10 months of age and three of the four at 24 months of age.

Franklin, Miller, & Ramer, 1976; Halliday, 1975). Yet the method employed in formulating underspecified phonetic elements has been informal and variable. A major methodological/theoretical challenge that faces child phonologists and semanticists in the next few years is the development of a workable and well-motivated set of criteria for categorization of young child words in both pragmatic and infraphonological terms.

Other data on the children in the pilot study have been collected to evaluate another characteristic of young child syllables that has been posited to be related to emerging segmentalization. MacNeilage and Davis (1990) argued that early phonological systems may be bound by mechanical constraints that are inconsistent with segmental function. According to data from the authors, early syllables are produced in "frames" that show tendencies to include predictive association of consonant-like onsets and vowel-like nuclei. The lack of free association of the onset and offset aspect of syllables is taken to mean that true segments are not involved. In particular, the frame hypothesis suggests that coronal consonants are, by mechanical association, most likely to co-occur with high and/or front vowels, whereas labial consonants are most likely to co-occur with nonhigh, nonfront vowels. Similarly, dorsal consonants are expected to show greater ties to back vowels than either labial or coronal consonants. According to the

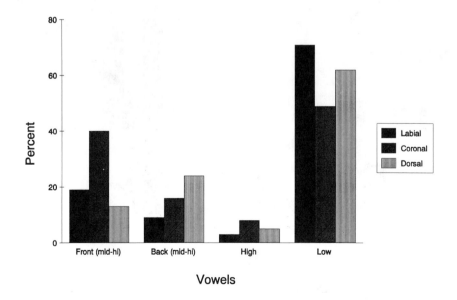

**Figure 2–3.** Consonant-vowel co-occurrence in four children 10–12 months of age.

frame hypothesis, only when a child has broken free of such mechanical constraints can there be a true segmental system.

Based on segmental transcriptions of the data from the four children, we performed an automatic analysis in LIPP in order to determine the extent of association of consonantal and vocalic gestures in the children. The data provided weak support for the frame hypothesis at 10–12 months of age as indicated by data from all four children in Figure 2–3. Coronal consonants were more frequently associated with front (mid to high) vowels than were labial or dorsal consonants. Dorsals were more closely associated with back (mid to high) vowels than were either labials or coronals. Coronals showed the highest association with high vowels as a whole, and labials showed the greatest association with low vowels. At the same time, none of the trends was characteristic of all four children's data at 10–12 months (see for example the data on Subject 09 in Figure 2–4), and it should be emphasized that the low vowels were the most

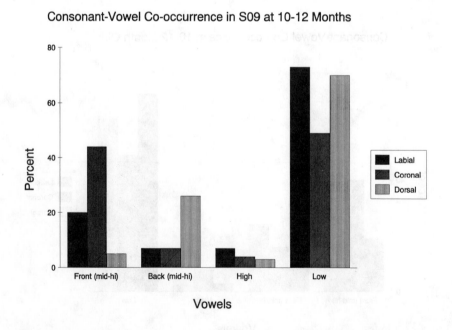

**Figure 2–4.** Consonant-vowel co-occurrence in one child (Subject S09) at 10–12 months of age.

frequent type with *all* the consonants for *all* the children. The data suggest that the mechanical constraints implied by the frame hypothesis impose inclinations toward certain connections but do not prevent production of syllables with a variety of consonant-vowel associations.

By 16–24 months of age, the pattern of mechanical inclinations appeared to have weakened further as indicated by data in Figure 2–5. Such a pattern of weakening would, of course, be consistent with the expectation that the children were readying their systems for more segmental function. By this age, coronal and other consonants were almost equally associated with front and high vowels, labials and dorsals were slightly more associated with low vowels, and coronals had replaced dorsals as the consonants most frequently associated with back vowels. Another indication of growing freedom of association is the fact that in the 16–24 month data, the children show much more balanced production of all vowel types, regardless of consonant place of articulation. In the coming months this analysis will be expanded to include data from 20 normal children.

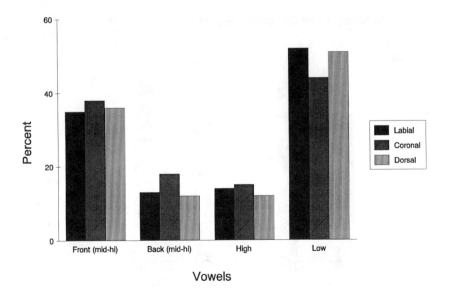

**Figure 2–5.** Consonant-vowel co-occurrence in three children 16–24 months of age.

Additional pilot data on the frame hypothesis have been collected in a study of deaf children's early vocabularies in speech. The data on six deaf children aged 2–5 years have been reported by Steffens, Fishman, Eilers, and Oller (1991) and are summarized in Figure 2–6. The general impression with all the data from the deaf children was that there were essentially only two syllable types utilized contrastively. One had a labial onset and one a coronal onset. The preferred vowel was mid to low and central in both cases. In fact, the two patterns of vowel usage look virtually identical in the context of the two consonants as indicated in the figure. One might argue that such data suggest a segmental system because there appears to be one vowel occurring in free association with two consonants. Our own preference is to assume that, when a system of production is so limited that it possesses only a single pair of syllables, it does not matter how those are constructed with regard to consonant-vowel pairings—they do not seem to provide sufficient weight of evidence to justify a segmental analysis. This preference may not, however, be shared by other colleagues. In Chapter 1, Vihman, Velleman, and McCune, for example, in analyzing the speech production of "Timmy," come to the conclusion that individual vowel

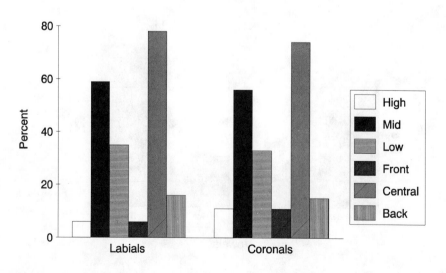

**Figure 2–6.** Consonant-vowel co-occurrence in six deaf children 2–5 years of age.

segments should be attributed to the child at the point at which the elements show some "autonomy." The challenge for all of us ultimately will be to establish a workable empirically based criterion by which the term "autonomy" can be defined, and by which other factors relevant to attribution of segmentalization can be systematically considered. In particular, we prefer a conservative criterion that would insist on not only evidence of autonomy, but also on evidence that there is an advantage of economy (in perception, production, or storage) that can be achieved by segmental reanalysis of a syllabic inventory.

Of course, our own analyses of co-occurrence begin with a segmental transcription, a fact that makes us a bit nervous, given that we conclude from the analyses that there is little reason to assume segmentalization in the child's intent. We reiterate that two issues are at stake in characterizing the child's forms. One issue has to do with the child's intents, the elements of primary interest in evaluating the progress of the young mind, a progress we now think begins with only a syllabic representation and is later split (although not necessarily suddenly) into a multitiered arrangement. The other issue has to do with the potential adult interpretations of child forms. In that domain there is room for segmental characterization, because well-formed syllables can be read as segmental sequences; and they may provide material through which parents can hurry their children along toward richer lexicons.

## ACKNOWLEDGMENT

This research is supported by NIH/NIDCD grant No. 5-R01-DC00484 to D. Kimbrough Oller.

## REFERENCES

Cruttenden, A. (1970). A phonetic study of babbling. *British Journal of Disorders of Communication, 5*, 110–118.

Dore, J., Franklin, M. B., Miller, R. T., & Ramer, A. L. H. (1976). Transitional phenomena in early language acquisition. *Journal of Child Language, 3*, 13–28.

Ferguson, C. A., & Farwell, C. B. (1975). Words and sounds in early language acquisition: English initial consonants in the first 50 words. *Language, 51*, 419–439.

Gasser, M. (1992). Phonology as a byproduct of learning to recognize and produce words: A connectionist model. In J. J. Ohala, T. M. Nearey, B. L. Derwing, M. M. Hodge, & G. E. Wiebe (Eds.), *ICSLP 92 proceedings* (Vol. 1, pp. 277–280). Edmonton, Canada: Personal Publishing Ltd.

Halliday, M. A. K. (1975). Learning how to mean. In E. Lenneberg & E. Lenneberg (Eds.), *Foundations of language development* (pp. 239–265). New York: Academic Press.

Holmgren, D., Lindblom, B., Aurelius, G., Jalling, B., & Zetterström, R. (1986). On the phonetics of infant vocalization. In B. Lindblom & R. Zetterström (Eds.), *Precursors of early speech* (pp. 51–63). New York: Stockton Press.

Ingram, D. (1974). Phonological rules in young children. *Journal of Child Language, 1*, 49–64.

Jakobson, R. (1962). Why "Mama" and "Papa"? In R. Jakobson, *Selected writings* (Vol. 1, pp. 538–545). The Hague: Mouton.

Kent, R. D., Osberger, M. J., Netsell, R., & Hustedde, C. (1987). Phonetic development in identical twins differing in auditory function. *Journal of Speech and Hearing Disorders, 52*, 64–75.

Lindblom, B. (1992). Phonological units as adaptive emergents of lexical development. In C. A. Ferguson, L. Menn, & C. Stoel-Gammon (Eds.), *Phonological development* (pp. 131–163). Timonium, MD: York Press.

Lindblom, B., MacNeilage, P., & Studdert-Kennedy, M. (1983). Self-organizing processes and the explanation of phonological universals. In B. Butterworth, B. Comrie, & Ö. Dahl (Eds.), *Explanations of linguistic universals.* The Hague: Mouton.

Lynch, M. P., Oller, D. K., Lewis, J. L., & Steffens, M. L. (1991, May). *Phonological phrase-like units in infant vocalizations: Evidence from normally developing and Down syndrome infants.* Paper presented at 24th annual Gatlinburg Conference, Key Biscayne, FL.

MacNeilage, P. F., & Davis, B. L. (1990). Acquisition of speech production: The achievement of segmental independence. In W. J. Hardcastel & A. Marchal (Eds.), *Speech production and speech modelling.* Dordrecht: Kluwer.

Mavilya, M. (1969). *Spontaneous vocalization and babbling in hearing impaired infants.* Unpublished doctoral dissertation, Columbia University, New York. (University Microfilms No. 70-12879).

Menyuk, P. (1968). The role of distinctive features in children's acquisition of phonology. *Journal of Speech and Hearing Research, 11*, 138–146.

Oller, D. K. (1980). The emergence of the sounds of speech in infancy. In G. Yeni-Komshian, J. Kavanagh, & C. Ferguson (Eds), *Child phonology: Volume 1 Production* (pp. 93–112). New York: Academic Press.

Oller, D. K. (1981). Infant vocalizations: Exploration and reflexivity. In R. E. Stark (Ed.), *Language behavior in infancy and early childhood* (pp. 85–103). New York: Elsevier/North-Holland.

Oller, D. K. (1991). Computational approaches to transcription and analysis in child phonology. *Journal for Computer Users in Speech and Hearing, 7*, 44–59.

Oller, D. K. (1992). *Development of the infrastructure of speech production abilities: Syllables and segments in early phonology* [Abstract]. In J. J. Ohala, T. M. Nearey, B. L. Derwing, M. M. Hodge, & G. E. Wiebe (Eds), *ICSLP 92 proceedings* (Addendum), (p. 5). Edmonton, Canada: Priority Printing.

Oller, D. K., & Eilers, R. E. (1988). The role of audition in infant babbling. *Child Development, 59*, 441–449.

Oller, D. K., Eilers, R. E., Bull, D. H., & Carney, A. E. (1985). Prespeech vocalizations of a deaf infant: A comparison with normal metaphonological development. *Journal of Speech and Hearing Research, 28*, 47–63.

Oller, D. K., Wieman, L., Doyle, W., & Ross, C. (1975). Infant babbling and speech. *Journal of Child Language, 3*, 1–11.

Papoušek, M. (1992, May). *Melodic gestures in maternal speech to preverbal infants: Similarities and differences across species.* Presented at 8th International Conferences on Infant Studies, Miami Beach, FL.

Smith, N. (1973). *The acquisition of phonology: a case study.* Cambridge, MA: Cambridge University Press.

Stark, R. E. (1980). Stages of speech development in the first year of life. In G. Yeni-Komshian, J. Kavanagh, & C. Ferguson (Eds), *Child phonology: Vol. 1. Production* (pp. 73–90). New York: Academic Press.

Steffens, M. L., Fishman, L. M., Eilers, R. E., & Oller, D. K. (1991, November). *Phonetic inventories of tactually aided deaf children.* Paper presented at American Speech-Language-Hearing Association Annual Convention, Atlanta.

Stoel-Gammon, C., & Otomo, K. (1986). Babbling development of hearing impaired and normally hearing subjects. *Journal of Speech and Hearing Disorders, 51*, 33–41.

Studdert-Kennedy, M. (1983). On learning to speak. *Human Neurobiology, 2*, 191–195.

Templin, M. C. (1957). *Certain language skills in children: Their development and interrelationships.* Minneapolis: University of Minnesota Press.

Vihman, M. M. (1978). Consonant harmony: Its scope and function in child language. In J. H. Greenberg, C. A. Ferguson, & E. A. Moravscik (Eds), *Universals of human language, Vol. 2: Phonology.* Palo Alto, CA: Stanford University Press.

Waterson, N. (1971). Child phonology: A prosodic view. *Journal of Linguistics, 7*, 170–221.

# CHAPTER    3

*Consonant Harmony and Phonological Underspecification in Child Speech*

CAROL STOEL-GAMMON, PH.D. AND JOSEPH PAUL STEMBERGER, PH.D.

A characteristic error pattern of early child speech is assimilation, whereby one speech sound in a word takes on one or more feature values of another sound. Thus, the /d/ of *doggie* might be fully assimilated to the following /g/ yielding the pronunciation [gagi], or the /p/ of *pin* might assimilate only the nasal feature of /n/ resulting in the form [mĩn]. Although there are examples of assimilatory patterns between consonants and vowels (Stoel-Gammon, 1983), assimilation occurs most frequently between noncontiguous consonants and is referred to as consonant harmony. Many researchers have noted the presence of consonant harmony in their studies of phonological development, and some have posited possible explanations, but our understanding of this phenomenon is far from complete. The major question to be examined in this chapter is: Is it possible to predict which consonant will assimilate to another, that is, is *doggie* typically [gagi], or is [dadi] just as likely to occur?

The question of whether there are any general biases across children in patterns of consonant harmony has been raised a number of times, but remains unanswered. In his often-cited diary study, Smith (1973) suggested that there are not. He proposed that a given child may assimilate alveolars to velars, for example, but another child may do the reverse. Lewis (1936), in contrast, proposed that there is a bias towards segments learned earlier; that is, children will assimilate newly learned sounds to sounds that have been in the child's system for a longer period of time. Vihman (1978) expressed some support for this bias. Menn (1976) and Cruttenden (1978) have argued for different biases, in examining harmony patterns among velars, labials, and alveolars. They each presented data from studies of one or a few children showing that: (1) alveolars were replaced by velars and labials; (2) velars and labials were never replaced by alveolars; and (3) velars and labials showed assimilation in one direction only. They differed on their observations of interactions between velars and labials, however, with Menn stating that labials assimilate to velars and Cruttenden stating that velars assimilate to labials (along with Ferguson, Peizer, & Weeks, 1973).

Both have suggested that their data reflect the most common case, citing several similar examples from the literature. No real explanation is given for these biases. Menn arranged the segments in a strength hierarchy, from weakest (alveolars) to strongest (velars), and noted that weak segments harmonize to stronger ones. Cruttenden suggested that alveolars are more difficult to produce than consonants at other places of articulation from a motor point of view, and that the bias is towards easier articulations; this bias would, then, also explain why velars assimilate to labials. Such ease of articulation arguments have the drawback of no phonetic underpinnings. In this case, they also seem highly unlikely. If alveolars are so difficult motorically, why are they so common in babbling (Locke, 1983) and early meaningful speech (Stoel-Gammon, 1985)? Thus, Menn and Cruttenden do not really provide us with an independent explanation for the asymmetries, and they disagree on exactly which asymmetry is expected for interactions between velars and labials.

Berg (1992), also investigating a single subject, agreed with Cruttenden that velars and alveolars assimilate to bilabials. Like Menn, he proposed a strength hierarchy, albeit with labials as the strongest segments. He has tried to attribute the high strength of labials to their high frequency of occurrence. This hypothesis is discussed further later.

There is also a drawback inherent in the single-subject type of study done by Menn, Cruttenden, and Berg. Such studies give us nice detail about what an individual child does, but are inconclusive about the issues raised here.

Phonological development can be influenced by a variety of factors, leading to a great deal of variability between children. Different factors can lead to opposite biases in different children. We need to be certain that the patterns shown by a given child are representative of children as a whole and then determine what factor, or set of factors, might underlie these patterns. Thus, to test a hypothesis adequately, we must examine data from many children. This has never been done for the type of hypothesis we are examining here. Although Menn and Cruttenden noted that velar harmony and labial harmony have often been reported in the literature, and that alveolar harmony has not, we really cannot be certain that there is a bias in this direction without a systematic look at a large number of children.

To date, the only published investigation based on more than a handful of subjects was done by Vihman (1978) who analyzed the productions of 13 young children from six different language communities. The study focused on three main issues related to assimilatory patterns in children: (1) the question of consonant harmony as a universal feature of early phonological development, (2) individual differences in the form and function of consonant harmony, and (3) the relationship between patterns of consonant harmony in child speech and the phonological system of the adult language being acquired. The question of patterns in terms of place and manner assimilations was not central to the study, although some of the examples cited are relevant to this issue. Thus, although Vihman's paper is based on data from a fair-sized subject population (fair-sized for child phonology studies, at least), it cannot answer the question of general biases posed earlier.

In this chapter, we propose an alternative explanation of consonant harmony in child speech, one based on the notion of **underspecification** of phonological segments. According to underspecification theory (e.g., Kiparsky, 1985), phonological segments in a lexical entry do not need to be fully specified. Some features are left blank in underlying representations, and the blanks are filled in during the course of a derivation, either through the assimilation of a feature from a nearby segment or through the operation of a feature-filling rule. Phonological underspecification has been shown to be useful in the analysis of phonological data from many languages (e.g., Archangeli, 1984; Pulleyblank, 1986).

## PHONOLOGICAL UNDERSPECIFICATION

To provide a background for the analyses presented here, we need to present some assumptions about which features are specified for which segments, assuming radical underspecification. Figure 3–1 presents the features discussed in this chapter, using the most common view of

| | /p,b/ | /f/ | /m/ | /t,d/ | /s/ | /n/ | /k,g/ | /ŋ/ |
|---|---|---|---|---|---|---|---|---|
| **Continuant** | | + | | | + | | | |
| **Nasal** | | | + | | | + | | + |
| **Coronal** | | | | | | | | |
| **Labial** | + | + | + | | | | | |
| **Dorsal** | | | | | | | + | + |

**Figure 3–1.** Place and manner specifications of selected obstruents.

universally unmarked features (e.g., Kiparsky, 1985). As shown, consonantal phonemes are specified (i.e., the cell is filled with a +) for varying numbers of features with, for example, /t/, being completely unspecified and /m/ specified for two features. For the manner features, only fricatives are specified for the feature [continuant] and nasals are specified as [nasal]. The place of articulation features presented in Figure 3–1 are based on proposals by Sagey (1986), and it should be noted that they are not binary; rather, consonants are either specified (as indicated by +) or unspecified (left blank). As shown, bilabial and labiodental consonants are specified as [Labial] and velars are [Dorsal]; alveolars are not specified for any place feature underlying, but are classified as [Coronal] later in the derivation.

Using the set of specified features in Figure 3–1, there are two ways in which a pair of segments can differ from one another. In the first case, the two segments might be identical except for the number of features that are specified. For example, /n/ differs from /t/ only in that /n/ is specified as [nasal] and /t/ is not; similarly, /s/ differs from /t/ only in that /s/ is specified as [continuant]. In these cases, we can say that /t/ is underspecified with respect to /s/ and /n/. The second way segments can differ from one another can be illustrated by comparing /s/ and /n/. They are similar in that neither is specified for place of articulation and both are specified for manner of articulation; however, the manner feature specified for /s/ is [continuant], whereas for /n/ it is [nasal]. In this comparison, then, we say that neither consonant is underspecified with respect to the other, or that both consonants are specified with respect to the other.

The two types of relationship between segments constrain the sorts of changes that can take place. In this example, /t/ can assimilate the manner feature [+nasal] simply by putting the feature into the blank spot where that feature can be specified. This converts the representation for /t/ into that of /n/. Similarly, putting in the feature [+continuant] converts the representation of /t/ into that of /s/. But, putting the feature [+continuant] into /n/ does not convert the representation into /s/, nor does putting the feature [+nasal] into /s/ convert it into /n/. The result instead is a nasalized fricative, a segment that does not occur in English or in most other languages. Similarly, if /k/ with the feature [Dorsal] assimilates to /p/ by adding the feature [Labial], a labiovelar stop results, another segment lacking in English. Converting /s/ to /n/ requires two steps: insertion of the feature [+ nasal] and deletion of the feature [+continuant]. Conversely, converting /n/ to /s/ requires insertion of [+continuant] and deletion of [+nasal]. These are more complex operations than converting an unspecified segment such as /t/ to a specified one such as /k/.

We predict that the different characterizations of these changes will affect the types of harmony that occur in child speech and will influence what assimilates to what (see below). Here we would like to point out that this view of underspecification naturally brings out three contrasts in terms of manner features: between oral stops and nasal stops ([nasal]), between oral stops and oral fricatives ([continuant]), and between nasal stops and oral fricatives (both [nasal] and [continuant]). More general comparisons, such as between oral and nasal phones (regardless of whether stops or fricatives are involved) or between stops and fricatives (regardless of whether they are oral or nasal) do not have any natural interpretation or form a coherent type of contrast. At all times, we will follow the groupings based on the representations of the sounds in question.

Underspecification leads to an asymmetry in the ease with which one phoneme assimilates to another. As noted above, for /t/ to assimilate to /p/, the feature [Labial] is added to /t/. The addition of a feature to an underspecified phoneme is a natural event. To provide proper articulatory instructions, some feature for place of articulation must be filled in. The feature can be provided by a nonassimilatory process (in which case it will be [Coronal]), or it can be filled in by an assimilatory process. In contrast, to assimilate /p/ to /t/, it is necessary to delete the feature [Labial] from /p/. In our view, deletion of features is not a natural operation, and we hypothesize that assimilations of specified segments to underspecified ones will be relatively uncommon. It is more natural for underspecified phonemes to assimilate to specified phonemes than the reverse. Although these hypotheses are grounded in modern phonological theory, Stemberger (1991) noted that they also can be derived from general properties of psychological processing.

In child speech, then, we predict that assimilatory processes will show a bias toward replacing underspecified elements with specified elements (i.e., we predict that this type of assimilation will occur more frequently than other types). On the basis of Figure 3–1, we make the following predictions: (1) given that alveolars have no specification for place of articulation, there should be a bias for alveolars to assimilate to velars and labials, which do have specifications for place; the reverse, where velars and labials assimilate to alveolars and thereby lose their specifications for place, should not be common; (2) there should be a bias for stops, which have no specification for manner of articulation, to assimilate to nasals and fricatives; the reverse, where nasals and fricatives assimilate to stops and thereby lose their specifications for manner, should not be common; and (3) in cases where a segment with one specification could assimilate to a segment with a different specification, we predict that no biases will be obtain since underspecification theory gives us no reason to predict any asymmetry; thus, labials should assimilate to velars just as frequently as velars assimilate to labials, and nasals should assimilate to fricatives just as often as fricatives assimilate to nasals We also predict that assimilations of this type will be less common than those involving assimilation of underspecified segments to specified ones (e.g., alveolars to labials or velars; stops to fricatives or nasals) because these assimilatory patterns are more complex, requiring that the original specifications be deleted and other specifications inserted.

## METHOD

This study is based on data from 51 children who were acquiring English. The children fall into two groups. The first group is made up of 33 children whose prelinguistic and early linguistic development was studied longitudinally by the first author. These subjects were audio- and videorecorded at 3-month intervals from 9 months to 2 years of age. The recordings were made in a laboratory setting as the child interacted with a parent in a play situation. (See Olswang, Stoel-Gammon, Coggins & Carpenter, 1987, for details.) Meaningful vocalizations produced by the subjects were identified, phonetically transcribed by a team of transcribers, and analyzed to determine various aspects of early phonological development (see Stoel-Gammon, 1985, 1987, for results). The present study examines the assimilation and substitution patterns in the speech of these 33 subjects.

The second group is made up of 18 children for whom enough detailed information was available to be of use to us. Four children are our own children (two each) who were followed in unpublished diary studies. The remaining 14 children have been reported in the literature in enough detail to give us a picture of their use of consonant harmony (Bleile, 1987; Cruttenden, 1978; Donahue, 1986; Ferguson et al., 1973; Fudge, 1969; Holmes, 1927; Leopold, 1947; Lewis, 1936; Matthei, 1989; Menn, 1971; Smith, 1973; Velten, 1943); the three English-speaking children included in Vihman (1978) are also included here.

This sample of 51 children, although quite large by usual standards, is of marginal but usable size to address the question of underspecification. We will use the full set of 51 children for statistical purposes. Since the longitudinal sample is more complete, however, we will give those data in parentheses as these numbers are useful in determining the frequency of assimilatory processes across children. The full sample is not as useful in that regard, because many of the children were preselected for the presence of harmony.

We first identified a given child's nonassimilatory substitutions. We then looked for possible cases of harmony, eliminating cases that could be attributed to nonassimilatory processes (following Vihman, 1978). For example, if a child replaced velars with alveolars everywhere (as in [di] *key*); a pronunciation such as [deyt] for *Kate*, which could a priori have been viewed as an instance of alveolar harmony, was instead analyzed as an instance of the nonassimilatory process of velar fronting (context-free substitution of alveolars for velars). There were a few cases of contiguous assimilation (i.e. assimilation between adjacent segments, including between consonants and vowels); these contact assimilations were excluded from the analysis here. We also excluded all cases of reduplication (i.e., assimilation of one syllable to another).

We encountered only a few unclear cases. One child in the longitudinal sample pronounced the word *down* as [dawt]. Is this oral harmony or (nonassimilatory) final denasalization? The child attempted no other words ending in nasals, so we could not be certain. Because all such cases went against our hypothesis about harmony, we treated them as instance of harmony; this is the most conservative decision in that it makes it more difficult to find support for our hypothesis.

There were five children who substituted velar stops for fricatives, producing [gowk] for *fork* or *soak*. We classified these forms as instances of place harmony rather than stopping harmony. Adult English contains no velar fricatives, and English-speaking children rarely produce velar fricatives in their speech. We reasoned that the fricatives were changing into stops as part of a nonassimilatory process of stopping, motivated by the lack of velar fricatives in the child's phonetic inventory. We considered pronunciations like [xowk] unlikely; as a general rule of thumb, a child will not have assimilatory processes that create segments that are not found elsewhere in the child's speech (although some cases have been reported). In the one child who showed a similar assimilation to a labial stop ([pʰiːp] for *sleep/sweep/sheep*), however, this was counted as an instance of stopping harmony, since the child had a bilabial fricative in her phonetic inventory at the time.

We will report the nonassimilatory processes as well as assimilations since these processes provide a control on the interpretation of harmonies. To rule out other explanations for the data, it is important that there not be general biases towards a particular place or manner of articulation that show up in all processes in the child's speech. If, for example, velar harmony is more common than alveolar harmony, it is important to show that there is no general bias for alveolars to become velars. If such a general bias were present, it could be accounted for in other ways.

After identifying the assimilatory and nonassimilatory processes for each child, we determined the number of subjects for whom an underspecified feature value was assimilated to another specified value. Some children showed assimilation in both directions (e.g., assimilating an alveolar to a velar in some words, but assimilating a velar to an alveolar in other words); the number of children showing such bidirectional harmonies is also reported. The results were evaluated using a two-tailed sign test over children, using only the data from children who showed harmony in one direction or the other; children showing bidirectional harmony were counted as ties and excluded from the statistical tests, as is standard.

The literature (e.g., Vihman, 1978) suggests that manner harmonies are much less common than place harmonies. We thought in advance that there might not be enough data to examine nasal harmony and fricative harmony separately, and planned to sum the data for a general test for asymmetries in manner harmony, to gain enough power for statistical purposes; this turned out to be unnecessary. Voicing harmony was not examined; none was observed in the longitudinal study, and we know of only one report in the literature of a child with voicing harmony (Matthei, 1989), although few examples were given. We also have not addressed harmonies involving laterals and glides as one or both of the segments involved (e.g., [zɪzowd] for *lizard* or [lɛlo] for *yellow*),because these are fairly uncommon across children.

# RESULTS

## *PLACE OF ARTICULATION*

The results of comparisons involving place of articulation appear in Table 3–1. The number of children for whom a particular process was observed is given for both the full sample of 51 subjects and, in

**Table 3–1.** Place of articulation features: Number of subjects from full sample ($n = 51$) using assimilatory and nonassimilatory processes; number of subjects from longitudinal sample ($n = 33$) shown in parentheses

| Context | Assimilatory | Nonassimilatory |
|---|---|---|
| Alveolar/Velar | | |
|     alveolar——>velar | 19 (10) | 1 (1) |
|     velar——>alveolar | 1 (0) | 24 (16) |
|     both directions | 3 (2) | 3 (2) |
| Alveolar/Labial | | |
|     alveolar——>labial | 18 (10) | 1 (0) |
|     labial——>alveolar | 2 (0) | 4 (0) |
|     both directions | 4 (0) | 2 (1) |
| Labial/Velar | | |
|     labial——>velar | 5 (2) | 1 (0) |
|     velar——>labial | 9 (2) | 1 (0) |
|     both directions | 4 (0) | 0 (0) |

parentheses, for the longitudinal subset ($n = 33$). Looking first at the comparisons of target velar and alveolar consonants in assimilatory contexts, it can be seen that the process of velar harmony only was observed in the samples of 18 children whereas alveolar harmony only was present for just one subject, a difference that is statistically significant ($p <.001$). The samples from three subjects evidenced both velar and alveolar harmony and consequently were not included in the statistical comparison. In nonassimilatory contexts, 24 subjects substituted alveolars for velars whereas only one evidenced the reverse pattern, a difference that was also statistically significant ($p < .01$). Both of these facts are predicted by our hypotheses listed above.

Comparisons of alveolars and labials in assimilatory contexts also revealed a statistically significant difference between the number of children who evidenced labial harmony only and the number with alveolar harmony only ($p < .01$). As was the case with the previous comparisons, a small group of children used both types of harmony processes. Analysis of the relatively few instances of substitutions in nonassimilatory contexts revealed that slightly more subjects replaced labials with alveolars than the reverse (a nonsignificant trend). Again, the facts are as predicted: Labial harmony was observed in more subjects than alveolar harmony, and (a few) more subjects evidenced substitutions of alveolars for labials than labials for alveolars in non-harmony contexts.

The findings comparing labial and velar places of articulation (Table 3–1) indicate that there is no significant difference in the numbers of subjects undergoing particular processes, although there is a small, nonsignificant difference, with more children assimilating velars to labials than the reverse. Thus, it is nearly as likely that velars will assimilate to labials as the reverse. As predicted, assimilations between velars and labials was less common than between alveolars and labials or velars. Non-harmony substitutions between labials and velars occurred infrequently.

## MANNER OF ARTICULATION

Comparisons of the numbers of subjects using processes involving manner of articulation are presented in Table 3–2. As shown, more children were observed to use nasal harmony (a stop assimilating to a nasal) than the reverse. Statistical analysis revealed that this difference just missed significance, due in part to the small set of subjects using either process ($p =$ .07). Just one subject evidenced oral harmony only (i.e., nasal assimilating to a stop); examination of this child's sample showed that the pattern occurred in the word *down*, the only word in the sample that included a word-final nasal. Thus it is possible that this was a nonassimilatory substitution. In clearly nonassimilatory substitutions, a few children substituted oral stops for nasals; none substituted nasals for oral stops.

As predicted, Table 3–2 shows that significantly more subjects assimilated stops to fricatives (fricative harmony) than vice versa ($p < .05$), and that substantially more subjects substituted stops for fricatives in nonassimilatory contexts ($p < .001$). The latter pattern, referred to as the phonological process of stopping, is well attested in the literature on child phonology (e.g., Stoel-Gammon & Dunn, 1985). As shown in Table 3–2, four children assimilated fricatives to nasals. Because two of these children evidenced a general patterns of substitution of stops for fricatives in nonassimilatory contexts, the assimilations of fricative to nasal could be interpreted as additional examples of stops assimilating to nasals.

## DISCUSSION

The results conform closely to the predictions based on phonological underspecification: (1) for place of articulation, we found that more children assimilated alveolars to velars and labials than the reverse; (2) for manner of articulation, we found that more children assimilated oral stops to nasals and fricatives than the reverse; and (3) we found that velars were no more likely to assimilate to labials than the reverse, clearing up some disagreement in the literature where conflicting statements had been made. In sum, underspecified phonemes assimilate

**Table 3–2.** Manner of articulation features: Number of subjects from full sample (*n* = 51) using assimilatory and nonassimilatory processes; number of subjects from longitudinal sample (*n* = 33) shown in parentheses

| Context | Assimilatory | Nonassimilatory |
|---|---|---|
| Stop/Nasal | | |
|    stop——>nasal | 7 (4) | 0 (0) |
|    nasal——>stop | 1 (1) | 4 (0) |
|    both directions | 2 (0) | 0 (0) |
| Stop/Fricative | | |
|    stop——>fricative | 8 (2) | 3 (1) |
|    fricative——>stop | 1 (0) | 37 (24) |
|    both directions | 0 (0) | 0 (0) |
| Nasal/Fricative | | |
|    nasal——>fricative | 0 (0) | 0 (0) |
|    fricative——>nasal | 4 (0) | 0 (0) |
|    both directions | 0 (0) | 0 (0) |

to specified phonemes. Assimilation between two specified phonemes is less common than between underspecified and specified phonemes, presumably because the former involves both deletion and addition of features whereas the latter involves only addition.

Although the results are precisely what underspecification predicts, we must examine other factors that might provide equally valid explanations. We can think of three other alternatives: the order of acquisition of the consonants involved, the frequencies of the consonants in assimilatory patterns, and a special type of regressive overgeneralization. Each of these is discussed in turn.

## ORDER OF ACQUISITION

One possible explanation for assimilatory patterns is that children show a bias toward consonants that they have learned earlier (Lewis, 1936). This is clearly wrong, as Cruttenden (1978) noted. It is well-known that children generally acquire alveolars before they acquire velars (e.g., Locke, 1983; Stoel-Gammon, 1985), a fact that is reflected in the high rate of nonassimilatory processes whereby velars are replaced by alveolars (see Table 3–1).

If order of acquisition is a reasonable explanation, we would need to assume that the children show a bias toward consonants that are acquired later. This would account for the biases to replace alveolars with velars and to replace stops with fricatives. However, it is clear that labials and alveolars are acquired at roughly the same time in many children (Stoel-Gammon, 1985), so the strong bias to replace alveolars with labials cannot be explained by order of acquisition. Further, because labials are acquired before velars, and nasals are acquired before fricatives, we would predict a bias for labials to be replaced by velars and for nasals to be replaced by fricatives. Both of these predictions are counter to our findings; the small, nonsignificant differences observed with these contrasts are, in fact, in the opposite direction from this prediction.

We would like to note that order of acquisition may play a small role in harmonies, accounting for some cases in which other places of articulation assimilate to alveolars. For example, one child originally showed the assimilation of intervocalic velars to word-final alveolars (e.g. *pocket* [pʰatət], just after intervocalic velars had appeared in the system. Several months later, after this harmony had ceased, the child showed the assimilation of alveolars to velars (e.g., *Canada geese* [kænəgəˈgiːs]). Initially, harmony was related to order of acquisition, but not later.

## FREQUENCY

The frequency of an element is a predictor of performance in many domains. Phoneme frequency in adult speech has been shown to be relevant for order of acquisition in cross-linguistic studies of child phonology (e.g., Pye, Ingram, & List, 1987). For example, /tʃ/ is relatively more frequent in Spanish than in English, and on average, Spanish-speaking children master it earlier than English-speaking children. It is possible that frequency has a further effect, with children showing a bias to replace less frequent phones with more frequent phones. We do not have any phoneme counts from these particular children, but we can use published counts of phoneme frequencies in adult and child speech to provide an idea of typical phoneme frequencies. Denes (1963) and Shriberg (1986) reported that in adult and child speech, respectively, alveolars occur more frequently than labials, which in turn are more frequent than velars. They also showed that stops are more frequent than fricatives, which are in turn more frequent than nasals. Given these data, it is clear that the children are not showing a bias towards more frequent phoneme types.

Berg (1992) presented data from a single child to support the hypothesis that less frequent phonemes are replaced the more frequent ones. He showed, for example, that both alveolars and velars assimilated to labials and that the child in question had a preponderance of words with labials. However, although few children have a preponderance of velars, assimilation of alveolars (and labials) to velars is quite frequent. Thus, although there might be a bias based on frequency in some cases (as with Berg's child), this is not the case for most children

The results in Tables 3–1 and 3–2 are much more compatible with a bias toward less frequent phoneme types. This would account for the bias for alveolars to be replaced by velars and labials and for the bias for stops to be replaced by fricatives and nasals. However, it would also predict that labials will be replaced by velars, and that fricatives will be replaced by nasals. Our finding indicate that the former prediction is false; there was no significant difference found between labials and velars (Table 3–1), and the small difference that occurred was in the opposite direction. Thus, frequency cannot account for this finding.

## *REGRESSIVE OVERGENERALIZATION*

There is one remaining hypothesis that might account for the data. Stemberger (1992) discusses various types of phonological regression documented in child phonology, that is, cases in which the pronunciation of particular phonemes or phoneme classes becomes less accurate rather then more accurate over time.One type of regression involves the overgeneralization of a more general change, leading to the loss of an earlier correct pronunciation. It is possible that assimilation patterns are a special case of this type of regression. This explanation can be viewed as a sophisticated version of the order of acquisition explanation for harmony, but one which predicts a bias towards sound types learned later.

Stemberger presented an interesting pattern of acquisition which has been observed in cases of phonological neutralization: When the phonemes A and B have been neutralized as A, it sometimes happens that subsequently both are neutralized as B for brief periods before they are accurately produced. For example, the sequence /or/ was optionally neutralized with /ə/ as [ə] at one stage, followed by a different stage where /ə/ was optionally neutralized with /or/ as [or]. Stemberger attributed this to low-level changes being made in the system that were designed to make [or] easier to produce when it was appropriate and [ə] harder to produce when it was inappropriate. If the changes being made are too heavy-handed, the child may overgeneralize and make [ə] harder to produce even where it is appropriate, so that it comes to be articulated as [or]. Thus, Stemberger suggested that consonant harmony may be a special and subtle form of overgeneralization.

This phenomenon could account for the bias to replace alveolars with velars in harmony, because large numbers (perhaps half) of the subjects evidenced the nonassimilatory process changing velars into alveolars (velar fronting). Data on particular children, as in our longitudinal sample, often showed the nonassimilatory process to replace velars with alveolars at one age, followed by a later harmonic process to replace alveolars with velars. Similarly, the bias toward replacing stops with fricatives in harmony could derive from overgeneralization; in trying to correct an earlier situation where fricatives were replaced by stops in a nonassimilatory process (which most children show), some stops are then replaced by fricatives in an assimilatory process. This hypothesis also accounts for the lack of bias in harmony processes involving the interaction of two specified places or manners of articulation, because, as the data above show, children rarely have nonassimilatory processes that neutralize velars and labials or nasals and fricatives. Overgeneralization occurs only if the two phones involved have been neutralized at an earlier period.

However, the hypothesis fails to account for the bias to replace alveolars with labials in harmony processes. As the data in Table 3–1 show, few children evidence a nonassimilatory process of replacing labials with alveolars. Thus, based on regressive overgeneralization, we would predict no bias toward either phone type here. However, we actually found a very strong bias; one that was as strong as that between velars and alveolars. Similarly, because nasals rarely denasalize in nonassimilatory processes, overgeneralization would not predict a bias towards replacing stops with nasals; yet, that is what we find in consonant harmony. The regressive overgeneralization hypothesis would also predict a general bias towards fricatives, once they appeared in a child's phonetic inventory. Although there was a tendency towards substituting fricatives for stops in assimilatory contents (Table 3–2), there was no evidence of this substitution pattern elsewhere.

## SUMMARY AND CONCLUSIONS

We have examined three possible explanations for the assimilatory and nonassimilatory error patterns observed in the speech of 51 children, namely, order of acquisition, phoneme frequency, and regressive overgeneralization, and found that none provided an adequate account of the data. Based on the analyses presented here, we conclude, then, that phonological underspecification offers the most principled explanation of the general biases that appear in the acquisition of English. It is of interest to note that these biases have been observed in the productions of English-speaking adults—not as consistent patterns, but as performance errors or slips of the tongue (Stemberger, 1991; Stemberger & Stoel-Gammon, 1991).

At present, we have insufficient data to comment on the universality of the biases documented for English; we need to obtain comparable sets of speech samples from children raised in other language environments to determine whether the same patterns obtain. It is our hope that such studies will be forthcoming so that we may examine in detail the relationship between the theoretical construct of underspecification in adult languages and the phenomenon of consonant harmony in the developing phonological system.

Although this chapter has focused on the relevance of underspecification for consonant harmony, we feel that it may also serve to explain other aspects of child phonology. A full discussion is obviously beyond the scope of this chapter; however, we would like to briefly discuss the role of underspecification in some additional aspects of phonological acquisition: (1) order of acquisition of segments, (2) error patterns, (3) consonant clusters, and (4) instances of disharmony.

First, there appears to be a relationship between degree of specification of a segment and order of acquisition in the developing phonological system. Thus, segments such as [t] and [d] that have little or no specification tend to occur frequently in babbling and appear early in development of meaningful speech. Bernhardt (1992a, b) has proposed a set of feature specifications for the phonemes of English and suggested that, all other things being equal, simpler segments (that is., those with fewer specified features) should be mastered earlier than complex ones.

Second, underspecified segments tend to serve as substitutes for later developing phones/phonemes. Numerous studies have shown that alveolar stops serve as substitutes for other consonants, particularly for velars (specified for the feature [Dorsal]), and for nonlabial fricatives (specified for the feature [continuant]). In terms of natural processes, these substitutions are viewed as two unrelated error patterns: Velar fronting, affecting /k, g, ŋ/, and stopping, affecting the fricatives . According to underspecification theory, these errors can be interpreted as a single phenomenon: The child has not yet acquired the specified features needed for velars and fricatives (i.e., [Dorsal] and [+continuant], respectively) and produces, instead, the underspecified segment /t/ in their place.

Third, the types of assimilation discussed here should not be limited to noncontiguous consonants. We expect that [Labial] and [Dorsal] should spread to coronal consonants within consonant clusters as well, as with [fm] for /sm/. Stemberger and Stoel-Gammon (1991) and Chin and Dinnsen (1992) have suggested that fusions, in which two consonants are combined into a single consonant, often combine just the specified features of the consonants. So, the cluster /sp/ will result in a segment with the specified features [+continuant] (from the /s/) and [Labial] (from the /p/), an [f]; it will not result in a segment with the underspecified values for place (coronal of /s/) and manner (stop of /p/) which would yield [t].

Finally Stemberger (1993) has argued that underspecification is involved with instances of disharmony, in which some process prevents identical phonological elements from being adjacent, either by deleting one of them or inserting another segment to keep them apart. Evidence of the latter process came from a set of productions from a young child who used schwa to break up some sequences of consonants in some instances, but not in others. The presence of "schwa epenthesis" appeared to depend on place of articulation of the consonants: Sequences of two coronal consonants (for which place is underspecified) did not usually trigger this pattern, while sequences of labials (specified for the feature [Labial]) did. The only other consonants which did not trigger schwa epenthesis were glottals ([h] and [ʔ]), which unambiguously lack specification for place features. Stemberger argued that the distinct patterns can be attributed to differences in the degree of specification of the consonants involved.

## ACKNOWLEDGMENT

This work was supported in part by grants from the Department of Education (No. G00-8002238) and NIDCD (No. DC00520) to Carol Stoel-Gammon, and a grant from NSF (No. BNS-8710288) to Joseph Paul Stemberger). We would like to thank Barbara Bernhardt and Margaret Kehoe for comments on a draft of this chapter.

## REFERENCES

Archangeli, D. (1986). *Underspecification in Yawelmani phonology and morphology.* New York: Garland Press.

Bernhardt, B. (1992a) Developmental implications of nonlinear phonological theory. *Clinical Linguistics and Phonetics, 6,* 259–281.

Bernhardt, B. (1992b) The application of nonlinear phonology to intervention with on phonologically disordered child. *Clinical Linguistics and Phonetics, 6,* 283–316

Berg, T. (1992). Phonological harmony as a processing problem. *Journal of Child Language, 19,* 225–257.

Bleile, K. M. (1987). *Regressions in the phonological development of two children.* Unpublished doctoral dissertation, University of Iowa, Ames.

Chin, S. & Dinnsen, D. (1992) Consonant clusters in disordered speech: Constraints and correspondence patterns. *Journal of Child Language, 19,* 259–285

Cruttenden, A. (1978). Assimilation in child language and elsewhere. *Journal of Child Language, 5,* 373–378.

Denes, P. B. (1963). On the statistics of spoken English. *Journal of the Acoustical Society of America 35,* 892–904.

Donahue, M. (1986). Phonological constraints on the emergence of two-word utterances. *Journal of Child Language, 5,* 373–378.

Ferguson, C. A., Peizer, D. B., & Weeks, T. E. (1973). Model-and-replica phonological grammar of a child's first words. *Lingua, 31,* 35–65.

Fudge, E. C. (1969). Syllables. *Journal of Linguistics, 5,* 193–320.

Holmes, U. T. (1927). The phonology of an English-speaking child. *American Speech, 2,* 219–225.

Kiparsky, P. (1985). Some consequences of Lexical phonology. *Phonology Yearbook 2,* 83–138.

Leopold, W. F. (1947). *Speech development of a bilingual child: A linguist's record, Vol. II: Sound learning in the first two years.* Chicago: Northwestern University Press.

Lewis, M. M. (1936). *Infant speech: A study of the beginnings of language.* New York: Harcourt Brace.

Locke, J. L. (1983). *Phonological acquisition and change.* New York: Academic Press.

Matthei, E. N. (1989). Crossing boundaries: More evidence for phonological constraints on early multi-word utterances. *Journal of Child Language, 16,* 41–54

Menn, L. (1971). Phonotactic rules in beginning speech. *Lingua, 26,* 225–251.

Menn, L. (1976). *Pattern, control, and contrast in beginning speech: A case study in the development of word form and word function.* Unpublished doctoral dissertation, University of Illinois, Champaign-Urbana.

Pulleyblank, D. (1986). *Tone in lexical phonology.* Dordrecht, Holland: Reidel.

Pye, C., Ingram, D., & List, H. (1987). A comparison of initial consonant acquisition in English and Quiche. In K. E. Nelson & A. van Kleek (Eds.), *Children's Language* (Vol. 6, pp. 175–190. Hillsdale, NJ: Lawrence Erlbaum.

Olswang, L., Stoel-Gammon, C., Coggins, T., & Carpenter, R. (1987). *Assessing prelinguistic and early linguistic behaviors in developmentaliv young children.* Seattle, WA: University of Washington Press.

Sagey, E. C. (1986). *The representation of features and relations in non-linear phonology.* Unpublished doctoral dissertation, Massachusetts Institute of Technology, Cambridge.

Shriberg, L. D. (1986). *Programs to examine phonetic and phonologic evaluation records.* Madison: University of Wisconsin.

Smith, N. (1973). *The acquisition of phonology.* Cambridge: Cambridge University Press.

Stemberger, J .P. (1991). Apparent anti-frequency biases in language production: The Addition Bias and phonological underspecification. *Journal of Memory and Language, 30,* 161–185.

Stemberger, J. P. (1992a). Vocalic underspecification in English language production. *Language, 68.*

Stemberger, J.P. (1992b). Regressive overgeneralizations in child phonology. Unpublished manuscript, Department of Communication Disorders, University of Minnesota.

Stemberger, J. P. (in press). Glottal transparency. *Phonology, 10.*

Stemberger, J. P., & Stoel-Gammon, C. (1991). The underspecification of coronals: Evidence from language acquisition and performance errors. In C. Paradis & J. F. Prunet (Eds.), *The special status of coronals* (pp. 181–199). New York: Academic Press.

Stoel-Gammon, C. (1983). Constraints on consonant-vowel sequences in early words. *Journal of Child Language, 10,* 455–458.

Stoel-Gammon, C. (1985). Phonetic inventories, 15–24 months: A longitudinal study. *Journal of Speech and Hearing Research, 28,* 505–512.

Stoel-Gammon, C. (1987). The phonological skills of two-year-olds. *Language, Speech, and Hearing Services in Schools, 18,* 323–329.

Stoel-Gammon, C., & Dunn, C. (1985). *Normal and disordered phonology in children.* Austin, TX: Pro-Ed.

Velten, H. V. (1943). The growth of phonemic and lexical patterns in infant language. *Language, 19,* 281–292.

Vihman, M. (1978). Consonant harmony: Its scope and function in child language. In J.H. Greenberg (Ed.), *Universals of human language Vol. 2: Phonology* (pp. 281–334). Stanford, CA: Stanford University Press.

# CHAPTER 4

## Intonation and Final Lengthening in Early Child Language

DAVID SNOW, PH.D.
CAROL STOEL-GAMMON, PH.D.

Speech prosody includes variations in three basic components of voice production: fundamental frequency, timing, and sound pressure level. The contour of pitch changes that occur throughout utterances corresponds to what we perceive as the intonation or melody of speech. Timing refers to the pattern of durations of syllables and pauses in sentences, and thus contributes to our sense of rhythm in speech. The sound pressure contour is related to the perceived loudness and softness of the voice. This chapter focuses on children's expressive development of the melodic (intonation) and rhythmic (timing) features that phonetically mark the edges of major grammatical units in spoken sentences such as phrases and clauses.

One of the most salient features of intonation is the prominent fall or rise in vocal pitch that occurs in the final syllables of statements and requests. As part of a sequence sometimes called the "nuclear tone," this pitch pattern, among other functions, marks major phrase boundaries in utterances (Cruttenden, 1986; Lieberman, 1967).

The corresponding aspect of speech rhythm is phrase-final lengthening, that is, a prolongation of the final syllables of both statements and requests. Although the significance of final lengthening is controversial (e.g., Lindblom, 1978), it is likely that the increased length of syllables at the boundaries of syntactic units helps the listener to perceive the phrasal segmentation of speech (Klatt, 1975; Oller, 1973).

Final lengthening and one of the major intonation patterns (falling contour) are among the few universals or near universals of speech prosody in the world's languages (Cruttenden, 1986). Because of their universality in speech and their central role in prosodic phonology, the development of these features in child speech is of special interest.

## ACQUISITION

Studies of prosodic development in young children have suggested that intonation is learned very early. For example, children use falling contours near the beginning of the one-word period (Dore, 1975; Scollon, 1976) or even before the onset of meaningful speech (Lenneberg, 1967). In addition to the basic falling contour, the full set of phrase-final contours, or nuclear tones, is acquired by 18 months (Crystal, 1986).

The development of phrasal timing during the period of meaningful speech has received less attention to date. Allen (1983) reported that 2-year-old French-speaking children showed control of this prosodic feature; studies of English-speaking children suggest that this aspect of timing is acquired around 2½ or 3 years of age (Allen & Hawkins, 1980; Smith, 1978). Some studies of prelinguistic vocal development, however, seem to show that final lengthening is evident in premeaningful utterances (Laufer, 1980; Robb & Saxman, 1990).

Two models of the relationship between tone and timing have been proposed. In one, the claim is that final lengthening is directly associated with the changes in the fundamental frequency ($F_0$) of the voice that are used for intonation. According to this "$F_0$-dependent" model, there are limits on the speed at which the fundamental frequency of the voice can change. Due to these restrictions on rate of vocal pitch change, phrase-final syllables are prolonged to allow enough time for the speaker to complete the prominent intonation contour that occurs at major phrase boundaries (Lindblom, 1978; Lyberg, 1979). Because this model interprets final lengthening to be a secondary and automatic effect of intonation, it implies that final lengthening and intonation skills emerge at the same time in child speech. This prediction would be consistent with an "association" model of prosodic development, that is, a model in which intonation and timing skills develop simultaneously.

The second model is built around the claim that final lengthening and intonation are acquired independently of one another. The strongest evidence in support of this "dissociation" model would be data showing that the two prosodic features are acquired at different ages or they change at different rates.

These competing views are important because they have very different implications about the significance of final lengthening in speech development. The association model implies that final lengthening is an unintentional phenomenon linked to intonation; thus it is not learned. In contrast, the dissociation model implies that final-syllable lengthening is a feature of prosodic phonology that is acquired independently from other skills and is therefore learned.

Previous studies of children's prosody during the early syntactic period have shown that phrase-final words are longer in duration and lower in fundamental frequency than nonfinal words (Branigan, 1979; Kubaska & Keating, 1981). However, three limitations of these studies make the results difficult to use as a test of the present models. First, previous studies did not isolate final lengthening as a specific prosodic variable. Thus, it is not known whether the observed temporal differences are due to contrasts in accent level (nuclear versus prenuclear), position-in-utterance (final versus nonfinal), or a combination of these effects. Second, studies of children before the age of two did not deal with the question of how temporal and tonal aspects of prosodic development are related. Finally, the effects of different pitch contour types have not been studied at this developmental period, although observations of 2-year-olds suggest that rising and falling contours are characterized by different developmental relationships between intonation and speech timing (Allen, 1983).

The study reported here is a longitudinal investigation designed to address these issues. The development of intonation and final-syllable lengthening was studied in three children from the ages of 1;6 to 2;0. Our main goal was to determine whether the acquisition data would support an association or dissociation model of prosodic development.

# METHODS

## THE DATABASE

Speech samples were selected from a longitudinal database of early child language that was created at the University of Washington in the early 1980s. The design of the original study and a description of the methods are given in Olswang, Stoel-Gammon, Coggins, and Carpenter (1987). The speech samples used in the present study were elicited in both structured and unstructured play activities involving the child and his or her mother; sometimes an adult female experimenter was also present.

High quality recordings of three children at 18 and 24 months (two females, one male) were selected for analysis. These participants were chosen after a review of transcripts showed that they produced some word combinations in free play activities at 18 months. Thus, at the outset of the study, they were at approximately the same point in linguistic development (beginning of combinatorial speech). The children's mean length-of-utterance data during the study period are listed in Table 4–1.

The sample analyzed included single-word utterances and accented, phrase-final words of multiword utterances. The sample included 103 one-syllable words and 80 two-syllable trochaic units (total of 263 syllables). The trochees consisted of words (e.g., *doggie*) and a lesser number of verb+pronoun phrases ( e.g., *find it*). The selection criteria emphasized words that were clearly audible, free from background noise, and used by more than one child or at more than one age. Examples of the types of words in the sample and data on their distribution are shown in Table 4–2. Word types are classified by number of syllables and phonetic characteristics of the word-final syllable coda. The categories reflect the phonetic forms used by the children; thus, *bottle* pronounced as [bado] was classified as a disyllable with final [o]. For each word type category, Table 4–2 shows the number of tokens sampled and their proportion with respect to the total sample for that age group.

All syllables were assigned to one of three categories of syllable weight and position: accented-final, accented-nonfinal, and unaccented-final. These three syllable types are shown with examples in Table 4–3. In each example, the relevant syllable is underlined and the accented syllable is written in capital letters.

**Table 4–1.** Descriptive data for the three child participants

|  |  | Mean Length of Utterance | |
| :---: | :---: | :---: | :---: |
| *Child* | *Sex* | *18 Months* | *24 Months* |
| EM | F | 1.50 | 2.05 |
| KW | F | 1.44 | 3.71 |
| RW | M | 1.49 | 3.32 |

**Table 4–2.** Description of words and phrases in the data sample

| Word/Phrase Type | Examples | Number and Proportion of Words | | | | | |
|---|---|---|---|---|---|---|---|
| | | 18 Months | | 24 Months | | Total | |
| Monosyllables | | 32 | .40 | 71 | .69 | 103 | .56 |
| final sonorant | toy, home | 12 | .15 | 29 | .28 | 41 | .22 |
| final obstruent | dog, cup | 20 | .25 | 42 | .41 | 62 | .34 |
| Disyllables | | 48 | .60 | 32 | .31 | 80 | .44 |
| final [ɪ] or [i] | baby, mommy | 41 | .51 | 16 | .16 | 57 | .31 |
| [u], [o], or [a] | table, bottle | 6 | .08 | 7 | .07 | 13 | .07 |
| [ɪn] or [ən] | open, button | 0 | .00 | 5 | .05 | 5 | .03 |
| verb + pronoun | see it | 1 | .01 | 4 | .04 | 5 | .03 |
| Total | | 80 | | 103 | | 183 | |

**Table 4–3.** Examples of syllable types*

| Type 1 Accented-final | Type 2 Accented-nonfinal | Type 3 Unaccented-final |
|---|---|---|
| I want a CAR. | This a TAble. | Brush ERnie. |
| JUICE? | Where BAby? | PUppy! |
| I making SOUP. | COOkie. | It's a BAby? |

*Note:* Nuclear accented syllables are written in capital letters. The syllables illustrated in each category are underlined.

## DATA ANALYSIS

All syllables were analyzed instrumentally to determine the fundamental frequency contour and the duration of the vocalic nucleus. The acoustic analysis was performed using the Interactive Laboratory Systems (ILS) computer system with a sampling frequency of 10 KHz. The domain for these measures included both the vowel and sonorant consonant segments in which voicing was detectable. Thus, the measures reflect the pitch contour and duration of the vocalic nucleus of each syllable.

The beginning and ending boundaries of each syllable were set at the first or last periodic pulse that was visually distinct in the time waveform. Generally, this occurred when the amplitude ratio of adjacent cycles was greater than 2:1. If voicing resumed for at least four cycles after periods of unvoicing, this continuation of periodicity was included in the boundary determination. By using these liberal criteria, we included as part of the syllable the very weak and breathy portion often occurring at the end of the syllable in infant speech (Oller & Smith, 1977).

Pitch contours were tracked using a combination of computerized and computer-assisted methods. First, the samples were analyzed by use of the analysis with pitch extraction command (API) whose algorithms are based on linear predictive coding and cepstral analysis. Second, we used a manual technique that involved sampling the signal at 25.6 msec intervals and determining the average fundamental frequency over each sampled interval by inspection of the time waveform. In the vicinity of peaks and valleys, the 25.6 msec analysis windows were spaced at every 12.8 msec to improve the resolution at these critical points. In some cases, the spectrum was also used. Due to imited clarity at high harmonics, typically the fourth or fifth harmonic was measured, with a resolution accuracy of 12.5 Hz. Thus, when the fourth harmonic was used, the measurement of the fundamental frequency was accurate within about 3 Hz.

## MEASURES OF FINAL LENTHENING AND INTONATION

### Final/Nonfinal Syllable Ratios

Final-lengthening typically is measured by comparing the duration of equally stressed syllables that differ only in phrase position. For example, we can compare the duration of final accented syllables (type 1 in Table 4–3) and nonfinal accented syllables (type 2) by expressing the difference as a ratio of syllable lengths. Typical final/nonfinal ratios for stressed syllables in English are about 1.6 or 1.7 (Delattre, 1966; Oller, 1973). We determined the final/nonfinal ratios that children used at 18 and 24 months. When these ratios were greater than 1.0 for at least two of the three children, we interpreted this as evidence that the children controlled or were beginning to control final lengthening at that age.

To have a comparable procedure for measuring the phrase-final fall in pitch, we compared the pitch changes that children used in final and nonfinal stressed syllables and expressed the difference as a ratio. We expected this ratio to be greater than 1.0 at both age levels. This prediction is supported by our theoretical framework for intonation which is discussed next.

**A Model of Intonation.** The analysis of intonation used in this study stems from the empirical work of Ashby (1978) and the theoretical model of Pierrehumbert (1980). In Pierrehumbert's model, contours are represented autosegmentally by a sequence of two levels of tone, high and low, marked H and L, respectively. The phrase-final contour is represented by a series of these target values, only two of which are discussed here. In Figure 4–1, these two pitch targets are shown for

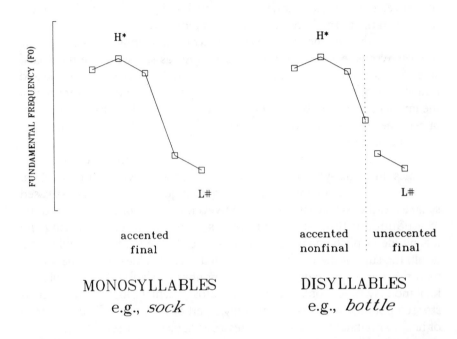

**Figure 4–1.** Falling intonation in phrase-final monosyllables and trochaic disyllables. The figure represents a schematic of the falling tone contour for monosyllabic nuclear-accented and phrase-final words on the left (e.g., "SOCK", "read BOOK"), and for trochaic disyllables in the same prosodic context on the right (e.g., "baby BOttle", "COOkies"). The dotted line indicates the final boundary of the accented syllable in the two-syllable word. H* is the high pitch accent, and L# is the low boundary tone. The contours are based on data from Ashby (1978), and the target tones are adapted from the framework of Pierrehumbert (1980).

single-syllable words on the left and two-syllable trochaic words on the right. The figure presents falling contours for single-word utterances and for the nuclear accented words of phrases, that is, words that receive the most prominent stress in a phrase.

Monosyllables such as *cup, juice,* and *dog* are shown on the left side of Figure 4–1. The first of the target tones defining the pitch contour is a pitch accent, which marks the highest peak of the nuclear syllable (H*). Then, a "boundary tone" (written L% in Pierrehumbert's model and L# in this chapter) represents the continuation of the phrase-final melody to the end of the final syllable. An important characteristic of the low boundary tone is that it is the lowest tone in the sequence. Even allowing for a characteristic downward drift in low tones throughout an utterance, the boundary tone is at a lower point in the speaker's pitch range than the normal downdrift would predict.

The melody sequence for one-syllable words also applies to two-syllable trochaic words (e.g., *bottle, baby*, and *puppy*), as shown in the right-hand side of Figure 4–1. These words consist of a nonfinal accented syllable and a final unaccented syllable. The autosegmental representation shows that the intonation pattern for the two-syllable words has the same sequence of target tones that is used for the single-syllable words. The tone sequence is independent of particular words or contexts. The difference between one- and two-syllable words has to do with the allocation of tones within syllables. In single-syllable words, both the high and low target tones are in the same syllable, giving a wide pitch change within a single stressed syllable. In the two-syllable words, however, the high pitch accent and the low boundary tone are in different syllables, thereby reducing the magnitude of pitch change that is carried out in the stressed syllable. As a result, the sum of the $F_0$ glides in accented-final syllables should be greater than the sum of $F_0$ glides in accented-nonfinal syllables, because phrase-final monosyllables contain the whole autosegmental tone pattern whereas stressed nonfinal syllables contain only a part of the pattern. Thus, the ratio of final to nonfinal $F_0$ changes in stressed syllables is expected to be greater than 1.00. When at least two of the children used $F_0$ changes in final syllables that were larger than those of equally accented nonfinal syllables (final/nonfinal tone ratio greater than 1.0), we interpreted this as evidence that they had acquired this general feature of intonation. Because this ratio is the tonal equivalent of the final lengthening ratio, a comparison of the timing and intonation ratios allows us to study the children's acquisition of the durational and tonal components of phrase-final prosody and to determine whether these two components develop at the same time (association model) or at different times (dissociation model).

The magnitude of $F_0$ glides in unaccented final syllables should be between the extremes given by the two accented syllable types. In our data set, unaccented syllables occur only in final position, so that ratio-based comparisons with unaccented nonfinal syllables were not possible. However, we were able to include these unaccented phrase-final syllables in a different type of analysis, using the regression slope.

## The Regression Slope Between $F_0$ Change and Syllable Timing

A second part of the investigation used regression analysis to study the relationship of $F_0$ characteristics and timing. This relationship is summarized by the slope of the regression line in a scatterplot. If there are any changes in the intonation of final syllables from 18 to 24 months, the association model predicts that there will be proportionally equivalent adjustments in the duration of these syllables. Thus, the relationship of $F_0$ change and timing should be constant from 18 to 24 months, and the slope of the regression line should be stable throughout the study period.

The dissociation model, on the other hand, predicts that final lengthening develops independently from intonation. This implies that the relationship of $F_0$ change and timing is not constant over time. In accordance with this model, the regression line should be tilted toward the $F_0$-change (horizontal) axis at 18 months. At 24 months, it should swing toward the timing (vertical) axis, reflecting the children's increasing emphasis on variations in syllable timing at the later age. The predicted age-related change in the relationship of intonation and timing is illustrated schematically in Figure 4–2. The figure depicts a hypothetical change in the variance of timing with respect to that of intonation from 18 to 24 months. The means may change or remain constant. What is important is the predicted difference in the relationship of the variances, for this is what affects the slope of the regression line.

Because previous studies have shown that the speed and magnitude of fundamental frequency change in final syllables are affected by the direction of the intonation contour (Allen, 1983), we divided the sampled words into rising and falling classes, based on the pitch direction of the final syllable. The analysis used only pitch changes of a magnitude greater than one semitone (100 cents). This criterion was adopted by Allen (1983) on the basis of evidence that a semitone roughly equals a just-noticeable difference in functional prosodic pitch perception. Thus, for each syllable, the measure of intonation is the sum of the absolute within-syllable $F_0$ glides having a magnitude of at least one semitone, a measure we will refer to as the "$F_0$ contour." For example, using data from EM at 18 months, the first syllable of *doggie* had an initial rise of 99 Hz (474 cents) and then a fall of 38 Hz (165 cents). The final syllable fell by 128 Hz (717 cents) and then had a slight rise of 13 Hz (89 cents). The $F_0$ contour of the first and second syllables, respectively, was analyzed as 137 and 128 Hz. Because the overall contour is a falling pattern, both syllables were analyzed within the category of "falling contours."

# RESULTS

## *FINAL VERSUS NONFINAL SYLLABLES*

The mean magnitudes of $F_0$ contours and syllable durations for words with falling intonation patterns are listed by syllable type in Table 4–4

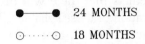

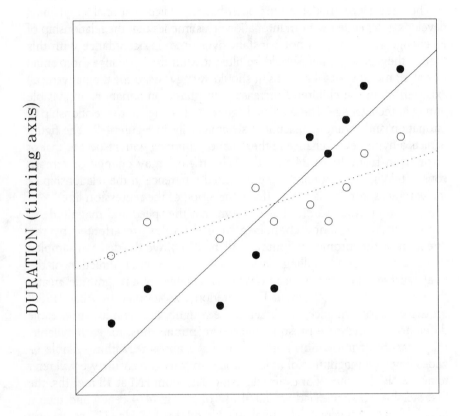

**Figure 4–2.** Schematic of the hypothesized shift of the $F_0$ change by timing regression slope toward the timing axis from 18 to 24 months.

(age 18 months) and Table 4–5 (24 months). The tables include ratios between the means for final and nonfinal accented syllables (column labeled "Ratio"). The final/nonfinal ratios in both tables are all greater than 1.0, indicating that the three children used larger $F_0$ contours and longer

**Table 4–4.** F₀ contour and duration measures by syllable type and child: Falling contours, age 18 months

| Syllable Type | N | F₀ Contour (Hz) | | | Duration (msec) | | | r | Slope |
|---|---|---|---|---|---|---|---|---|---|
| | | Mean | Ratio | S.D. | Mean | Ratio | S.D. | | |
| Accented-final | | | | | | | | | |
| EM | 7 | 174 | 1.03 | 92 | 468 | 1.79 | 207 | | |
| KW | 8 | 100 | 2.70 | 77 | 233 | 1.19 | 82 | | |
| RW | 9 | 270 | 1.05 | 169 | 495 | 1.44 | 279 | | |
| Group | 24 | 185 | 1.18 | 139 | 400 | 1.50 | 234 | .52 | .88 |
| Accented-nonfinal | | | | | | | | | |
| EM | 13 | 169 | | 84 | 261 | | 125 | | |
| KW | 9 | 37 | | 23 | 195 | | 48 | | |
| RW | 9 | 258 | | 257 | 344 | | 91 | | |
| Group | 31 | 157 | | 168 | 266 | | 112 | .14 | .09 |
| Unaccented-final | | | | | | | | | |
| EM | 13 | 131 | | 74 | 225 | | 57 | | |
| KW | 9 | 33 | | 25 | 187 | | 71 | | |
| RW | 9 | 208 | | 82 | 398 | | 119 | | |
| Group | 31 | 125 | | 94 | 264 | | 120 | .63 | .80 |
| Total (all types) | | | | | | | | | |
| EM | 33 | 155 | | 82 | 291 | | 155 | .37 | .70 |
| KW | 26 | 55 | | 54 | 204 | | 68 | .47 | .59 |
| RW | 27 | 245 | | 179 | 412 | | 187 | .08 | .08 |
| Group | 86 | 153 | | 137 | 303 | | 167 | .40 | .49 |

*Note:* Group = data for all three children combined; *N* = number of syllables; F₀ Contour = sum of F₀ glides of at least one semitone in magnitude (100 cents); S.D. = standard deviation; Ratio = mean Accented-final/mean Accented-nonfinal; *r* = Pearson correlation coefficient (duration by F₀ contour); Slope = slope of the duration (Y axis) by F₀ contour (X axis) regression line.

durations for final syllables than nonfinal syllables at both ages. These findings for falling contours are consistent with the association model.

The corresponding data for rising contours are listed in Tables 4–6 and 4–7. At 18 months, two of the children have a tone ratio greater than 1.00 (RW and EM), but there is evidence of final lengthening only for RW (duration ratio = 1.29). At the 24 month session, KW did not produce any two-syllable words with rising contours; thus, there is complete data only for EM and RW. Both the intonation and final lengthening indices for these two children are greater than 1.00. The criterion we used to determine that a given prosodic feature has been acquired is that at least two of the three children demonstrated a final/nonfinal ratio greater than

**Table 4–5.** $F_0$ contour and duration measures by syllable type and child: Falling contours, age 24 months

| Syllable Type | N | $F_0$ Contour (Hz) | | | Duration (msec) | | | r | Slope |
|---|---|---|---|---|---|---|---|---|---|
| | | Mean | Ratio | S.D. | Mean | Ratio | S.D. | | |
| Accented-final | | | | | | | | | |
| EM | 16 | 132 | 1.38 | 80 | 448 | 1.71 | 222 | | |
| KW | 19 | 169 | 2.64 | 76 | 354 | 1.36 | 136 | | |
| RW | 17 | 203 | 2.71 | 106 | 479 | 1.72 | 227 | | |
| Group | 52 | 168 | 2.13 | 91 | 424 | 1.59 | 200 | .34 | .74 |
| Accented-nonfinal | | | | | | | | | |
| EM | 9 | 96 | | 72 | 262 | | 94 | | |
| KW | 9 | 64 | | 28 | 261 | | 121 | | |
| RW | 5 | 75 | | 74 | 279 | | 114 | | |
| Group | 23 | 79 | | 58 | 266 | | 105 | .71 | 1.29 |
| Unaccented-final | | | | | | | | | |
| EM | 9 | 154 | | 65 | 354 | | 228 | | |
| KW | 9 | 59 | | 39 | 203 | | 56 | | |
| RW | 5 | 109 | | 70 | 337 | | 209 | | |
| Group | 23 | 107 | | 69 | 291 | | 182 | .60 | 1.58 |
| Total (all types) | | | | | | | | | |
| EM | 34 | 128 | | 75 | 374 | | 208 | .42 | 1.16 |
| KW | 37 | 116 | | 80 | 295 | | 132 | .54 | .89 |
| RW | 27 | 162 | | 108 | 416 | | 219 | .57 | 1.15 |
| Group | 98 | 133 | | 88 | 356 | | 191 | .52 | 1.13 |

*Note:* Group = data for all three children combined; $N$ = number of syllables; $F_0$ Contour = sum of $F_0$ glides of at least one semitone in magnitude (100 cents); S.D. = standard deviation; Ratio = mean Accented-final/mean Accented-nonfinal; $r$ = Pearson correlation coefficient (duration by $F_0$ contour); Slope = slope of the duration (Y axis) by $F_0$ contour (X axis) regression line.

1.00 for that feature. In accordance with this criterion, we find that the intonation feature is acquired at 18 months, but final lengthening is not acquired until 24 months. This pattern of findings for rising contours is consistent with the dissociation model.

## $F_0$ CHANGE BY DURATION RELATIONSHIPS

Tables 4–4 through 4–7 also list correlation and regression slope coefficients that describe the relationship between $F_0$ contour and timing. The scatterplots and regression lines for all three children and both contour types are displayed in Figures 4–3 through 4–5. The

**Table 4–6.** $F_0$ contour and duration measures by syllable type and child: Rising contours, age 18 months

| Syllable Type | N | $F_0$ Contour (Hz) | | | Duration (msec) | | | r | Slope |
| | | Mean | Ratio | S.D. | Mean | Ratio | S.D. | | |
|---|---|---|---|---|---|---|---|---|---|
| Accented-final | | | | | | | | | |
| EM | 3 | 192 | 1.42 | 124 | 228 | .77 | 62 | | |
| KW | 2 | 24 | .45 | 9 | 219 | .86 | 40 | | |
| RW | 3 | 637 | 7.08 | 426 | 358 | 1.29 | 122 | | |
| Group | 8 | 317 | 3.73 | 363 | 275 | 1.01 | 102 | .88 | .25 |
| Accented-nonfinal | | | | | | | | | |
| EM | 4 | 135 | | 87 | 295 | | 130 | | |
| KW | 7 | 53 | | 56 | 256 | | 94 | | |
| RW | 5 | 90 | | 42 | 277 | | 75 | | |
| Group | 16 | 85 | | 66 | 272 | | 93 | .52 | .73 |
| Unaccented-final | | | | | | | | | |
| EM | 4 | 139 | | 93 | 366 | | 126 | | |
| KW | 7 | 19 | | 16 | 196 | | 78 | | |
| RW | 5 | 79 | | 48 | 358 | | 104 | | |
| Group | 16 | 67 | | 70 | 289 | | 125 | .34 | .61 |
| Total (all types) | | | | | | | | | |
| EM | 11 | 152 | | 93 | 303 | | 118 | .03 | .04 |
| KW | 16 | 34 | | 41 | 225 | | 83 | .69 | 1.40 |
| RW | 13 | 212 | | 301 | 327 | | 98 | .38 | .12 |
| Group | 40 | 124 | | 192 | 279 | | 106 | .39 | .22 |

*Note:* Group = data for all three children combined; $N$ = number of syllables; $F_0$ Contour = sum of $F_0$ glides of at least one semitone in magnitude (100 cents); S.D. = standard deviation; Ratio = mean Accented-final/mean Accented-nonfinal; $r$ = Pearson correlation coefficient (duration by $F_0$ contour); Slope = slope of the duration (Y axis) by $F_0$ contour (X axis) regression line.

regression lines summarize the complete data set for each child (see rows for "Total" under syllable type in the tables).

For falling contours, scatterplots are shown for all three children in Figure 4–3. Each graph shows the distribution of data points and the regression line at 18 months and at 24 months. For all three children, the slopes of the regression show a change over time. The magnitude of the change is quite different across children, but the direction of change is consistently toward the timing axis (steeper slope). For example, using data for KW, the regression slope is .59 at 18 months and .89 at 24 months (the larger coefficient indicates a steeper slope). The corresponding slope coefficients for all children combined (row for "Group" under "Total") are .49 and 1.13 at 18 and 24 months, respectively.

**Table 4–7.** $F_0$ contour and duration measures by syllable type and child: Rising contours, age 24 months

| Syllable Type | N | $F_0$ Contour (Hz) | | | Duration (msec) | | | r | Slope |
| | | Mean | Ratio | S.D. | Mean | Ratio | S.D. | | |
|---|---|---|---|---|---|---|---|---|---|
| Accented-final | | | | | | | | | |
| EM | 7 | 150 | 2.27 | 129 | 285 | 1.34 | 82 | | |
| KW | 6 | 123 | — | 164 | 295 | — | 64 | | |
| RW | 6 | 138 | 1.64 | 118 | 403 | 1.29 | 90 | | |
| Group | 19 | 138 | 1.86 | 130 | 325 | 1.26 | 93 | .40 | .29 |
| Accented-nonfinal | | | | | | | | | |
| EM | 5 | 66 | | 41 | 213 | | 81 | | |
| KW | 0 | | | | | | | | |
| RW | 4 | 84 | | 29 | 312 | | 119 | | |
| Group | 9 | 74 | | 35 | 257 | | 107 | .00 | .00 |
| Unaccented-final | | | | | | | | | |
| EM | 5 | 153 | | 44 | 264 | | 78 | | |
| KW | 0 | | | | | | | | |
| RW | 4 | 135 | | 61 | 327 | | 115 | | |
| Group | 9 | 145 | | 49 | 292 | | 96 | –.13 | –.25 |
| Total (all types) | | | | | | | | | |
| EM | 17 | 126 | | 93 | 258 | | 82 | .16 | .14 |
| KW | 6 | 123 | | 164 | 295 | | 64 | .68 | .27 |
| RW | 14 | 122 | | 84 | 355 | | 106 | .47 | .59 |
| Group | 37 | 124 | | 101 | 301 | | 98 | .30 | .29 |

*Note:* Group = data for all three children combined; $N$ = number of syllables; $F_0$ Contour = sum of $F_0$ glides of at least one semitone in magnitude (100 cents); S.D. = standard deviation; Ratio = mean Accented-final/mean Accented-nonfinal; $r$ = Pearson correlation coefficient (duration by $F_0$ contour); Slope = slope of the duration (Y axis) by $F_0$ contour (X axis) regression line.

The scatterplots for rising contours are compared to those of falling contours in Figures 4–4 and 4–5. Because the data are incomplete for KW at 24 months, plots are shown only for EM (Figure 4–4) and RW (Figure 4–5). The figures indicate a developmental shift towards steeper regression lines in both children, although the magnitude of change is not as great for rising contours as it is for falling contours. For all children combined, the regression slope is .21 at 18 months and .29 at 24 months. The shift in the slope of the regression line toward the timing axis is consistent with the dissociation model. A similar shift occurs for both rising and falling contours, but the change is much less marked for rising contours than for falling contours.

In summary, our observations looked at developmental changes in the prosody of three children. Data were presented for two intonational

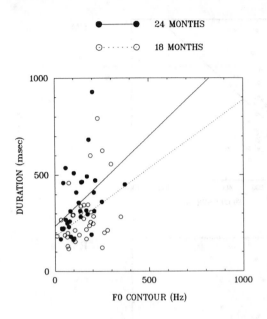

## Falling Contours

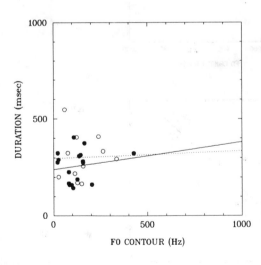

## Rising Contours

**Figure 4–3.** Syllable duration by $F_0$ contour in falling intonation patterns by child and age.

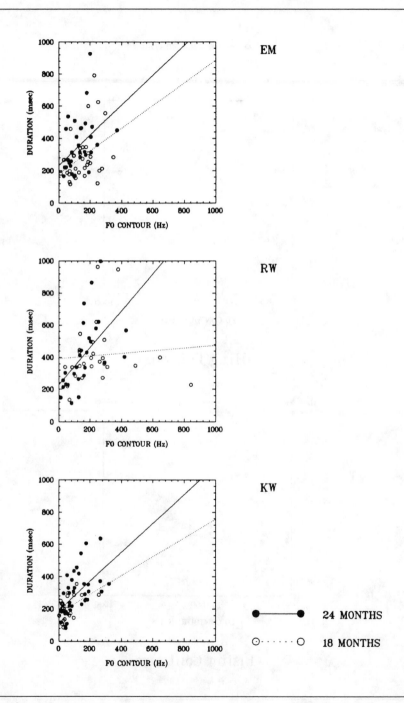

**Figure 4–4.** Syllable duration by $F_0$ contour for EM, by contour type and age.

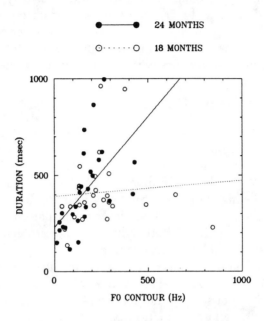

## Falling Contours

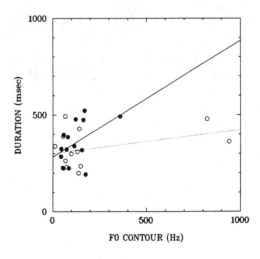

## Rising Contours

**Figure 4–5.** Syllable duration by $F_0$ contour for RW, by contour type and age.

contexts (falling and rising intonation) and in two types of analysis (final/nonfinal ratios and regression slopes), four observation conditions in all. The findings in one of these observation conditions are in accordance with the association model. The findings for the other three observations are in accordance with the dissociation model.

## INDIVIDUAL DIFFERENCES

The results just summarized characterized the prosodic development of all three children, but there were some striking individual differences, especially in regard to intonation. In two-syllable words like *baby, bottle,* and *daddy*, RW and EM at 18 months frequently used a very high pitch accent, with the high point occurring very near the final boundary of the stressed syllable. The use of complex rise-fall patterns like this, with relatively wide $F_0$ glides in both syllables, suggests that these children were emphasizing the emotional aspects of intonation. In contrast, KW at 18 months tended to use very flat contours on similar words, minimizing the emotional expressiveness of the pitch accents. On the other hand, the data suggest that KW emphasized the grammatical tone contrasts of the falling intonation pattern. Evidence for this claim is shown in Table 4–4, which lists the mean magnitudes of F0 contours on accented final and nonfinal syllables. At 18 months, KW used a much flatter $F_0$ contour than either of the other children on accented nonfinal syllables (37 Hz versus 169 and 258). To a lesser extent, this was also true of final accented syllables (100 Hz versus 174 and 270). Because affect is related to the extent of $F_0$ contours in both final and nonfinal stressed syllables, the data show that KW used much less emotional expressiveness than the other two children.

The grammatical use of tone is reflected in the $F_0$-change contrast between equally accented final and nonfinal syllables. An index of this grammatical contrastivity is the $F_0$ contour ratio of final to nonfinal syllables (shown under the column labeled "Ratio" in Tables 4–4 through 4–7). At 18 months, KW used grammatical contrasts of intonation to a greater extent than the other children (ratio of 2.70 versus 1.03 and 1.05). Although the absolute magnitudes of both final and nonfinal $F_0$ contours were small (affective component), the contrast between final and nonfinal syllables was quite prominent (grammatical component). This pattern of results supports the claim that KW's productions emphasized the grammatical functions of intonation rather than the emotionally expressive ones. This results in a large intonation ratio at 18 months (2.70). At 24 months, RW's speech reflects a similar grammatical intonation ratio, again in falling contours (2.71).

Because phrase-final prosodic features are linguistically related to syntactic structure, it is possible that children's acquisition of these features may be paced by the same learning factors that guide the induction of syntactic regularities. To investigate this possibility, we computed a grammatical index of intonation for each child by averaging the intonation ratio over the two observation sessions (18 and 24 months), and correlated this index with the children's mean length of utterance (MLU) at 24 months. For example, the average intonation index for EM is 1.21 (average of 1.03 at 18 months and 1.38 at 24 months), and her MLU at 24 months is 2.05. The intonation index correlated very well with MLU at 24 months (Pearson $r = .94$). Thus, there may be a relation between children's acquisition of grammatical intonation contrasts and their general development of syntactic skills as measured globally by MLU. However, we are not able to draw any strong conclusions because of the small number of subjects in our study. The corresponding average index for final lengthening was also computed, but it was not positively correlated with MLU at 24 months ($r = -.93$).

## DISCUSSION

This study investigated the development of phrase-final prosodic patterns in the speech of three English-speaking children. The intonation feature of interest is the fall or rise in the fundamental frequency of the voice that occurs in the final syllables of statements and requests. The corresponding feature of speech timing is phrase-final lengthening, which occurs in the final syllables of both statements and requests. Using methods stemming from an autosegmental approach, these features were compared in a longitudinal study of the children's speech between the ages of 18 and 24 months. The results support the claim that intonation is learned very early. Our theoretical model of intonation implied that the magnitude of $F_0$ contours is greater in final syllables than in equally accented nonfinal syllables. The results showed that, at 18 months of age, this intonation feature characterized the speech of all children in falling contours and at least two of the three children in rising contours.

The syllable timing aspects of prosody seem to develop more slowly than intonation. The most consistent evidence for this was found in an age-related shift in the slope of the $F_0$ by timing regression line. From 18 months to 24 months, the regression line tilted away from the $F_0$ axis and towards the timing axis. Most importantly, this effect was observed in all three children for falling contours, and in two of the three children for rising contours. The data on rising contours for the third child imply the opposite pattern, but they are insufficient to make any conclusion.

The change in steepness of the regression slope resulted from two effects: (1) an age-related increase in the correlation between $F_0$ change and syllable timing, and (2) an increase in the variance of syllable timing with respect to the variance of $F_0$ changes. The latter effect indicated that, at 24 months, the timing domain used by the children became more spread out, without a proportional increase in the $F_0$ domain. This is consistent with the dissociation model of prosodic development, because such a model predicts that the children at first emphasize the $F_0$ contrasts between syllables and later focus on the temporal differences.

The most important implication of these findings is that features of prosodic timing such as final lengthening are acquired independently from intonation. Thus, final lengthening is not merely an epiphenomenon of tone production. Instead, it must be learned, like other aspects of speech timing. Overall, the outcomes of our study indicate that the period from $1\frac{1}{2}$ to 2 years of age represents an important stage in the child's learning of basic phrase rhythm skills.

The results were quite different for the two types of intonation contours. The data suggest that final lengthening is acquired more slowly in the context of rising contours than in falling contours (see Allen, 1983 for similar data for French-speaking 2-year-olds). All of the children demonstrated control of final lengthening at 18 months in falling contours (as measured by ratio indices), but only one did so in utterances using a rising intonation pattern. This suggests that, at the beginning of the study, the children had already taken major steps toward the acquisition of the final lengthening contrast in the context of falling contours and were gradually extending it to rising patterns during the 6-month period of this study. For this reason, differences in the children's development of tone versus timing skills were observed most clearly in the developmentally more advanced utterances using rising intonation.

The difficulty associated with rising contours is also shown in some of the findings for intonation, especially the data pertaining to variability within and between children. Generally, variability tends to decrease from 18 to 24 months. The intonation measures show that variability in rising contours at 18 months is quite marked (overall standard deviation of 363 Hz for final stressed syllables, compared to 139 Hz for falling contours). However, at 24 months, the variability of rising contours is closer to that of falling contours (e.g., 130 Hz for stressed monosyllables in rising contexts and 91 Hz for equivalent syllables in falling patterns). The large variability in children's use of rising intonation contours at 18 months suggests that the rising pattern is acquired more slowly than the falling pattern, a finding that supports previously reported evidence that children learn the grammatical pattern of intonation first in the context of falling contours and then in rising contours (Crystal, 1986). Thus, both intonation patterns and final lengthening seem to be acquired first in the context of falling intonational contours. Another generalization, that was discussed above, is that intonation is acquired before final lengthening. As a result of the interaction of these two developmental trends, the most difficult skill to be acquired should be final lengthening in the context of rising contours. The data focusing on final/nonfinal ratios, regression slopes, and variability all seem to confirm this expectation.

The first skill to be acquired, on the other hand, should be intonation in falling contours. The results generally confirm this (although the ratio indices are only slightly above 1.00 for two of the children at 18 months), and they point to something perhaps even more significant about intonation. The grammatical use of falling intonation (i.e., a distinctive melody pattern at the edges of phrase boundaries) may be related to the child's syntactic development generally. During the period of 18 to 24 months, this feature seems to be a good predictor of the child's overall syntactic development at 24 months.

The results of the study were generally less conclusive about final lengthening than about intonation. Although the data suggest that final lengthening follows intonation in development, the study certainly indicates that the children had already begun to acquire final lengthening before 18 months, at least for falling intonation patterns. The answer to the question of when it begins to develop remains elusive. Finally, as an additional contrast to the findings for intonation, the study did not find any evidence that final lengthening is related to syntax acquisition. In order to observe the emergence of final lengthening in child language more clearly (and thus to evaluate the acquisition models discussed here), future research needs to investigate prosodic skills development in children at earlier stages of development—before the onset of syntax, and perhaps before the beginning of meaningful speech.

## IMPLICATIONS FOR CHILD LANGUAGE DISORDERS

As discussed the introductory remarks, final lengthening and the falling intonation pattern are expressed to varying degrees in all of the world's languages (Cruttenden, 1986), suggesting how closely linked they are to communication. Findings about the normal acquisition of these early-developing linguistic universals have potential applications in the diagnosis and treatment of language disorders in children. A notable example of childhood language disorders is specific language impairment

(SLI), which is characterized especially by slow development of morpho-logical and syntactic patterns (Leonard, Bortolini, Caselli, McGregor, & Sabbadini, 1992). Because the morphological and syntactic features that are used to distinguish between normal and impaired language development are relatively advanced acquisitions, SLI is usually not identified formally until about age 3 or 4. From clinical and social perspectives, it would be desirable to identify children at risk for SLI much earlier, that is, at the time they are beginning to use first words or early word combinations. Although parents of children with SLI retrospectively report that they felt something was wrong with their children's language development at age 1;6 to 3;0 (Plante, Swisher, Vance, & Rapcsak, 1991), the onset and characteristics of first words and two-word utterances usually are unremarkable (Elena Plante, personal communication). Because language characteristics at these major milestones often fail to reflect later-developing difficulties with language acquisition, there are few early indicators that can be used at age 1 or 2 to predict that language impairment is likely to be identified later in the preschool or early school years.

Prosodic features may provide a window through which future stages of syntax acquisition can be predicted. Prior to and during the one-word period, normally developing children acquire a suprasegmental foundation for syntax based mostly on intonation. Intonation pattern is related to syntax because one of its functions—perhaps its most basic and primitive one—is to mark the primary units of grammatical structure, that is, phrases, clauses, and sentences. In this sense, intonation is the first correlate of syntax that children express, even when they are using only one word at a time. Thus, restricted or atypical use of intonation during the presyntactic period of early meaningful speech might be the first warning sign that the child is having difficulty with the acquisition of syntax.

Data presented in this chapter suggest that phrase-final lengthening develops later than intonation. Accordingly, the development of final lengthening may help to predict SLI at linguistic stages following the one-word period, that is, after children have begun combining words into phrases. Indeed, seriously delayed acquisition of final lengthening at this stage might be the most robust of the early prosodic indicators of SLI. This prediction stems partly from our observations of normal prosodic development and partly from inferences about the language-learning straegy that SLI children seem to use, as discussed next.

We pointed out earlier that children with SLI have particular difficulty with the acquisition of morphological and syntactic features, for example, inflections and auxiliary verbs. Formal descriptions of normal grammatical development (Brown, 1973) imply that children's syntax and morphology have a highly sequential or hierarchical organization.

For this reason, morphological and syntactic patterns exemplify the types of features that are acquired most easily by an analytic, linguistic learning strategy (Peters, 1977). A plausible inference is that children with SLI have difficulty using some of the skills that underlie an analytic approach to language acquisition.

Final lengthening is part of a hierarchically organized system that is closely linked to the syntactic organization of sentences (Cooper & Paccia-Cooper, 1980; Klatt, 1975). Due to its formal, linguistic characteristics, final lengthening seems to be learned most parsimoniously by the same kind of strategy that is needed to acquire morphological and syntactic patterns, that is, an analytic strategy that children with SLI may not use proficiently. Intonation, on the other hand, has a continuous, musical form that is compatible with a holistic learning strategy, and such a strategy may still be available to children who have difficulty using an analytic approach (Peters, 1977). For this reason, children at risk for SLI might demonstrate good control of intonation in the early syntactic period, but could have serious and persistent delays in the acquisition of final lengthening. Thus, children's use of speech melody (intonation) and rhythm (final lengthening) at different developmental levels of early meaningful speech may be viewed as precursors of their eventual approach to syntax and discourse at later linguistic stages. Current research efforts addressing these issues may help us to identify children with SLI and to initiate appropriate clinical or parent-assisted intervention in a much more timely way than is now possible.

## ACKNOWLEDGMENTS

This work was supported by grants from the Department of Education (No. G00-8002238) and the National Institute on Deafness and other Communication Disorders (No. DC00520) awarded to the second author. We would like to thank George Allen for his helpful comments on an earlier draft of the study reported in this chapter.

## REFERENCES

Allen, G. D. (1983). Some suprasegmental contours in French two-year-old children's speech. *Phonetica, 40,* 269–292.

Allen, G. D., & Hawkins, S. (1980). Phonological rhythm: definition and development. In G. H. Yeni-Komshian, J. F. Kavanagh, & C. A. Ferguson (eds.), *Child phonology. Vol. 1: Production* (pp. 227–256). New York: Academic Press.

Ashby, M. (1978). A study of two English nuclear tones. *Language and Speech, 21,* 326–336.

Branigan, G. (1979). Some reasons why successive single-word utterances are not. *Journal of Child Language, 6*, 411–421.

Brown, R. (1973). *A first language: The early stages.* Cambridge, MA: Harvard University Press.

Cooper, W. E., & Paccia-Cooper, J. M. (1980). *Syntax and Speech.* Cambridge, MA: Harvard University Pess.

Cruttenden, A. (1986). Intonation. Cambridge: Cambridge University Press.

Crystal, D. (1986). Prosodic development. In P. J. Fletcher & M. Garman (Eds.), *Studies in first language development* (pp. 174–197). New York: Cambridge University Press.

Delattre, P. (1966). A comparison of syllable length conditioning among languages. *International Review of Applied Linguistics, 4*, 183–198.

Dore, J. (1975). Holophrases, speech acts and language universals. *Journal of Child Language, 2*, 21–40.

Klatt, D. H. (1975). Vowel lengthening is syntactically determined in a connected discourse. *Journal of Phonetics, 3*, 129–140.

Kubaska, C. A., & Keating, P. A. (1981). Word duration in early child speech. *Journal of Speech and Hearing Research, 24*, 615–621.

Laufer, M. (1980). Temporal regularity in prespeech. In T. Murry & J. Murry (eds.), *Infant communication: Cry and early speech* (pp. 284–309). Houston, TX: College-Hill Press.

Lenneberg, E. H. (1967). *Biological foundations of language.* New York: John Wiley.

Leonard, L. B., Bortolini, U., Caselli, M. C., McGregor, K. K., & Sabbadini, L. (1992). Morphological deficits in children with specific language impairment: The status of features in the underlying grammar. *Language Acquisition, 2*, 151–179.

Lieberman, P. (1967). Intonation and the syntactic processing of speech. In W. Wathen-Dunn (Ed.), *Models for the perception of speech and visual form: Proceedings of a symposium* (pp. 314–319). Cambridge, MA: M.I.T. Press.

Lindblom, B. (1978). Final lengthening in speech and music. In E. Garding, G. Bruce, & R. Bannert (Eds.), *Nordic prosody: Papers from a symposium* (pp. 86–101). Lund, Sweden: Department of Linguistics, Lund University.

Lyberg, B. (1979). Final lengthening—partly a consequence of restrictions on the speed of fundamental frequency change? *Journal of Phonetics, 7*, 187–196.

Oller, D. K. (1973). The effect of position in utterance on speech segment duration in English. *Journal of the Acoustical Society of America, 54*, 1235–1237.

Oller, D. K., & Smith, B. L. (1977). The effect of final-syllable position on vowel duration in infant babbling. *Journal of the Acoustical Society of America, 62*, 994–997.

Olswang, L. B., Stoel-Gammon, C., Coggins, T. E., & Carpenter, R. L. (1987). Assessing linguistic behaviors (ALB): *Assessing prelinguistic and early linguistic behaviors in developmentally young children.* Seattle: University of Washington Press.

Pierrehumbert, J. (1980). *The phonology and phonetics of English intonation.* Unpublished doctoral dissertation, Massachusetts Institute of Technology, Cambridge.

Plante, E., Swisher, L., Vance, R., & Rapcsak, S. (1991). MRI findings in boys with specific language impairment. *Brain and Language, 41*, 52–66.

Robb, M. P., & Saxman, J. H. (1990). Syllable duration of preword and early word vocalizations. *Journal of Speech and Hearing Research, 33*, 583–593.

Scollon, R. (1976). *Conversations with a one year old: A case study of the developmental foundation of syntax.* Honolulu: The University Press of Hawaii.

Smith, B. L. (1978). Temporal aspects of English speech production: a developmental perspective. *Journal of Phonetics, 6,* 37–67.

# CHAPTER 5

## From Lexical Access to Lexical Output: What is the Problem for Children with Impaired Phonology?

SHULA CHIAT, Ph.D.

Studies of children's phonology, both normal and impaired, have until recently been dominated by linguistic rather than psycholinguistic perspectives. The object of this chapter is to switch the focus to psycholinguistic questions about the output of children with impaired phonology. This leads into an exploration of the relationship between metrical and segmental factors in children's output planning, and the implications for the modeling of speech processes.

Scanning the past two decades of work on children's phonology, it is clear that children's phonological output has provided a rich source of data for measuring the fit of different phonological theories. Patterns in children's output, and their relation to patterns in adult input, have been described in terms of generative phonology (e.g., Smith, 1973), prosodic phonology (e.g., Waterson, 1971), and autosegmental phonology or feature geometry (e.g., Bernhardt & Gilbert, 1992; Chin & Dinnsen, 1991;

Spencer, 1988). The purpose of such studies generally is to show that the particular phonological theory can account for the scope and limits of children's phonological contrasts and structures. Theorization sometimes extends to debate about whether the child's underlying representations differ from their surface representations and whether constraints on the child's phonology arise in perception, storage, or motor production (e.g., Braine, 1976; Ingram, 1974; Smith, 1973; Spencer, 1988). By and large, these questions have been considered on the basis of how the observed pattern of output data can best be explained. Until recently, there has been little interest in direct evidence of the child's input and output processing.

Yet the data concerned clearly are the product of psycholinguistic processing. As the child receives spoken input, she must identify word shapes within the stream of speech, relate these to word meanings, and work out how to produce the word shapes required to express particular word meanings. Differences between the child's phonological output and that of adults must arise at some point in this processing. The distinction that is sometimes postulated between underlying representations of words and their production is relevant to psycholinguistic processing, but constitutes a very simplistic psycholinguistic model, entailing just two stages of processing whose structure and relations to each other remain unspecified. Real-time speech processing involves perception and production of complex representations mapping acoustic signals onto meanings, and meanings onto articulatory gestures. If we are to gain insights into the locus of the problem resulting in disordered phonological output, we need theoretical models of the processes involved, specifying the nature of representations and their interrelations in input and output.

In this chapter, I argue that psycholinguistic studies of children with phonological problems can throw light on the locus of the delay or impairment in development and can contribute to the modeling of speech processes. I consider two major sources of evidence. In each case, I discuss the methodology used, the findings which have emerged, and the implications for psycholinguistic processing. These bring into question certain aspects of current information-processing models and point towards a connectionist approach to modeling which could better accommodate the patterns observed in the psycholinguistic studies. I conclude with some indications for future research into developmental phonological disorders which might yield detailed insights into speech processing.

## INVESTIGATION INTO LEVELS OF PROCESSING

The psycholinguistic processing that underlies phonological impairment has been approached through the theory and methodology developed in cognitive neuropsychology, particularly in the study of single-word reading by adults (Coltheart, Patterson, & Marshall, 1980), and increasingly in studies of developmental dyslexia (Hulme & Snowling, 1992; Snowling & Hulme, 1989; Snowling, Stackhouse, & Rack, 1986). Such research assumes that cognitive processing involves the mapping of one type of information, such as orthographic information, onto another type of information, such as phonological information. Different types of information characteristically are represented by different boxes, and their interconnections by arrows between the boxes (e.g., see the logogen model in Morton & Patterson, 1980). On the basis of models of particular cognitive processes, such as single-word reading, predictions can be made about how the system might break down, specifying which behaviors will be affected by disruption of a particular component in the model, and which will be independent of that component and so will be spared. For example, if the model has an orthographic component and a phonological component, it may be predicted that single word reading might be impaired in the presence of intact phonological representations. Observation of such dissociations between related representations provides some of the crucial evidence for separate components within models or for connections between components. In the case of single-word reading, for example, dissociation between the reading of words with regular and irregular orthography has generated models with two routes to single-word reading, a visual and a phonological route.

The phonological processing of children whose output is impaired can be explored in relation to such psycholinguistic theories and models. Starting from an existing model of phonological processing, tasks can be devised to tap children's control of different levels within the model. Conversely, observations of dissociations between intact and impaired behaviors in these children may point to extensions or modifications of existing models and theories.

Psycholinguistic questions about normal and impaired phonological development have been posed, and models of children's output processing have been postulated. In a review of normal phonological development, Menn (1983) suggested that the "defining question" of research had changed from "What linguistic theory will explain the order in which the various language behaviors develop?" to "What behavioral predispositions and abilities does the child bring to the task of learning to communicate with language, and how does the individual go about solving the articulatory and phonological problems posed by the language to be learned?" (Menn, 1983, p. 45). Menn's response to this new question included a model of processing and storage. The model consists of a "collection of percepts" which feed into an "input lexicon," to which "rules" apply, giving rise to an "output lexicon." The entries in the output lexicon are "ways-to-say-words," specifying a canonical form together with certain variable parameters of that form. These entries then plug into an articulatory program for realising the relevant canonical form. Menn presented evidence of perceptual and articulatory constraints that affect the input and output lexicons in the course of normal development.

Hewlett (1990) has proposed a more elaborated model of phonological processing. The structure of the model closely resembles information-processing models of adult single-word processing, particularly the logogen model. It assumes an input lexicon, which consists of perceptual representations. The perceptual representations of the input lexicon feed into a motor programmer which devises motor plans. The motor plans are relayed to a motor processing component containing the information required for the articulatory execution of the motor plan. But the motor programmer also relays its motor plans to an output lexicon, which provides a faster route to motor processing: A word can be selected directly from the output lexicon and implemented by "highly learned combinations of muscle commands." The components and organization of Hewlett's model are motivated by a wide range of observations of normal and disordered development of speech. Focusing on the specific case of impaired phonological development, how might the different levels be investigated and how far does the model enable us to account for observed dissociations in behavior?

Phonological impairment is identified on the basis of deviations in output. Clinical assessment would include informal observation or standardized testing of input phonology. However, compared with the detailed description of output, systematic investigation into different levels of input processing in children with phonological impairment is quite limited. Clinical observation typically shows the child discriminating and recognizing distinctions even when these are neutralized in output. Systematic investigation has produced similar findings. Chaney (1988b) reported a study of normally developing children aged 4;0–4;9 and articulation-impaired children aged 6;4–7;5, all of whom made substitutions for semivowel targets. Both groups of children were able to identify adult semivowels. Brett, Chiat, and Pilcher (1988) presented an investigation into groups of children aged 3–7 years whose output showed voicing of voiceless stop targets or fronting of velar stop targets. Neither the voicing nor the fronting group showed problems in distinguishing words that differed in the relevant parameter (voiced/voiceless or alveolar/velar). It might be concluded that perception and input representations were intact, and could not be responsible for impaired output. Dodd, Leahy, and Hambly (1989) studied three subgroups of children in the age range 3;5–5;2 years whose phonology was identified as "delayed," "deviant consistent," or "deviant inconsistent." Discrimination was investigated by presenting the children with audiotapes of their own production of adult targets and asking them to select a picture from a set of four, including the target and three distractors which were phonologically related to the child's pronunciation. All three subgroups of children were better at identifying the adult pronunciation of words than their own pronunciation, and when their own pronunciation resulted in a real-word homophone (e.g. *tree* pronounced [ti]), they chose the distractor picture corresponding to that homophone. Dodd et al. inferred that auditory discrimination and word recognition were intact, and that "The impaired mental process causing the disorders must lie in output" (p. 66).

From such studies, it would appear that input processing is not the dominant problem for children identified as having phonological disorders. However, some caution must be exercised, given the limitations of the evidence. First, it may be that similar deviations in output can arise from different underlying deficits, and that in some cases (although not those discussed above) phonological disorder may indeed be due to deficient input processing. On the other hand, the fact that Dodd et al. obtained similar results on the input task across the three subgroups investigated strengthens the generality of the findings. Another possibility is that the role of input is different for different contrasts. Studies of normally developing children (Edwards, 1974; Eilers & Oller, 1976) have suggested that some contrasts are perceived earlier than others, and that perceptual confusions may play a role in speech errors (although substitutions in production do not necessarily involve contrasts which are most difficult perceptually). Accordingly, it is possible that phonologically impaired children's problems with certain contrasts do arise at the input stage. However, the role of input can be discounted for a particular contrast where it can be shown that the contrast is neutralized in output but discriminated in input, as in the Brett et al. study.

A different reason for cautious interpretation of the findings is the relatively gross nature of the tasks used to investigate input. In general, the child is required to discriminate between categories which are apparently neutralized in output. It may be that the child's output does distinguish the relevant categories (e.g., voiced/voiceless), but does so on the basis of acoustic features that are different from or more limited than those used by adults. This would result in correct performance on discrimination tasks, but loss of detectable distinctions in output—precisely the pattern of response observed. However, the problem would not then be confined to output; in fact, the output limitation might itself be due to the distorted identification of features in input. Furthermore, the child would be making a systematic distinction in representations, and the apparent limitation in the phonological system would actually reflect a limitation in the features on which that system is based. There is evidence to suggest that normally developing children sometimes rely on different features to distinguish adult categories. That evidence is that, at least in some cases, children whose realizations of distinct targets are perceived as the same are in fact making a distinction, which is revealed by spectrographic analysis or by the children's ability to distinguish their apparently neutralized targets. This has been observed for children who appear to be making semivowel substitutions such as [w] for [r] (Chaney, 1998a, 1988b; Hoffman, Stager & Daniloff, 1983; Kornfeld, 1971; Kornfeld & Goehl, 1974), or voiced stops for voiceless stops (Macken & Barton, 1980). An imperceptible voicing contrast has also been observed in an analysis of a phonologically disordered child (Maxwell & Weismer, 1982). In a study of three children who omitted word-final stops (Weismer, Dinnsen, & Elbert, 1981), acoustic analysis revealed that two of the children, aged 7, produced vowel durations that were reliably sensitive to the voicing characteristics of the omitted final stop. It is clear that these children were distinguishing between voiced and voiceless stops, even if this was based on limited cues to the distinction.

The possibility that the child is making distinctions on the basis of acoustic features that are different from or more limited than those used by adults is not, however, compatible with Dodd et al.'s (1989) findings. The input task in their study presented children with their own realizations of targets; if these realizations were based on the child's selective perception of certain features in the input, one would expect the child to recognize those features in their own realization and identify the original target. As pointed out earlier, the children had more difficulty identifying their own production of targets than the adult production; and where their own production was homophonous with a different real word, they identified it as that real word. This suggests that the children were relying on the features adults use to discriminate and recognize words, rather than features they might have selected for production. This does not rule out the possibility that the child is selecting limited or different features for targeting in production, but it does mean that any such limitation or difference does not have its origins in perception or recognition processes.

If problems in perception or in the internal lexicon can be excluded, lexical retrieval and subsequent stages of output planning must be considered. Could it be that, although the children discriminate words and map them onto lexical semantics on the basis of the same perceptual parameters as adults, when they come to map that lexical semantics onto output, they retrieve a phonological representation that is limited or different from their input representation? Such a possibility appears to be excluded in Menn's and Hewlett's models. These models do include an output lexicon, but the entries in the output lexicon appear to be articulatory representations or motor programs, rather than abstract phonological representations which are distinct from those accessed in input and also independent of motor programming. There is some evidence, from experimental tasks and from analysis of spontaneous output, that children's failure to mark distinctions in output does not reflect a failure to map semantic representations onto distinct phonological representations. This can be tested by a task that presents children with pictures of words containing targets which they fail to distinguish in their output, and asking the children to think of the words for the pictures and classify them according to which sound is in the word. Brett et al. (1988) devised such an "internal judgment" task, in which phonologically impaired children who fronted velar stops were asked to sort pictures representing words that began with alveolar or velar stops. The phonologically disordered group performed no differently from a matched control group on this task. This indicated that any neutralization between targets such as *cart* and *tart* was not due to mapping of the different meanings onto the same phonological representation. Of course, this finding cannot be generalized without similar investigation into groups of children showing different and more deviant processes. It is possible that the subgroups identified by Dodd et al. (1989) as deviant consistent and deviant inconsistent would show problems in this task. If this were the case, an impairment in mapping of semantic representations onto phonological representations could not be ruled out as the source of their deviant phonological output.

An internal judgment task of the sort described is not ideal for investigating the nature of phonological representations accessed in output. It is a metalinguistic task which taps representations very indirectly: As well as accessing the word for the picture, the child must hold onto the word, segment the initial sound of the word, and match that initial to one of two given sounds. If the child succeeds in making the judgment, it can be inferred that the child has distinct representations for the targets. But, as is generally the case with such tasks, failure could reflect problems with other aspects of the task, and so yield no evidence of the representations the child accesses. It is therefore important to find other sources of evidence.

Analysis of patterns in the child's output may provide evidence. As pointed out above, spectrographic analysis has been known to reveal differences between targets that appear to be neutralized by a child.

Where such differences are observed, we again have clear evidence that the child is mapping the different semantic representations onto distinct phonological representations. However, failure to identify such differences is again inconclusive. The child may be making a distinction that has not been considered in the spectrographic analysis. Or she may be retrieving distinct representations, which become identical at a subsequent stage of output.

The mapping of semantic representations onto phonological representations might also be investigated by eliciting phonological output **independently** of semantic representations and comparing this with phonological output elicited from semantics. Repetition, as opposed to naming or spontaneous production, does not require that semantic representations be accessed; a word or sentence can be repeated by mapping input phonology onto output phonology without necessarily accessing the semantic representations they encode. Where the stimuli are nonsense words, by definition, there is no connection to semantics. If a child's problem is in the mapping of semantic representations onto phonological representations, she might bypass the semantic route in a repetition task, and production might be closer to the adult model. Systematic comparison between repetition and spontaneous or elicited production has produced mixed results. The Brett et al. (1988) study of children fronting velar stops compared their repetition and naming of words with a matched control group and found that the performance of velar fronters was significantly lower on both tasks. Single case studies of fronting (Chiat, 1983) and stopping (Chiat, 1989) revealed the same pattern of errors in repetition and spontaneous production. In the Dodd et al. (1989) study of three subgroups of phonologically disordered children, the number of errors in repetition, picture naming, and description of absurd pictures were compared. Although there was no difference between these tasks for the phonologically delayed subgroup, both the deviant subgroups made fewer errors on repetition than on naming and picture description. Williams and Chiat (1993) compared the number of errors in naming with those in repetition of real words, nonwords, and sentences in groups identified as "phonologically delayed" and "phonologically disordered." The delayed group was consistent across tasks, producing similar numbers and types of errors. As a whole, the disordered group showed a difference between tasks, making fewer errors in the repetition tasks than in the naming task. But they appeared to fall into two subgroups. One showed the same consistency across tasks as the delayed group. The other subgroup was responsible for the overall finding that performance on repetition was superior to performance on other output tasks.

The results from these studies are not clear-cut. The relation between responses to an auditory model (repetition) and responses to a semantic stimulus (naming or spontaneous output) appears to vary between children. There appears to be some connection between patterns of response to different tasks and patterns of error in spontaneous output, but the evidence is limited and not altogether consistent. Dodd et al. (1989) and Williams and Chiat (1993) both found that children whose output was characterized by phonological processes typical of those used by younger children showed similar patterns across different production tasks. However, the two studies diverge with respect to children whose output deviates from normal developmental processes. Dodd et al. found that such children made fewer errors in repetition, and this was true for both their consistent and inconsistent subgroups. Williams and Chiat, on the other hand, found that their deviant group divided into a subgroup of children who behaved like the delayed group, making similar errors across production tasks, and a subgroup of children who behaved like Dodd et al.'s deviant subgroups, making fewer errors in repetition. The divergence between findings of the two studies could be due to a number of factors, with different implications for the locus of impairment and its effect on patterns of error. It may be that the deviant groups in the two studies were distinct, even though the criteria used to identify deviance were similar. Criteria based on the range of phonological processes used are not absolute, and different underlying deficits may produce sufficiently similar ranges of behaviors that they are indistinguishable on these criteria. Williams and Chiat's deviant group appears to have included a subgroup of children whose problems were at the same point in processing as those in the delayed group, but more severe (i.e., with more extreme effects on that level of processing). Perhaps the Dodd et al. study did not include such "severely delayed" children, or did not identify them as deviant.

Whether or not it turns out that clinical subgroups show distinct and predictable patterns of response to different output tasks, we may consider the implications of the observed patterns for the locus of impairment. For children who show no difference, it may be inferred that the problem is not in retrieval of phonological representations, but arises in the planning of articulatory output. This might be situated in Hewlett's motor programmer. Hewlett's model has the motor programmer feeding into an output lexicon. This would imply that the impaired motor plans devised by the motor programmer are sent to the output lexicon. Once established there, an impaired motor plan can be accessed directly for output. Presumably the output lexicon can be accessed from an input representation (as in repetition of real words) or from a semantic representation (as in naming or spontaneous production). This is not altogether clear in Hewlett's model, because it does not include semantic representations and their relation to other processing components. A possible source of evidence for the storage of impaired motor plans in an output lexicon is the observation that when a distinction eventually emerges in the child's output, it may do so gradually (Menn, 1983), suggesting that the child is programming words as established wholes rather than filtering them through the newly developed motor programming skills.

For children who show fewer errors in repetition than in responses to a semantic stimulus, the processing implications are not quite the same. Since repetition does show problems, it may be inferred that these children, too, have difficulty in planning articulatory output. The question is why the difficulty is less marked when the child has received an auditory model. Following Hewlett's model, it may be that these children have a further problem in relaying the motor plan to the output lexicon, resulting in an output representation that is further degraded. When the child seeks the output representation for a particular meaning, this degraded representation would be retrieved. Interpreted in this way, the implication would be that the child has two independent problems: an impairment in motor planning and an impairment in storing the resulting motor plans. It may be, however, that the two problems are integrally related. For example, the child's problem may lie not in the motor plans themselves, but in the connections between motor plans and other representations, with the connection to auditory representations being less impaired than the connection to semantic representations. It is difficult to see how an information-processing model of the sort just discussed could accommodate such differences of degree in the routes between components. I return to this issue below, and suggest how connectionist modeling may provide more insight into the observed behaviors.

Drawing together the findings discussed in this section, it may be tentatively concluded that children typically described as "phonologically impaired" do not have problems in perception, storage, and retrieval of input phonological representations or retrieval of phonological representations for output; their problems arise at a later point in output, in planning the articulation of those representations, and hence in stored motor plans. It may be that the children as a group all have problems in these particular aspects of output processing, but differ in the severity and/or range of impairment within these output processes. It may also be that children are identified as "phonologically impaired" who *do* have problems in input processing. This would be detected by different responses to input and internal judgment tasks from those documented here, and might be expected to give rise to different patterns of output.

These tentative conclusions have implications for models of output processing. They suggest that there may be a number of routes to "phonological output." One maps a semantic representation onto an internal phonological representation (as evidenced by internal judgment). Another maps an input phonological representation onto a plan for articulatory output (as evidenced by repetition of nonwords and, potentially, repetition of real words). Another maps a semantic representation onto a stored output plan (as evidenced by naming and spontaneous production). The latter two routes appear to be most compatible with models of children's output processing, such as Hewlett's and Menn's, and with models of adult processing such as the logogen model, all of which include separate input and output lexicons, and allow a lexical and nonlexical route to articulatory output. The route from semantic representation to internal phonological representation, on the other hand, appears to be more compatible with a single-lexicon model (e.g., Butterworth, 1980; Forster, 1976) where the same internal representation is accessed in input and output. This route perhaps could be accommodated in the two-lexicon model by building in a route from semantic representation to the input lexicon. The child evidence thus suggests a combination of the components in the two types of model. It also suggests that routes between different inputs and the same output may be impaired to different degrees. Such a proliferation of representations, along with variations in the strength of routes between those representations, might be considered undesirable or even incompatible with information-processing models that postulate a flow of information from one "box" to the next. A similar point was made by Menn and Matthei (1992) when they observed that "As with many other box-and-arrow models, the two-lexicon model was forced to undergo a fair amount of proliferation to deal . . . with additional types of variability in behavior" (p. 219). Such variability may be more compatible with a connectionist model which allows for multiple interconnections of variable weightings, a possibility which will be discussed later.

## INVESTIGATION INTO PATTERNS OF ERRORS AT PARTICULAR LEVELS

In the previous section, we have seen how some light can be shed on the level(s) of processing affected in phonologically impaired children by comparing behaviors that tap different levels of input and output processing. Such investigations generally compare the **number** of errors on particular targets, such as "consonants" or "word-initial consonants," in different behaviors, such as discrimination, repetition, or spontaneous output. They do not explore the **pattern** of errors. The pattern of errors provides a major source of insights into the level of processing that is impaired and the nature of the impairment at that level. Such insights may be gained by focusing on one particular behavior and investigating which distinctions are affected, the ways in which they are affected, and the contexts in which they are affected. Studies of the type discussed earlier pointed to output planning as the locus of impairment. Output planning and the way in which it is impaired may be further explored by investigating the pattern of errors in output behaviors and the variables these reflect.

Children's output data provide a particularly rich source of evidence. First, the data are a relatively direct reflection of the child's language processing, being much less liable to contamination by extraneous factors of the sort which affect the more metalinguistic tasks required to tap input. Furthermore, the data reveal systematic patterns, reflecting variables of a far more subtle nature than the variables that can be investigated in input tasks. This is precisely why output data have attracted the interest of phonologists, have been subjected to competing phonological descriptions, and have been seen as a possible testing ground for competing theories. The point is that, when children's output patterns differ from those of adults, the relation between the two is neither random nor simple. Children generally do not replace or omit target categories piecemeal or wholesale. They replace or omit certain categories, and do so in certain contexts. Phonological theories—from generative phonology to autosegmental phonology and feature geometry—have been used to characterize the regularities in children's output, and thereby to account for the scope of substitutions/omissions and the domains in which these occur. Such theory-based descriptions have led to the identification of certain typical substitutions and omissions, and these have come to be known as "phonological processes," such as "stopping," "fronting," "consonant harmony," "cluster reduction." Phonological process analysis, which analyses data in terms of these phonological processes, is commonly used in assessing children with phonological disorder (Grunwell, 1985; Ingram, 1981). Such phonological descriptions of the data, be they theory-specific or eclectic, are not in themselves descriptions of psycholinguistic processing, since they seek to characterize the **product** of processing without reference to that processing and the mapping between input and output representations involved. But they do have implications for processing.

For example, phonological descriptions, and the phonological processes derived from them, indicate the domains in which a substitution or omission occurs. The factors that define the domain have implications for the representations which are being processed at the point where the "error" arises, and the interrelations between these representations at that point. This can be illustrated by studies which have investigated the factors affecting substitutions or omissions in children with phonological impairment. Chiat (1983, 1989) carried out case studies of children who realized particular segmental targets differently depending on whether they occurred word-initially or word-finally. The first study focused on velar stop targets, which were fronted initially, but correct finally. For example, /g/ in *go* was fronted, resulting in [dəu], whereas in *egg* it was realized correctly. The second study focused on fricative targets, which were stopped initially, but correct finally. For example, /s/ in *sea* was stopped, resulting in [ti], whereas in *ice* it was realized correctly. In both cases, it was found that the realization of word-medial stop and fricative targets was affected by the metrical structure of the word. They were treated like initials, being fronted or stopped, if they preceded the stressed vowel. For example, the velar fronting child produced /k/ correctly in 'record but fronted it in re'cord; the stopping child produced /f/ correctly in 'toffee, but stopped it in be'fore. This stress effect did not cross word boundaries. In connected speech, where the target preceded an unstressed vowel, but as the initial of a function word rather than the medial of a word, it was treated like other word-initials and was not realized correctly. So, for example, /k/ in /'hi kən 'dɑns/ was fronted, in contrast to /k/ in the single word /'bikən/, which was correct. From this, it was concluded that at the point in processing where fronting and stopping occurred, the unit being processed was the word, and features such as velar or fricative were being planned as parameters of the metrical structure of the word. This conclusion calls to mind Menn's proposal (Menn, 1983) that entries in the output lexicon consist of canonical forms within which the values of variable parameters are set.

The case study of stopping (Chiat, 1989) probed further the effects of word structure on the realization of targets. The treatment of targets that occurred in trisyllabic words between the penultimate and final unstressed vowels, such as /f/ in *elephant*, was investigated. It was found that these were stopped, and so treated in the same way as initials. Thus, while /f/ was correct between the stressed and unstressed vowels of a word such as *difficult*, behaving in the same way as a final, it was stopped between the unstressed vowels of *beautiful*, behaving in the same way as an initial. From this, it was inferred that the feature "fricative" was planned as a parameter of a metrical subunit of the word, which consisted maximally of stressed+unstressed syllables; in a trisyllabic word, an unstressed syllable following this metrical structure was separate. Such a metrical subunit is similar, although not identical, to the metrical foot posited by some metrical theories (Selkirk, 1984). A further finding of this study was that the treatment of intervocalic targets within this subunit was affected by their phonotactic position. Where the target fricative occurred in a sequence of consonants, it was correct if it followed a consonant with which it could form a legal word-final cluster (e.g., /f/ in *selfish*). However, where the fricative followed a consonant with which it could not form a legal word-final cluster (e.g., /f/ in *infant*), it was stopped, suggesting that it was planned as an initial rather than final. Although some of the words, such as *selfish*, *beautiful*, and *carefully*, may contain morpheme boundaries, this did not appear to affect realization of targets. Drawing together the findings of this study, it appeared that the feature "fricative" was planned as a parameter of a subunit of the word whose boundaries depend on the metrical and phonotactic structure of the word.

A recent study (in preparation) has been carried out to explore further the effects of metrical and phonotactic structure observed in these earlier case studies. The subjects were two phonologically impaired children. Joseph omitted all stops and fricatives word-initially, but not word-finally, such that *sea* was [i] but *ice* was [aɪs]. In contrast, Luke omitted all stops, fricatives, and nasals word-finally, but not word-initially, such that *sea* was [si] but *ice* was [aɪ]. The treatment of word-medial stops and fricatives was investigated. These were again affected by metrical structure. Both children treated pre-stress medials in the same way as initials (i.e., Joseph omitted the /z/ of *deserve*, while Luke produced it). Conversely, Joseph treated post-stress medials in the same way as finals, so that /z/ in *easy* was produced. Luke, on the other hand, showed variability in this position, often treating a post-stress target like a final and omitting it as in [mjuʔɪʔ] for *music*, but sometimes treating it as an initial and producing it as in [tʌdʊ] for *cuddle*. These findings give further weight to the inference that features are planned on metrical structures, but suggest a degree of variability in the relation between segmental and metrical structure.

An analysis of phonotactic effects also pointed to a degree of variability in the relation between feature context and syllabification. In contrast to the subject in Chiat (1989), Joseph showed no effects of phonotactic position on post-stress word-medial targets. These were always treated as finals, whether or not they could form a legal final with a preceding consonant. So, Joseph treated the /f/ in *infant* in the same way as the /f/ in *selfish*; he did not omit either. Phonotactic effects did however emerge in his treatment of pre-stress consonant sequences. But in this case the effects were not related to the legality of the sequence as a word-initial or final. In words such as *disturb* and *mistake,* Joseph varied in his realization of the medial sequence. If he were treating it definitively as an initial cluster (which it could legally be), he would omit it as he did word-initial clusters and pre-stress singletons. This did happen, but not consistently. He sometimes did produce the /s/, implying that he was treating it as the final of the unstressed syllable, overriding the clear attraction of consonants to a following stressed vowel which applied consistently where /s/ occurred as a singleton before a stressed vowel. The inconsistency with the /s/+stop sequences suggests that stress and phonotactic structure may have conflicting effects on word structure, producing ambivalence in the planning of a feature within the word. A different interaction between these factors was observed in Luke's output. As with Joseph, phonotactic structure did not affect Luke's treatment of post-stress word-medial consonant sequences. Whether or not the sequence would be legal word-finally, Luke showed the same inconsistency with these as he did with word-medial singletons. Thus, the /f/ in *selfish* and *infant* might be omitted or might be produced. Unlike Joseph, on the other hand, his treatment of pre-stress consonant sequences such as /st/ in *mistake* was also unaffected by phonotactic structure and was consistent: he always treated these in the same way as word-initial clusters, and realized them as he would in word-initial position, in a word such as *stay,* rather than treating the first element as a final and omitting it. Thus, for Luke, stress appeared to be the overriding factor in determining syllabification and realization of intervocalic targets.

The common thread through these four cases is that place and manner features are realized according to their position in the metrical structure of the word and their relation to other place and manner features within the word. Although the specific interactions between these aspects of the word vary, they do so within limits. For example, a stressed vowel attracted a preceding consonant across a wide range of the data. The only instance of this stress effect being overridden involved obstruent sequences such as /st/ where the first obstruent was sometimes treated as a final of a preceding unstressed syllable. Even here, the stress effect was evident in the ambivalent syllabification of that first obstruent. The implication of these observations for psycholinguistic processing is that place and manner features are planned word by word, and are planned as parameters of subunits of the word defined by metrical and phonotactic structure.

In the first of these studies (Chiat, 1983), it was noted that "voicing," unlike "fronting" and "stopping," was affected by context beyond the word boundary. It appeared that voiceless stops were voiced preceding a vowel, whether the vowel was in the same word or a following word. Thus, the /k/ of *back* was voiced in the construction *back out,* where it preceded the stressed vowel of the following word. In contrast, the /k/ was not fronted, even though it preceded a stressed vowel; fronting only occurred if the velar preceded a stressed vowel **within** the word. This observation was followed up with a systematic investigation into the domain of voicing in a group of phonologically impaired children (Brett et al., 1988). The sensitivity of voicing to a following vowel, independently of word boundaries, was confirmed. Furthermore, it was found that voicing was affected by vowel stress: More voiceless targets were produced correctly before an unstressed vowel than before a stressed one, whether within or beyond the word boundary. From this it was inferred that voicing occurred at a later stage of output processing where word boundaries are no longer specified. This was taken to be the stage of articulatory execution.

There is nothing very original about the findings in these studies. The literature on normal and disordered phonological development abounds in examples of individual children applying a generally specified "phonological process" in subtly different domains. Current studies continue to reveal the interaction between segmental features, segmental context, and metrical position (although these aspects are not always explicitly identified). Chin and Dinnsen (1992), in a large-scale study of cluster reduction in speech-disordered children aged 3;4–6;8, found that the realization of particular segments sometimes depended on their feature context and that the effects of feature context varied between children. Berg (1992), in a case study of consonant harmony in a normal child between 2;7 and 2;11 years, found that the process affected targets in particular positions relative to word boundaries and other segments in the word and did not cross word boundaries. Thus, there is an increasing body of data revealing the contexts in which particular substitutions or omissions occur. The patterns observed are often advanced as arguments for analysing children's phonological output in terms of nonlinear phonology, where representations consist of relatively autonomous tiers and associations between these (Bernhardt & Gilbert, 1992; Chin & Dinnsen, 1991). However, there has been little exploitation of these data from a psycholinguistic point of view, as possible evidence of the structure of output processing. Psycholinguistic questions tend to be overlooked or are confined to considering whether the deficit occurs in "underlying representations" versus "phonetic representations," or "representations" versus "processing." The Chiat studies discussed in detail above seek to extend the insights into processing that can be gained from such data, by evaluating them against theories of output planning.

How do the inferences from these data relate to the evidence derived from investigations into stages of processing discussed in the preceding section? Those investigations led to the conclusion that children with impaired phonology have problems in devising motor programs and that these problems may vary according to the input to the motor program (auditory or semantic). Investigations into the factors that affect segmental realization in some of these children have suggested that place and manner features are planned at a stage where the word is the unit of planning and as parameters of subunits within the word which are defined by metrical and segmental features of the word. Voicing, on the other hand, appeared to be planned at a later stage of articulatory execution, where word boundaries were no longer relevant and the stress of a vowel following the target within or beyond the word boundary could affect it. Drawing together these different conclusions, it might be inferred that phonological impairment arises at various points in output planning: in mapping auditory input or semantic representations onto a motor program, or in the articulatory execution of a motor program.

## TOWARD A CONNECTIONIST MODEL OF IMPAIRED DEVELOPMENT OF PHONOLOGICAL OUTPUT

The analysis of phonological impairment in terms of stages of processing has produced a proliferation of stages of output planning and a rather odd dispersion of problems across these stages. The apparent dispersion of problems may reflect the limitations of the information-processing theory and models within which they have been analysed. These models have forced an interpretation in which different types of information (boxes) or the routes between them (arrows) are impaired. They treat the representations within a box as a single level, which means they do not provide a framework for specifying the processing of structures **within** a box. This could, of course, be remedied by specifying subcomponents within a box. For example, the motor programmer component could be broken down into metrical and segmental levels. This would allow for one level of phonological planning, such as planning of certain segmental features, to be subsequent to and contingent on an earlier level, such as metrical structure, enabling one to account for the sensitivity of children's segmental substitutions and omissions to metrical structure. Somewhat analogously, Hewlett (1990) divided motor processing into two components, one specifying the syllable level and feeding into the other, specifying the segmental level. Such modeling of subcomponents begs further specification. However, even if it were possible to elaborate subcomponents, it is questionable whether the box model framework can accommodate the patterns of behavior which have been observed. The above discussion included three patterns of behavior which suggested differential effects of features within one component or subcomponent on features within a separate component or subcomponent. These effects call to mind recent observations about adult speech errors: Dell (1989), for example, claims that "errors occurring at one level of processing can be affected by factors outside that level" (p. 138). It is as if a component or subcomponent can "reach into" another component or subcomponent and affect its contents selectively. Such interactions appear to conflict with the core assumption of information-processing models which map one type of representation onto another, each type being in a closed box. (See Stemberger, 1985, and Chiat and Jones, 1988, for more wide-ranging evidence and discussion.)

These interactions point towards a "connectionist" model that transcends the box model structure. Indeed, the point recently has been made with respect to the phonological development of normal children. Menn and Matthei (1992) argued that a variety of "unruly" phenomena were indescribable with box-and-arrow models; such models are "deterministic, and there is no straightforward way to graft probabilistic processes onto them" (p. 228). Menn, Markey, Mozer, and Lewis (1993) have proposed that the basic features of connectionist models lead one to expect fuzzy boundaries, interactions, and frequency effects, as well as apparently rule-governed behavior. They outlined a connectionist model that seeks to simulate properties of phonological development, including a range of unruly phenomena.

A connectionist approach has also been advocated by Stemberger (1992), who claims that most phenomena observed in child phonology can be described in terms of effects on the accessibility of units within a connectionist network. He identified three sources of difference between the child's and the adult's production: incorrect weighting between units on different levels; incorrect inhibition of nontarget units; or different settings of parameters such as feedback between levels. Berg (1992) analyzed a child's consonant harmony in terms of the strength of connections within the child's processing system, presumably exemplifying the first of the sources of difference suggested by Stemberger. According to Berg's interpretation, the error arises from underdeveloped connections between a node at the segmental level and a node at the feature level, such that "onset activation cannot spread from the segment to the feature level and reverberate from the feature to the segment level" (p. 244). The child therefore seeks a substitution by selecting the most highly activated node in the domain. Any nodes that share features with the problematic segment will be more highly activated (e.g., an initial velar stop which is problematic will activate a following bilabial stop rather than a liquid, resulting in harmonization of the velar target with the bilabial). Berg also identified position in syllable structure as a feature which, if shared by segmental nodes, will result in them activating each other. So, if a feature is problematic, it is more likely to be replaced with a feature of a segment that is highly activated by virtue of sharing position in syllable structure, such as occurring prevocalically, than a feature occupying a different position in syllable structure. Leonard (1992) considered the possibility of modeling phonological disorder from a connectionist point of view. He followed up just one possible source of disruption, where activation fed back from lower to higher levels is disproportionately high. Such a disruption presumably falls into the last of the categories of difference identified by Stemberger.

It would seem that, at the present point, connectionism offers the possibility of accounting for phenomena that cannot be accommodated by box models. However, the possibilities it offers are open-ended. A connectionist approach to phonological development must be instantiated through particular models, specifying layers of nodes, weighting of nodes, and the mechanisms for activation and inhibition between nodes. A connectionist approach to disordered development must also be instantiated through such models, but must, furthermore, specify possible source(s) of impairment in the normal architecture or weighting of nodes or in the mechanisms for activation and inhibition between nodes. The connectionist project undoubtedly is a long-term one. However, it is promising, and the way forward can, to some extent, be mapped out. Hypotheses about the organization and activation of connections must be advanced, and can be tested against the very data that have been the motivation for a connectionist approach to phonological development. The model developed by Menn et al. (Menn & Matthei, 1992; Menn et al., 1993) provides an example of a connectionist learning system that seeks to demonstrate patterns observed in early phonological development. The model simulates connections between simultaneous motor, auditory, and kinesthetic experiences; between sequential experiences within each of these modalities; and between sequential links across the different modalities.

At this stage in the connectionist enterprise, limited consideration has been given to the nature of phonological representations within the network. According to Stemberger (1992), "There is presently insufficient information to determine reliably what phonological representations are like" (p. 171); he assumes features, segments, syllable units, and a coarse phonological representation that codes number of segments. Menn and Matthei (1992) pointed out the challenge of modeling the development of autosegmental structure which, they suggest, "will require a rich representation of auditory and articulatory axes of similarity" (p. 243). In modeling the emergence of connections between experiences in different modalities (e.g., auditory, motor, kinesthetic), one of the questions which must, then, be addressed is the precise nature of representations of those experiences. I suggest that this aspect of connectionist modeling may be informed by detailed investigation of the **interactions** between phonological features in input and output. Children with phonological disorder are likely to provide a rich source of evidence, because such children have larger vocabularies and are amenable to more active investigation than children in the earliest stages of phonological development. This is exemplified by the detailed patterns of errors which emerged from the studies discussed in this chapter. Such patterns of errors have implications for the network of connections giving rise to speech output. It is striking, for example, that metrical factors which were found to affect segmental realization have not been incorporated into connectionist models considered above.

I now return to the patterns that led me to propose a connectionist approach to phonological disorder and to explore the implications for connectionist modeling of phonological processing. The purpose of this discussion is not to propose specific models or hypotheses, which would be premature at this stage. Rather, the purpose is to point out observed interactions that must somehow be explained by the organization and activation of nodes within a network. In this discussion, I identify connections which appear to be impaired, and connections to which those impaired connections appear to be sensitive in certain children, which must be taken into account in any connectionist architecture. I do not, however, consider the activation mechanisms which might be responsible for impairments in connections.

## ROUTES TO OUTPUT

In the discussion of levels of processing, it was observed that output arising from repetition, naming, and spontaneous production shows consistent errors, quantitatively and qualitatively, for some children. For other children, there is a difference between repetition and output elicited in other ways. It was suggested that the latter group of children, who are inconsistent across behaviors, may have two independent problems: one in devising motor programs and another in relaying these to an output lexicon. However, an alternative view was that these problems may be related, and may both arise from impaired routes between motor plans and other representations, with the connection to auditory representations being less impaired than the connection to semantic representations. Such differences in the degree of activation between representations in different boxes could be compatible with a "box" model, but go beyond its machinery. We can only begin to account for relative effects of different inputs on output if we have theories about the organization and weighting of connections between relevant features in development and how these might be disrupted.

Children who show differential problems with repetition and naming may contribute significantly to the development of such theories. For example, we might go beyond observing a quantitative difference between repetition and naming, and investigate where that difference lies, determining which connections are affected in repetition and naming and, more specifically, whether inferior performance in naming involves impairment to particular connections that are not affected in repetition. This would have implications for the establishment of connections between auditory and articulatory features on the one hand, and between semantic and articulatory features on the other.

## PLACE, MANNER, VOICING, AND METRICAL FEATURES IN OUTPUT

In the discussion of patterns in children's output, it was observed that some children realize place, manner, and voicing features differently depending on their relation to surrounding vowels. Where place and manner features were affected by processes such as fronting, stopping, or consonant deletion, their realization might vary according to whether they attached to a following vowel or a preceding vowel (i.e., whether they were involved in a C-V transition or a V-C transition). This was determined by their position relative to word boundaries and word stress. Voicing, on the other hand, was always affected by a following vowel, regardless of word boundaries. This difference in the factors affecting place/manner and voicing features led to the suggestion that voicing is planned at a later stage than place/manner features. Voicing was attributed to a problem at the stage of articulatory execution, where word boundaries are no longer specified, following the stage of articulatory planning, which operates on words. This could certainly account for the different domains of the two processes. But it raises the question why "errors" which occur at such distinct stages (motor programming vs. motor execution) should so typically co-occur in a child.

Again, if the notion of "levels" of processing is transcended, and the interaction between features is considered in connectionist terms, we might gain more insight into the processing underlying these patterns of error. It may be hypothesized that when children make errors in place/manner or voice, these errors are affected by the weighting of the connection of these features to other features. The sensitivity of place/manner errors to word boundaries suggests that there are relatively strong connections between place/manner and semantic features of words. The connections between voicing and semantic features appear to be less heavily weighted, because voicing is realized independently of word boundaries.

This interpretation has implications which invite further investigation. It has been hypothesized that the different domains of processes affecting place/manner and voicing arise from differences in the weighting of their connection to the semantic features of the word. This assumes that the relative weighting of these connections to semantic features is normal and intact in children who show these patterns of error. This assumption is supported by the observation that, for these children, output in repetition, naming, and spontaneous production shows the same patterns of error. Where, on the other hand, it is hypothesized that connections to semantic features are themselves impaired (see previous section), we might predict that errors in place/manner features will not be subject to consistent effects of word boundaries. For example, substitutions in a particular word might vary according to context and might be affected by factors beyond the boundaries of the word. Detailed exploration of the phonological factors affecting place/manner features in children who show impaired connections between semantic features and articulatory output, and comparison with children for whom these connections are intact, might throw more light on the complex interconnections between semantic features and articulatory features.

## PLACE/MANNER FEATURES, METRICAL FEATURES, AND PHONOTACTIC STRUCTURE

It has been observed that place/manner features may be realized differently according to whether they occur in transition to or from a vowel, and that this in turn depends on their position relative to word stress. The effect of word stress on the syllabification and realization of consonants was evidenced by all the children who treated word-initial and word-final targets differently. This implies relatively strong connections between metrical position and place/manner features, which override other interconnections. To accommodate this, a connectionist model should incorporate connections between metrical position and place/manner features and explain how the weighting of interconnections between different articulatory features and different metrical positions is established in normal development and may be affected by impairment.

The patterns in children's output outlined above also revealed certain effects of phonotactic structure on the realization of place/manner features. Where a sequence of consonants occurred at a particular point in the metrical structure of the word, a feature of one of these consonants might be realized differently depending on features of the other consonant. Unlike the stress effect, these phonotactic effects were subject to variation between children. For example, one child might realize the feature "fricative" within a consonant sequence differently depending on the place/manner features of the adjacent consonant, whereas another child might show no such difference. This suggests that the strength of connections between consonants in a sequence may vary, determining whether their features are planned as independent transitions, one from a vowel and one towards a vowel, or as interdependent transitions, both from a vowel or both towards a vowel (depending on their metrical position). The weighting of connections between consonants in a sequence presumably depends on other interconnections. These might include the weighting of connections between the same feature sequences and other metrical positions (e.g., whether strong connections have been established between those feature sequences in word-initial or word-final position) or the weighting of connections between the relevant features and surrounding vowels (e.g., whether strong connections have been established between the features of one of the consonants and the preceding or following vowel). Variation in the treatment of consonant sequences could arise because of different interactions between these factors. Such differences could be due to differences in the input received by the child. However, they are more likely due to differences in the connections that are impaired and have repercussions for the establishment of further interconnections. More extensive investigation is needed to explore this possibility. This would involve detailed analysis of individual children's output to reveal the treatment of problematic features in different phonotactic contexts, and comparison between children whose problems involve different connections to infer the effects of one problematic connection on other connections. For example, do children who have problems with initial consonants show different effects of phonotactic structure from children who have problems with final consonants? Do children who deal with a problematic connection by omitting a consonant show different effects of phonotactic structure from children who seek a substitution for the problematic connection? If we find a predictable relation between types of error (e.g., omission or substitution), position of error (e.g., word-initial or word-final), and effects of phonotactic position, this will have implications for the organization and weighting of interconnections between features.

## CONCLUSION

Clearly, a connectionist approach to speech processing and to impairments in its development generates a wide and as yet underspecified range of possibilities for research. Once we go beyond models that identify gross levels of representation, hypotheses about interconnections between and within levels are not adequately constrained. However, by focusing on fragments of a network, it should be possible to develop and test detailed models within this framework.

At this early stage in the development of connectionist models of speech processing, the above discussion of specific interconnections and their weighting can be no more than exploratory. It points the direction that research might take and suggests how children with impaired phonology may provide important evidence of interconnections in speech processing. Until recently, variation between and within children has been of peripheral interest; the principal interest has been in general patterns which abstract from individual variation. But variation within the general patterns now becomes the key to generalizations about the organization and weighting of connections between input and output phonological features and semantic features. As Stemberger (1992) has pointed out, "If progress is to be made, more longitudinal and cross-sectional studies of large numbers of children will have to be performed to increase our data base" (p. 186). Detailed case studies of impaired connections between phonological features (metrical and segmental) and semantic features, and connections which are preserved and exploited to compensate for the impairment, can reveal possible interconnections between these different features. As such detailed case studies accumulate, generalizations about the organization and relative weighting of connections between features in speech processing will emerge. Beyond "levels" of processing, there is a rich future in the microscopic exploration of impaired phonological development.

## REFERENCES

Berg, T. (1992). Phonological harmony as a processing problem. *Journal of Child Language, 19,* 225–257.

Bernhardt, B., & Gilbert, J. (1992). Applying linguistic theory to speech-language pathology: The case for nonlinear phonology. *Clinical Linguistics and Phonetics, 6,* 123–145.

Braine, M. D. S. (1976). Review of N.V. Smith, The acquisition of phonology. *Language, 52,* 482–498.

Brett, L., Chiat, S., & Pilcher, C. (1988). Stages and units in output processing: Some evidence from voicing and fronting processes in children. *Language and Cognitive Processes, 2,* 165–177.

Butterworth, B. (1980). Some constraints on models of language production. In B. Butterworth (Ed.), *Language production* (Vol 1, pp. 423–459). London: Academic Press.

Chaney, C. (1988a). Acoustic analysis of correct and misarticulated semivowels. *Journal of Speech and Hearing Research, 31,* 275–287.

Chaney, C. (1988b). Identification of correct and misarticulated semivowels. *Journal of Speech and Hearing Disorders, 53,* 252–261.

Chiat, S. (1983). Why *Mikey's* right and *my key's* wrong: The significance of stress and word boundaries in a child's output system. *Cognition, 14,* 275–300.

Chiat, S. (1989). The relation between prosodic structure, syllabification and segmental realization: Evidence from a child with fricative stopping. *Clinical Linguistics and Phonetics, 3,* 223–242.

Chiat, S., & Jones, E. V. (1988). Processing languagebreakdown. In M. J. Ball (Ed.), *Theoretical linguistics and disordered language* (pp. 31–50). London: Croom Helm.

Chin, S. B., & Dinnsen, D. A. (1991). Feature geometry in disordered phonologies. *Clinical Linguistics and Phonetics, 5,* 329–337.

Chin, S. B., & Dinnsen, D. A. (1992). Consonant clusters in disordered speech: constraints and correspondence patterns. *Journal of Child Language, 19,* 259–285.

Coltheart, M., Patterson, K., & Marshall, J. C. (1980). *Deep dyslexia.* London: Routledge & Kegan Paul.

Dell, G. S. (1989). The retrieval of phonological forms in production: Tests of predictions from a connectionist model. In W. Marslen-Wilson (Ed.), *Lexical representation and process* (pp. 136–165). Cambridge, MA: MIT Press.

Dodd, B., Leahy, J., & Hambly, G. (1989). Phonological disorders in children: underlying cognitive deficits. *British Journal of Developmental Psychology, 7,* 55–71.

Edwards, M. L. (1974). Perception and production in child phonology: The testing of four hypotheses. *Journal of Child Language, 1,* 205–219.

Eilers, R. E., & Oller, D. K. (1976). The role of speech discrimination in developmental sound substitutions. *Journal of Child Language, 3,* 319–329.

Forster, K. I. (1976). Accessing the mental lexicon. In R. J. Wales & E. Walker (Eds.), *New approaches to language mechanisms* (pp. 257–287). Amsterdam: North-Holland.

Grunwell, P. (1985). *Phonological assessment of child speech (PACS).* Windsor, England: NFER-Nelson.

Hewlett, N. (1990). Processes of development and production. In P. Grunwell (Ed.), *Developmental speech disorders* (pp. 15–38). Edinburgh, Scotland: Churchill Livingstone.

Hoffman, P. R., Stager, S., & Daniloff, R. G. (1983). Perception and production of misarticulated /r/. *Journal of Speech and Hearing Disorders, 48,* 210–215.

Hulme, C., & Snowling, M. (1992). Deficits in output phonology: an explanation of reading failure? *Cognitive Neuropsychology, 9,* 47–72.

Ingram, D. (1974). Phonological rules in young children. *Journal of Child Language, 1,* 49–64.

Ingram, D. (1981). *Procedures for the phonological analysis of children's language.* Baltimore: University Park Press.

Kornfeld, J. (1971). Theoretical issues in child phonology. In *Papers from the Seventh Regional Meeting, Chicago Linguistics Society* (pp. 454–468).

Kornfeld, J., & Goehl, H. (1974). A new twist to an old observation: Kids know more than they say. Parasession on Natural Phonology, *Chicago Linguistics Society Meeting, 10,* 210–219.

Leonard, L. B. (1992). Models of phonological development and children with phonological disorders. In C. A. Ferguson, L. Menn, & C. Stoel-Gammon (Eds.), *Phonological development: Models, research, implications* (pp. 495–507). Timonium, MD: York Press.

Macken, M. A., & Barton, D. (1980). The acquisition of the voicing contrast in English: A study of voice onset time in word-initial stop consonants. *Journal of Child Language, 7,* 41–74.

Maxwell, E., & Weismer, G. (1982). The contribution of phonological, acoustic, and perceptual techniques to the characterization of a misarticulating child's voice onset time for stops. *Applied Psycholinguistics, 3,* 29–34.

Menn, L. (1983). Development of articulatory, phonetic, and phonological capabilities. In B. Butterworth (Ed.), *Language production* (Vol. 2, pp. 3–50). London: Academic Press.

Menn, L., & Matthei, E. (1992). The "two-lexicon" account of child phonology: Looking back, looking ahead. In C. A. Ferguson, L. Menn, & C. Stoel-Gammon (Eds.), *Phonological development: Models, research, implications* (pp. 211–247). Timonium, MD: York Press.

Menn, L., Markey, K., Mozer, M., & Lewis, C. (1993). Connectionist modeling and the microstructure of phonological development: A progress report. In B. de Boysson-Bardies, P. Jusczykk, P. MacNeilage, J. Morton, & S. de Schonen (Eds.), *Changes in speech and face processing in infancy: A glimpse at developmental mechanisms of cognition* (NATO Conference, Carry-le-Rouet, 1992). Kluwer Academic Publishers.

Morton, J., & Patterson, K. (1980). A new attempt at an interpretation, or, an attempt at a new interpretation. In M. Coltheart, K. Patterson, & J. C. Marshall (Eds.), *Deep dyslexia* (pp. 91–118). London: Routledge & Kegan Paul.

Selkirk, E. O. (1984). *Phonology and syntax: The relation sound and structure.* Cambridge, MA: MIT Press.

Smith, N. V. (1973). *The acquisition of phonology: a case study.* Cambridge, England: Cambridge University Press.

Snowling, M., & Hulme, C. (1989). A longitudinal case study of developmental phonological dyslexia. *Cognitive Neuropsychology, 6,* 379–401.

Snowling, M., Stackhouse, J., & Rack, J. (1986). Phonological dyslexia and dysgraphia: a developmental analysis. *Cognitive Neuropsychology, 3,* 309–339.

Spencer, A. (1988). A phonological theory of phonological development. In M. J. Ball (Ed.), *Theoretical linguistics and disordered language* (pp.115–151). London: Croom Helm.

Stemberger, J. P. (1985). An interactive activation model of language production. In A. W. Ellis (Ed.), *Progress in the psychology of language* (Vol. 1, pp. 143–186). London: Lawrence Erlbaum.

Stemberger, J. P. (1992). A connectionist view of child phonology: Phonological processing without phonological processes. In C. A. Ferguson, L. Menn, & C.

Stoel-Gammon (Eds.), *Phonological development: Models, research, implications* (pp. 165–189). Timonium, MD: York Press.

Waterson, N. (1971). Child phonology: *A prosodic view. Journal of Linguistics, 7,* 179–221.

Weismer, G., Dinnsen, D., & Elbert, M. (1981). A study of the voicing distinction associated with omitted, word-final stops. *Journal of Speech and Hearing Disorders, 46,* 320–327.

Williams, N., & Chiat, S. (1993). Processing deficits in children with phonological disorder and delay: A comparison of responses to a series of output tasks. *Clinical Linguistic and Phonetics, 7,* 145–160.

# CHAPTER 6

# Independent and Relational Accounts of Phonological Disorders

DANIEL A. DINNSEN, Ph.D.
STEVEN B. CHIN, Ph.D.

Phonological disorders have been described from two very different perspectives: in relation to the target sound system or independent of it. These two approaches have yielded very different claims about the nature of disordered sound systems. Relational accounts (e.g., Edwards & Shriberg, 1983; Ingram, 1989) have been advanced primarily within the framework of Natural Phonology (Donegan & Stampe, 1979), although this perspective has at times also been evident in other theoretical frameworks and in the description of other developing sound systems (e.g., Gandour, 1981; Lorentz, 1976; Menn, 1976; Spencer, 1986). The relational perspective has for years dominated clinical research and practice. This approach maintains that there is a systematic relationship or correspondence between the target system and the child's erred productions. This presumed systematic relationship is accounted for by assuming that the child's underlying mental representations of words are correct and that a finite set of innate natural processes convert those underlying representations into the child's erred substitutes. A phonological disorder thus is characterized as a phonetically simplified derivative of the target system. The problem is seen as unidimensional, requiring a focus on the more superficial aspects of the system, namely the persisting natural processes that when eliminated should result in entirely corrrect productions. Although this approach may seem attractive, it is admittedly quite abstract in terms of its claims about children's underlying representations. Many of the postulated distinctions attributed to the child are absolutely neutralized by the natural processes and thus are never realized phonetically in the child's speech.

The other approach (sometimes referred to as the Indiana perspective) analyzes disordered systems independently of the target system, just as fully developed sound systems are analyzed in generative theory (Chomsky & Halle, 1968). Claims about what a child knows about his or her sound system thus are based on facts evident only in that child's speech, without regard to any presumed relationship with the sound system of the surrounding speech community. These claims tend to be much less abstract compared with those made in relational accounts. For examples of detailed analyses within this framework, see Chin (1993), Gierut (1985), and Maxwell (1979, 1981). This framework has resulted in a very different characterization of disorders. The principal difference is the finding that children's errors can, in some cases, be attributed to underlying representations that are in some sense "incorrect," at least relative to the target system. The nature of children's underlying representations thus need not be assumed a priori to be correct. Rather, the correctness of underlying representations can be determined on empirical grounds. The possibility that children's errors may be attributed in part to the nature of their underlying representations broadens the scope of the problem, requiring a focus on both rules and representations.

This broadened focus is based on four general arguments which suggest that it is not possible in certain cases to postulate correct underlying representations in the characterization of phonological disorders. One argument relates to the need to differentiate among seemingly identical error patterns for different children. For example, final consonant omissions have been found (Weismer, Dinnsen & Elbert, 1981) to fall into two distinct subtypes depending on the relative correctness of underlying representations. The subtype of final consonant omission associated with correct underlying representations exhibits the following two empirical characteristics: an alternation with word-medial consonants and a vowel length alternation that is sensitive to the voicing of the underlying omitted final consonant. The subtype of final consonant omission associated with incorrect underlying representations exhibits neither a consonantal alternation nor a vowel length alternation. Empirical differences of this sort associated with a single error pattern cannot be explained if all underlying representations are assumed to be correct. Another argument for distinguishing between correct and incorrect underlying representations derives from observed differences in children's learning patterns (e.g., Dinnsen & Elbert, 1984; Gierut, Elbert & Dinnsen, 1987). That is, the remediation of children's errors is highly dependent on the relative correctness of their underlying representations. Regardless of which errors are targeted for treatment, the greatest improvements are observed in errors associated with correct underlying representations. Also, when treatment is directed at errors associated with correct underlying representations, improvements tend to be limited to that class of errors. However, when treatment is directed at errors associated with incorrect underlying representations, improvements are observed across the child's entire system. A third argument for postulating incorrect underlying representations relates to the existence of nonsystematic correspondences between the target system and the child's system (e.g., Gierut, 1989; Leonard & Brown, 1984). If underlying representations are assumed to be correct in cases of nonsystematic correspondence, competing (and even contradictory) processes with unexplained or optional applicability would have to be postulated. Finally, the existence of certain allophonic phenomena (e.g., Camarata & Gandour, 1984; Gierut, 1986b; Williams & Dinnsen, 1987) requires the postulation of at least some incorrect underlying representations. That is, if children's underlying representations were assumed to be correct in these cases, the nontarget complementary distribution of sounds would have to be viewed as accidental. It thus appears that there are several empirical reasons for distinguishing between correct and incorrect underlying representations as essential properties of these systems. For further discussion of these and related issues, see Gierut (1986a).

## PURPOSE

Given that the proper characterization of phonological disorders may depend on the postulation of incorrect underlying representations in certain circumstances, it is important to specify what those circumstances are and determine what the extent or magnitude of this problem is for disorders. That is, do all phonologically disordered children evidence at least some incorrect underlying representations? Also, for any given child, what proportion of that child's underlying representations is correct? This chapter will attempt to answer these and other related questions by briefly reviewing the empirical criteria for determining the nature of underlying representations and then by advancing a procedure for quantifying the resultant claims. These procedures then will be applied in the analysis of 40 phonologically disordered children to determine the prevalence of incorrect underlying representations in phonological disorders.

## SUBJECTS

The subjects for this study represent the initial 40 children drawn from a large scale investigation of the sound systems and learning patterns of young children with functional (nonorganic) speech disorders. The children ranged in age from 3 years 4 months to 6 years 8 months. To be included in the study, each child exhibited six sounds in error across three manner classes on the *Goldman Fristoe Test of Articulation* (GFTA) (Goldman & Fristoe, 1986). Of the 40 children, 21 scored below the 1st percentile on the GFTA, and no child scored above the 34th percentile. All children evidenced normal hearing. Various aspects of these children's phonologies have been described elsewhere (Chin & Dinnsen, 1991, 1992; Dinnsen, 1992; Dinnsen & Chin, 1993; Dinnsen, Chin, & Elbert, 1992; Dinnsen, Chin, Elbert, & Powell, 1990; Elbert, Dinnsen, Swartzlander, & Chin, 1990).

## DETERMINATION OF
## UNDERLYING REPRESENTATIONS

All contemporary theories of phonology allow for at least two levels of representation, namely a phonetic and an underlying level of representation. The character of the phonetic level is relatively clear, but details of the underlying level can only be hypothesized. The underlying level is a theoretical abstraction that is intended to represent a speaker's mental representation of the morphemes and words of the language. The underlying level incorporates all and only the idiosyncratic, learned properties of pronunciation. Thus, only contrastive (unpredictable) information is represented at the underlying level. The noncontrastive (predictable) properties of pronunciation then are specified by phonological rules, thus relating the two levels. The task of describing any phonological system, then, is to determine which properties of pronunciation are contrastive and must then be specified at the underlying level and which properties are noncontrastive and thus are specified by rule. The general procedures for making these determinations in fully developed languages have been detailed in many generative phonology textbooks (e.g., Kenstowicz & Kisseberth, 1979). The extension of the same procedures to the description of phonological disorders has also been detailed in Dinnsen (1984).

Within this framework, a child is credited with knowledge of a target distinction only if the child's productions offer evidence of the distinction.

Two general conditions in a child's speech will fail to provide any positive evidence for a target distinction and thus result in the claim that that aspect of the child's underlying representations is incorrect. First, if a target sound fails to occur in any context, then that sound is not represented anywhere in the child's phonology. The nonoccurrence of that sound is taken to be a nonaccidental property of pronunciation and is thus predicted to be excluded by an inventory constraint. These inventory constraints may be very general to account for the nonoccurrence of whole classes of sounds, or they may be more limited in scope to account for the nonoccurrence of one or two sounds. For example, the rule in (1) below would account for the exclusion of all fricatives and affricates from a child's system.

(1) [+consonantal] —> [–continuant, –delayed release]

This rule expresses the generalization that all consonants are (non-affricated) stops and was characteristic of two children in this study (see Dinnsen et al., 1990 for details). The rule in (2) is less general, accounting for the nonoccurrence of [ʃ] and [ʒ] and the fact that all fricatives are anterior.

(2) [–sonorant, +continuant] —> [+anterior]

This rule was characteristic of 23 children in this study.

    The second condition that will fail to support a claim of correct underlying representations relates to the occurrence of a target sound or class of sounds in only certain contexts. That is, the target sound occurs in the child's phonetic inventory and is produced correctly in some contexts but fails to occur in certain other contexts. The fact that the target sound is produced correctly in some contexts certainly can be taken as support for the claim that the child has underlying knowledge of the target sound, at least in those contexts where it does occur. However, the systematic nonoccurrence of a target sound in the other contexts would appear to be nonaccidental, and thus would be accounted for by a positional (or phonotactic) constraint that holds at all levels of representation, including the underlying level. This means that a given target sound may be represented correctly in some word positions but incorrectly in other word positions. Such constraints were evident in 37 of the 40 children in this study (Dinnsen et al., 1990). In sum, incorrect underlying representations will be posited in cases where a child's errors can be accounted for by either inventory constraints or positional constraints.

    On the other hand, the postulation of correct underlying representations is especially well supported under two other general circumstances: (a) in phonological contexts where a target sound is produced correctly (although see Dinnsen & Chin, 1993, for certain well-defined exceptions), and (b) in contexts where an error alternates with a correct production in morphophonemically related forms. The former circumstance is relatively uncontroversial because the child is not producing any errors, and the two systems are congruent, at least with regard to those sounds in those contexts. The forms in (3) below illustrate a child's (S3; age 3;6) correct productions of target /k/ in all phonological contexts (word-initial, -medial, and -final), even though other target segments may not be produced correctly. For example, [s] did not occur in the child's system and appeared to have [θ] as its substitute. Similarly, [r] did not occur and appeared to have [w] as its substitute. In the case of S3, it is apparent that target /k/ was represented correctly at the underlying level in all three word positions. Notice that the medial and final /k/ occur in morphophonemically related forms, which are potentially subject to rule-induced errors; such, however, was not the case.

(3) a.  Target initial /k/: kʰɪdð "kids," kʰɔθɪŋ "coughing"
    b.  Target medial /k/: θɑki "sockie," wɑki "rocky"
    c.  Target final /k/: θɑk "sock," wɑk "rock"

As regards /k/, then, the child's system and the target system are in congruence at both the underlying and the phonetic levels of representation.

The other cases in which correct underlying representations are especially well supported involve the operation of a phonological rule. This can be exemplified by considering the following forms from child S22 (age 4;6) from this study:

(4) a.  [bʌs]/[bʌʃin] "brush/brushing"
        [wɪts]/[wɪtʃi] "witch/witchie"
        [kʰeɪdz]/[kʰeɪdʒi] "cage/cagey"
    b.  [bʌs]/[bʌsi] "bus/bussy"

The forms in (4a) show an alternation between a (correct) palatoalveolar in intervocalic position and an (incorrect) alveolar in final position. These forms are considered to have a correct underlying representation (at least as regards the postvocalic segment in question), and the incorrect production in final position is accounted for by a rule requiring that all [+coronal] segments also be [+anterior] in final position. Evidence for the correctness of this analysis in given in (4b), where it is seen that it is not the case that alveolars become palatoalveolars in intervocalic position. Also, a comparison of the (4a) forms with (4b) shows that alveolar and palatoalveolar segments do indeed contrast intervocalically. Thus, although the forms in (4a) show an erred production in final position, the occurence of correct productions in intervocalic position in morphophonemically related forms speaks for the correctness of the underlying representation.

   In sum, many empirical considerations of the sort just discussed can be brought to bear in postulating children's underlying representations. In certain instances, correct underlying representations can be supported; in other circumstances they cannot.

## DATA FOR ANALYSIS

To support the claims of an independent analysis empirically, an extensive speech sample that tests a full range of target sounds in a variety of contexts and provides multiple opportunities for each sound in each given context is needed. It is also especially important to examine how the sounds of any given morpheme are realized when the contexts for that morpheme are varied. The latter concern relates to the identification of morphophonemic alternations and provides the clearest evidence about the underlying representation of those morphemes. These general points have been integrated into the design of a probe and elicitation procedure first developed by Gierut (1985) and subsequently adapted for this and related studies (as noted above in the description of subjects). This probe consists of 306 picturable words that are likely to be known to children in this age range. All English consonants (except /ʒ/) and glides are tested in word-initial, word-medial and word-final positions, except as limited by the phonotactic restrictions of English (e.g., the velar nasal is not probed in word-initial position). Wherever possible, words that allowed for possible morphophonemic alternations were selected. The full set of pictures depicting these words was presented to each child for spontaneous naming. Each child's responses were tape-recorded and phonetically transcribed by trained listeners with high levels of reliability.

## ANALYSIS

The phonological system of each child was analyzed within this framework based on the speech sample described above with special emphasis on determining the nature of underlying representations. For illustration purposes, these criteria are applied in the description of a particular child, S4, age 3;7. This child produced the glides [w j h] and the velar nasal [ŋ] correctly in all probed word positions; therefore, he was credited with correct underlying representations in all word positions. The alveolar nasal

[n] occurred correctly in initial and final position, but did not occur in intervocalic position. However, the word-final occurrences alternated with null intervocalically in morphophonemically related forms. Therefore [n] was represented correctly at the underlying level in all word positions. The segments [m b d] occurred correctly in word-initial position, but were either missing or had substitution sounds in both postvocalic positions (intervocalic and word-final positions). Therefore, these sounds were correct underlyingly only in initial position. Finally, all other target English segments were never produced at all and were thus determined to be incorrectly represented underlyingly.

## QUANTIFICATION OF CLAIMS ABOUT UNDERLYING REPRESENTATIONS

Based on the description of the above child's phonological system and the general considerations noted earlier, it appears that certain target sounds can be represented incorrectly in all contexts, certain other target sounds can be represented correctly only in certain contexts, and yet other target sounds can be represented correctly in all contexts. The possibility thus exists for considerable variation both within and across children along this dimension with no established measure for quantifying the difference (or distance) between the child's system and the target system. To address this concern, a measure has been developed which attempts to quantify the percentage of correct underlying representations (PCUR).

The calculation of the PCUR is as follows. Each target English phoneme is assigned a value of 1 for each context in which it can occur as sampled in the probe described above. The number of phonemes (by context) is divided by the total number of possible target phonemes (by context) and multiplied by 100, yielding the PCUR. For the specific probe described above, 23 target English sounds were sampled in from one to three word positions. Using the procedure just described, the maximum number of points that could accrue to any one child for representing all sounds correctly in all contexts at the underlying level was 63, which would correspond to a PCUR of 100%.

## RESULTS AND DISCUSSION

For illustration purposes, this quantification procedure is applied to the description of child S4, described above, to yield a measure of the correctness of his underlying representations. In this case, the target appropriate production of the three glides and the velar nasal credited 7 points toward the PCUR; the glides were probed in two contexts, word-intial and intervocalic, and the velar nasal in final position. Because [n] alternated with null intervocalically due to a phonological rule and otherwise occurred correctly in initial and final position, the alveolar nasal was considered to be correctly represented underlyingly in all positions; 3 points thus accrued toward the PCUR. The situation with [m b d] is different, however. In this case, these segments were represented correctly in initial position but incorrectly in intervocalic and final position. The representations in initial position therefore added 1 point each for the three sounds to the determination of the PCUR, and no points were given for postvocalic underlying representations. In all, then, 13 points accrued toward the PCUR, which was then determined to be $13/63 \times 100 = 21\%$. The remaining sounds by context (50 points) were not considered to be correctly represented at the underlying level and thus did not contribute to the PCUR.

A PCUR was calculated in a like manner for each child in this study based on the independent analysis. The results are reported in Table 6–1 on page 142.

It can be seen from Table 6–1 that children exhibited considerable variation in the correctness of their underlying representations. The range in PCUR was from a high of 92% to a low of 18%. The mean PCUR score for the group was 58%, and importantly, all subjects in this study evidenced at least some incorrect underlying representations. This is in sharp contrast to what would be expected from relational accounts which simply assume a priori that underlying representations are correct. The fact is that the incidence of incorrect underlying representations in these phonologies is quite high, and the magnitude of the problem in at least some cases is considerable.

The measure PCUR differs in important respects from another current measure, namely "Percentage of Consonants Correct" (PCC) (Shriberg & Kwiatkowski, 1982). PCC provides a superficial measure of a child's errors based on a conversational speech sample, although it is equally possible to compute PCC on other types of speech samples such as those used in this study. The important difference is that PCC weights all errors equally. PCUR, on the other hand, weights errors differently depending on the source of the error. That is, errors associated with correct underlying representations do not in some sense count as errors. Errors associated with incorrect underlying representations do, however, count as errors. The value in making this distinction is evident in the results of treatment studies (e.g., Dinnsen & Elbert, 1984; Gierut, Elbert & Dinnsen, 1987), which have found characteristically different learning patterns in accord with the nature of the underlying representations. Specifically, errors associated with correct underlying

**Table 6–1.** Ages and Percentage of Correct Underlying Representations (PCUR) of 40 functionally misarticulating children

| Child | Age (years;months) | PCUR |
|:-----:|:------------------:|:----:|
| S1 | 3;4 | 61 |
| S2 | 3;6 | 64 |
| S3 | 3;6 | 54 |
| S4 | 3;7 | 21 |
| S5 | 3;8 | 84 |
| S6 | 3;8 | 70 |
| S7 | 3;8 | 47 |
| S8 | 3;9 | 65 |
| S9 | 3;9 | 89 |
| S10 | 3;9 | 65 |
| S11 | 3;10 | 41 |
| S12 | 3;11 | 76 |
| S13 | 4;1 | 40 |
| S14 | 4;1 | 65 |
| S15 | 4;2 | 65 |
| S16 | 4;2 | 33 |
| S17 | 4;3 | 78 |
| S18 | 4;3 | 18 |
| S19 | 4;3 | 92 |
| S20 | 4;4 | 59 |
| S21 | 4;5 | 79 |
| S22 | 4;6 | 63 |
| S23 | 4;8 | 73 |
| S24 | 4;8 | 43 |
| S25 | 4;10 | 62 |
| S26 | 4;11 | 21 |
| S27 | 4;11 | 48 |
| S28 | 4;11 | 25 |
| S29 | 4;11 | 51 |
| S30 | 5;0 | 73 |
| S31 | 5;1 | 70 |
| S32 | 5;2 | 70 |
| S33 | 5;4 | 51 |
| S34 | 5;5 | 73 |
| S35 | 5;7 | 84 |
| S36 | 5;9 | 27 |
| S37 | 5;10 | 41 |
| S38 | 5;11 | 57 |
| S39 | 6;3 | 83 |
| S40 | 6;8 | 53 |

representations are overcome more easily (i.e., achieve higher levels of accuracy) than errors associated with incorrect underlying representations. Additionally, when treatment targets are selected from the set of errors associated with correct underlying repres    tations, improvements tend to be limited to that class. That is, treatment focused on these errors does not generally yield improvements in errors associated with incorrect underlying representations. On the other hand, when treatment targets are selected from errors associated with incorrect underlying representations, improvements tend to be more widespread, occurring across both error types. Thus, clinical treatment that recognizes that not all errors are equal and moreover focuses on errors associated with incorrect underlying representations can be expected to yield improvement across the entire system.

The difference between the two measures is further highlighted by considering the possibility that two children could have identical PCC scores but significantly different PCURs. This situation could arise if one child produced most errors by phonological rules that operated on correct underlying representations, and the other child produced most of the errors due to inventory and positional constraints associated with incorrrect underlying representations. Precisely this situation was reported by Connell, Elbert, and Dinnsen (1991) in a study of two subgroups of children from this study. The two subgroups exhibited PCC scores that were not significantly different. Their PCURs did, however, differ significantly. One subgroup of 10 children was identified as "syntax-delayed," and the other subgroup of 13 children was identified as "syntax-normal." The average PCUR for the syntax-delayed group was 48% and for the syntax-normal group 63%. This suggests that the measure PCUR may have certain advantages over other measures as a diagnostic and/or as a measure of severity.

PCUR appears to provide a gross measure of the difference between a child's system and the target system, at least at the underlying level of representation. There are, however, certain limitations that must be noted in the interpretation of these measurements. This method for quantifying claims about underlying representations may, in certain cases, overestimate a child's knowledge of the target system. The case that is problematic in this regard is where a child represents a target sound correctly in a particular context but not necessarily in all morphemes. In other words, even if a target sound is represented correctly in most (but not all) morphemes, the child will be given credit for correct underlying representations of that target sound in that context for all morphemes. Similarly, a degree of underestimation is also possible in the case where a child represents a target sound correctly in only a few morphemes. In this case, the child would not be credited anywhere with knowledge of the target sound. It remains to be determined whether these potential over- and underestimations are critical in any sense.

# CONCLUSION

When analyzed independently of the target system, children's phonological systems can be seen to differ from the target sound system in ways not evident from relational accounts proposed thus far. Although the PCUR is a relational claim, it becomes relational only after the child's system has been established independently of the target system. Within this framework of independence, the problem for the child may not be limited to rules but may also involve, to some extent, the nature of the child's underlying representations. Errors may come about because of nontarget phonological rules and/or because of nontarget underlying representations. This is important clinically because it suggests that not all errors are equal and may respond differently to different forms of treatment. The quantification of claims about underlying representations suggests that the incidence of incorrect underlying representations is high in general and that, for at least some children, incorrect underlying representations outnumber correct underlying representations.

# ACKNOWLEDGMENTS

We are especially grateful to Phil Connell, Mary Elbert, Judith Gierut, and Tom Powell for their comments throughout this project. This work was supported in part by a grant from the National Institutes of Health (No. DC00260), to Indiana University.

# REFERENCES

Camarata, S., & Gandour, J. (1984). On describing idiosyncratic phonological systems. *Journal of Speech and Hearing Disorders, 49,* 262–266.

Chin, S. B. (1993). *The organization and specification of features in functionally disordered phonologies.* Unpublished doctoral dissertation, Indiana University.

Chin, S. B., & Dinnsen, D. A. 1991. Feature geometry in disordered phonologies. *Clinical Linguistics and Phonetics, 5,* 329–337.

Chin, S. B., & Dinnsen, D. A. 1992. Consonant clusters in disordered speech: Constraints and correspondence patterns. *Journal of Child Language, 19,* 259–286.

Chomsky, N., & Halle, M. (1968). *The sound pattern of English.* New York: Harper & Row.

Connell, P., Elbert, M., & Dinnsen, D. A. (1991, June). *A syntax delayed subgroup of phonologically-delayed children.* Paper presented at the 12th Annual Symposium for Research on Child Language Disorders, Madison, WI.

Dinnsen, D. A. (1984). Methods and empirical issues in analyzing functional misarticulations. In M. Elbert, D. A. Dinnsen, & G. Weismer (Eds.), *Phonological theory and the misarticulating child, ASHA Mongraphs 22,* 5–17.

Dinnsen, D. A. (1992). Variation in developing and fully developed phonetic inventories. In C. A. Ferguson, L. Menn, & C. Stoel-Gammon (Eds.), *Phonological development: Theories, research, implications* (pp. 191–210). Timonium, MD: York Press.

Dinnsen, D. A., & Chin, S. B. (1993). Individual differences in phonological disorders and implications for a theory of acquisition. In F. R. Eckman (Ed.), *Confluence: Linguistic theory, L2, and speech pathology* (pp. 137–152). Amsterdam/Philadelphia: John Benjamins.

Dinnsen, D. A., Chin, S. B., & Elbert, M. (1992). On the lawfulness of change in phonetic inventories. *Lingua, 86,* 207–222.

Dinnsen, D. A., Chin, S. B., Elbert, M., & Powell, T. W. (1990). Some constraints on functionally disordered phonologies: Phonetic inventories and phonotactics. *Journal of Speech and Hearing Research, 33,* 28–37.

Dinnsen, D. A., & Elbert, M. (1984). On the relationship between phonology and learning. In M. Elbert, D. A. Dinnsen, & G. Weismer (Eds.), *Phonological theory and the misarticulating child, ASHA Monographs 22,* 59–68.

Donegan, P. J., & Stampe, D. (1979). The study of Natural Phonology. In D. A. Dinnsen (Ed.), *Current approaches to phonological theory* (pp. 126–173). Bloomington: Indiana University Press.

Edwards, M. L., & Shriberg, L. D. (1983). *Phonology: Applications in communicative disorders.* San Diego, CA: College-Hill Press.

Elbert, M., Dinnsen, D. A., Swartzlander, P., & Chin, S. B. (1990). Generalization to conversational speech. *Journal of Speech and Hearing Disorders, 55,* 694–699.

Gandour, J. (1981). The nondeviant nature of deviant phonological systems. *Journal of Communication Disorders, 14,* 11–29.

Gierut, J. A. (1985). *On the relationship between phonological knowledge and generalization learning in misarticulating children.* Unpublished doctoral dissertation, Indiana University, Bloomington.

Gierut, J. A. (1986a). Generative phonology and error pattern analysis: Empirical claims and differences. *Research on Speech Perception, 12,* 175–203.

Gierut, J. A. (1986b). Sound change: A phonemic split in a misarticulating child. *Applied Psycholinguistics, 7,* 57–68.

Gierut, J. A. (1989). Describing developing systems: A surrebuttal. *Applied Psycholinguistics, 10,* 469–473.

Gierut, J. A., Elbert, M., & Dinnsen, D. A. (1987). A functional analysis of phonological knowledge and generalization learning in misarticulating children. *Journal of Speech and Hearing Research, 30,* 462–479.

Goldman, R., & Fristoe, M. (1986). *Goldman-Fristoe Test of Articulation.* Circle Pines, MN: American Guidance Service.

Ingram, D. (1989). *Phonological disability in children* (2nd ed.). London: Cole & Whurr.

Kenstowicz, M., & Kisseberth, C. (1979). *Generative phonology: Description and theory.* New York: Academic Press.

Leonard, L. B., & Brown, B. L. (1984). Nature and boundaries of phonologic categories: A case study of an unusual phonologic pattern in a language-impaired child. *Journal of Speech and Hearing Disorders, 49,* 419–428.

Lorentz, J. (1976). An analysis of some deviant phonological rules of English. In D. Morehead & A. Morehead (Eds.), *Normal and deficient child language* (pp. 29–59). Baltimore: University Park Press.

Maxwell, E. M. (1979). Competing analyses of a deviant phonology. *Glossa, 13,* 181–214.

Maxwell, E. M. (1981). *A study of misarticulation from a linguistic perspective.* Unpublished doctoral dissertation, Indiana University, Bloomington.

Menn, L. (1976). *Pattern, control and contrast in beginning speech: A case study in the development of word form and word function.* Unpublished doctoral dissertation, University of Illinois at Urbana-Champaign.

Shriberg, L., & Kwiatkowski, J. (1982). Phonological disorders: III. A procedure for assessing severity of involvement. *Journal of Speech and Hearing Disorders, 47,* 256–270.

Spencer, A. (1986). Towards a theory of phonological development. *Lingua, 68,* 3–38.

Weismer, G., Dinnsen, D., & Elbert, M. (1981). A study of the voicing distinction associated with omitted, word-final stops. *Journal of Speech and Hearing Disorders, 46,* 320–328.

Williams, A. L., & Dinnsen, D. A. (1987). A problem of allophonic variation in a speech disordered child. *Innovations in Linguistics Education, 5*(1), 85–90.

# CHAPTER 7

## The Prosodic Tier and Phonological Disorders

BARBARA BERNHARDT, Ph.D.

Children with severe phonological disorders commonly have restricted word/syllable structure (see Chiat, 1989; Grunwell, 1985; Ingram, 1976). Characterization of this aspect of "disordered" systems has evolved as phonological theories have evolved. The purpose of this chapter is to demonstrate application of current nonlinear phonological theories to the description of the syllable/word structure of disordered phonological systems. The chapter begins with a brief overview of the evolution of description of the syllable/word structure of disordered speech, then outlines major aspects of current theories with respect to syllable/word structure, and, finally, provides data demonstrating the utility of the nonlinear frameworks for description and derivation of intervention methodologies.

## THE HISTORICAL PERSPECTIVE

Description of the syllable/word structure aspect of children's disordered phonological systems has evolved as linguistic theories have changed. In early characterizations of disordered systems, note was made of the presence of omissions versus substitutions versus distortions. In this taxonomy, omission was the primary descriptor relating to word structure, although its application was in terms of individual phonemes.

In the evolution of phonological disorder descriptions, distinctive feature theory was utilized in the early 1970s. In applying this theory to phonological intervention, focus moved from individual segments to features common to several segments (sound classes). In application, this often resulted in a focus on substitution errors. Researchers such as Dinnsen (1984) and Elbert and Gierut (1986) utilized more extensive rule-based analyses of standard generative phonology (still using features) to characterize phonological patterns, including those of "omission" (i.e., deletions). They characterized systems in terms of underlying phonological "knowledge," and described "constraints" on output and representations, for example, inventory constraints (against certain phonemes and features), positional constraints (against realization of phonemes in certain word positions only), and phonotactic constraints (against realization of certain combinations of phonemes and syllable/word shapes).

Since the mid-1970s, another linguistically based approach has had a wide impact on description of phonological disorders: phonological process analysis, based on Stampe's Natural Phonology theory (Stampe, 1969). Phonological process analysis encompasses errors in both phonemes and syllable/word shapes. Substitution processes (and sometimes assimilation processes) describe the phonemic mismatches between the adult and child forms (e.g., velar fronting). Errors in syllable/word shapes are accounted for with syllable structure processes, (e.g., final or initial consonant deletion; weak syllable deletion).

Although standard generative phonology and phonological process theory can be used to characterize aspects of the syllable/word structure of disordered systems, in recent years changes in phonological theory have provided opportunities to develop new analyses of disordered systems. These can be assistive, not only because they deepen our understanding of complex phonological systems, but because they can provide us with new ways to set intervention targets and, perhaps, generate new therapeutic techniques. The remainder of this chapter is dedicated to discussion of parts of the new theories and their application.

## SYLLABLE/WORD STRUCTURE IN NONLINEAR PHONOLOGICAL THEORIES

### GENERAL ASPECTS OF NONLINEAR PHONOLOGICAL THEORIES

Nonlinear phonology developed in the late 1970s, with the major impetus provided by Goldsmith's dissertation on tone (1976). The principal elements of "linear" phonological theories (standard generative and phonological process theories) are sequentially organized segments and sets of rules (or processes) which account for observable sound pattern alternations. Because spoken language is subject to sequence in the time dimension, linear description of phonological elements cannot be abandoned. Nonlinear phonological theory, however, posits more than sequential organization. Relationships among segments are accounted for in terms of (1) an hierarchical organization of words, syllables, segments, and features and (2) sets of universal principles/conventions. By accounting for more aspects of the phonological system in terms of hierarchical representation and principles/conventions, phonologists have been able to (1) reduce the numbers and types of phonological rules necessary to describe sound patterns of a language and (2) provide motivations for rules that exist. This is considered desirable, because many rules, although they may be descriptive, are seen as *ad hoc*, or unmotivated in terms of the entire phonological system. (See Durand, 1990; Goldsmith, 1990; and Kaye, 1989, for further discussion of this topic.)

Separate hierarchically organized descriptive levels ("tiers") are posited for both prosodic and "melodic" (segmental) units. *Prosodic structure* refers to all structure above the level of the segment, to the level of the phrase, and relates to the stress and intonation patterns (suprasegmental, hence prosodic patterns) of the language. In standard generative phonology prosodic aspects of words and segments were represented by features (e.g.,[+/–stress]; [+/–long]; [+/–syllabic]). In nonlinear phonology, these aspects of phonology are represented independently of segments in an hierarchical prosodic structure.

Prosodic phenomena such as syllabification and stress assignment are seen to occur in accordance with predictable principles. Different proposals exist regarding these various principles, although certain observations lead to commonalities among them. Goldsmith (1990) summarized proposals regarding syllabification. He suggested that syllabification applies throughout the derivation "in a minimal fashion (that is, with the minimum number of syllables) to cover the maximum number of segments possible" (p. 123), until all elements of a word are taken into account. Syllabification principles interact with the syllable well-formedness constraints of a particular language, resulting in phonological "rules." For example, when a language with no word-initial clusters "borrows" a word from English containing such a cluster, an epenthetic vowel may be inserted between the cluster elements to produce well-formed (CV) syllables in the borrowing language (e.g., *ski* > [səki]). General abstract principles provide motivation for language-specific phonological rules, leading to a more explanatory linguistic theory. Fewer rules are needed to explain phonological alternations, resulting in a more parsimonious description of phonological systems. Both explanation and parsimony are valued aspects of theory construction.

Although phonologists currently agree on the need for hierarchical representation and association of the various levels or tiers, alternate proposals have been offered to account for structure and linkages. Different proposals exist for mediating structure between the segment and the syllable (e.g., onset-rime, moras, skeletal tier), and suprasyllabic structure (metrical feet versus grids; see Durand, 1990; Goldsmith, 1990). In this chapter, the focus is on proposals that relate to structure between the syllable and the segment, because many children with severe phonological disorders have minimally developed structure even at that level of prosodic structure.

## THE SYLLABLE AS CONSTITUENT

Goldsmith (1990) comments: "The syllable is a unit of phonological description which has never ceased to be discussed at length in the phonological literature of this century" (p. 103). Chomsky and Halle (1968), in *The Sound Pattern of English* (the hallmark work of standard generative phonology) attempted to build a theory without the notion of syllable. However, subsequent researchers have returned to the notion of a syllable as a constituent, because many phonological rules, particularly those referring to prosodic phenomena such as stress and tone, are more elegantly described with reference to that unit of description. (See Goldsmith, 1990, and Kaye, 1989, for further discussion of this topic.)

According to Goldsmith (1990), words should be "factorable into sequences of syllables, which should have a specifiable internal structure that is roughly constant across the language" (p. 107). Within any language a syllable is composed of zero or more consonants, a sonorous peak, and zero or more consonants. In a given language, each of these three syllable units has restrictions on type and number of segments that may occur within them.

How best to describe structure between the syllable and the segment is a current topic of debate and the focus of the remainder of this chapter. In particular, description and contrasts among skeletal tier theory, onset-rime theory, and moraic theory are provided.

## THE SKELETAL ("TIMING") TIER

In Kahn's (1976) version of the syllable, internal structure was not described (see representation for the word *key* [ki:] in Figure 7–1A). Segments dominated by a syllable were directly linked to the syllable node. Clements and Keyser (1983) demonstrated the need for a

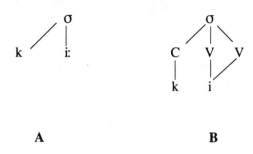

**Figure 7–1.** Association of segments to syllables with and without a skeletal tier. **A** shows no intervening structure between the segments and the syllable node. Length of the vowel is represented segmentally only. **B** shows an intervening CV-tier, with a long vowel linked to two V-slots. Representation of length is on the skeletal tier rather than at the level of the segment.

mediating representational level between syllable node and segments. They proposed a CV-tier (as in Figure 7–1B), in which segments were associated to C or V skeletal positions or slots, which then were grouped into syllables. Note that, in the Clements and Keyser proposal, two V-"slots" are linked to one segment [i]. By representing length in the prosodic domain (a logical domain for a prosodic timing phenomenon), the feature [+long] can be eliminated from segmental representation.

Rules such as compensatory lengthening can be described in terms of the skeletal tier. For example, in Figure 7–2, if *tip* /tɪp/ > [tɪː], the number of units on the CV-tier does not change: CVC is realized as CVV (that is, three phonological units are present in both the target and the output). The skeletal representation does not change in terms of number of units, only in type. Because /p/ is not available to provide segmental content for the existing C-slot, content spreads from the adjacent V-slot. The C-slot becomes a V-slot.

An alternative skeletal tier proposal is the *x*-tier (e.g., Levin, 1985). Segments are linked to the syllable node through a mediating tier which has no feature content, (that is, not even a designation of vowel or consonant). The *x*s are merely segment indicators, or "timing" units. One advantage of this description is that consonant slots on the skeletal tier do not have to be redefined as vowel slots in compensatory lengthening rules, as is necessary in the CV-tier formulation (see Figure 7–2B).

In summary, one possible mediating level between the syllable and segments is a skeletal or "timing" tier, one theory of which includes one aspect of major class definition (i.e., whether the elements are con-

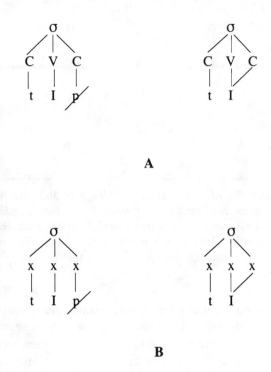

**A**

**B**

**Figure 7–2.** Alternate skeletal tier representations of a closed monosyllable with a missing final consonant and compensatory lengthening. **A** shows a CV-tier representation in which deletion of the final consonant results in association of the C-slot to the vowel. **B** shows the same phenomenon, but with x-slots.

sonants or vowels), and another which only notes the presence of segments. Because syllabification needs to identify syllable peaks, more information about this operation would be available in terms of a CV-tier than an x-tier. The latter theory is dependent on other intervening structure between the skeleton and the syllable, such as in the onset-rime theory discussed in the following section.

## ONSET-RIME THEORY

Onset-rime (alternate spelling, rhyme) theory has been discussed since Pike and Pike (1947). Halle and Vergnaud (1980), Kaye, Lowenstamm, and Vergnaud (in press), and Steriade (1988) are among those who have developed the onset-rime theory recently.

In an hierarchical structure, the onset (O) node dominates the pre-vocalic consonant(s) (see Figure 7–3). The other major constituent, the rime (R), dominates the nucleus (N)—a node intervening between the rime node and the most sonorant segment (usually a vowel)—and any postnuclear consonants. Phonological data demonstrating independent functioning of segments from the vowel to the right edge of the syllable compared with segments preceding the vowel lend support to an onset-rime division. For example, stress is never assigned with reference to units preceding the vowel, no matter how numerous, whereas the number of "rime" elements often is relevant in stress assignment.

The internal structure of the rime is also a subject of discussion. The syllable nucleus contains the most sonorous element(s) of the syllable, and may be composed of one or more sonorant elements. For example, Figure 7–3 demonstrates the difference between nuclei with short vowels (no branch) and long vowels (one branch). Diphthongs may be represented with one or no branch, depending on whether they are considered "heavy" (branching) or "light" (no branch) in terms of stress assignment. The nucleus is sometimes described as the "head" of the syllable, a term borrowed from syntactic theory, where, for example, a noun may be described as the head of a noun phrase (Durand, 1990, p . 203).

Postnuclear consonants are represented in various ways. Alternate descriptions of the postnuclear consonants are appendix, coda, and *x*-slots. An appendix is a specifically a *word*-final consonant or set of consonants that is *extra*-syllabic (outside the domain of the syllable). Goldsmith (1990) described stress rules of Arabic that appear to refer to

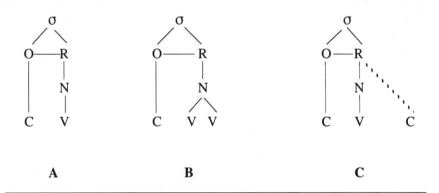

**Figure 7–3. A**. Onset-rime representations of monosyllables with short vowels. **B**. Final consonants. **C**. Long vowels. (O = onset, R = rime, N = nucleus.)

the appendix. The coda is a designation of postnuclear consonants in a syllable. Kaye et al. (in press) do not give postnuclear consonants any particular constituent status, designating them only as *x*-slots adjoined to the rime node. They present several arguments against codas, for example, (1) postnuclear consonants are not universally present in syllable inventories as are onset, nucleus, and rime; (2) phonological processes are not sensitive to coda branching (see below for relevance of branching); and (3) postnuclear consonants have a syllabic mobility atypical of other constituents. (They can occur sometimes under the rime node, sometimes as an appendix of the word as a unit, and sometimes, through resyllabification, as onset of the following syllable.)

Complexity in syllable structure is expressed in terms of number of branches in the tree structure. More complex syllable shapes (such as those with clusters or diphthongs) have more branches.

Stress assignment can be described in terms of sensitivity to branching in the rime in many languages. In Figure 7–3, both long vowels (VV) and VC rimes are branching rime units. Although different in terms of *level* of branching, both units may correlate with stress assignment in a given language, (branching rimes attract stress). The different levels of branching may also be relevant, so that, in some languages, only branching nuclei may attract stress.

*Government* is a hierarchical concept defining phonological domains and interactions which Kaye et al. (in press) imported from recent generative syntactic theory. In terms of phonology, Kaye et. al suggested that government is a directional and binary asymmetric relationship between two adjacent units. Within the domain of a major constituent (i.e., within the onset, rime, or nucleus), direction of government proceeds from left to right. The first element of a constituent is then the head/governor of that constituent (head-initial domain). Between constituents, government proceeds from right to left (giving a head-final domain). In this case, the rime governs the onset *within* a syllable, but, between consecutive syllables, the onset of the second syllable governs the rime of the first. The notion of government designates targets of rules: Governed constituents are more likely to be targets of phonological phenomena (e.g., deletion of /r/ rather than /b/ when constraints on onset element number require cluster reduction). The Kaye, Lowenstamm, and Vergnaud hypotheses about government also can account for absent structures in language. For example, in languages without branching onsets (word-initial clusters), stop-liquid sequences do not even occur within words. Their theory, by other principles, suggests that stops always govern liquids. If stop-liquid sequences were to occur, they then would have to be in the same syllable (hence as onsets), because of the principle of left-to-right intraconstituent government (stops governing liquids). Because the language has no word-initial clusters, the sequence cannot then occur without violating the government principles for segments and constituents.

Overall, onset-rime theory has greater power than skeletal theory as a proposed mediating tier between syllable and segment. Separate subdomains are postulated for various parts of the syllable. Hypotheses extend to describe constraints on rules relating to the various parts of the syllable, and possible relationships of government between those syllable constituents. Although the rime is recognized as the relevant domain for prosodic phenomena such as stress assignment, the onset is also considered a constituent with a distinct set of functions and principles.

## MORAIC THEORY

Another theory of syllable constituency is moraic theory (see particularly Hayes, 1989; McCarthy & Prince, 1986). In this proposal, prosodic *weight units* (Hyman, 1985) or *moras* (M) are considered the critical constituents of syllables for stress assignment and other phonological phenomena (see Figure 7–4).

Light syllables have one mora, heavy syllables two. Hyman (1985) argued that branching may not be the critical factor for stress assignment, as suggested in onset-rime theory. He commented that, in some languages, stress is assigned to syllables with branching nuclei but not to

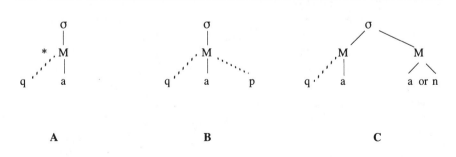

**Figure 7–4.** Moraic representation. **A** shows a monosyllable with a short vowel. **B** shows a light closed monosyllable (one mora, vowel only). **C** shows a heavy syllable, where the mora is projected from either a second vowel or consonant. (*The adjunction of consonants is to the mora rather than the syllable node, although either position has been suggested as a plausible representation.)

syllables with branching at the level of the rime node itself (p. 8). (As suggested above, the difference in level of branching may be a possible option for languages in terms of stress assignment, that is, stress is assigned either to any branching units or only to branching nuclei.) Branching is not eliminated from the formal representation; other constituents can be singly or doubly associated to moras. However, the branch is not the crucial element relating to stress assignment, but rather the number of moras.

Another difference between onset-rime and mora theory relates to the association of segments to the moraic tier. Segments are not "counted" by assigning them skeletal slot positions in moraic theory, but are directly linked to the moraic tier. Hayes (1989) claimed that "no known phonological processes [such as compensatory lengthening] count segments, although many count moras or syllables" (p. 254), and thus a mediating skeletal tier is superfluous.

Moras are realized primarily through resonant segments (usually vowels). The resonant segment is directly associated to the mora, without intervening skeletal or nucleus nodes. As Figure 7–4 shows, they also may be realized through postvocalic consonants in *weight-sensitive* languages. For example, in weight-sensitive languages such as Latin and English, CVV and CVC syllables are usually heavy syllables (with two moras), and CV is a light syllable (one mora). Thus *algebra* is stressed on the first VC syllable, because the other two CV syllables are light, whereas *veranda* is stressed on the second CVC syllable. In other languages such as Lardil, only CVV is heavy (has two moras), whereas both CV and CVC are light (have one mora).

Prevocalic and postvocalic consonants that do not contribute to syllable weight are adjoined directly to the mora or syllable (and not to any intervening node, such as an onset or coda). The level of consonant adjunction (whether to the mora or syllable node) is unresolved. If prevocalic consonants and the moras are adjoined to the syllable node and all other segments are adjoined to the mora(s), representational structure for moraic theory is roughly equivalent to that of onset-rime theory. (Recall that the onset and rime are linked to the syllable node, and all other segments are adjoined to the rime.) This is advantageous because a structure of that type has been shown to be relevant in phonological rules (Hayes, 1989, p. 298). The difference between theories relates to the representation of consonant adjunction. In onset-rime theory, the consonants form a constituent under an onset node which itself is linked to the syllable node. In moraic theory the consonants are directly adjoined to the syllable node.

If rules apply to the prevocalic consonant and the adjacent mora (such as in reduplication described in Stonham, 1990), it may be advantageous to represent the immediately adjacent prevocalic consonant as linked to the mora rather than to the syllable node. (See also the later discussion on integrated theories.) In either case, prevocalic consonants and postvocalic consonants, which do not contribute to prosodic phenomena such as stress attraction, must be represented with a hierarchical formalism that makes them dependents of the prosodically prominent units—the moras and syllables. In onset-rime theory, it needs to be stipulated separately that an onset, although it may be branching, cannot attract stress to a syllable, unlike a structurally equivalent branching rime unit.

Moras are grouped together to form syllables with a postulated maximum of two moras per syllable. (Rare cases with three moras exist.) Following McCarthy and Prince (1986), a bimoraic word is considered to be the primary word level unit available from Universal Grammar.

## THEORY INTEGRATION AND IMPLICATIONS

### Skeletal Tier and Onset-Rime Theories

As noted earlier, onset-rime theory and skeletal tier theory are frequently integrated, with both levels of structure formally represented. X-tier theory by necessity requires another level of representation before the syllable, because syllabification is not predictable from undefined x-slots. Skeletal tier theory gains power by integrating another level of complex structure before the syllable level, because phonological phenomena have been shown to relate to constituents such as the rime. The integration of both theories allows rules such as compensatory lengthening to be encoded abstractly (without reference to segmental content), while still retaining a distinction between onset and rime constituents.

### Integration of Onset-Rime and Moraic Theories

As noted, mora theorists such as Hayes (1989) and McCarthy and Prince (1986) have eliminated the skeletal tier in representation, utilizing the moraic tier to fulfill that role. Prevocalic consonants are adjoined directly to syllables or moras, without mediation through another level of representation. If no rule can be described that crucially demonstrates the need for "onset" as constituent, or that crucially requires the "counting" of segments (prevocalic or moraic), this theory will be favored over the others in terms of its parsimony.

Recently, Stonham (1990) and Shaw (in press) proposed slightly different integrated versions of onset-rime and moraic theories (see Figures 7–5 and 7–6), based on templatic analyses of reduplication.

Stonham uses N-bar notation (see Figure 7–5). N″ is equivalent to the syllable. N′ is equivalent to the rime node, but this N′ branches to

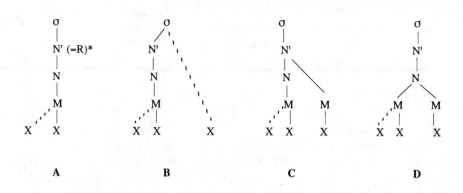

**Figure 7–5.** Representation in Stonham's (1990) integrated version of onset-rime and mora theories. **A** shows an open monosyllable with a short vowel; **B** shows a closed light syllable; **C** shows a closed heavy syllable; and **D** shows an open heavy syllable. (*Note: N' is equivalent to rime node.)

dominate N (nucleus) and consonantal moras. The nucleus then dominates one or more moras. Finally, a nuclear mora may branch, yielding two segments with one mora, such as for a "light" diphthong. Prevocalic consonants are adjoined to the first mora. Postvocalic nonmoraic (weightless) consonants adjoin to the syllable node. As can be seen, Stonham (1990) is positing intervening structure between the mora and the syllable node, which are directly linked in more standard moraic theories. He further distinguished between moras that are consonantal and resonant in type. Weight units are maintained as primes, but the hierarchical structure of the onset-rime theory is also maintained.

Shaw's (in press) proposal (see Figure 7–6) also distinguished between nuclear and non-nuclear moras, but eliminated some of the other onset-rime structure. Only a nuclear node intervenes between the mora and the syllable node. Furthermore, the prevocalic consonant is adjoined to the syllable node, not the mora.

Shaw described how reduplicative morphological templates distinguish between types of copied units, indicating a need to posit different constituent status to the different types of moras. For example, in Nisgha, the copied material involves a monomoraic nucleus, whether the base form has a long vowel or not. (In this case, the post-nuclear content transfers whether moraic or not.)

qá:p > qap-qá:p       "to scratch something"
híx > hax -(h)íx       "to be fat"

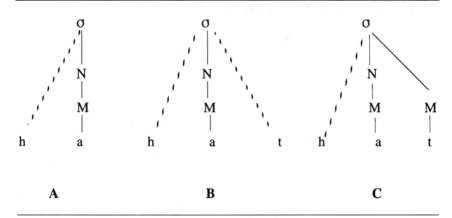

**Figure 7–6.** Representation in Shaw's (in press) integrated version of onset-rime and mora theories. **A** shows an open monosyllable with a short vowel; **B** shows a closed light syllable; and **C** shows a closed heavy syllable.

In Nootka, only nuclear material reduplicates, even when consonants (in this case, nasals) are moraic.

t∫ims > t∫i-t∫ims- 'iːh     "hunting bear"

Both of these integrated theories maintain the onset-rime distinction between the syllable "head" and other types of "rime" units, while maintaining the notion of syllable weight. However, in congruence with moraic theory, neither of these revised versions gives the onset independent status.

# DEVELOPMENT AND PROSODIC THEORIES

## GENERAL ASSUMPTIONS FOR DEVELOPMENTAL PHONOLOGY

If a child comes to the language-learning situation with a representational framework and a set of universal principles, "templates" are then available to utilize for decoding and encoding (Menn, 1978). Exposure to the input language(s) will both confirm the universally-determined representation (e.g., that, as expected, the language has CV units and stop consonants) and also result in "setting" of parameters where options are available (e.g., that the language has final consonants and that stress is syllable-initial in a given language).

## PROSODIC REPRESENTATION

Ingram (1986) and others have shown that children typically use CV words at early stages of development. CVs are considered the most common syllable shapes across languages, some languages having no other more complex syllable shapes. Taking a universalist perspective, a child will come to language learning with a set of principles and given structures/representations (e.g., CV syllables) in place. Exposure to the input language results in the child learning all possible syllable and word shapes for the language, how stress relates to the prosodic constituents (e.g., whether stress is word-final or word-initial), and other prosodic phenomena for the language. The following section discusses some of the implications for development derived from the theories outlined above, as a prelude to the examination of some data from children with phonological disorders.

## ONSET-RIME VERSUS MORAIC STRUCTURE

Depending on the theory, somewhat different predictions could be made about development, both in predetermined structure and type and timing of learned units. In O-R terms, the developmentally early CV unit equals the predetermined unbranching O-R syllable: O=C, R=N=V. Learning language-specific prosodic structure would mean: (1) learning the conditions for and results of branching for onsets and rimes (e.g., maximum onsets, nuclei, or rimes) plus (2) stress assignment relationships to branching. If the language has phonological phenomena which crucially relate to branching of the rime node, one might expect the establishment of branching rimes first. One also might expect branching at higher (less embedded) levels of representation first, namely, at the onset or rime node levels versus nucleus or coda levels. The establishment of diphthongs (nuclear branch) and final consonants (rime branch) could occur independently, because these two types of structures are represented at different levels of branching. One also might expect independent development of onsets, with observable rules and functions specific to the onset.

In moraic terms, the early CV unit is the most basic moraic unit—one mora, with one adjoined prevocalic consonant. Because onsets are not obligatory in moraic theory, the motivation for the observed C of CV has to come from higher levels of representation (universal minimal syllable or word). McCarthy and Prince (1986) postulated such "core syllables" (CV) and minimal (bimoraic) words. Phonological development would involve learning at a minimum: (1) the maximum constituency of syllables and words in terms of moras and feet, (2) the weight sensitivity of the language in terms of vowels and consonants, and (3) maximum consonant adjunction possibilities premoraically and postmoraically. One might expect refinement of the moraic constituency of the syllables prior to that of the nonmoraic constituents. Thus, moraic units may appear before initial clusters or non-weightbearing postvocalic consonants. For weight-sensitive languages, learning that bimoraic syllables can be constructed with both vowels and consonants could result in simultaneous acquisition of final consonants and long vowels/diphthongs. Differences in stress assignment might result in developmental differences across languages. For example, children acquiring weight-sensitive languages might acquire final consonants and diphthongs earlier in development than children acquiring non-weight-sensitive languages. Nonmoraic consonants (whether prevocalic or postvocalic) may have no organized developmental sequence as units.

The integrated onset-rime/moraic proposals of Stonham (1990) and Shaw (in press) might suggest that both moraic and branching level differences are significant for development, since moras can be realized at different levels, either in subnuclear positions, or at a higher level of branching, that is, under the rime node. Development might progress in terms of branching structures (maximally and/or minimally, that is, at the level of the onset or rime, or at a subnuclear level), or in terms of weight unit specification, or in some integrated version of the two.

## DEVELOPMENTAL IMPLICATIONS OF A SKELETAL TIER

Both onset-rime and moraic theories provide motivated analyses of prosodic phenomena such as stress assignment. However, the concept of skeletal tier is unsupported in moraic theory, and not necessarily motivated as a result of onset-rime theory, although it does provide a mechanism for describing segment length independent of features (e.g., two segmental slots to one prosodic position). If it is possible to show the need for "segment-counting" in the course of acquisition that cannot be accounted for in terms of moraic or onset-rime structure, the skeletal tier might be supported.

According to principles of tier association, unlinked constituents cannot appear in surface form. At the time a child produces only CVs and has no other prosodic structural representation, word-final consonants of a CVC target word are unrealized because they are not underlylingly present. A skeletal tier seems unmotivated in this case. The two skeletal slots (CV) are equivalent to the predictable syllable units, onset and rime, or the core syllable of mora theory.

If structure is, however, underlyingly present, but unrealized in surface form, there may be more reason to posit a skeletal tier. According to principles of association, if a syllable constituent is linked to a skeletal slot, it will not be subject to deletion. In Figure 7–2B, the CVC word /tɪp/ is realized as [tɪː ] or $CV_1V_1$. The child is capable of producing two rime elements as long as they are both the same vowel. Without a skeletal tier, the rime consonant /p/ would have to be delinked from the rime node, and relinked below the nucleus as a vowel. This is perhaps less formally elegant than double linking of *x*-slots as in Figure 7–2B, or even reclassification of C as V/V_# (CV-tier theory). However, in mora theory, the consonantal mora of /p/ would be delinked and then relinked to the vowel mora. No segments are counted, thus obviating the need for a skeletal tier and maintaining integrity at the moraic level. The proof of the need for a skeletal tier in such cases of unrealized underlying representation thus might not come from the weight-bearing part of the syllable. However, compensatory lengthening in the onset might demonstrate the utility of a skeletal tier, since no moraic links can be present, except extrasyllabically, a highly marked phenomonen (Hayes, 1989, p. 302).

## THEORIES OF SYLLABLE STRUCTURE AND PHONOLOGICAL DISORDER DATA

The data presented here were derived from Bernhardt (1990), a phonological intervention study with six children aged 3–6 years old with severe phonological disorders. Aspects of nonlinear phonological theory were utilized to analyze the children's speech samples, set intervention targets, and develop therapeutic strategies. Several questions were addressed in that study, but in this chapter only results pertinent to subsyllabic structure are discussed. In the first section, outcomes for contrasting intervention methodologies based on onset-rime theory versus moraic theory are discussed. The next section describes final consonant and diphthong data that are relevant to the two theories.

## *APPLICATION OF THEORY TO INTERVENTION TECHNIQUES*

In portions of the intervention program devoted to syllable/word structure development, a main question asked was whether there would be a difference in proportion and rate of syllable/word shapes acquired as a result of interventions that contrast the onset and rime versus those that emphasize the mora as a weight unit constituent. Basic assumptions were that such constituents can be identified at the surface level of representation and that children learn from the type of evidence provided in direct therapy.

Acknowledging that onset-rime and moraic theories converge in their focus on the syllable peak and postvocalic consonant representation, they are, however, distinct in their focus with respect to onsets. Thus, intervention methodologies respected this distinction.

In the onset-rime condition, the units of focus were the maximal onset and maximal rime in both perception and production activities. For example, when focusing on cluster onsets in perception activities, instructions might be given such as "Here are some names that start with [st]—*stan, stew, stick.* Here is a name that doesn't start with [st], only with [t]—*tick.*" After several training items, the child would be asked to sort words into [t] versus [st] piles. Other awareness activities involved reading the children poems that were alliterative or rhyming and drawing attention to the alliteration or rhyme. In imitative production tasks focusing on cluster development, one way of presenting stimuli for a word such as *snow* was as CC and V, for example, [sn]—PAUSE—[oʊ], with gradual increase of the rate of articulation to produce [snoʊ]. Another method utilized alternations of VCC—[ɛɪst]—PAUSE—[ɛɪst]—PAUSE [ɛɪst], with gradually increasing rate to produce [stɛɪ] (*stay*). (VCC#VCC becomes CCV in alternation by onset maximization.) For development of the CVC word shape, C and VC units were presented for imitation , for example, [tʰhh]-PAUSE-[ɑp], with gradual increase of the rate of articulation, yielding [tʰɑp] (*top*). Another method utilized alternations of VC, for example, [oʊk-oʊk-oʊk] becomes [koʊk] (*coke*), by onset maximization.

In the moraic condition, the immediately prevocalic consonant was considered "attached" to the following vowel, making the basic constituent CV (similar to the Stonham [1990] hypothesis). Consonants were added to this inseparable CV core syllable unit. To establish word-initial clusters, a CCV word was presented as a C and a CV, for example, [s]—PAUSE—[noʊ], with gradually increasing rate of articulation, yielding [snoʊ]. The utility of preconsonantal adjunction was emphasized through demonstration of the "magic" of the added constituent (e.g., *wick* becomes *quick*, when you add "magic" [k]). To establish the CVC word shape, separate CV and C stimuli were presented, for example, [tʰɑ]—PAUSE—[p], with gradual increase in rate of articulation. Addition of moras was assumed to be addition of "weight units" or "beats," and, hence, various rhythmic methods were used to accentuate the additional moras.

One could conceivably construe either stimulus presentation method as its counterpart. For example, the onset-rime CC—V presentation could also be construed as moraic because the moraic unit (V) was presented separately from the prevocalic adjoined consonant(s) CC. However, the major assumption for stimulus presentation was that *constituent status* of the various elements is the crucial variable for contrasting the two theories. Presenting CC as a cluster unit makes its constituent status as an onset salient, in comparison with adding C to CV, because the added C is not a constituent at the subsyllabic level in either theory. Because onset clusters are not constituents in moraic theory, they were not presented as such in the moraic condition. One could arguably also construe the CV moraic unit as an onset-rime combination. However, presentation of the onset-rime combination does not focus on the onset and rime as separate and independent constituents, which was the objective in the onset-rime condition.

## Statistical Analysis Contrasting Outcomes for the Onset-Rime and Mora Conditions

In seeking to determine whether the children had greater success for targets in the onset-rime or moraic conditions, the nonparametric Kolmogorov-Smirnov statistic was used. Cumulative proportional frequency distributions of the children's matching imitative responses (to adult stimuli) in treatment sessions and probes were compared for onset-rime and moraic conditions. No significant differences were found, either for individuals or the group of six children:

$$\text{Group data: } (4)(.18)^2_{57,63}(57)(63)/57 + 63 = 3.878, \text{ d.f. 2.}$$

In explaining the lack of difference, recall that, although different types of constituent stimuli were used in the two conditions, they may not have been contrastive in reality, and thus may have confounded each other; that is, the similar outcomes may reflect similarity of stimuli. Another training factor confounding results may have been response-related. Once able to imitate a word correctly without imitating its separate constituents (e.g., [swɪm] versus [s]—PAUSE—[wɪm]), a child may ignore any other aspect of the condition that focuses on the stimuli in a particular way.

The observed lack of difference is not an unwelcome therapeutic outcome, because stimuli and methods derived from both theories facilitated advances in syllable/word structure development, the ultimate objective of intervention. The use of contrasting methodologies, whether legitimate or not in terms of their assumptions, may have helped the children learn the prosodic structure of English by "breaking up" words in different ways. The children, overall, progressed significantly more quickly in syllable/word structure development than in segmental (feature) development, according to a Sign test statistic of 2.886 (significant at the .005 level, one-tailed). Thus the two syllable theories motivated intervention strategies, which, although not ultimately comparable, provided impetus for change in the children's syllable/word structure.

## Final Consonant and Diphthong Development in English

Data from the individual children have some bearing on moraic and onset-rime theories, however, without recourse to statistical analysis. In this chapter, the focus is solely on outcomes for final consonants and diphthongs. The reader is referred to Bernhardt (1990) and Bernhardt (1992b) for discussion of other outcomes with respect to the theories.

## SEAN'S PROSODIC STRUCTURE DEVELOPMENT

Sean's (fictional name, *S4* in Bernhardt, 1990) prosodic development could be characterized as "step-like," with the "steps" being "plateaus." Learning one targeted word/syllable type did not immediately lead to production of other theoretically related word/syllable types. Although one could attribute this lack of prosodic generalization to his phonological disorder, an examination of the specific failures to generalize may lead to elucidation of or new questions about development in terms of onset-rime and moraic theories.

## Relationship of CVV and CVC Monosyllabic Words

At the onset of intervention, the open monosyllable CV(V) accounted for 54.65% of all monosyllables (see examples below). The CVC word shape was beginning to develop: CVC child forms matched the adult targets 29% of the time in terms of CVC slots (excluding adult targets with word-final /l/ or /r/, and including segmental substitutions, such as the overgeneralized sibliant).

| | |
|---|---|
| big | [bægi], [bɛ:kʰ] |
| boy | [bɔə], [bo] |
| broke | [bɔ:], [bokʰ] |
| cake | [kʰaʃ] |
| eye | [ʔaɪ] |
| man, mad | [mæə], [mæ] |
| me | [mi:] |
| mitt | [mæəs>] |
| pie | [pɑ:ə] |
| thumb | [hɑ:ə] |
| way | [wæ], [wæ:] |

In a sample of 83 *monosyllabic* utterances with tense and lax vowels, 15 of 17 tense vowels were noticeably long, and 28 of 30 lax vowels had offglides. In the sample, most of the 36 CVC words contained lax vowels, about half of which were extended with offglides (14/32). The four instances of CVC with tense vowels did not have offglides or any obvious lengthening. For syllables with monophthongs, it is difficult to determine whether the offglides were phonologically based compensations for the missing C2s, or merely a type of surface articulatory habit (as [mæᵊs] for *mitt* might suggest, where an offglide is unmotivated phonologically). However, a more obvious example of restricted V2 slot development was noted with the diphthongs; 15 of 27 open syllable diphthong targets appeared with monophthongs (see *pie, way* versus *eye* above). For CVVC targets, (where VV = diphthong), only 2 of 17 child forms were matches with the adult targets, (e.g., *bike* > [baik] and *noise* > [nɔɛˆs]).

One goal in the first 6-week block of intervention was to strengthen the CVC word shape (V=tense or lax vowel). At the end of this 6-week block, 58 of 72 (81%) of the child CVC forms matched the adult targets for CV-slots in a probe with words not used during training.

The CVV word shape, where $V_1V_2$ = diphthong, did not arise spontaneously through generalization of skeletal slots. An actual *decrease* in matches for $CV_1V_2$ and $CV_1V_2C$ word shapes was noted. Overall, only 13 of 56 (23%) monosyllabic targets had diphthongs. Matching diphthongs were /ou/ (alternatively labeled a tense or *long* vowel) and /ɑɪ/ (40%). By contrast, however, cluster production was incipient, with two /sn/ onset clusters produced (*snake* > [snæk], *snakey* > [snæki]) and three final liquid-stop clusters produced, showing that increase in skeletal positions was not limited to *final* consonants, although it was limited to consonants.

## Intervention Results and the Theories of Subsyllabic Structure.

Skeletal *x*-tier theory does not provide an explanatory account of this developmental pattern, because $CV_1V_2$, CVC, and CCV all have three elements per syllable. The alternate skeletal theory, CV-tier theory, does however, acknowledge the difference between the structures in terms of C- and V-elements, and branching of vowels.

In onset-rime theory, CVC, CCV, and $CV_1V_2$ structures differ in that $CV_1V_2$ has branching at a more deeply embedded level (under the nucleus, a constituent dominated by the rime node, rather than at the level of the rime node itself). Onset-rime theory would not predict necessary generalization from $CV_1V_1$ to CVC, or CVC to $CV_1V_2$ because the two structures, although branching, have different levels of branching.

According to moraic theory, CVV is bimoraic in English. We can start with two different assumptions about CVC in English. If we first assume that CVC is bimoraic, then establishment of one realization of bimoraic structure, CVV, could logically imply establishment of the other. With this assumption, moraic theory fails to explain the lack of generalization noted. Differences need to be seen as general developmental asynchronies for varying members of a category.

If, on the other hand, we assume that $C_2$ of CVC monosyllables is only an adjunct of the vocalic mora, lack of generalization from $CV_1V_1$ to CVC, or CVC to $CV_1V_2$, is logically predictable, because adjunction is prosodically different from morafication. Although Sean may have learned final consonant adjunction, his monosyllabic moraic structure did not change, and therefore, $CV_1V_2$ did not generalize from CVC learning. Because assumptions regarding moraic status of various structures for the language in question also create implications for development, prediction of developmental patterns is difficult. In comparison, the structure of onset-rime theory is more straightforward, because the relationship of structures to weight sensitivity is not in question.

Developmental differences noted between final consonant and diphthong establishment in monosyllables could be predicted from Stonham's (1990) and Shaw's (1992) integrated proposals for onset-rime and moraic theory. In both proposals, two types of moraic constituents are suggested—nuclear versus consonantal. Such differences appear to have relevance in Sean's developmental patterns, which demonstrate a difference between CVV and CVC.

## Relationship of CVVC and CVCC in Monosyllabic Words

Because diphthongs did not appear after targeting CVC structures, they became targets of intervention in the subsequent 6-week treatment block, both in open and closed monosyllables. Only those in open syllables became established, even though CVC (V = tense or lax vowel) and $CV_1V_1$ were already well established.

In both onset-rime and moraic theories, establishment of CVVC from CVV involves single consonant adjunction; thus predictions are equivalent in that final consonant adjunction would be a later developmental step. Skeletal tier theories would be similar in predictions: four-element syllables (x-x-x-x) should be acquired later than three-element syllables (x-x-x).

Once retargeted in a subsequent treatment block, CVVC became established, but the CVCC syllable/word shape did not emerge until specifically targeted 6 months later (except with plurals, which involves morphological learning, and, is therefore, arguably, different). Contiguous consonant production (CC) did not appear to be an articulatorily based difficulty, because Sean produced plural morphemes on consonant-final words, and mastered the targeted word shape CCV(C) with word-initial clusters at the same time that CVVC emerged.

Skeletal tier theory might predict appearance of four-element syllables more or less simultaneously. Although CVVC and CCVC were simultaneous in appearance, CVCC was much later, making skeletal theory unreliable in this prediction.

According to onset-rime theory, CVVC and CVCC are structurally different. CVCC involves consonant adjunction of the last consonant to an already branching rime node, whereas CVVC involves single branches under both the rime and nucleus. It is not clear whether the consonant adjunction for CVCC is more complex (and therefore expected to develop later) than the two levels of branching for CVVC. However, the onset-rime explanation does at least demonstrate a structural difference (an extension of the difference between CVC and CVV), which may be developmentally relevant.

In terms of moraic theory, if one assumes that CVC is bimoraic, then CVCC involves single consonant adjunction to the second mora. This makes the lack of generalization from CVVC to the moraically equivalent CVCC unexpected, except as developmental delay, just as the lack of generalization from CVC to moraically equivalent CVV (VV = diphthong) was unexpected.

If one assumes that CVC monosyllables are monomoraic, however, double consonant adjunction is required for production of CVCC, perhaps a more marked phenomenon (and a predictably later development) than the single consonant adjunction required for CVVC. This is more explanatory than the moraic interpretation with a bimoraic CVC monosyllable hypothesis, and possibly more explanatory than the onset-rime interpretation, in which CVC involves single branching of the rime node and CVCC requires single consonant adjunction to that branching rime node.

As noted above for variations in CVV and CVC development, integrated versions of moraic and onset-rime theories may be predictive of developmental patterns, because of their separation of mora types into nuclear and consonantal moras.

## Summary

Sean's prosodic structure development was step-like. His monosyllables progressed as targeted from $CV_1V_1$ to CVC to $CV_1V_2$ to CVVC and CCVC to CVCC without spontaneous generalization from one structure to the next. This developmental pattern appears to support onset-rime theory and integrated versions of onset-rime and mora theories, all of which attribute independent constituent status to the vocalic nucleus.

# DIRECTIONS IN INTERVENTION

Exploration of current theoretical developments in syllable and word structure is both challenging and rewarding for intervention. Literature on the subject is primarily on adult language and includes data from many languages unfamiliar to the average North American. This makes interpretation and application challenging. What can be extracted from this literature, however, provides an impetus for new ways of analyzing data from children with phonological disorders, setting targets for intervention, and providing input in therapy. At the same time, we are able to evaluate aspects of the theories in the light of developmental data to test their relevance in developmental theory construction.

# REFERENCES

Bernhardt, B. (1990). *Application of nonlinear phonological theory to intervention with six phonologically disordered children.* Unpublished doctoral dissertation, University of British Columbia, Vancouver, BC.

Bernhardt, B. (1992a). Developmental implications of nonlinear phonological theory. *Clinical Linguistics and Phonetics, 6,* 259–281.

Bernhardt, B. (1992b). The application of nonlinear phonological theory to intervention with one phonologically disordered child. *Clinical Linguistics and Phonetics, 6,* 283–316.

Chiat, S. (1989). The relation between prosodic structure, syllabification and segmental realization: Evidence from a child with fricative stopping. *Clinical Linguistics & Phonetics, 3,* 223–242.

Chomsky, N., & Halle, M. (1968). *The sound pattern of English.* New York: Harper and Row.

Clements, G., & Keyser, S. (1983). *CV-phonology: A generative theory of the syllable.* Cambridge, MA: MIT Press.

Dinnsen, D. (1984). Methods and empirical issues in analyzing functional misarticulation. In M. Elbert, D.A. Dinnsen, & G. Weismer (Eds.), *Phonological theory and the misarticulating child. ASHA Monograph, 22,* 5–17.

Durand, J. (1990). *Generative and non-linear phonology.* London: Longman.

Elbert, M., & Gierut, J. (1986). *Handbook of clinical phonology.* San Diego, CA: College-Hill Press.

Goldsmith, J. (1976). *Autosegmental phonology.* Doctoral dissertation, Indiana University, Bloomington; [Published, 1979. New York: Garland Press].

Goldsmith, J. (1990). *Autosegmental and metrical phonology.* Cambridge, MA: Basil Blackwell.

Grunwell, P. (1985). *Phonological assessment of child speech.* San Diego, CA: College-Hill Press.

Halle, M., & Vergnaud, J. (1980). Three dimensional phonology. *Journal of Linguistic Research, 1,* 83–105.

Hayes, B. (1989). Compensatory lengthening in moraic phonology. *Linguistic Inquiry, 20,* 253–306.

Hyman, L. (1985). *A theory of phonological weight.* Dordrecht: Foris.

Ingram, D. (1976). *Phonological disability in children.* London: Edward Arnold.

Ingram, D. (1986). Phonological development: Production. In P. Fletcher & M. Garman (Eds.), *Language acquisition: Studies in first language development* (pp. 223–239). Cambridge, Great Britain: Cambridge University Press.

Kahn, D. (1976). Syllable-based generalizations in English phonology. Indiana University Linguistics Club.

Kaye, J. (1989). *Phonology: A cognitive view.* Hillsdale, NJ: Lawrence Erlbaum.

Kaye, J., Lowenstamm, J., & Vergnaud, J. -R. (in press). Constituent structure and government in phonology. In M. Prinzhorn (Ed.), *Linguistiche Berichte.*

Levin, J. (1985). *A metrical theory of syllabicity.* Unpublished doctoral dissertation, Massachusetts Institute of Technology, Cambridge.

McCarthy, J., & Prince, A. (1986). *Prosodic morphology.* Unpublished manuscript, University of Massachusetts and Brandeis University.

Pike, K., & Pike, E. (1947). Immediate constituents of Mazateco syllables. *International Journal of American Linguistics, 13,* 78–91.

Menn, L. (1978). Phonological units in beginning speech. In A. Bell & J. Bybee Hooper (Eds.), *Syllables and segments* (pp. 157–171). Amsterdam: North-Holland.

Shaw, P. (in press). Templatic evidence for the syllable nucleus. *Proceedings from the North Eastern Linguistic Society Meeting,* Chicago, Illinois, October, 1992.

Stampe, D. (1969). The acquisition of phonetic representation. In R. T. Binnick et al. (Eds.) *Papers from the Fifth Regional Meeting of the Chicago Linguistic Society* (pp. 433–444). Chicago: Chicago Linguistic Society.

Steriade, D. (1988). Reduplication and syllable transfer in Sanskrit and elsewhere. *Phonology, 5,* 73–155.

Stonham, J. (1990). *Current issues in morphological theory.* Unpublished doctoral dissertation, Stanford University, Palo Alto, CA.

# PART                II

*Second Language Phonology*

# INTRODUCTION

## *L1 and L2 Phonology: Looking Ahead*

HENNING WODE, PH.D.

Continuing along the same lines as Menn in her preface to Part I, the reader will notice that one of the strong points of this book is that it attempts to bring L1 and L2 acquisition research together. In doing this, the chapters contribute to a very important development in both phonology and developmental linguistics. Human beings can learn more than one language (i.e., as L1s, L2s etc.); they can forget and relearn languages and there does not seem to be any biologically based restrictions to the number of languages that can be acquired. Note that there would be no methodological reason at all to consider L2 acquisition if all that is worth knowing about the language capacity of homo sapiens could be identified by looking at young monolingual children struggling with their L1. Linguists, and phonologists in particular, held essentially this view until the early 1970s, and many developmental phonologists still do today. Newcomers to the field, in particular graduate students, are, therefore, advised to bear in mind that crucial insights into the nature of L1 acquisition of young children are available from research in L2 acquisition by adults. An example is the development of speech perception.

Why do many adults L2 learners retain a foreign accent when child L2 learners do not, and why do adults have difficulties in perceiving non-native phonic distinctions? Lenneberg's (1967) critical period hypothesis would suggest that adults lose their child language learning abilities around puberty and that this loss is due to physiological changes in the brain. Recent research by Werker and her associates (see Werker & Pegg, 1992, for a summary), however, has suggested that what is involved is not physiological changes but changes in processing abilities; that these changes occur between 0;7–0;12 years (i.e., before the onset of speech); and that before children begin to speak they probably can identify all the phonic contrasts of their ambient language. Two points are important here: In terms of methodology, note that this discovery was made possible only by moving outside the paradigm of L1 acquisition; in terms of research results, Werker's findings on speech perception in infants require a reassessment of one of the most central issues in developmental phonology, namely, the nature of the mental representation of the learner's perception and/or production of lexical items. How close are they to adult forms, and are there one or two lexicons—one for perception and one for production? (see Wode, in press-a, for some suggestions.)

Throughout its development (i.e., since the early 1970s), L2 acquisition research has always been integrated with L1 acquisition. The chapters in Part II bear out this tradition. In Chapter 8, Major provides a thoughtful introduction. He lists the major issues and results, and also provides some historical depth. Patkowski reviews the recent studies concerning the age issue in Chapter 9. His focus is on the level of L2 attainment and the impact of age at first contact with the L2 rather than on the nature of language learning abilities and how they change with age. The reader, therefore, may want to compare the approach illustrated in Chapter 9 with the research that attempts to explain how age-dependent changes come about, such as speech perception research (e.g., Werker & Tees, 1984; Wode, in press-b).

The remaining chapters in Part II are not focused on individual segments but take various theoretical notions as their starting points. In Chapter 13, Weinberger reviews data on syllable structure and vowel epenthesis. He suggests that L2 learners have access to the Principle of Recoverability of universal grammar and that L1 children do not, because only the former rely heavily on epenthesis in their production. Weinberger claims that this principle needs to mature in children, which explains why it does not surface in L1 data. The reader may wonder from which functional biological basis the Recoverability Principle develops and how this information ever got into the genes of homo sapiens in the first place.

The contributions by Carlisle, Eckman and Iverson, and Yavas (Chapters 10, 11, and 12) are attempts to refine the impact of markedness on L2 phonology. Carlisle reviews data that suggest that the phonological environment interacts with markedness to produce the kind of variation characteristic of L2 phonology. In fact, Carlisle suggests that environments themselves may be ordered according to a markedness scale. In a similar vein, Eckman and Iverson present data from adult Korean, Japanese, and Cantonese speakers of English to argue that both markedness constraints and the phonetic properties of segments determine the nature of L2 phonological variation. Yavas, in turn, focuses on the devoicing of final stops. He observes parallels between L1 and L2 acquisition and finds that vowel height and consonantal place of articulation interact conspicuously.

Obviously, a book such as this cannot reflect the entire field (i.e., include the full range of issues in L1 and L2 phonology, the different languages, nor the various national research traditions). The reader should, therefore, take note that the chapters in this book are written by researchers in the United States and that the book is addressed primarily to an English-speaking audience. Consequently, the focus is on English, and the literature acknowledged in the contributions is predominantly English.

A volume bridging L1 and L2 acquisition, almost by necessity, challenges readers to identify areas that have been neglected by mainstream L1 and/or L2 researchers. Such issues include, among others, the relationship between perception and production, the status of "phonological processes," the maturational issue, and the (in)adequacy of presently available models/theories. As for perception and production, learning the phonological system of a language means to learn to pronounce. Under normal circumstances perception is what allows learners to tune into the language, whatever the type of acquisition. Unfortunately, in the past both L1 and L2 acquisition research dealt almost exclusively with production phonology. Research on speech perception in infants and more mature learners has, with few exceptions (notably Flege, 1992a, 1992b), not been taken note of (for speech perception cf. recent volumes such as Tohkura, Vatikiotis-Bateson, & Sagisaka, 1992; Strange, in press). It needs to be explored whether or not some of the notorious problems that developmental phonologists have wrestled with in the past can be clarified by reference to the development of speech perception. For example, it appears like a painful detour to propose that L1 children first develop two lexicon (see Menn's perfect to the Part I) so that, later, on they need to develop the appropriate machinery to reduce the two to a single one. Perception research may provide a way of showing how perception may be ahead of production during early L1 acquisition without assuming a dual lexicon.

Another point is that to date developmental phonologists have failed to clarify the nature and status of the so-called phonological processes. Are they merely descriptive devices (see Menn's preface to Part I) or are the psycholinguistically real? If the latter, how do they originate ontogenetically and phylogenetically? Some research is under way in Germany that attempts to explore the possibility that the nature of early L1 phonological processess may be derived in a systematic way from the nature of the perception of lexical items in early infancy. The hypothesis is that variation in early L1 phonology and the phonological processes derives from fuzzy representation of the phonological component of lexical items of the target language.

All types of language acquisition need to be integrated into one developmental theory of phonology. Such an approach would allow researchers to determine more precisely how language learning abilities change, or do not change, as a function of age; to what extent languages can be relearned, and whether the same abilities are reactivated for such purposes. For example, if vowel epenthesis is found to be extremely prevalent in L2 acquisition but occurs only very sporadically in L1 acquisition, is it justifiable to conclude with Weinberger that vowel epenthesis relates to universal grammar and that L1 children at first do not have access to this principle? Such a conclusion depends on the interpretation of Weinberger's evidence. He correctly points out that vowel epenthesis abounds in L2 acquisition and that it occurs only very rarely in L1 acquisition. But what happens in between? Are differences of this sort sufficient to claim nonaccess to principles of a more universal sort? Or should we assume that, because both L1 and L2 speakers show evidence for vowel epenthesis, the ability is there from the very start, but surfaces in different quantities due to other intervening factors?

Perhaps most importantly, the development of phonological theories needs to be much more closely related to acquisition data,. Current theories are based almost exclusively on the production of fully mature monolingual speakers. There is no guarantee that such theories also apply to bilingual speakers. Moreover, one way or another, all theories are built on some notion of phonological segment (the phoneme or the like). The evidence is growing that, at least during the early stages of development, speakers who are not mature do not operate on the basis of segments. If so, traditional phonology based on mature speakers needs to be revised so that theories mirror the way the basic phonological constructs evolve ontogenetically within sound systems. Acquisition data present an exciting challenge to phonologists, especially to newcomers to the field.

# REFERENCES

Flege, J. E. (1992a). The intelligibility of English vowels spoken by British and Dutch talkers. In R. D. Kent (Ed.), *Intelligibility in speech disorders: Theory, measurement and management* (pp. 157–232) Amsterdam: John Benjamins.

Flege, J. E. (1992b). Speech learning in a second language. In C. Ferguson, L. Menn, & C. Stoel-Gammon (Eds.), *Phonological development: Models, research, implications* (pp. 565–604). Timonium, MD: York Press.

Lenneberg, E. (1967). *Biological foundations of language.* New York: John Wiley.

Strange, W. (in press). *Speech perception and linguistic experience: Theoretical and methodological issues*. Timonium, MD: York Press.

Tohkura, Y., Vatikiotis-Bateson, E., & Sagisaka, Y. (Eds.). (1992). *Speech perception, production and linguistic structure*. Tokyo: Ohmsha.

Werker, J. F., & Pegg, J. E. (1992). Infant speech perception and phonological acquisition. In C. Ferguson, L. Menn, & C. Stoel-Gammon (Eds.), *Phonological development: Models, research, implications* (pp. 285–311). Timonium, MD: York Press.

Werker, J. F., & Tees, R. (1984). Phonemic and phonetic factors in adult cross-language speech perception. *Journal of the Acoustical Society of America, 75*, 1866–1878.

Wode, H. (1981). *Learning a second language: An integrated view of language acquisition*. Tubingen: Narr.

Wode, H. (in press-a). Perzeption, Produktion und die Lernbarkeit von Sprachen. In H. Vater, K. H. Ramers, & H. Wode (Eds.), *Universale phonologische Strukturen*. Wiesbaden: Niemeyer.

Wode, H. (in press-b). Nature, nurture and age in language acquisition: The case of speech perception. *Studies in Second Language Acquisition*.

# CHAPTER 8

## Current Trends in
## Interlanguage Phonology

ROY C. MAJOR, PH.D.

The study of interlanguage phonology has undergone considerable changes in the last few decades, due to both the cumulative research in interlanguage phonology itself, as well as to research in related areas. Recent developments in linguistic theory, psychology, first language acquisition (see earlier chapters in this book), and technology in experimental phonetics have made feasible kinds of research that even as recently as a decade ago were neither possible nor even considered. The purpose of this chapter is to sketch the development of second language phonology up to the present and to suggest some future trends. This sketch is not meant to exhaust all avenues of interlanguage phonology research (for a comprehensive review, see Leather & James, 1991). Rather, it will cover several common themes and approaches that have been pursued over the years and describe how these theories have been modified. Such recurrent themes include age; personality; transfer and contrastive analysis; phonological similarity; markedness; universal developmental factors; style; perception, production, and underlying representation; attrition; and only very recently, nonlinear phonology.

# AGE

Second language L2 acquisition researchers, as well as the lay public, have observed that it is extremely difficult, if not impossible, for adults to acquire a second or foreign language with a native-like accent. The period after which it is supposedly impossible to acquire a native-like accent has been termed the "critical period" or it has often been framed in the form of the "critical period hypothesis." Originally proposed for first language (L1) acquisition, the hypothesis claims that after a certain period it is impossible to learn an L1 natively (see Curtiss, 1977). In terms of L2 acquisition, the hypothesis claims that after a certain age it is impossible to acquire native-like proficiency in a second language. Even without empirical data to lend support, it seems logical that there would be such maturational constraints; it would be odd if there were not biologically determined constraints on one of the most important characteristics of human beings—language—because in almost every other higher organism there are maturational constraints dealing with important aspects of their being, be it nest building, mating calls, or food gathering techniques. Yet, in human beings the question has hardly been settled. However, it is largely uncontested that in early bilingual acquisition learners eventually reach native-like proficiency in two languages. One of the best known studies of simultaneous acquisition is of Leopold's daughter Hildegard learning English and German simultaneously (Leopold, 1939, 1944, 1949a, 1949b). Other studies of simultaneous acquisition include Bergman (1976), Burling (1973), Contreras (1961), Fantini (1985), Imedadze (1967), Major (1977), and Swain and Wesche (1973). In older children the acquisition of a native-like accent still seems possible, for example, Wode (1981) documented his children's acquisition of native-like English pronunciation (their first language is German).

A volume of 12 papers treating different aspects of L2 acquisition (Krashen, Scarella, & Long,1982) presented documentation that older learners progress faster at first but early exposure in natural settings ultimately produces higher proficiency in all areas. Although there is much disagreement whether proficiency in nonphonological areas (e.g., syntax and semantics) is possible after the critical period, there is more agreement that, after a certain age, the attainment of native-like accent is not possible. This has been called the "Joseph Conrad phenomenon" (Scovel, 1981, 1988; updated by Brown, 1987 as the "Henry Kissinger phenomenon") because Conrad, a Polish novelist who wrote in English and learned English as a second language, possessed a tremendous command of written English, yet spoke English with a Polish accent. Scovel (1988) argued strongly that after puberty attainment of native accent becomes impossible; and Long (1990), in an excellent review article, suggested that even as early as age six, acquisition of a second language native accent may not be possible. Although Flege (1987a) found differences in proficiency according to age, he suggested that they might be due to other mediating factors, which cannot be controlled for in such research, such as sociocultural considerations. Likewise, Banu (1986) discussed the role of socio-psychological factors in addition to age. Finally, in Chapter 9, Patkowski updates research on the critical period.

## PERSONALITY

One's native language (NL) accent is intimately tied to one's sense of identity and personality; likewise one's personality has been linked to pronunciation proficiency in an L2. However, no study, to my knowledge, has claimed that personality variables alter specific linguistic processes; instead the claim is that these variables are mediating factors, affecting rate and ultimate attainment, rather than the nature of linguistic processes. That is, on the continuum of heavy foreign accent to native-like accent, personality factors are claimed to affect the learner's position on the continuum, rather than the nature of the continuum.

Personality variables typically considered are self-esteem, risk-taking, anxiety, empathy, extroversion, ego permeability, and motivation. (See Brown, 1987 for a useful summary.) Motivation has been categorized by Gardner and Lambert (1972) into integrative (when a learner wants to become a fullfledged member of the L2 culture) and instrumental motivation (when a learner wants to use the L2 as a tool for some specific purpose), although this distinction has been questioned by many. It is generally believed that integrative motivation, as opposed to instrumental, fosters better pronunciation; however, Coates (1986) did not find this to be true. In fact, Gardner himself and MacIntyre (1991) found instrumentally motivated students to be effective learners, although their study did not involve pronunciation. They claimed that it is not the orientation per se that promotes learning but rather the effect of the motivation. If neither instrumental nor integrative motivation is tied to motivation to learn a language, it is difficult to argue how it could promote learning. (In another study, Gardner, Day, and MacIntyre [1992] found integrative motivation aided vocabulary acquisition.) Even if motivation is strong, inhibition can often block it. In an often cited study, Guiora, Beit-Hallami, Brannon, and Dull (1972) found that small amounts of alcohol (1 ounce) improved subjects' pronunciation, which they attribute to a decrease in inhibition, but larger doses of alcohol hindered pronunciation. Guiora and his associates have done a number of other studies that administer drugs to the subjects, with varied results, such as a study using valium (Guiora, Acton, Erard, & Strickland, 1980).

Coates (1986) investigated the English of 143 German students learning English and considered the factors of musicality, motivation, extroversion, need for achievement, and overall educational success as measured by grade point average. Although the author admitted that there were methodological problems in his study, he reported some interesting results. Popular belief has it that integrative motivation, extroversion, and musicality are correlated with pronunciation proficiency, but Coates' study showed no such correlations; however, Coates did find strongly positive correlations in pronunciation proficiency for two factors: grade point average and the need for achievement.

Because the results of personality studies are so mixed, one must be cautious in interpreting their results, because the ways of measuring personality traits are so varied and complex. Most likely, research that attempts to correlate personality with pronunciation will continue to produce diverse results.

## TRANSFER AND CONTRASTIVE ANALYSIS

One of the most important factors governing second language acquisition is L1 transfer to L2 pronunciation (for a condensed review of transfer, see Odlin, 1989). The awareness of the important role of transfer took the form of contrastive analysis (CA), the early version of which claimed all nonnative deviations were due to interference or negative transfer. This philosophy is exemplified in some of the early works on languages in contact e.g., Weinreich (1953). Weinreich described interference at the phonotactic, suprasegmental, and phonic levels. The phonic level is further subdivided into *sound substitution* (e.g., an English speaker using alveolar stops for Italians dentals), *under differentiation* (a Japanese speaker using one liquid for both English /r/ and /l/), *over differentiation* (an English speaker conceptualizing the allophonic differences of Spanish /d/, that is [d] and [ð] as phonemic differences /d/ and [ð]), and *reinterpretation of distinctions* (a German speaker of English perceiving the tense/lax distinctions in American English vowels as primarily quantitative rather than qualitative because in German quantitative distinctions are primary).

Lado's landmark work, *Linguistics Across Cultures* (1957), was an attempt to explain and predict all substitutions based on NL transfer. A weaker version of CA was later proposed which was less predictive but instead explained substitutions after the fact (Wardhaugh, 1970). But in both the "strong" (predictive) and "weak" (after the fact) versions, researchers seemed to accept unquestioningly the notion that all nonnative substitutions were due to transfer, and because of this assumption they were able to fit all substitutions into the Procrustean bed of transfer. Substitutions not obviously due to transfer were just swept into the transfer category because it was axiomatic that transfer was the only cause. The exact nature of the substitutions did not matter, because they were unquestionably due to transfer.

In the 1960s and 1970s several problems with the CA notion that all nonnative substitutions were due to transfer became apparent. First, CA could not explain why some errors occurred whereas others did not. At best one could merely state that speakers just happened to learn certain things but not others. Second, there was an increasing awareness that transfer did not explain all substitutions (Brière, 1966; Nemser, 1971). Furthermore, transfer by itself could not explain why certain phenomena were generally acquired before others.

A refinement of CA, incorporating the notion of similarity, attempted to explain why some phenomena are more difficult than others: If phenomenon $x$ occurs in L1 and $y$ in L2, it is more difficult to learn $y$ if $x$ and $y$ are very similar than if they are very dissimilar. For example, learning dental unaspirated stops in French would be difficult for an English speaker because English alveolar aspirated stops are very similar to French; on the other hand, learning the French uvular /R/ may be easier because English and French $rs$ are so dissimilar.

## PHONOLOGICAL SIMILARITY

The notion of phonetic and phonological similarity, although originally from CA, has developed further and taken on different forms. Although not dealing with phonology, Oller and Ziahosseiny (1970) applied this notion to spelling systems, finding that speakers whose native language did not use a Roman alphabet made fewer spelling mistakes than those whose languages did. Wode (1981) elaborated on the notion of similarity by attempting to explain which sounds are more likely to show L1 influence (transfer) and which are not: If an L2 sound meets certain similarity requirements compared to the L1 sound it will show L1 influence, whereas dissimilar sounds will not show this L1 influence; in fact, for the latter case (dissimilar sounds), substitutions that are not due to the L1 will be used . Along these lines, in a study of German second graders whose teacher spoke the Swabian dialect, Young-Scholten (1985) found that errors in phonology and morphology were due to developmental differences or to interference because of crucial similarity. Further, she claimed that errors due to interference will persist due to similarity.

Flege, in a series of sound empirically based articles (e.g., 1985, 1987b, 1987c, 1990), used the concept of similarity for his "equivalence classification" hypothesis and found that, among more advanced speakers, nonequivalent sounds (i.e., "new" categories) are learned more completely than equivalent or "similar" categories. For example, he (Flege, 1987b) found that L1 English speakers who were advanced learners of French were more successful with French /y/ (no equivalent in English) than with /u/ (equivalent to English /u/).

Continuing this line of research, Bohn and Flege (1992) found that, in German speakers of English, experienced speakers did not produce /i I ɛ/ (the "similar" English vowels) more accurately than inexperienced speakers. On the other hand, for the vowel /æ/ (the "new" vowel), experienced, as opposed to inexperienced, speakers produced it similarly to native speakers.

However, Wode (1981) pointed out that we do not have a good definition of similarity requirements. Similarly, Flege (personal communication, 1990) has admitted that there is still a lack of rigorous definitions of similarity and equivalence, and until there are such definitions, one has to safeguard against circular reasoning: *x* is difficult to learn because *y* is equivalent. How do we know it is equivalent? Because it is difficult to learn. Ultimately, such classifications must come from perceptual, acoustic, articulatory, and perhaps orthographic evidence.

## MARKEDNESS

One of the drawbacks of CA was its failure to predict level of difficulty or order of acquisition. Eckman (1977) attempted to salvage CA by adding the dimension of markedness. His markedness differential hypothesis (MDH), encompassing both syntax and phonology, claims that markedness can predict order of acquisition: The less marked phenomenon is acquired before the more marked. Markedness has been variously defined, from statistical frequencies (i.e., the more marked the less frequent), to a strict implicational hierarchy (i.e., *x* is more marked than *y* if the presence of *x* implies the presence of *y* but not vice versa). Eckman used the latter definition to make his hypothesis a very strong one: If *x* has been acquired, *y* necessarily has also been acquired. Thus, the hypothesis is stated in a way that it can easily be disconfirmed, or to put it another way, it is easy to state what counterevidence would be. For example, voiced obstruents are more marked in wordfinal position than they are in initial and medial positions. Therefore, if an L2 learner (whose NL had no voiced obstruents) were to acquire them in final position before the other two positions, it would be clear counterevidence.

To date, the MDH has found good support in studies of phonology (Anderson, 1983; Carlisle, 1988, 1991); other studies have provided limited support but no strong counterevidence (Benson, 1988; Hodne, 1985; Riney, 1989); however, see Sato (1984) for some apparent counter-evidence in a syllable structure study. Although not directly testing Eckman's hypothesis, Broselow and Finer (1991), in a study of consonant clusters (as well as some syntactic phenomena), found that speakers transferred their NL parameter settings (with various markedness relationships) to the target language (TL), and for some L2 learners ,the parameter settings were midway between the NL and TL. Their results may be interpreted as indirectly supporting Eckman's claims.

In nonphonological studies, support for Eckman's hypothesis seems to be somewhat weaker. Chaudron and Parker (1990) found support in a discourse study; other studies supporting the MDH are Berent (1985), Macedo (1986), and Rutherford (1982); Bardovi-Harlig (1987) gave an apparent counterexample. Other studies seem to neither strongly support nor refute the hypothesis (e.g., White [1987], rather than directly supporting or refuting the MDH, suggested that markedness covers a whole range of phenomena that needs to be clarified). White's study is telling because, in all fairness, some of the apparent counterevidence in nonphonological studies is perhaps due to the fact that there is less agreement among linguists as to exact markedness relationships.

A number of other works by Eckman (1984, 1985, 1987) relate to the issue of markedness and universals. More recently, Eckman (1991) proposed the interlanguage structural conformity hypothesis (SCH), which is more encompassing than the MDH. The SCH claims that universals of primary languages also hold for interlanguages. This is indeed a very powerful claim: Interlanguages are in fact languages, there is nothing intrinsically different about interlanguages, and principles characterizing primary languages also hold true for interlanguages. His data from consonant clusters of second language learners (Eckman, 1991) largely support his claims.

Eckman has argued that the SCH is a stronger hypothesis than the MDH because the former is more easily falsifiable. The MDH makes predictions on the basis of universals and the differences between the NL and TL, whereas the SCH makes predictions only on the basis of universals. Thus, if there are no differences for a given phenomenon the MDH makes no predictions, whereas the SCH predicts that universals will still obtain. For example, Eckman reported (1991) that Altenberg and Vago (1983) found that Hungarian learners of English devoiced word final obstruents, even though Hungarian has a voiceless/voiced contrast in this position. It is noteworthy that the Hungarian learners maintained the contrast in English in word-initial and medial-positions, a universal pattern of voicing (voicing in final position implies voicing in the other two positions but not vice versa). If, however, it was found that speakers devoiced obstruents in initial but not in final position, this would have falsified the SCH because no primary language has such voicing constraints. To date there appear to be no data that have falsified Eckman's claims.

## UNIVERSAL DEVELOPMENTAL FACTORS

Using markedness to explain and predict order of acquisition was a significant step forward from CA's straight transfer predictions. CA predicted that all differences between the NL and TL would cause difficulty, whereas markedness predicted order of difficulty. However, neither point of view was concerned with the types of substitutions that occurred: CA attributed all errors to NL transfer, and most studies of markedness were not concerned with classifying the types of substitutions. However, even though the types of substitutions L2 learners used were not studied, it became apparent that not all substitutions could be attributed to NL transfer.

As early as 1971 Nemser reported that some Hungarian learners of English produced sounds occurring neither in native English nor Hungarian (e.g., [sθ] for English [θ]). Johansson (1973) noted that L2 learners of Swedish used sounds that occurred in neither Swedish nor the NL. For example, some German and American English speakers used [ʉ] for Swedish [ɯ], even though [ʉ] does not occur in Swedish, English, or German; other subjects overgeneralized by using one Swedish sound for another Swedish sound when neither occurred in their NLs. Such processes can be categorized as *overgeneralization* and *approximation*, respectively, processes that commonly occur in L1 acquisition. These and similar processes that cannot be directly attributed to the NL often are lumped together as *developmental* because they are similar or identical to what occurs in L1 acquisition of the language in question.

A number of other L2 studies have revealed the presence of developmental processes. In general, the types of developmental processes occurring are similar to those in L1 acquisition of the language under consideration, among them being English obstruent devoicing, consonant cluster simplifications, preference for open versus closed syllables, and in other languages various types of substitutions (Altenberg & Vago, 1983; Benson, 1988; Edge, 1991; Flege & Davidian, 1984; Hecht & Mulford, 1982; Hodne, 1985; Major, 1986; Piper, 1984; Riney, 1989; Wode, 1980). Major's "Ontogeny Model" (1987a), recognizing the strong influence of both transfer and developmental factors, proposed a hierarchical relationship between transfer and developmental processes, claiming that transfer decreases over time while concurrently developmental processes first increase and then decrease.

Although not dealing with phonology, Andersen (1983) argued that in order for transfer to operate in the TL, there have to be corresponding structures in L1 and L2; otherwise, nontransfer processes (developmental, not Andersen's term) operate. Extrapolating to phonology, this would imply that English speakers learning Bantu clicks would use developmental substitutions, because there are no readily apparent corresponding phonemes in English; in contrast, the same speakers learning French dental stops quite naturally substitute English alveolar stops.

Whereas CA maintained that L2 substitutions could be explained solely on the basis of transfer, awareness of these developmental processes demonstrated that not all substitutions could be attributed to the L1. In this way, the types of substitutions that were swept under the carpet because they did not fit the transfer category were now open to examination. Furthermore, perhaps the most important contribution made by the discovery of developmental processes was that researchers began to realize that L1 and L2 acquisition share some very fundamental characteristics. The earlier notion, taking for granted that L1 and L2 acquisition were basically different, was now called into question. The unity of language, be it a first or second language, began to be established. Currently there are many debates concerning the role of Universal Grammar (UG) and other universals in L2 acquisition (Bley-Vroman; 1989, Eckman, Moravosik, & Worth, 1989; Flynn, 1987; Tarone, 1987; White, 1987, 1989, 1990). Without the impetus of having uncovered developmental processes, whether they concern phonology or the rest of grammar, perhaps the current investigations of universals in L2 acquisition and their relationship to language universals in general would not now be taking place.

## STYLE

Just as primary languages vary, so too do interlanguages. Beebe's (1977) study of Chinese Thai bilinguals showed that their accent was directly correlated to their interlocutors: Speakers more often used a Thai accent when speaking to Thai listeners and a Chinese accent when speaking to Chinese listeners. Such interlocutor accommodation has been observed widely and has been formalized in the Accommodation Theory of Giles and his associates (Beebe & Giles, 1984; Giles, 1973; Giles & Johnson, 1987; Giles, Mulac, Bradac, & Johnson 1987). A further study of Beebe's (1980), involving prestige and nonprestige variants, found that Thai speakers of English pronounced English /r/ more correctly in conversation than in word lists, where speakers used a trill more often, a high-prestige variant in Thai.

Nemser (1971), in a study of Hungarian learners of English, found significant variation in the amount of transfer as a function of formality; likewise Wilson and Møllergard's (1981) study of Norwegians' production of English described variation in reading and speaking. All other things being equal, the more formal the style, the more target-like the production (Dickerson & Dickerson, 1977; Gatbonton, 1978; Sato, 1985; Schmidt, 1977; Wenk, 1979; ) and further, the less transfer is likely to occur (Dickerson & Dickerson, 1977; Major, 1987b; Preston, 1989; Schmidt, 1977; Tarone, 1979, 1988; but see Beebe, 1980). Teachers of second and foreign languages commonly observe this, noticing students' native-like pronunciation in word lists but NL transfer in conversation.

However, a preponderance of transfer processes does not necessarily mean non-native-like pronunciation. If a formal process in the NL produces a nonnative TL variant but fortuitously a casual process produces the nativelike output, accuracy is greater as style becomes less formal. For example, Japanese learners of English frequently insert [u] in consonant clusters as in [sukay] *sky*. However, in normal running speech in native Japanese, high vowels between voiceless obstruents are devoiced and then often deleted. Thus, *sky* would tend to be pronounced correctly as [skay]. This example brings home the fact that, to thoroughly evaluate the influence of NL on the T, one must be completely familiar with the stylistic variants of the NL.

Variations due to gender in native speaker investigations have been known for a long time and need not be reiterated here. For example, as early as 1958 Fischer investigated children aged 3–10 in their use of the -*ing* morpheme found that boys used the [n] variant (as opposed to [ŋ], e.g., *runnin'* vs. *running*) much more frequently than girls, but both sexes used [ŋ] more frequently as style became more formal. The general finding—that females tend to use prestige forms more frequently than males and both sexes use prestige forms more frequently as formality increases—has been substantiated in a number of later studies (Labov, 1963, 1972; Trudgill, 1974). The increased use of prestige forms as a function of formality has been attributed to individuals monitoring their speech more closely in formal styles.

In second language acquisition research involving gender differences, Gussenhoven (1979, reported in Leather and James, 1991) found females more favorably disposed to use prestige forms than males. In another study involving prestige and nonprestige forms, Adamson and Regan (1991) investigated Cambodian immigrants in their use of the *-ing* morpheme in two speech styles, with some surprising results. Two of their findings closely correlate to what is found in English native speakers: first, the total frequency of [ŋ] (the so-called prestige variant) was greater for females compared to males; second, for females the frequency of [ŋ] increased as style became more formal. However, the most striking finding was that for males the frequency of [ŋ] actually decreased as style became more formal. Apparently, the males (quite correctly) perceived the [n] variant as more of a male native speaker variant, and therefore, to them it was the prestige variant. Therefore, in monitoring their speech (the more formal variety) they accommodated to the male native speaker norm (i.e., more [n]), rather than to the overall norm, which for both sexes shows a greater frequency of [ŋ] in formal styles.

## PERCEPTION, PRODUCTION, AND UNDERLYING REPRESENTATION

The interrelationship between perception, production, and underlying representation in native speakers is far from clear and has been a source of debate for decades. In nonnative speakers the picture is even less settled because there are a number of possible relationships in both underlying representations and processes that produce surface forms. Both perceptual categories and processes that produce surface forms can be identical to the learner's native language, target language, or neither like the NL nor TL.

In L1 acquisition there is much evidence that the Underlying Representation (UR, also called mental representation) of the child is identical or nearly identical to that of the adult and that the child's mispronunciations are due to processes causing deviations from the adult target rather than to perceptual inabilities. The Natural Phonology of David Stampe (1969, 1987) promotes this view. Thus, a child who says [gak] for *dog* is trying to say [dag] but, due to consonant harmony and terminal obstruent devoicing, the word is pronounced as [gak].

In terms of the target or what is intended, in L1 acquisition, there are important differences between phonology and morphology and syntax. As discussed above, in phonological acquisition the target is approximately the same as the adult's, whereas in morphology and syntax it can be different. A child who says [fɪs] for fish knows the word is supposed to be pronounced [fɪš] (the so-called *fis* phenomenon). In contrast, a child who says, "Daddy go work?" with rising intonation is trying to say exactly that, not "Did Daddy go to work?" or "Is Daddy going to work?" That is, the syntactic intention is the same as the syntactic output (this, of course, ignores performance, which is a factor in all acquisition).

Second language acquisition of morphology and syntax shares a number of similarities with L1 acquisition of morphology and syntax. In both L1 and L2 acquisition there is a close correspondence between the intention and what is produced. The intention reflects the L1 learner's grammar or the L2 learner's grammar or interlanguage. Therefore, nonnative forms for both the L1 and L2 learner are due to a nonnative target.

However, in phonology there are a number of differences between L1 and L2 acquisition. Whereas the child "knows" the adult target, the L2 learner may or may not know (i.e., the UR may or may not be different from the native speakers). In L2 phonology a nonnative target usually results in nonnative pronunciation, yet a nativelike target does not necessarily produce nativelike pronunciation (i.e., the speaker may know what it is supposed to sound like but is unable to produce it).

Leather (1987, 1990), in investigations of perception and production of Chinese tones by Dutch and English speakers, found relationships between perception and production but not a 1:1 relationship; rather they depended on the tones being acquired. These and similar studies have illustrated that, in spite of the fact that one would expect some logical connection between perception and production (because the target has to come from somewhere and in production one has to have a target to aim at), there never can be a predictable clear-cut relationship, since both underlying representations and processes can be identical to the learner's native language (NL) or target language (YL) or something intermediate. For the L2 learner, there seem to be three possibilities with respect to the UR: the UR may be the same as the L2 learner's NL, the same as the TL, or something intermediate. Furthermore, just as URs can vary in these three ways, so too can the processes that act on URs to produce surface forms. That is, these processes may be the same as the NL (transfer processes), different from the NL and TL (universal developmental processes), or the same as the TL. Considering these three possibilities for URs and the three possibilities for processes give us nine possibilities (for a more complete treatment of these relationships, see Major, in press):

1. UR (of interlanguage) = UR of NL (NSs of NL)
   a. processes = NL processes (processes of NSs of NL)
   b. processes ≠ NL or TL processes
   c. processes = TL processes (processes of NSs of the TL)

2. UR ≠ NL or TL (something intermediate)
    a. processes = NL processes
    b. processes ≠ NL or TL processes
    c. processes = TL processes
3. UR = UR of TL (NSs of the TL)
    a. processes = NL processes
    b. processes ≠ NL or TL processes
    c. processes = TL processes

Let us consider examples of these nine possibilities.

(1)a.  UR = UR of NL and processes = NL processes

Usually the result is nonnative pronunciation (e.g., a Japanese learner of English who pronounces *hearing* and *healing* both as [hiɾiŋ] because English /l/ and /r/ are represented as Japanese /ɾ/ and the Japanese processes apply; a French NS learning Spanish produces a uvular /R/ for the Spanish trilled /r/). However, native pronunciation may be fortuitously produced even when the UR and processes are different from the TL. A Spanish speaker of English who represents English /ð/ as /d/ would pronounce it incorrectly as [d] in nonpostvocalic position (e.g., [dem]) *them* but in postvocalic position the speaker would correctly pronounce the sound, due to native Spanish postvocalic spirantization (e.g. mo[ð]e)*r*. Many Brazilian Portuguese speakers of English tend to represent English *few* as /fil/ (pronounced [fiw]) as they would in their NL. However, in running speech it may be correctly pronounced as [fyu], due to syllabicity shift occurring in native Portuguese in running speech (Major 1985). A third example of a nonnative UR resulting in native pronunciation is an English learner of Spanish who thinks of Spanish intervocalic /d/ as /ð/, rather than /d/ as a native Spanish speaker would (where [ð] is an allophone of /d/). For this English speaker, the intervocalic /d/ in Spanish would then be correctly produced as [ð] ( e.g., [naða] *nada* 'nothing'). What these three examples illustrate is that, even though one has URs and processes the same as one's NL, they can fortuitously produce native-like pronunciation in the L2.

(1)b.  UR = UR of NL and processes ≠ NL or TL processes

Because Portuguese does not have syllable final stops, in loan words, [i] is inserted as in *Rock*[i] music. In word-final position, Portuguese speakers may correctly perceive voiced stops as voiced, and if the speakers do not insert [i], they may devoice the final voiced stops, due to a universal developmental process of final devoicing, which is not a native Portuguese process: *sad* [sæt̪]. Thus, the UR of the final sound is identical to the NL (dental and voiced), but the source of the devoicing process is neither the NL nor the TL.

(1)c.  UR = UR of NL and processes = TL processes

This condition does not seem to be logically possible because when the UR is the same as the speaker's NL, and therefore different from the TL, it is impossible for TL processes to apply because the conditions for the processes to apply are not met because the input is different.

(2)a.  UR ≠ NL or TL and processes = NL processes

A Korean learner of English has a UR of English /r/ that is neither like native Korean nor English, yet in production a Korean liquid is produced, which to English speakers sounds intermediate between [r] and [l]. An American learning Portuguese /ɔ̃w̃/ often knows it as a nasalized /ɔ̃w̃/ but when pronouncing it denasalizes it to [aw] as in [saw] *Paolo São Paolo.*

(2)b.  UR ≠ NL or TL and processes ≠ NL or TL processes

A number of Flege's studies illustrate this condition (especially 1987b) illustrate this condition. A native speaker of English learning French thinks of /ü/ as different from a native speaker of French but still unlike English /u/ and in production it may be intermediate between French /ü/ and /u/. A number of voice onset time (VOT) studies of English, French, Spanish, and Portuguese suggest that both the UR and processes are intermediate between the NL and TL (Caramazza, Yeni-Komshian, Zurif, & Carbone, 1973; Flege, 1987b; Major, 1987c).

(2)c.  UR ≠ NL or TL and processes = TL processes

Similar to 1c above, this appears to be an impossible condition because for the TL processes to apply the UR has to be native.

(3)a.  UR = UR of TL and processes = NL processes

A native speaker of English has a UR alveolar trilled /r/ in Spanish but in production produces English [ɹ]. A native speaker of Portuguese has UR /o/ in English in word final position (e.g., *veto*) but produces [u], because of the Portuguese raising process.

(3)b.  UR = UR of TL and processes ≠ NL or TL processes

A native speaker of English has a UR trilled /r/ in Spanish yet produces a voiced retroflex sibilant (Major 1986). In word-final position Portuguese speakers represent /d/ as voiced and alveolar, but they devoice the /d/, *sad* [sæt] (cf. 1b above).

(3)c.  UR = UR of TL and processes = TL processes

Everything is native-like (e.g., a native speaker of Spanish who represents natively and accurately produces English /v/ and /b/).

## FIRST LANGUAGE ATTRITION

Attrition can take various forms from complete loss ( Dorian, 1981; Dressler & Wodak-Leodoter, 1977) to modification in contact situations (Caramazza et al., 1973; Clyne, 1980; Flege & Hillenbrand, 1984; Puppel & Marton, 1991; Thomason & Kaufman, 1988; Van Coetsem, 1988; Weinreich, 1953) to a decrease in proficiency (Freed, 1980; Kaufman & Aronoff, 1991; Sharwood Smith, 1983a, 1983b; Sharwood Smith & van Buren, 1991). Most of the studies deal with nonphonological phenomena. In fact, in a recent issue of *Studies in Second Language Acquisition* (1989, vol. 11, no. 2), devoted entirely to language attrition, none of the six articles even mentioned phonology.

A very prevalent factor in L2 acquisition is L1 transfer and so too in L1 attrition is L2 transfer important. Caramazza et al. (1973) found VOTs for /p t k/ in English and French Canadian bilinguals to be intermediate between monolingual English speakers and French speakers. In this study it is perhaps improper to term the languages L1 and L2, but in any case, it is obvious that there is mutual influence between the two languages. Other studies have also shown the influence of L2 on L1 (Flege, 1987b; Flege & Hillenbrand, 1984; Major, 1992). However, in all of the studies to date, it seems that the notion of transfer is the dominating factor; there is no discussion of whether universal developmental factors in fact could operate. If they do operate, do they exhibit similar patterns as L2?

## NONLINEAR PHONOLOGY

For more than a decade, much of the research in phonology has been termed nonlinear, which includes autosegmental, metrical, CV, and lexical phonology (see Goldsmith, 1990), in which representations have complex geometric structures somewhat similar to chemistry models.

Only quite recently has this approach been used in L2 phonology, perhaps not so much because L2 researchers have been behind mainstream phonology but because much of the L2 research might more properly be categorized as phonetic. Even the journals where much of L2 research is published are telling, such as the *Journal of the Acoustical Society of America* and the *Journal of Phonetics*.

However, a number of researchers have approached L2 phonology in a nonlinear fashion. Broselow (1985), in a production and perception study of Arabic learners of English, found that by employing principles of metrical phonology she could explain the patterns of Arabic speakers breaking up consonant clusters. Furthermore, she claimed that L2 substitutions can provide new evidence for testing general linguistic hypotheses. In various works, James (1986, 1987, 1988, 1989, 1990) has employed nonlinear approaches. For example, the 1987 study used metrical phonology to map out the prosodic structure of Dutch learners of English; in the 1990 study he proposed a model of L2 phonological acquisition employing nonlinear principles; the 1990 article used autosegmental notions of skeletal tier and parameter settings. Other nonlinear research includes Carlisle (1991), who in examining vowel epenthesis in the environment /sC/ in Spanish speakers of English, used CV phonology (Clements & Keyser, 1983) to account for the more frequent epenthesis after word-final consonants than after final vowels. Archibald (1992) utilized metrical parameters similar to those used by Carlisle to account for Polish speakers stress assignment in English (see Archibald, in press, for a study of Spanish learners of English), and Vogel (1991) used Italian speakers of English as evidence for issues in prosodic phonology. Finally, Weinberger (1990) used underspecification theory in a study of various languages.

These recent articles suggest that future studies in abstract L2 phonology, as opposed to purely phonetic, will continue to employ principles of nonlinear phonology, which have been part of mainstream phonology for some time.

## CONCLUSION

Interlanguage phonology research has widened its scope from the early nearly exclusively contrastive analysis approach, with the assumption that all errors were due to native language transfer, to a more broadly based approach incorporating general linguistic theory. More recent research has taken into account developmental errors, which are not due to native language but rather to universal factors that have been found to occur both in first and second language acquisition. In addition, studies have taken into account sociolinguistic variables as well as markedness theory. Much of the very recent work considers L2 acquisition from the standpoint of universal grammar, such as parameter settings and nonlinear approaches.

Whereas much current L2 research employs linguistic theory, mainstream linguistics has been largely immune to L2 research. More recently L2 researchers have tried to demonstrate that the relationship should be a two way street—that L2 research provides relevant data for testing linguistic theories, not merely that L2 research should use linguistic theory. In fact, Huebner has called L2 research a "litmus test" for linguistic theory (Huebner & Ferguson, 1991). Even *Language*, a mainstream linguistics journal, has published L2 research (e.g., Birdsong, 1992). But even now there is a reluctance on the part of most linguists to consider L2 data, in part probably due to the concentration of research on monolingual native speakers. This is unfortunate because monolingual speakers clearly are a minority in the world, and it has been shown that in contact situations there is a mutual influence of L1 and L2, the effect of which has to be taken into account in learnability theory and historical change—certainly concerns of general linguistic theory. With L2 learners prevalent and alive and well in the world, L2 researchers must continue to urge mainstream linguists to take into account their insights. It is hoped that the future will find mutual cooperation and mutually rewarding discoveries between L2 researchers and mainstream linguists.

# REFERENCES

Adamson, H. D., & Regan, V. (1991). The acquisition of community speech norms by Asian immigrants. *Studies in Second Language Acquisition, 13,* 1–22.

Altenberg, E., & Vago, R. (1983). Theoretical implications of an error analysis of second language phonology production. *Language Learning, 33,* 427–447.

Andersen, R. W. (1983). Transfer to somewhere. In S. Gass & L. Selinker (Eds.), *Language transfer and language learning* (pp. 177–201). Rowley, MA: Newbury House.

Anderson, J. L. (1983). The markedness differential hypothesis and syllable structure difficulty. In G. S. Nathan (Ed.), *Proceedings of the Conference on the Uses of Phonology* (pp. 85–89). Carbondale: Southern Illinois University.

Archibald, J. (1992). Transfer of L1 parameter settings: some empirical evidence from Polish metrics. *Canadian Journal of Linguistics, 37,* 301–339

Archibald, J. (in press). The learnability of English metrical parameters by Spanish speakers. *International Review of Applied Linguistics* (in press).

Banu, R. (1986). Child vs. adult in second language acquisition: Some reflections. *WATESOL Working Papers, 3.* [ERIC Document Reproduction Service No. ED 274-207]

Bardovi-Harlig, K. (1987). Markedness and salience in second-language learning. *Language Learning, 37*, 385–407.

Beebe, L. M. (1977). The influence of the listener on code-switching. *Language Learning, 27*, 332–339.

Beebe, L. M. (1980). Sociolinguistic variation and style shifting in second language acquisition. *Language Learning, 30*, 433–447.

Beebe, L., & Giles, H. (1984). Speech accommodation theory: A discussion in terms of second-language acquisition. *International Journal of the Sociology of Language, 46*, 5–32.

Benson, B. (1988). Universal preference for the open syllable as an independent process in interlanguage phonology. *Language Learning, 38*, 221–242.

Berent, G. P. (1985). Markedness considerations in the acquisition of conditional sentences. *Language Learning, 335*, 337–372.

Bergman, C. (1976). Interference vs. dependent development in infant bilingualism. In G. Keller, R. Teschner, & S. Viera (Eds.), *Bilingualism in the bicentennial and beyond* (pp. 86–96). New York: Bilingual Press.

Birdsong, D. (1992). Ultimate attainment in second language acquisition. *Language, 68*, 706–755.

Bley-Vroman, R. (1989). What is the logical problem of foreign language learning? In S. Gass & J. Schachter (Eds.), *Linguistic perspectives on second language acquisition* (pp. 41–68). Cambridge: Cambridge University Press.

Bohn, O -S., & Flege, J. E. (1992). The production of new similar vowels by adult German learners of English. *Studies in Second Language Acquisition, 14*, 131–158.

Brière, E. (1966). An investigation of phonological interference. *Language, 42*, 768–796.

Broselow, E. (1985, December). *Metrical phonology and the acquisition of a second language.* Paper presented at the Annual Meeting of the Linguistic Society of America, Seattle, WA.

Broselow, E., & Finer, D. (1991). Parameter setting in second language phonology and syntax. *Second Language Research, 7*, 35–59.

Brown, H. D. (1987). *Principles of language learning and teaching* (2nd ed.). Englewood Cliffs, NJ: Prentice-Hall.

Burling, R. (1973). Language development of a Garo and English-speaking child. In A. Bar-Adon & W. Leopold (Eds.), *Child language: A book of readings* (pp. 170–184). Englewood Cliffs, NJ: Prentice-Hall.

Caramazza, A., Yeni-Komshian, G. H., Zurif, E. B., & Carbone, E. (1973). The acquisition of a new phonological contrast: The case of stop consonants in French English bilinguals. *Journal of the Acoustical Society of America, 54*, 421–428.

Carlisle, R. (1988). The effect of markedness on epenthesis in Spanish/English interlanguage phonology. *IDEAL 3*, 15–23.

Carlisle, R. (1991). The influence of environment on vowel epenthesis in Spanish/English interphonology. *Applied Linguistics, 12*, 76–95.

Chaudron, C., & Parker, K. (1990). Discourse markedness and structural markedness. *Studies in Second Language Acquisition, 12*, 43–64.

Clements, G., & Keyser, S. (1983). *CV phonology: A generative theory of the syllable.* Cambridge, MA: MIT Press.

Clyne, M. (1980). Typology and grammatical convergence among related languages in contact. *Review of Applied Linguistics, 49,* 21–35.

Coates, J. (1986). *Fremdsprachen in Lehre un Forschung* [Pronunciation and personality]. (Vol. 3). Bochum, West Germany: AKS-Verlag.

Contreras, H. (1961). *The phonological system of a bilingual child.* Unpublished doctoral dissertation, Indiana University, Bloomington.

Curtiss, S. (1977). *Genie: A pycholinguistic study of a modern-day "wild child."* New York: Academic Press.

Dickerson, L. J., & Dickerson, W. B. (1977). Interlanguage phonology: Current research and future directions. In S. P. Corder & E. Roulet (Eds.), *The notions of simplification, interlanguages, and pidgins, and their relation to second language pedagogy* (pp. 18–30). Neuchâtel, Switzerland: Faculté des Lettres.

Dorian, N. C. (1981). *Language death: The life cycle of a Scottish Gaelic dialect.* Philadelphia: University of Pennsylvania Press.

Dressler, W. U., & Wodak-Leodolter, R. (1977). *Language death.* The Hague: Mouton.

Eckman, F. R. (1977). Markedness and the contrastive analysis hypothesis. *Language Learning 27,* 315–330.

Eckman, F. R. (1984). Universals, typologies and interlanguage. In W. Rutherford (Ed.), *Language universals and second language acquisition* (pp. 79–105). Amsterdam: John Benjamins.

Eckman, F. R. (1985). Some theoretical and pedagogical implications of the markedness differential hypothesis. *Studies in Second Language Acquisition 7,* 289–307.

Eckman, F. R. (1987). The reduction of word final consonant clusters in interlanguage. In A. James, & J. Leather (Eds.), *Sound patterns in second language acquisition* (pp. 143–162). Dordrecht: Foris.

Eckman, F. R. (1991). The structural conformity hypothesis and the acquisition of consonant clusters in the interlanguage of ESL learners. *Studies in Second Language Acquisition, 13,* 23–41.

Eckman, F. R., Moravcsik, E., & Wirth, J. (1989). Implicational universals and interrogative structures in the interlanguage of ESL learners. *Language Learning, 39,* 173–205.

Edge, B. A. (1991). The production of word-final voiced obstruents in English by L1 speakers of Japanese and Cantonese. *Studies in Second Language Acquisition, 13,* 377–393.

Fantini, A. (1985). *Language acquisition of a bilingual child: A sociolinguistic perspective.* Clevedon, Avon, England: Multilingual Matters.

Fischer, J. L. (1958). Social influences in the choice of a linguistic variant. *Word, 14,* 47–56.

Flege, J. E. (1985). The production and perception of foreign language speech sounds. *Biocommunication Research Reports 4.* (Birmingham, Alabama: University of Alabama at Birmingham), (Also published [1988] in H. Winitz (Ed.), *Human communication and its disorders,* [pp. 224–401], Norwood, NJ: Ablex.)

Flege, J. E. (1987a). A critical period for learning to pronounce foreign languages. *Applied Linguistics, 8,* 162–177.

Flege, J. E. (1987b). The production of "new" and "similar" phones in a foreign language: Evidence for the effect of equivalence classification. *Journal of Phonetics, 15*, 47–65.

Flege, J. E. (1987c). Effects of equivalence classification on the production of foreign language speech sounds. In A. James & J. Leather (Eds.), *Sound patterns in second language acquisition* (pp. 9–39). Dordrecht: Foris.

Flege, J. E. (1990). English vowel production by Dutch talkers: More evidence for the "similar" vs. "new" distinction. In J. Leather & A. James (Eds.), *New sounds 90: Proceedings of the Amsterdam Symposium on the Acquisition of Second-Language Speech* (pp. 255–293). Amsterdam: University of Amsterdam.

Flege, J. E., & Davidian, R. (1984). Transfer and developmental processes in adult foreign language speech production. *Applied Psycholinguistics, 5*, 323–347

Flege, J. E., & Hillenbrand, J. (1984). Limits of phonetic accuracy in foreign language production. *Journal of the Acoustical Society of America, 76*, 708–721.

Flynn, S. (1987). *A parameter-setting model of L2 acquisition.* Dordrecht: D. Reidel.

Freed, B. F. (1980, November). *The problem of language skill loss.* Paper presented at the Annual Meeting of Modern Language Association, New York.

Gardner, R. C., & Lambert, W. E. (1972). *Attitudes and motivation in second language learning.* Rowley, MA: Newbury House.

Gardner, R. C., & MacIntyre, P. D. (1991). An instrumental motivation language study: Who says it isn't effective? *Studies in Second Language Acquisition, 13*, 57–72.

Gardner, R. C., Day, J. B., & MacIntyre, P. D. (1992). Integrative motivation, induced anxiety, and language learning in a controlled environment. *Studies in Second Language Acquisition, 14*, 197–214.

Gatbonton, E. (1978). Patterned phonetic variability inn second-language speech: A gradual diffusion model. *Canadian Modern Language Review, 34*, 335–347.

Giles, H. (1973), Accent mobility: A model and some data. *Anthropological Linguistics, 15*, 247–252.

Giles, H., & Johnson, P. (1987). Ethnolinguistic identity theory: A social psychological approach to language maintenance. *International Journal of the Sociology of Language, 68*, 69–100.

Giles, H., Mulac, A., Bradac, J. J., & Johnson, P. (1987). Speech accommodation theory: .The first decade and beyond. In M. L. McLaughlin (Ed.), *Communication yearbook 10* (pp. 13–48). Beverly Hills: Sage.

Goldsmith, J. (1990). *Autosegmental and metrical phonology.* Cambridge, MA: Basil Blackwell.

Guiora, A. Z., Acton, W. R., Erard, R., & Strickland, F. W. (1980). The effects of benzodiazepine (Valium) on permeability of language ego boundaries. *Language Learning, 2*, 111–130.

Guiora, A. Z., Beit-Hallami, B., Brannon, R. C. L., & Dull, C. Y. (1972) The effects of experimentally induced changes in ego states on pronunciation ability in second language: An exploratory study. *Comprehensive Psychiatry, 30*, 351–364.

Gussenhoven, C. (1979). *Pronunciation preference among Dutch students.* Paper presented at the Second International Conference on the Teaching of Spoken English, University of Leeds.

Hecht, B., & Mulford, R. (1982). The acquisition of a second-language phonology: Interaction of transfer and developmental factors. *Applied Psycholinguistics, 3*, 313–328.

Hodne, B. (1985). Yet another look at interlanguage phonology: The modification of English syllable structure by native speakers of Polish. *Language Learning, 35,* 405–422.

Huebner, T., & Ferguson, C. (Eds.). (1991). *Crosscurrents in second language acquisition and linguistic theories. (Language acquisition and language disorders 2).* Amsterdam & Philadelphia: John Benjamins.

Imedadze, N. V. (1967). On the psychological nature of child speech formation under condition of exposure to two languages. *International Journal of Psychology, 2,* 129–132.

James, A. (1986). *Suprasegmental phonology and segmental form.* Tübingen: Niemeyer.

James, A. (1987). Prosodic structure in phonological acquisition. *Second Language Research, 3,* 118–140.

James, A. (1988). *The acquisition of a second language phonology.* Tübingen: Narr.

James, A. (1989). Linguistic theory and second language phonological learning: A perspective and some proposals. *Applied Linguistics, 10,* 367–381.

James, A. (1990). A parameter-setting model for second language phonological acquisition? In J. Leather & A. James (Eds.), *New sounds 90: Proceedings of the Amsterdam Symposium on the Acquisition of Second-Language Speech* (pp. 180–188). Amsterdam: University of Amsterdam.

Johansson, F. A. (1973). *Immigrant Swedish phonology.* Lund, Sweden: Gleerup.

Kaufman, D., & Aronoff, M. (1991). Morphological disintegration and reconstruction in first language attrition. In H. W. Seliger, & R. M. Vago (Eds.), *First language attrition: Structural and theoretical perspectives.* Cambridge: Cambridge University Press.

Krashen, S. D., Scarcella, R. C., & Long, M. H. (Eds.). (1982). *Child-adult differences in second language acquisition.* Rowley, MA: Newbury House.

Labov, W. (1963), The social motivation of sound change. *Word, 19,* 273–309.

Labov, W. (1972), *Sociolinguistic patterns.* Philadelphia: University of Pennsylvania Press.

Lado, R. (1957). *Linguistics across cultures.* Ann Arbor: University of Michigan Press.

Leather, J. (1987). Fo pattern inference in the perceptual acquisition of second language tone. In J. Leather & A. James (Eds.), *New sounds 90: Proceedings of the Amsterdam Symposium on the Acquisition of Second-Language Speech* (pp. 59–80). Amsterdam: University of Amsterdam.

Leather, J. (1990). Perceptual and productive learning of Chinese lexical tone by Dutch and English speakers. In J. Leather & A. James (Eds.), *New sounds 90: Proceedings of the Amsterdam Symposium on the Acquisition of Second-Language Speech* (pp. 72–97). Amsterdam: University of Amsterdam.

Leather, J., & James, A. (1991). The acquisition of second language speech. *Studies in Second Language Acquisition, 13,* 305–341.

Leopold, W. (1939, 1944, 1949a, 1949b). *Speech development of a bilingual child: A linguist's record. Vol. 1: Vocabulary growth in the first two years. Vol. 2: Sound learning in the first two years. Vol. 3: Grammar and general problems in the first two years. Vol. 4: Diary from age two.* Evanston , IL: Northwestern University Press.

Long, M. H. (1990). Maturational constraints on language development. *Studies in Second Language Acquisition, 12,* 251–285.

Macedo, D. P. (1986). The role of core grammar in pidgin development. *Language Learning, 36,* 65–75.

Major, R. C. (1977). Phonological differentiation of a bilingual child. Ohio State University Working *Papers in Linguistics, 22*, 88–122. [ERIC Document Reproduction Service No. ED 149 644.]

Major, R. C. (1985). Stress and rhythm in Brazilian Portuguese. *Language, 61*, 259–282.

Major, R. C. (1986). The ontogeny model: Evidence from L2 acquisition of Spanish *r*. *Language Learning, 36*, 453–504.

Major, R. C. (1987a). A model for interlanguage phonology. In G. Ioup & S. H. Weinberger (Eds.), *Interlanguage Phonology: The acquisition of a second language sound system* (pp. 101–124). New York: Newbury House/Harper & Row.

Major, R. C. (1987b). Foreign accent: Recent research and theory. IRAL: *International Review of Applied Linguistics in Language Teaching, 25*, 185–202.

Major, R. C. (1987c). English voiceless stop production by Brazilian speakers of English. *Journal of Phonetics, 15*, 197–202.

Major, R. C. (1992). Losing English as a first language. *Modern Language Journal, 76*, 190–208.

Major, R. C. (in press). Native and nonnative phonological representations. In *Proceedings of the Natural Phonology Workshop at the 1990 Annual Meeting of the Societas Linguistica Europaea*. B. Hurch & R. Rhodes (Eds.). The Hague: Mouton.

Nemser, W. (1971). *An experimental study of phonological interference in the English of Hungarians*. Bloomington: Indiana University Press.

Odlin, T. (1989). *Language transfer: Cross linguistic influence in language learning*. Cambridge: Cambridge University Press.

Oller, J. W., & Ziahosseiny, S. M. (1970). The contrastive analysis hypothesis and spelling errors. *Language Learning, 20*, 183–189.

Piper, T. (1984). Observations on the second-language acquisition of the English sound system. *Canadian Modern Language Review, 40*, 542–551.

Preston, D. R. (1989). *Sociolinguistics and Second Language Acquisition*. New York: Basil Blackwell.

Puppel, S., & Marton, W. (1991). Towards a dynamic model of acquisition of second language phonology. *International Journal of Applied Linguistics, 1*, 89–103.

Riney, T. (1989). Syllable structure and interlanguage phonology. *Kansas Working Papers in Linguistics, 14*. Lawrence: University of Kansas.

Rutherford, W. (1982). Markedness in second language acquisition. *Language Learning, 32*, 85–108.

Sato, C. J. (1984). Phonological processes in second language acquisition: Another look at interlanguage syllable structure. *Language Learning, 34*, 43–57.

Sato, C. J. (1985). Task variation in interlanguage phonology. In S. Gass & C. Madden (Eds.), *Input in second language acquisition* (pp. 181–196). Rowley, MA: Newbury House.

Schmidt, R. W. (1977). Sociolinguistic variation and transfer in phonology. *Working Papers in Bilingualism, 12*, 79–95.

Scovel, T. (1981). The recognition of foreign accents in English and its implications for psycholinguistic theories of language acquisition. In *Proceedings of the 5th International Association of Applied Linguistics* (pp. 389–401). Montreal: Laval University Press.

Scovel, T. (1988). *A time to speak: A psycholinguistic inquiry in to the critical period for human speech.* New York: Newbury House/Harper & Row.

Sharwood Smith, M. (1983a). On explaining language loss. In S. Felix & S. Wode (Eds.), *Language development at the crossroads: Papers for the Interdisciplinary Conference on Language Acquisition at Passau* (pp. 49–59). Tübingen: Narr.

Sharwood Smith, M. (1983b). On first language loss in the second language acquirer: Problems of transfer. In S. Gass, & L. Selinker (Eds.), *Language transfer in language learning* (pp. 222–231). Rowley, MA: Newbury House.

Sharwood Smith, M., & van Buren, P. (1991). First language attrition and the parameter-setting model. In H. W. Seliger & R. M. Vago (Eds.), *First language attrition: Structural and theoretical perspectives.* Cambridge: Cambridge University Press.

Stampe, D. (1969). The acquisition of phonetic representation. *Papers from the Fifth Regional Meeting of the Chicago Linguistic Society* (pp. 443–453). Chicago: University of Chicago Press.

Stampe, D. (1987). On phonological representations. In W. U. Dressler, H. C. Luschützky, O. E. Pfeiffer, & J. R. Rennison (Eds.), *Phonologica 1984: Proceedings of the First International Phonology Meeting Eisentadt* (pp. 287–299). London: Cambridge University Press.

Swain, M., & Wesche, M. (1973). Linguistic interaction: A case study of a bilingual child. *Working Papers in Bilingualism, 1,* 10–34.

Tarone, E. (1979). Interlanguage as chameleon. *Language Learning, 29,* 181–191.

Tarone, E. (1987). Some influences on the syllable structure of interlanguage phonology. In G. Ioup & S. H. Weinberger (Eds.), *Interlanguage phonology: The acquisition of a second language sound system* (pp. 232–247). New York: Newbury House.

Tarone, E. (1988). *Variation in interlanguage.* London: Edward Arnold.

Thomason, S. G., & Kaufman, T. (1988). *Language contact, creolization, and genetic linguistics.* Berkeley: University of California Press.

Trudgill, P. (1974). *The social differentiation of English in Norwich.* Cambridge: Cambridge University Press.

Van Coetsem, F. (1988). *Loan phonology and the two transfer types in language contact.* Dordrecht: Foris.

Vogel, I. (1991). Prosodic phonology: second language acquisition data as evidence in theoretical phonology. In T. Huebner & C. Ferguson (Eds.), *Crosscurrents in second language acquisition and linguistic theories* (pp. 47–65). Amsterdam/Philadelphia: John Benjamins.

Wardhaugh, R. (1970). The contrastive analysis hypothesis. *TESOL Quarterly, 4,* 123–130

Weinberger, S. (1990). Minimal segments in L2 phonology. In J. Leather & A. James (Eds.), *New sounds 90: Proceedings of the Amsterdam Symposium on the Acquisition of Second-Language Speech* (pp. 137–179). Amsterdam: University of Amsterdam.

Weinreich, U. (1953). *Languages in contact.* New York: Linguistic Circle of New York.

Wenk, B. (1979). Articulatory setting and de-fossilization. *Interlanguage Studies Bulletin, 4,* 202–220.

White, L. (1987). Markedness and second language transfer: The question of transfer. *Studies in Second Language Acquisition, 9,* 261–266.

White, L. (1989). *Universal grammar and second language acquisition*. Amsterdam: John Benjamins.

White, L. (1990). Second language acquisition and universal grammar. *Studies in Second Language Acquisition 12*, 121–133.

Wilson, D., & Møllergard, E. (1981). Errors in the production of vowel no. 10 /ɐ/ by Norwegian learners of English. *IRAL: International Review of Applied Linguistics in Language Teaching: International Review of Applied Linguistics, 19*, 69–76.

Wode, H. (1980). Phonology in L2 acquisition. In S. Felix (Ed.), *Second language development* (pp. 123–136). Tübingen: Narr.

Wode, H. (1981). *Learning a second language*. Tübingen: Narr.

Young-Scholten, M. (1985). Interference reconsidered: The role of similarity in second language acquisition. *Selecta, 6*, 6–12.

# CHAPTER 9

## The Critical Age Hypothesis and Interlanguage Phonology

MARK S. PATKOWSKI, Ph.D.

It will be argued here that the findings from studies on age-related differences in the ability to acquire the phonological system of a second language are highly consistent with the notion of an optimal period for such acquisition. To be more precise, it will be argued that the research focused on ultimate, or at least long-term, attainment of the sound system of a second language provides robust evidence of the superiority of younger learners over older learners, while uncovering no counter-evidence to this claim.

This task is made easier by the recent publication of two texts (Scovel, 1988; Singleton, 1989) and an exhaustive review article (Long, 1990), which are devoted entirely to examining the evidence for and against the critical period hypothesis (though the terms "critical," "sensitive" or "optimal" will be used interchangeably herein). These three sources, therefore, will first be examined for their conclusions relevant to the issue of an optimal period specifically for phonological acquisition in second languages. Then, three recent studies (Flege, 1991; Flege & Fletcher, 1992; Thompson, 1991) which directly compare the acquisition of early and late learners will be similarly scrutinized.

To state it formally, the assertion that is claimed to be sustained by all the relevant research is the following:

> There is a period, ending around the time of puberty (operationally defined to mean somewhere between the ages of 12 and 15 years), during which it is possible, but not inevitable, for learners to acquire, as an end-product of a naturalistic L2 acquisition process, full native-like fluency in the phonological system of a second language, and after which such a possibility does not exist anymore. Thus, a comparison between younger and older learners of their long-term achievement (operationally defined to mean that naturalistic exposure has occurred for at least 5 years or so under "advantaged" sociological, cultural, psychological, and affective circumstances) should reveal (a) that only younger learners can sometimes be shown to attain full native-like phonological L2 competence, and (b) that, overall, there is a strong statistical difference in the long-term achievement of younger and older learners.

This definition, although wordier, is essentially that used in Oyama's (1976) seminal study in which the optimal period was defined as stretching from about 18 months to puberty, and as being a time during which a learner can master the phonology of a second language but after which complete acquisition becomes very unlikely if not impossible. This definition, furthermore, is consonant with Lenneberg's (1967) view of the critical period as being a time of "peculiar sensitivities, response propensities, or learning *potentials*" (p. 175, emphasis added).

The evidence for such a period is examined without delving into possible causes (neurological, psychosocial, cognitive, or other); thus, the claim being made here is clearly a limited but nevertheless important one, because even this limited claim has been highly controversial in the field of second language acquisition for decades. The author believes, however, that the time has come for the field to accept the notion of an age-related constraint on language acquisition, and for the controversy to circumscribe itself to the discussion of its causes.

## REVIEW OF THREE RECENT REVIEWS

Attention will now be turned to the three aforementioned reviews; the purpose is not to examine in detail all aspects and claims put forth in these texts, but to focus on the aspects most relevant to the issue at hand, namely, the research evidence concerning long-term attainment in second language phonology. Scovel (1988), Singleton (1989), and Long (1990) will be reviewed in their chronological order of publication.

Scovel, in *A Time to Speak: A Psycholinguistic Inquiry into the Critical Period for Human Speech*, places great emphasis on what he terms the "Conrad phenomenon," named after the Polish-born author whose control of the written form of the English language allowed him to produce some of the great masterpieces of the English language literature, while at the same time his spoken language remained so poor throughout his life that he decided to forego the well-remunerated American lecture circuit that so many of his contemporaries and successors plied to their financial advantage. This term thus refers to Scovel's strongly held notion that there is a clear critical period for the acquisition of second language phonology whereas there are no such constraints on the acquisition of various other aspects of a second language, such as syntax in particular. Indeed, that is the fundamental thesis of his book, which reviews evidence from paleontology, ethology, sociobiology, neurology, the study of feral children (ferology?), and language acquisition studies. For the purposes of this discussion, attention will be devoted primarily to those chapters most directly relevant to the issue under consideration, namely Chapters 3 and 6 which present the Conrad phenomenon and discuss evidence from language acquisition research.

In Chapter 3, after discussing Penfield and Roberts' (1959) and Lenneberg's (1967) classic notions of a neurologically based optimal age for the acquisition of language, Scovel presents one of his own early accent recognition studies (Scovel, 1969) which demonstrated that 117 untrained, native-speaking, junior high school students could easily and accurately identify non-native speakers of English on the basis of hearing a short, taped greeting spoken twice by 10 subjects. Five subjects were native speakers of American English, and five were L2 speakers who had learned the language "after childhood," and who knew English "very well and wrote so competently that it would be impossible to ascertain whether they were 'native writers' of American English given their written work alone" (pp. 59–60).

Later experiments, reported in Chapter 6, illustrated that 146 even younger native children could just as easily recognize accented speech, reaching an adult level of accuracy (which Scovel set at 95%) by the age of 9 or 10 years. In contrast, 92 ESL college students performed so poorly that even advanced level non-natives were outperformed both by 6-year-old natives and by a group of 23 native aphasics. In this case, there were 20 subjects, 10 natives and 10 nonnatives. The latter group had all lived in an English-speaking country for at least 5 years and were or had been graduate students in the United States; age at the start of acquisition is not given but can be deduced from other information as being above 15 in all cases. In contrast to the accent recognition tasks, Scovel also found that essays written by his subjects could not be distinguished by the judges as native or non-native; indeed, 31 adult American English judges achieved a 95% accuracy rate in the accent recognition task, but only a 57% accuracy rate (more or less chance level) in correctly appraising whether compositions were written by natives or not, thus demonstrating that the subjects' English language competence had reached a high level.

Scovel presents his results to demonstrate the validity of the Conrad phenomenon. For the purposes of this discussion, and leaving aside the issue of whether the composition task in question truly demonstrated "full-native syntactic competence," it is clear that the results are fully consistent with the hypothesis presented in this paper's introduction.

Scovel then reviews the collective evidence from other studies, including such well known ones as Asher and Garcia (1969); Seliger, Krashen, and Ladefoged (1975); Oyama (1976); and Tahta, Wood and Loewenthal (1981). The methodologies varied, but all four of these studies dealt with the phonological attainment of immigrants to various countries. Oyama's study is the most clearly focused on eventual achievement, as her sample included only subjects whose length of residence in the L2 country ranged above 5 years. However, even though the other studies included subjects whose length of residence was as low as 1 or 2 years, because of large sample sizes (which range from 60 for Oyama to 394 for Seliger et al.) and because of upper ranges of length of residence as high as 55 years, the information gathered can still be considered as germane to the issue of eventual achievement, and clearly is relevant to the question concerning the abilities of younger and older learners to "pass for native." In addition, it should be noted that Oyama's findings were fully replicated with a similar size sample of subjects who had also resided in the L2 country for a minimum of 5 years (Patkowski, 1990, pp. 78–80).

It is noteworthy that all the above studies found a marked phonological advantage for earlier L2 learners, and none found any effects on long-term achievement for other practice or motivational factors when tested for. Scovel came to a similar conclusion, and considered the evidence for a critical period for the ability to sound like a native speaker "so overwhelming that (he) cannot see how its existence can be denied; so compelling that non-biological factors alone cannot account for its etiology" (p. 122).

Singleton (1989) takes a far more skeptical view in his *Language Acquisition: The Age Factor*. Indeed, the theme of his book seems to be that the evidence on age-related differences is murky and contradictory. Singleton does, however, find some consistent results in the language acquisition literature. For example, in Chapter 2, his reading of the evidence on (first) language development in infants and children is that it clearly supports the notion of stable speech milestones that unfold within relatively well defined age ranges. He notes that findings in abnormal first language development also support the concept of speech milestones, as when, for example, normal babbling and cooing occur in deaf babies. The existence of speech milestones had been one of the arguments advanced by Lenneberg for the biological basis of language. On the other hand, Singleton also finds first language evidence to support the notion that L1 acquisition continues well beyond the purported critical period into late adulthood, particularly in the areas of lexical acquisition and of "meta-memorial skills," although it is unclear to this writer why vocabulary development and certain memory tasks are considered relevant to the issue of a critical period for language.

Be that as it may, the chapter which is by far the most relevant to this review is clearly Chapter 4, which is devoted to second language evidence. In this chapter, Singleton reviews four positions which, according to him, have been at the center of the critical period debate. The positions are the following: (1) The "younger = better" position; (2) its opposite, the "older = better" position; (3) the "younger = better at acquiring accent and basic interpersonal communicative skills (BICS)" position; (4) the "younger = better in the long run" position. A final section of this chapter deals with possible age-related differences in the process of second language acquisition. It can be seen that the fourth position is most relevant to this discussion, and it will be reviewed last and in the greatest detail.

The problem, to this writer at least, with the first three positions is that they fail to differentiate between short- and long-term studies and between naturalistic and formal language exposure conditions, although Singleton does allude to these factors when reviewing studies under each category. Thus, in considering position 1, Singleton begins by referring to observations made in 1925 concerning the common habit of adult British residents in India of bringing along their 4- or 5-year- old children to act as interpreters in their dealings with the house-servants. He then switches to a discussion of American studies of the effects of the foreign languages in elementary schools (FLES) programs of the 1960s. This back and forth continues, eventually covering the long-term studies mentioned above such as Oyama, Seliger et al., and so on. Not surprisingly, Singleton concludes that hypothesis 1 is not supported by the available evidence.

A similar pattern unfolds with respect to position 2, which is after all only the opposite of the first. Here the tendency is in fact to examine short-term studies involving formal instruction, although not to the absolute exclusion of naturalistic long-term investigations. Again, the evidence is found inconclusive. Position 3 fares no better, although Singleton does refine the parameters somewhat; thus position 3 seeks to examine findings relevant to the question of whether L2 learners of different ages enjoy selective advantages, and in particular, whether younger learners are more efficient in acquiring native-like L2 pronunciation. However, studies involving naturalistic exposure as well as formal instruction in real or even artificial languages are again discussed side by side, and again, the evidence is found inconclusive. With respect to the last issue which Singleton examines in the chapter, namely whether differences in the process of L2 acquisition can be uncovered between younger and older learners, some limited evidence is found in favor of such differences. For example, the author feels that studies have demonstrated a greater contribution of IQ to L2 acquisition with older learners; nevertheless, the overall evidence on process is again found contradictory and difficult to interpret.

It is thus, in this writer's opinion, particularly revealing to note that Singleton does find clear supportive evidence, and no actual counter-evidence, for the notion that learners who begin second language acquisition as children and under naturalistic conditions achieve higher levels of proficiency in the long run. Here, Singleton, like Scovel, quotes the immigrant studies (e.g., Asher and Garcia, 1969; Seliger et al., 1975; Oyama, 1976; Patkowski, 1980). Although Singleton does not really separate his discussions of long-term attainment in syntactic, morphological, and phonological aspects of a second language, as has been seen earlier, the above studies (with the exception of Patkowski, 1980) do focus on accent.

In this section, Singleton pays special attention to Snow and Hoefnagel-Hohle (1978) who examined English speakers residing in Holland and learning Dutch and found that, despite initial higher gains for older learners, in the longer run the advantage returned to their younger counterparts, in what was a natural exposure situation. To this writer, a most interesting finding from the Snow and Hoefnagel-Hohle research, which Singleton does not discuss, concerns the significant differences which were uncovered in the speech rates of younger and older learners. Learners aged 5 to 15 years reached approximately (the figures quoted here are read from a diagram) 1.4 words per second, up from initial rates of .15 to .8 words per second. The adults, in contrast, attained only a rate of .8, up from .6 words per second a year earlier. Thus, subjects who acquired a second language before the close of puberty appeared to speak considerably faster than their adult counterparts; it seems intuitively plausible to posit that this difference reflected, to some degree, a greater control of the L2 phonological system of the early acquirers.

Singleton concludes the section on eventual attainment as follows: "to sum up . . . there is a fair amount of evidence suggestive of a long-term advantage for learners whose experience of the target language begins in their childhood years. Most of this relates to natural exposure situations... There is no counter-evidence from natural exposure studies" (p. 122).

Although not as ringing an endorsement as Scovel's, it is nevertheless a significant one, given the author's highly skeptical approach to the critical period hypothesis.

For Long (1990), the evidence is neither murky nor contradictory; it is in fact seen as being very strongly supportive of the following hypothesis:

> There are sensitive periods governing the ultimate level of first or second language attainment possible in different linguistic domains, not just phonology, with cumulative declines in learning capacity, not a catastrophic one-time loss, and beginning as early as age 6 in many individuals, not at puberty as is often claimed. (p. 255)

Long further argues that while many critics reject the notion of maturational constraints as counter-intuitive in itself, it is in fact the opposite hypothesis, that there are no such constraints, which is the marked hypothesis, given the well established maturationally based constraints which have been uncovered in the development of other animal species, in other kinds of human learning, and in other human neurological abilities. Of course, Lenneberg and Scovel have both presented a similar point of view.

Long then turns his attention to the relevant first and second language literature and, as already mentioned, finds the facts convincing. With respect to normal first language acquisition, he notes, like Singleton, that the existence of a language-specific maturational schedule, which is independent of general cognitive development, is well established. With respect to abnormal first language acquisition, his review of two cases of feral children (Curtiss, 1977; Mason, 1942), and of several studies involving the acquisition of American Sign Language by deaf subjects of various ages (in particular, Newport, 1984) leads him to conclude that the findings "combine to provide compelling evidence of maturational constraints" (p. 259)

As before, it is Long's view on the issue of long-term L2 phonological attainment that is of interest. Again, the Oyama, Asher, and Garcia, and Tahta et al. studies, among others, are reviewed. Long concludes unequivocally in support of maturational constraints but, interestingly, suggests that these constraints begin to set in as early as age 6. In fact, Long states that "exposure needs to occur before age 6 to guarantee that an L2 phonology can become native-like" (p. 274).

To this writer, Long's assertion is worded too strongly to be supported by the data. Tahta et al. (1981) found 31 of 60 learners whose ages at the start of L2 acquisition ranged from 7 to 12 years to be accent-free (Table 1, p. 268). Oyama (1973) found 8 of 25 learners, within the same age range at the start of L2, to be accent-free on the more demanding of her two accent tasks (Figure 1, p. 68). Patkowski (1990) found 8 of 23 learners whose ages at L2 ranged from 7 to 15 years (or 7 of 19 learners with an age range of 7–12 years) whose pronunciation was also judged accent-free (Figure 2, p. 79). Long does, in fact, allow that, at least in some learners, the onset of maturational constraints may come as late as age 12; it therefore seems to this writer that Long's assertion about the need for exposure before age 6 to "guarantee" a native accent in a second language is insufficiently supported by the data.

Returning to the three studies discussed in the preceding paragraph, it should be noted that, in all cases, not a single adult learner obtained an accent-free rating. The subjects with the highest age at the start of L2 acquisition to acquire native ratings were 12 years old for Tahta et al. (with 109 subjects), 11 years old for Oyama (with 60 subjects), and 15 years old for Patkowski (one case, with the next two cases being 11 years old, with 67 subjects). The other two-long term studies, Asher and Garcia (1969) and Seliger et al. (1975), did not provide any evidence relevant to this issue. The former found that none of 71 subjects received a native accent rating; the latter employed self-ratings by 394 subjects, and although 12 of 173 learners who had begun L2 acquisition after the age of 15 years considered themselves to have no accent, the unreliability of a self-assessment measure for this purpose seems self-evident (although there is no reason to think that, with such a large sample size, the vagaries of personal reporting would essentially alter the general comparison between the L2 abilities of the younger and older learners).

Thus, the available evidence does seem to bear out the twin claims, made in the introduction, that (a) only younger learners can sometimes be shown to attain full native-like phonological L2 competence and (b) overall, there is a strong statistical difference in the long-term achievement of younger and older learners. In addition, it does clearly emerge from this review of Scovel (1988), Singleton (1989), and Long (1990), that all three authors, having extensively reviewed the available evidence on the notion of an age-related limitation on language acquisition, are essentially in agreement on the second claim, and that two (Scovel and Long) are in essential agreement on the first claim while Singleton does not specifically either refute or accept this assertion. The question to which we now turn, then, is whether any counter-evidence has appeared since the publication of the three reviews.

# THREE RECENT LONG-TERM ATTAINMENT STUDIES

A search of the relevant literature from 1990 to 1992 (i.e., since the publication of the three reviews just discussed), found three further studies germane to the issue of long-term L2 phonological achievement by learners of different ages.

A study by Thompson (1991) clearly falls into the mold of the long-term accent research of Oyama (1973, 1976) and Tahta et al. (1981). Speech samples of Russian immigrants to the United States were collected according to three procedures (free speech, reading of a prose passage, and reading of sentences constructed to contain difficult sounds) and were rated for accentedness. Thompson also examined a wide range of independent variables (including age at arrival, length of residence, degree of English-language usage, sex, self-reported characteristics such as ability to mimic, musicality, motivation, extraversion). The data were gathered by a questionnaire.

A correlational analysis showed that age at arrival was the best predictor of degree of accent; other variables, including length of residence, years of education in English, and English language usage were correlated among themselves and confounded with age at arrival. Therefore, a multiple regression analysis was carried out, and age at arrival again emerged as the most significant predictor variable, contributing to 66% of the variance in accent scores. Length of residence and English exposure variables dropped out of the multiple regression.

One difference between this study and previous long-term studies is that the sample size was markedly smaller (36 subjects, as opposed to 60 to 394 subjects for the earlier studies), and another that the distribution of age at the onset of L2 seems rather unbalanced, based on the information which is revealed. Thus, we are only told that the range was from 4 to 42 years, and that just six of the subjects had arrived in the United States before the age of 10. Clearly, both a larger sample size and a more balanced range of age at arrival would be preferred. Nevertheless, Thompson's results clearly show that age of arrival

> was the best indicator of the accuracy of (subjects') pronunciation in English, accounting for well over half the variance in their accent scores.

> The effect of Age at Arrival in the U.S. was so great that most other
> independent variables had relatively little to contribute to the prediction of
> success in mastering English pronunciation. (p. 195)

Thus, assertion (b) of the hypothesis stated in this paper's introduction
is supported.

At the same time, there is no confirming evidence to be found here for
assertion (a), as even those six subjects who had arrived in this country
before the age of 10 were not consistently judged to be accent-free. These
results, then, are similar to those reported by Asher and Garcia (1969), but
unlike those uncovered by Oyama (1973, 1976), Tahta et al. (1981), and
Patkowski (1990). It would be appropriate to reiterate, at this point, that
the sensitive period hypothesis does not "guarantee" accent-free speech
for younger L2 learners, but merely states that the *potential* exists until
the close of the sensitive period and ceases to exist thereafter. For that
potential to be realized, socio-affective, cognitive, and other factors must
be optimal. As was seen in section 2 of this paper, the available evidence
does show that only L2 learners who began naturalistic exposure before
the close of the hypothesized sensitive period have received accent-less
ratings, and that the eventual performance of younger learners is
consistently higher than that of older learners.

Furthermore, assertion (b) is supported by findings in Flege (1991),
and assertions (a) and (b) are both supported by findings in Flege and
Fletcher (1992). Thus, Flege (1991) examined how well 10 early and 10
late learners of English would produce the English /t/ and whether
learning English would affect the production of their native Spanish /t/.
Again, the sample size in this study (as well as in the following) was
somewhat limited, but the early and late groups are of equal size.
Subjects read words beginning with /t/ at the end of a brief carrier
phrase ("Take a _____" or "Tengo un _____") and voice onset time
(VOT) was measured. Four of the early learners had been born in Mexico
and the other six in border towns in Texas. All were unable to speak
English when they began school, but all had native-speaking American
teachers in the first three grades and/or a majority of native-speaking
classmates, and Flege reported that they spoke without accent. The late
learners' mean age of arrival in the United States was 20 years.

Results showed that early learners did not differ significantly from
monolingual native VOT norms in their production of both the English and
Spanish /t/. In contrast, late learners produced the English /t/ with VOT
values considerably shorter than those of monolingual English speakers.

In a second experiment, seven subjects each from the original groups
were required to produce Spanish and English /t/ in words, phrases, and

sentences in alternation. A "switching time" difference was uncovered favoring early learners. Flege interpreted his results to support the position that learners who begin L2 acquisition in early childhood, but not older learners, are able to establish phonetic categories in L2 that are independent of the speakers' corresponding L1 categories.

Flege and Fletcher (1992) report on four experiments, but one in particular is of the most direct relevance to the issue under consideration. In this experiment, three groups of 10 native Spanish speakers each were rated for accent by 10 native speakers of American English who indicated the degree of perceived accent by positioning a lever on a response box (yielding a total of 256 possible values) after hearing sentences. The first group consisted of early learners, similar to those described above, whose age of L2 learning ranged from 0 to 6 years; the next two groups consisted of late learners whose age at L2 ranged from 11 to 35 years and who were either experienced (mean length of residence in the United States = 7 years) or inexperienced (mean length of residence = 0.3 year).

The scores of the early learners were almost identical to the scores obtained by native speakers, leading Flege and Fletcher to conclude that the early learners had no perceptible foreign accent. On the other hand, the late learners' scores were considerably lower than those of both natives and early L2 learners (50–80% lower, based on Figure 1, p. 375). Flege and Fletcher (1992) also correlated various independent variables with degree of accent, and found no effect for gender or degree of English-language usage. Age at arrival again showed the highest degree of correlation with accent; and as in Thompson (1991), length of residence and formal education also were correlated with accent as well as with each other and with age at arrival. Thus, a multiple regression analysis was also carried out in which age at arrival again emerged as the most significant independent variable, accounting for 79.8% of the variance in accent scores. English language instruction increased the $R^2$ value to 85%, and none of the other variables were found to be significant predictors of accent.

Other experiments discussed in this paper examined listener- and talker-related factors which affected native perceptions of foreign accent. Although range effects were found (i.e., it was found that perceptions can be influenced by the proportion of native speech samples included in the set to be evaluated), the authors concluded that listeners can make reliable judgments of degree of accent. Another finding was that native Chinese subjects with an average age at L2 acquisition of 7.6 years did have detectable non-native accents, unlike the early Spanish learners. The authors interpreted this as tentative support for Long's hypothesis that foreign accents emerge as early as age 6.

In their general discussion, Flege and Fletcher (1992) propose the following scheme, with respect to the age factor in the acquisition of L2 phonology.

> One might hypothesize that a perceptible foreign accent is highly unusual for individuals who begin learning an L2 before reaching the age of six years, is almost always evident for post-pubescent learners, and is evident in an increasing proportion of individuals who begin L2 learning between the ages of about 6 to 12 years. (p. 385)

In addition, Flege and Fletcher propose that variability in learners' degree of accent increases progressively from age 6, when foreign accents first emerge, until some time after the teens. They further speculate that foreign accents become increasingly marked after puberty. Finally, the authors note that their "hypotheses are consistent with observations . . . concerning sensitive periods" (p. 386).

## CONCLUSION

The relevant literature concerning the ultimate phonological attainment of second language learners who began L2 acquisition under conditions of naturalistic exposure at different ages is compelling; the claim, as worded in the introduction, that a sensitive period exists for the acquisition of phonology in a second language is strongly supported, and no counter-evidence exists. It seems, to this writer at least, that the time has come for the controversy which has surrounded this issue to move to the area of providing an explanation for the observed phenomenon, rather than to continue questioning the existence of the phenomenon itself.

As every participant in this controversy knows, there is still plenty left to debate. For example, despite the quotes from Flege and Fletcher reported above, Flege (1992) clearly continues to reject the notion of a neurological or biological basis to this sensitive period. He finds that the relationship between lateralization and language learning ability, which was proposed by Lenneberg as an explanation for the critical period, has not been established and that chronological age is confounded with too many other factors to make it possible to persuasively demonstrate the existence of maturational constraints. He seeks to explain the difficulties of late learners on the basis of the development and stabilization of the L1 phonetic system itself, perhaps as a consequence of the onset of the Piagetian stage of concrete operations.

Scovel (1988), on the other hand, finds that studies in aphasiology, as well as dichotic studies and studies concerning the results of hemispherectomies, may contradict some of the details of Lenneberg's formulation, but leave his essential thesis mostly intact. Scovel thus considers the evidence convincing in explaining the existence of a critical period, but one which is solely limited to the acquisition of phonology. Singleton (1989), not surprisingly, considers the evidence from aphasiology contradictory and basically rejects attempts at explaining the critical period hypothesis with reference to the process of cerebral lateralization and neuroplasticity. Yet, he does admit that, as Lenneberg had asserted, similar cerebral lesions cause different aphasic disorders depending on whether the victim is a child or an adult and that the younger brain is more adaptable and more capable of transferring functions than the older brain. Long (1990) and Patkowski (1990) believe that maturational constraints are linked to a loss of the brain's plasticity (as Lenneberg had proposed) but that this loss is not necessarily due to the process of lateralization as envisaged by Lenneberg. Indeed, Long favors the myelination of neural pathways as a potential explanation for the decline in language learning capacity, but recognizes the speculative nature of this position. However, he does consider that the cumulative evidence from feral children, from the acquisition of sign language by deaf children, from first language acquisition by normal and mentally retarded children, and from second language acquisition studies to be overwhelmingly in support of his notion of multiple critical periods for language acquisition; and he finds affective, input, and cognitive explanations unconvincing.

Clearly, proposals to explain what this writer takes to now be a statistically well-established claim in favor of age-related constraints on eventual L2 phonological attainment will continue to generate debate and controversy for the foreseeable future.

## INSTRUCTIONAL IMPLICATIONS

Before examining the role of age in language learning from a pedagogical point of view, it is useful to reiterate that the notion of an age-related advantage applies only to L2 acquisition under "naturalistic conditions" and is essentially irrelevant to issues surrounding traditional foreign or second language instruction in the classroom. In fact, it is for this very reason that the failure of the FLES (Foreign Languages in the Elementary School) programs of the 1960s and early 70s in Britain and the United States (as documented, for example, by Burstall, 1975, who compared the proficiency of students who had begun the study of French in elementary school to students who had begun later and found no advantage for younger learners and disappointing results for all) cannot be taken as counter-evidence to the critical period hypothesis.

Additionally, it also must be reiterated that a myriad of psychosocial and cognitive factors clearly do affect second language development in fundamental ways; thus, as stated in the introduction, the age factor emerges only in naturalistic situations under "advantaged" sociological, cultural, psychological, and affective circumstances. The following, brief discussion is therefore be limited to aspects of language education policy that involve contexts which most closely approximate naturalistic acquisition, namely immersion programs, particularly when they involve language majority children who do not face the kind of sociocultural barriers that their language minority counterparts can encounter, or in the case of language minority children from middle- or upper-class backgrounds in their native countries.

Given these caveats, the critical period hypothesis clearly seems consistent with the positive results found in studies of immersion programs. For example, Lambert and Tucker (1972), in a well-known and influential report, carried out a longitudinal investigation of the impact of schooling Anglo-Canadian children mainly in a second language (French) from kindergarten to the fourth grade. The results showed no deficit in the children's English language development, but striking progress in French, although native levels were not attained in syntactic or phonological proficiency.

Genesee (1987), in a comprehensive review of second language immersion programs in Canada and the United States, confirmed the effectiveness of immersion programs for majority group, English-speaking students. Such students achieved levels of L2 proficiency far above those achieved in traditional foreign language instruction programs such as FLES, but which still fell short of native standards in vocabulary, grammar, and phonology. Because teachers are usually the pupils' only language models in these immersion programs, it seems that an insufficient amount of interaction with native speakers, particularly with native speaking peers, largely accounts for these limitations. Genesee recognized the language-learning limitations of most school environments and saw a need for more "discourse-rich" pedagogical approaches so that immersion programs may more fully realize their potential.

Immersion for minority language students is a controversial issue in the United States and approaches such as ESL pull-out classes (which are effectively equivalent to traditional foreign language instruction) and bilingual education programs (which usually involve both ESL instruction and content-matter instruction in the students' native language) are more common. In Britain, however, educational policy since 1985 has favored placing language minority students in the mainstream with the support of

English-as-a-second-language (ESL) specialists who assist the regular teaching staff by working individually with language minority students in the mainstream class (McKay & Freedman, 1990). This approach allows for significant interaction with native speakers, unlike the North American immersion programs, but does not provide the language minority students with native language development and support. This writer is not aware of any longitudinal data concerning the outcomes of this approach at this time.

However, similar approaches are not completely unknown in the United States, and research results have been published. For example, Collier (1987) examined the length of time second language students needed to become proficient in English in a large public school system on the East Coast that did not offer self-contained ESL classes. The language minority students were described as an "advantaged group" from an upper- or middle-income background in their country of origin. Students spent part of their day receiving special assistance from ESL teachers and the rest of the day in the mainstream classroom. No native language instruction was available in the school. Most students were mainstreamed within 2 or 3 years of entry into the school system, and national norms in language and content areas generally were approached within 4 to 8 years. Students who had arrived at ages 12 to 15 years experienced the most difficulty in L2 acquisition under conditions of immersion, and the authors concluded that such students most needed alternatives to that approach, including content instruction in L1 and content area ESL classes taught at the students' level of proficiency (sheltered instruction).

As can be seen from this brief review, the essential implication of the critical period hypothesis for educational policy is that an immersion approach, given an appropriate sociocultural context, has a potential for yielding results in the L2 acquisition of students whose age at arrival falls below the 12–15 year age range, that are far superior to the results usually obtained in traditional, formal, second or foreign language self-contained instruction. At the same time, it has to be recognized that the hard questions about how this potential can be realized, particularly when the students involved do not fall into the "advantaged" category and the sociocultural context is less than optimal, can be answered only with reference to factors largely unrelated to age. As Genesee (1987) put it, "It is widely recognized that the success of *any* (emphasis added) educational program for minority language students . . . will depend on socio-cultural factors" (p. 194).

To conclude, current research evidence strongly supports the notion of an age-based limitation on the ability to acquire native-like control of an L2; yet, to posit the existence of a sensitive period is not to claim that nothing else matters with respect to issues of language education; indeed, such a belief misconstrues the ethological meaning of the term "sensitive period" with its implications of potentiality, not certitude, of propensity, not inevitability.

## REFERENCES

Asher, J., & Garcia, R. (1969). The optimal age to learn a foreign language. *Modern Language Journal, 53*, 334–341.

Burstall, C. (1975). Primary French in the balance. *Educational Research, 17*, 193–197.

Collier, V. (1987). Age and rate of acquisition of second language for academic purposes. *TESOL Quarterly, 21*(4), 617–642.

Curtiss, S. (1977). *Genie: A linguistic study of a modern day "wild child."* New York: Academic Press.

Flege, J. (1991). Age of learning affects the authenticity of voice-onset time (VOT) in stop consonants produced in a second language. *Journal of the Acoustical Society of America, 89*, 395–411.

Flege, J. (1992). Speech learning in a second language. In C. Ferguson, L. Menn, & C. Stoel-Gammon (Eds.), *Phonological development: Models, research, implications* (pp. 565–604). Timonium, MD: York Press.

Flege, J., & Fletcher, K. (1992). Talker and listener effects on degree of perceived accent. *Journal of the Acoustical Society of America, 91*, 370–389.

Genesee, F. (1987). *Learning through two languages: Studies of immersion and bilingual education.* Cambridge, MA: Newbury House.

Lambert, W., & Tucker, G.(1972). *Bilingual education of children: The St. Lambert experiment.* Cambridge, MA.: Newbury House.

Lenneberg, E. (1967). *Biological foundations of language.* New York: John Wiley.

Long, M. (1990). Maturational constraints on language development. *Studies in Second Language Acquisition, 12*, 251–285.

Mason, M. (1942). Learning to speak after six and one half years of silence. *Journal of Speech Disorders, 7*, 295–304.

McKay, S., & Freedman, S. (1990). Language minority education in Great Britain: A challenge to current U.S. policy. *TESOL Quarterly, 24*(3), 385–406.

Newport, E. (1984). Constraints on learning: Studies in the acquisition of American Sign Language. *Paper and Reports on Child Language Development, 23*, 1–22.

Oyama, S. (1973). *A sensitive period for the acquisition of a second language.* Unpublished doctoral dissertation, Harvard University, Cambridge, MA.

Oyama, S. (1976). A sensitive period for the acquisition of a phonological system. *Journal of Psycholinguistic Research, 5*, 261–283.

Patkowski, M. (1980). The sensitive period for the acquisition of syntax in a second language. *Language Learning, 30*, 449–472.

Patkowski, M. (1990). Age and accent in a second language: A reply to James Emil Flege. *Applied Linguistics, 11*, 73–89.

Penfield, W., & Roberts, L. (1959). *Speech and brain mechanisms.* New York: Atheneum.

Scovel, T. (1969). Foreign accents, language acquisition, and cerebral dominance. *Language Learning, 19*, 245–254.

Scovel, T. (1988). *A time to speak: A psycholinguistic inquiry into the critical period for human speech.* Cambridge, MA: Newbury House.

Seliger, H., Krashen, S., & Ladefoged, P. (1975). Maturational constraints in the acquisition of second language accent. *Language Sciences, 36,* 20–22.

Singleton, D. (1989). *Language acquisition: The age factor.* Clevedon, England: Multilingual Matters.

Snow, C., & Hoefnagel-Hohle, M. (1978). The critical period for language acquisition: Evidence from second language learning. *Child Development, 49*, 1114–1128.

Tahta, S., Wood, M., & Loewenthal, K. (1981). Foreign accents: Factors relating to transfer of accent from the first language to a second language. *Language and Speech, 24*(3), 265–272.

Thompson, I. (1991). Foreign accents revisited: The English pronunciation of Russian immigrants. *Language Learning, 41*, 177–204.

# CHAPTER 10

*Markedness and Environment as Internal Constraints on the Variability of Interlanguage Phonology*

ROBERT S. CARLISLE, Ph.D

One of the major findings of research in second language acquisition is that interlanguage is characterized by variability. Certain linguistic structures can have a number of surface realizations, or variants, whose frequency of occurrence is determined by both internal linguistic constraints and external stylistic and social constraints. Most of the work in interlanguage phonology has examined the influence of external constraints (Ellis, 1988; Tarone, 1988), with the most commonly examined variable being task. In general, tasks that allow subjects to attend more closely to the form of their speech rather than to its content elicit a higher frequency of target variants, a phenomenon generally referred to as style shifting (Beebe, 1980; L. Dickerson, 1975; L. Dickerson & W. Dickerson, 1977; Gatbonton, 1978; Major, 1987; Sato, 1985; Schmidt, 1987; Weinberger, 1987). In one of the first studies of style shifting in second language acquisition, L. Dickerson (1975) found the highest frequency of the target variant occurred in the reading of word lists, the next highest in the reading of a text, and the least frequent in free speaking. Subsequent studies have found similar interrelationships between the frequency of target variants and style.

Other research has indicated that the frequency of variants can also be influenced by the background of the person to whom a speaker is conversing (Beebe, 1977a, 1977b). For example, Beebe (1977a) found that native Chinese speakers who were fluent in Thai used a higher frequency of Thai variants when speaking to a native Thai speaker and a higher frequency of Chinese variants to Chinese speakers of Thai, even though the latter spoke Thai without any obvious influence from Chinese.

The length of time students spend in studying the L2 and length of residence in an L2 environment also appear to be relevant external constraints influencing variability. Students with more years of experience in the formal study of English produce a higher frequency of target variants (Major, 1987). Also, L2 learners who reside longer in the L2 environment may produce a higher frequency of target variants than do those who have lived for less time in the same environment (Major, 1987).[1] Finally, in a longitudinal study over a 9-month period, L. Dickerson (1975) found that Japanese speakers of English produced a higher frequency of target variants over time; all subjects were studying in an intensive English institute as well as living in the L2 environment.

As important as external constraints are for understanding the variability of interlanguage, the present chapter is concerned with the internal linguistic constraints that structure the interlanguage. Specifically, the current study examines the influence of markedness relationships and environment. In addition, this chapter reviews recent research on the interaction between markedness relationships and environment, an area of study which has received very little attention.

## MARKEDNESS

Within the last decade, much of the work in interlanguage phonology has been concerned with the influence of language universals in structuring the interlanguage phonology. As has been well documented by Comrie (1989), there are currently two general approaches to the study of language universals. The first approach is associated with Chomsky's

---

[1] At least one other study has found no significant relationship between length of residence and the production of target variants although it did find a relationship between the frequency of target variants and age of arrival to an area where the L2 is spoken (Riney, 1990).

more recent versions of generative grammar. In this paradigm, which is generally referred to as universal grammar, language universals are regarded as innate principles and parameters that facilitate the learning of the L1 by children. Differences among languages are partially the result of the diverse settings each language has for the parameters. Adherents of this approach believe that it is possible to discover language universals through an in-depth analysis of only a few languages.

As influential as the theory of universal grammar has been in research on the acquisition of the L1 and on the acquisition of L2 syntax, it has not been influential in the study of the the acquisition of L2 phonology. In fact, only one article has attempted to account for the acquisition of an L2 phonological structure through an appeal to universal grammar (Broselow & Finer, 1991).

The second major methodological approach for studying language universals is to examine the structure of a representatively large and appropriately sampled range of languages to determine what properties they share (Comrie, 1989); the universals uncovered in this approach are often called taxonomic universals. In phonology this approach has uncovered a number of important absolute and implicational universals. Absolute universals are properties inherent in all languages, such as the presence of oral vowels and simple open (CV) syllables. In contrast, implicational universals always involve at least two properties in a conditional relationship: if X then Y. For example, some languages have both voiced and voiceless obstruents whereas others have only voiceless obstruents, but no language has only voiced obstruents. Thus, the presence of voiced obstruents implies the presence of voiceless obstruents. In such cases, the implicated property is regarded as the less marked of the two.

Important insights from research into taxonomic universals have stimulated research into the possible relationship between universals and second language acquisition. Many researchers in L2 acquisition are interested in determining whether taxonomic language universals are reflections of innate predilections that both first and second language learners bring to the process of language acquisition (Comrie, 1984, 1990). The first prominent hypothesis emanating from this interest was the Markedness Differential Hypothesis (Eckman, 1977), which essentially claims that L2 learners will acquire less marked structures more readily than they will more marked structures.

The Marked Differential Hypothesis as first proposed 15 years ago explicitly asserted that languages can differ in that one language (A) may have a structure that is more marked than a corresponding structure in another language (B). As a consequence, speakers of B would have more difficulty acquiring the structure in A than speakers of A would have acquiring the structure in B. A concrete example that has often been cited is the case of word-final obstruents. A voicing contrast between obstruents in word-final position is more marked than is the occurrence of only voiceless obstruents in the same position. Consequently, if the Markedness Differential Hypothesis is valid, speakers of German should have a more difficult time maintaining a voicing contrast while learning a language such as English than should speakers of English learning German which has a rule of terminal devoicing. This cross-linguistic nature of the Markedness Differential Hypothesis prompted some criticism of it. Two researchers have pointed out that the markedness relationship may not be between the L1 and the L2, but rather within the L2 (Carlisle, 1988; Hammarberg, 1990). Carlisle, for example, examined the production of three English onsets by native Spanish speakers. None of the onsets is found in Spanish, yet they are in a markedness relationship according to the work of Greenberg (1965). The results of the study revealed that the Spanish-speaking subjects modified the more marked onsets (/sm/ and /sn/) significantly more frequently than they modified the less marked onset, /sl/, demonstrating that markedness relationships within the L2 are just as relevant as markedness relationships between the L1 and the L2. In all honesty, however, Eckman (1984) was also aware of this problem with the original version of the Markedness Differential Hypothesis and commented on it in an article published before those of Carlisle and Hammarberg. And even though the Markedness Differential Hypothesis was never rewritten to incorporate the markedness relationship within the L2, Eckman (1991) has developed a new hypothesis, the Structural Conformity Hypothesis which takes into account the markedness relationships both between the L1 and the L2 and within the L2.

All of the research on the relationship between markedness and the acquisition of a second language phonology reviewed below can be regarded as tests of the Structural Conformity Hypothesis as it both encompasses the old Markedness Differential Hypothesis and accounts for the markedness relationships within the L2.

## UNIVERSAL PREFERENCE FOR THE CV SYLLABLE

The universally least marked syllable type in the primary languages of the world is the CV syllable; all languages have CV syllables, and many languages have only CV syllables. Thus, this syllable type is an absolute substantive universal, and the presence of any other syllable type implies the presence of the CV syllable. All theories of syllable markedness accept the CV syllable as primary (Battistella, 1990; Cairns & Feinstein, 1982; Kaye & Lowenstamm, 1981; Vennemann, 1988).

In the last dozen years, five studies have tested for a universal preference for the simple open syllable, the hypothesis being that because the CV syllable is the least marked syllable in natural languages, it should occur in interlanguage independent of native language transfer. There has been some positive, albeit weak, evidence for this hypothesis. In her seminal study, Tarone (1980) transcribed the English narratives of two speakers each of Korean, Cantonese, and Portuguese and found that the subjects modified 137 syllables (about 20% of the syllables that they produced) either through epenthesis, deletion, or the insertion of a glottal stop. Although most of the modifications could be attributed to native language transfer, 30 could not and were therefore interpreted as evidence for a preference for the CV syllable.

Following the same procedures used by Tarone, Hodne (1985) examined the English syllable structure of two native speakers of Polish. Polish was chosen because it has syllable structures at least as complex as those found in English; in fact, Polish and English share at least 26 complex onsets and 26 complex codas. Hodne collected 666 syllables in an interview task and a narrative. The corpus of data contained 66 syllable structure errors; of those a mere 11 (about 16%) resulted in CV syllables, the derivation of which could not be attributed to L1 transfer.

The final three studies that tested for a possible universal preference for the simple open syllable all used native speakers of Vietnamese as subjects. Sato (1984) examined the spontaneous and informal English conversations of two Vietnamese children. Data were gathered at three different points over a 10-month period. Sato selected Vietnamese because over 81% of the phonemic syllables in the language are closed. Given that Tarone (1980) had found that transfer was more prevalent in accounting for the syllable structure of the interlanguage than was any possible preference for the simple open syllable, speakers of Vietnamese offered an interesting case because a transfer hypothesis would predict that the subjects would favor closed rather than simple open syllables in the interlanguage. Sato examined the production of two-member codas by the subjects and found that of the 489 two-member codas produced over the 10 months, 363 were reduced (one member of the coda was deleted) and 61 were completely deleted. In other words, approximately 12% of the target syllables with two-member codas were pronounced as open syllables.

Benson (1988) taped two adult native speakers of Vietnamese in informal conversation with the investigator. Benson investigated both monosyllabic words consisting of an open syllable and a closed syllable ending in [p, t, k, m, n] or [ŋ] as Vietnamese has closed syllables ending in those segments. Three types of errors were examined: the insertion of a consonantal segment after a word-final V, the occurrence of an epenthetic vowel after a word final C, and the deletion of a word-final C.

Two types of errors essentially did not occur in the interlanguage of the two subjects; insertion of a word-final consonant occurred once and word-final epenthesis never occurred at all. However, of the 537 target closed syllables, 92 were modified towards CV syllables through deletion, but only 11 of those resulting CV syllables could not be attributed to transfer.

In the most recent study to examine a universal preference for the CV syllable, Riney (1990) examined the syllable production of 40 native speakers of Vietnamese who were distributed equally among four age groups: 10–12, 15–18, 20–25, and 35–55. Riney restricted his examination to stressed monosyllabic words ending in the word-final singleton codas /t/, /k/, and /v/; environment was controlled so that only items followed by a vowel or a pause were examined. Riney tabulated the frequency of epenthesis for all four groups and found a positive linear relationship between the frequency of epenthesis and age at time of data collection: the older the subject the more frequent the epenthesis. From youngest to oldest group the frequencies of epenthesis were 5.6, 16.3, 20.4, and 32.4%. An ANOVA revealed a significant difference among groups. In addition, the groups differed in the frequency with which they deleted the word-final singleton codas. Again, from youngest to oldest group, the frequencies were 10.2, 18.5, 9.6, and 6.3%. In other words, whereas all age groups simplified final closed syllables, they did so with different frequencies and with different strategies. The youngest group simplified the least frequently (15.8%) and used the strategy of deletion nearly twice as much as epenthesis. The next three groups each modified approximately one third of the target items (34.8, 30, and 38.7%, respectively), but they differed on the strategies that they used. The 15- to 18-year-old age group used both strategies about equally, but the two eldest age groups used epenthesis more frequently than they did deletion. In fact, the eldest group used epenthesis five times more frequently than deletion. In conclusion, this study indicates that even speakers of languages having word-final closed syllables will variably reduce some more complex syllable structures in the L2 to CV syllables. However, the strategies may vary according to the age of the subjects.

Several other studies that did not specifically study the preference for the CV syllable type may, nevertheless, offer insights into the modification of word-final syllables. Eckman investigated the strategies that native Japanese speakers (1981b, 1984) and native Mandarin speakers (1981a) used to modify word-final voiced obstruents. He found that the subjects either produced the word-final obstruent without modification or else used schwa paragoge. The use of schwa paragoge may be attributable to the preference for the CV syllable. However, Eckman (1981a) noted that schwa paragoge also preserves more of the underlying structure and may be preferable for communicative reasons, rather than for phonological ones.

Several generalizations can be made from these studies. They have revealed, and the researchers have acknowledged, that transfer is the primary process involved in modifying the syllable structure of the interlanguage; clearly, most modifications of syllable structure found in the studies just described could be attributed to transfer rather than to any preference for the CV syllable. Other researchers have commented on how susceptible the interlanguage phonology is to transfer from the L1. Broselow (1984) studied the Arabic of native English speakers and found that they resyllabified Arabic to conform to English syllable structure conditions and rules that derive underlying syllables into acceptable surface structure forms. The tendency was so strong that Broselow developed the Syllable Structure Transfer Hypothesis to account for the cases discussed in her article and to provide other researchers with a means to further study syllable structure in interlanguage phonology. In addition, Ioup (1984), in a comparison of phonological and syntactic modifications in interlanguage, remarked that transfer appears to be more influential in structuring interlanguage phonology than in structuring interlanguage syntax. In fact, she went on to state "that transfer is the major influence on interlanguage phonology" (p. 13).

A study that clearly demonstrates the influence of transfer on the structuring of interlanguage phonology has been conducted by Broselow (1983). Broselow investigated syllabification errors in the English of native speakers of Arabic who spoke two distinct dialects: Iraqi and Egyptian. Both dialects have syllable structure conditions that disallow consonant clusters in word-initial position. Yet speakers of each dialect modify English words with initial consonant clusters in a different manner. Egyptian speakers will pronounce *flow* as [filo] whereas Iraqi speakers will pronounce it as [iflo]. Both pronunciations can be attributed to rules of epenthesis in the native language which bring underlying syllable structures into conformity with surface structure restrictions on syllable structure. In a word such as *flow*, the first consonant is extrasyllabic (unassociated with a nucleus) and a vowel must be inserted to which the consonant is resyllabified according to convention before it reaches surface structure (Clements & Keyser, 1983). The Egyptian rule of epenthesis inserts a vowel to the right of the extrasyllabic consonant to which it resyllabifies forming a CV syllable. In contrast, the Iraqi rule of epenthesis inserts a vowel to the left of the extrasyllabic consonant to which it resyllabifies forming a VC syllable. If the preference for the CV syllable had been powerful, Iraqi speakers might have been expected to pronounce words such as flow as [filo] at least some of the time because such a strategy would have created a CV syllable independent of L1 transfer; however, such pronunciation was not evident for Iraqi speakers.

More evidence for the strength of L1 transfer over a preference for the CV syllable also comes from studies on the English of native Spanish speakers. In four independent studies, Carlisle (1988, 1991a, 1991b) examined the production of /sC-/ onsets in English. Spanish has a large number of words that begin with the sequence /esC/ such as *escuela, estampa,* and *espia.* For each word, the /e/ is predictable and consequently inserted by phonological rule. Because the epenthesis of /e/ takes place in the derivation of the words, the underlying representations begin with the sequence /sk/, /st/, and /sp/ which are prohibited onsets according to the syllable structure conditions of Spanish (Harris, 1983). In the underlying representations, therefore, /s/ is an extrasyllabic consonant. Spanish speakers respond to this consonant by inserting a vowel before it. The resyllabification convention then applies forming a syllable of the extrasyllabic consonant and the epenthetic vowel. The result, of course, it that the relevant derived words in Spanish begin with a VC syllable. This same rule of epenthesis is transferred into Spanish/English interlanguage phonology. Spanish speakers will variably pronounce words such as *snow, slow,* and *steep* as as [esno], [eslo], and [estip], a pronunciation that results in the words beginning with a VC syllable. In none of the studies did the subjects ever produce forms such as [seno], [selo], or [setip] as might be expected if the subjects really had a preference for the CV syllable independent of language transfer.

A second point emerging from the studies investigating a possible universal preference for the CV syllable is that they have resulted in contradictory results as to the relative strength of epenthesis as opposed to deletion in modifying syllables. Tarone's (1980) study with all adult subjects from three different language backgrounds indicated that the strategy used by language learners to modify syllables seems very much dependent on the L1 of the language learner. In modifying word-final consonants, the Korean subjects preferred deletion; the Portuguese preferred epenthesis; and the Cantonese used the two strategies about equally. However, in the modification of word-internal consonant clusters, deletion was the strategy almost exclusively used by all subjects. Hodne's (1985) adult Polish subjects used epenthesis more than twice as frequently as they used deletion. In her examination of two Vietnamese children learning English, Sato (1984) found that epenthesis was hardly ever used; instead the subjects relied on deletion of either one or both members of both word-initial and word-final two-member clusters. The work of Riney apparently resolved some of the discrepancy; as mentioned previously, Riney (1990) examined 40

Vietnamese subjects in four different age groups and found that the older subjects used more epenthesis than did the younger subjects. Such a finding would then account for Sato's finding that epenthesis was rarely used because her subjects were minors. However, Riney did not take into account the findings of Benson (1988) whose article had been published two years before Riney's appeared. Benson's subjects were two Vietnamese speakers, ages 16 and 26. Their ages would have placed the younger subject into Riney's second youngest group, and the second subject would have been in the second oldest group. In Riney's study the second youngest group used epenthesis and deletion with nearly equal frequency, but the next oldest group used epenthesis twice as frequently as they did deletion. However, in Benson's study neither subject used epenthesis at all to resolve word-final consonants even though Benson's and Riney's studies examined some of the same structures, specifically monosyllabic words ending in [t] and [k]. Another interesting discrepancy in these studies is that even subjects from the same language background and approximately the same age used different frequencies of epenthesis and deletion. Eckman (1981a), Anderson (1987), and Weinberger (1987) all examined the simplification of English word-final codas by native speakers of Mandarin, but whereas Eckman's subjects nearly exclusively used epenthesis, Anderson's used deletion, and Weinberger's used the two strategies about equally.

Several researchers have offered possible explanations for which strategy would be used more often. Major (1987) suggested that epenthesis would be used in more formal styles because it preserves more of the structure of the word. And there is some evidence for this hypothesis; Edge (1991) found that her Japanese and Cantonese subjects used a higher frequency of epenthesis in word lists than in other types of tasks. And Weinberger (1987) found that his four Mandarin speaking subjects used epenthesis twice as frequently as they used deletion in reading lists of words, a very formal style. However, Weinberger also stated that formality is not the crucial variable involved, but rather linguistic context. That is, the proportion of epenthesis to deletion will be reduced in spoken text because other factors in the text allow an interlocutor to recover or repair what has been lost through deletion. Again, Weinberger's study provided some documentation for this hypothesis because the proportion of epenthesis to deletions was twice as great in the context-free list task as in the two context-bound tasks used in the same study. Weinberger has also suggested that the proportion of epenthesis to deletion will increase with the proficiency of the L2 learners as they will become more aware of potential ambiguity in the L2 and seek to avoid it; no one has yet tested for this possibility. Obviously, there is no current answer as to which strategy is more prevalent in modifying the syllable structure of the L2; the answer will probably be found in a complex configuration of intralinguistic and extralinguistic variables including the age of the subjects, their native language background, level of proficiency, length of residence, task, and linguistic environment.

As a final comment on this research, it has obviously provided little evidence for a "universal" preference for the simple open syllable. The reason that the evidence may appear so slight is that the case for the CV syllable has probably been overstated. Because the CV syllable is the maximally least marked syllable in natural languages, researchers apparently have assumed that syllable modifications in the L2 would most naturally result in CV syllables, but syllable structures fall along a continuum of markedness, a matter of more or less marked rather than marked and unmarked. This begin true, it would not be necessary for an L2 learner to produce simple open syllables to demonstrate that language universals were an influence. If L2 learners produce less marked structures, rather than the least marked, independent of language transfer, then linguistic universals can reasonably be claimed to be an influence. For example, if L2 learners whose native language has only CV syllables produce a CVC syllable instead of a CVCC target syllable, they have not only produced a syllable not found in their native language, but one that is also less marked. This point is brought out clearly in the following section.

## THE MARKEDNESS OF ONSETS AND CODAS BY LENGTH

All descriptive and theoretical studies of the syllable have found that the markedness of both onsets and codas increases with length (Cairns & Feinstein, 1982; Greenberg, 1965; Kaye & Lowenstamm, 1981; Vennemann, 1988), a fact captured by the observation that the presence of an onset or coda of length $n$ implies the presence of $n - 1$ (Greenberg, 1965; Kaye & Lowenstamm, 1981). A few studies in interlanguage phonology have revealed that shorter onsets and codas are preferred over longer onsets and codas; one obvious point from all of the studies discussed in this section is that, when complex clusters are modified, it is through deletion, not expansion. That is, whereas three-member onsets may be reduced to two-members, and two-member-onsets may be reduced to one, the reverse never occurs. In other words, if the length of clusters is modified, less marked, not more marked, clusters result.

Anderson (1987) examined the casual conversation of 29 speakers of colloquial Egyptian Arabic, and 10 speakers each of Amoy and Mandarin Chinese. In general, all groups of subjects made significantly more modifications (either by deletion or epenthesis) of both onsets and codas as their length increased. In fact, whereas the Arabic-speaking subjects modified only about 2% of one-member codas, they modified over 30% of three-member codas. The difference for the Chinese speakers was even greater; they modified 50% more of the three-member codas than the one-member codas. In another study, Weinberger (1987) examined word-final codas produced by four adult speakers of Mandarin and found that the frequency of modification increased linearly with the length of the coda; 5.5% of one-member codas were modified, 29.8% of two-member codas, and 42% of three-member codas. In other words, as markedness increased, so did the frequency of the syllable simplification strategies.

Eckman (1987) examined the production of two-member and three-member codas by six subjects, two speakers each of Korean, Japanese, and Cantonese. An examination of the subjects' production revealed that both two-member and three-member codas were reduced as expected. Although Eckman did not provide the frequencies with which two-member codas were reduced in relation to three-member codas, his study provides a revealing insight about the reduction of the codas. One of Greenberg's implicational universals is that, if a language has a word-final two-member coda consisting of a stop-stop, then it will also have one consisting of a fricative-stop. A second universal is that, if a language has a word-final coda consisting of a fricative-fricative, then it will also have one consisting of a stop-fricative or fricative-stop. Eckman found that when his subjects reduced three-member codas they tended to delete that member which would result in one of the less marked subsequences. For example, a word such as *clasped* has a coda of the form [spt], which could be reduced to [sp], [pt], or [st]. In actual production, however, the subjects normally produced the first and third variant; the second variant, the more marked one, rarely occurred. However, exceptions to the above generalization appear quite regularly and may be influenced more by morphology than phonology. In the rare cases in which a three-member coda, such as [pts] in *opts*, was reduced to the more marked subsequence consisting of a stop-stop, rather than to the less marked subsequence, the deleted fricative was always an allomorph of an inflectional morpheme—that is, one that marked plurality or the third person singular of the present tense. In fact, if a three-member cluster consisted of two stops and a fricative, the fricative was deleted only if it were an allomorph of an inflectional morpheme; the fricative in such codas as [kst] as in *waxed* was never deleted. A number of studies have demonstrated that inflectional morphemes are frequently dropped by non-native English speakers (Moore & Marzano, 1979; Politzer & Ramirez, 1973) and even by some native English speakers as the morphemes, in context anyway, carry redundant information (Whiteman, 1981). This behavior is apparently so strong that it will be done even if the result is a more marked structure on the phonological level.

In another study, Eckman (1991) examined the reduction of complex codas and onsets by 11 subjects from three different language backgrounds: Japanese, Cantonese, and Korean. None of these languages allow complex codas or onsets. Unlike other studies, Eckman did not compare the frequency with which two-member and three-member onsets and codas occurred relative to each other as did Anderson (1987) and Weinberger (1987). Instead, Eckman used a criterion measure, 80%, to determine the presence or absence of a particular structure. For example, if a subject produced onsets of the form /spr-/ correctly 80% of the time, the structure was regarded as present in the interlanguage phonology. And if either or both of the two subsequences were present 80% of the time, then they were also present and the Interlanguage Structural Conformity Hypothesis was confirmed. The hypothesis could have been falsified if the three-member onset or coda was present and both of the two-member subsequences were absent according to the the 80% criterion. Eckman examined three three-member onsets and eight three-member codas across 11 subjects and four tasks and found three falsifications; that is, in three cases, a three-member cluster was present at the criterion level, but both two-member subsequences were absent. It should be stated, however, that these three falsifications were by two subjects and did not occur in all tasks. Even with the falsifications, this study provides very strong evidence for the Interlanguage Structural Conformity Hypothesis.

## MARKED ONSETS AND CODAS OF EQUAL LENGTH

As previously mentioned, onsets and codas are in markedness relationships according to their length. However, both structures can participate in markedness relationships even when length is held constant, a point cogently demonstrated by Greenberg (1965). One of Greenberg's universals was that, if a language has an obstruent-nasal onset, then it will also have an obstruent-liquid onset. In other words, the presence of the first onset implies the presence of the latter, indicating that the latter is less marked than the first. To test the possible influence of this implicational universal in L2 acquisition, Carlisle (1988) examined the frequency of epenthesis before the onsets /sl/, /sm/, and /sn/, the hypothesis being that epenthesis would occur less frequently before the obstruent-liquid onset than the obstruent-nasal onsets as the former is less marked than the latter.

For this study, 14 native Spanish speakers read a list of 435 topically unrelated and randomly ordered sentences, 145 sentences each for /sl/, /sm/, and /sn/. Twenty-eight environments and silence occurred five times each before each onset. The environments were controlled because two previous independent studies had revealed that epenthesis occurred significantly more frequently after consonants than after vowels before word-initial /sC/ onsets in Spanish/English interlanguage phonology (Carlisle, 1991a).

The mean proportions of epenthesis before the three onsets were .29 for /sl/, .38 for /sm/, and .33 for /sn/; an ANOVA revealed a significant difference among the three means. Pairwise comparisons revealed that the mean frequency of epenthesis before /sl/ was significantly less than those before /sm/ and /sn/ as hypothesized. In addition, /sm-/ was also more frequently modified than was /sn-/, although the two onsets are not in any known markedness relationship. However, the segments in the latter onset are homorganic and may be easier to articulate, as indicated by Greenberg (1965) who found that for codas a sequence of a nasal and a homorganic obstruent is less marked than a nasal followed by a heterorganic obstruent; and although no similar universal relationship has been expressed for onsets the same relationship may hold in a richer theory of markedness.

Eckman (1991) also investigated another of Greenberg's implicational universals: If a language has a word-final two-member coda consisting of a stop-stop, then it will also have one consisting of a fricative-stop. Again, using a criterion measure of 80% to determine the presence of a particular structure from the data of 11 subjects and four different tasks, Eckman found only two falsifications out of 44 cases for the acquisition of the codas. In other words, in two cases the less marked coda failed to reach the criterion level, whereas the more marked coda did. Despite the two falsifications, 95% of the cases either supported the Interlangauge Structural Conformity Hypothesis or were consistent with it, providing strong evidence that less marked structures are more easily acquired than are more marked structures.

## MARKEDNESS DISTINCTIONS BETWEEN ONSETS AND CODAS

In their theory of markedness for the syllable, Kaye and Lowenstamm (1981) demonstrated that closed syllables are more marked than open syllables and consequently that, if onsets and codas have the same number of segments in them, the latter will always be more marked than the former. A number of studies have revealed that onsets are less frequently modified than are codas when length is held constant.

Anderson (1987) found that, when the length of onsets and codas was held constant, the subjects made significantly more modifications of codas than of onsets. Her Chinese subjects modified less than 1% of one-member onsets, but over 20% of the one-member codas. They also modified about 10% of two-member onsets, but 50% of the two-member codas; the differences between the onsets and codas of both lengths were also significant for the Arabic speakers.

In her longitudinal study of two Vietnamese youths learning English, Sato (1984) found that both subjects modified two-member codas much more frequently than they did two-member onsets. At the end the the final data gathering session, one subject was modifying only 12% of the two-member onsets, but 81% of the two-member codas; the other subject was modifying 14% of the same onsets, but 79% of the codas. In the last study that provided information on this topic, Tropf (1987) examined the German of 11 native Spanish speakers and found that his subjects more frequently modified two-member codas than two-member onsets.[2]

## UNIVERSAL CANONICAL SYLLABLE STRUCTURE

Some researchers have noted that there is a Universal Canonical Syllable Structure (UCSS) for onsets and codas based on sonority (Cairns & Feinstein, 1982; Hooper, 1976; Kiparsky, 1979; Selkirk; 1984; Vennemann, 1988). Onsets and codas abide by the UCSS if there is a continuous rise in sonority from the most peripheral member of both structures through the nucleus of the syllable. The UCSS is not an absolute universal, but rather a universal tendency, as a few languages, such as English, have language-specific syllable structures that violate the UCSS.

To examine whether the the frequency of the modification of onsets and codas depends on whether they abide by the (UCSS), Tropf (1987) examined the production of these structures in German by 11 adult native Spanish speakers in actual conversation, finding that there was a tendency for onsets and codas that abided by the UCSS to be less frequently modified than those that did not abide by it. For example, Tropf's subjects infrequently modified word-final two-member codas consisting of a lateral-fricative; codas consisting of a nasal-fricative were modified a little more frequently; and those consisting of a plosive-fricative, a structure which violates the UCSS, were modified the most frequently. Of further interest is that the nasal-fricative coda was modified more frequently than the lateral-fricative, even though both structures abide by the UCSS. Vennemann (1988) has pointed out a preference in language change for codas that that display a greater drop

---

[2] Although it was not Tropf's explicit intention to examine the question of whether codas are more frequently modified than onsets, an examination of the tables in the article provide evidence for the question.

in sonority from the member closest to the nucleus to the peripheral member. The distance in sonority between a lateral and a fricative is greater than that between a nasal and a fricative; and in Tropf's study, the preferred structure was less frequently modified.

## FINAL OBSTRUENT DEVOICING

A well-established observation of markedness is that voiceless obstruents are less marked than are voiced obstruents. Some languages such as English, German, and Spanish have both voiced and voiceless obstruents; others such as Cantonese have only voiceless obstruents; but no language has only voiced obstruents. In addition, even though some languages have a voicing contrast in either word-initial or word-medial position, they may not have one in word-final position; quite a few languages (e.g., German and Polish) have a rule of terminal devoicing which neutralizes the voicing contrast in word-final position. Terminal devoicing is also a developmental feature of children learning languages that maintain the voice contrast in word-final position; many children learning English as their first language will devoice at least some word-final obstruents until the age of four (Smith & Stoel-Gammon, 1983), and adult speakers of English will devoice final obstruents in casual speech (Shockey, 1974) and even in reading style (Edge, 1991), although such devoicing is heavily influenced by environment, occurring most frequently before a pause or a voiceless obstruent than before another voiced segment (Edge, 1991; Ladefoged, 1982).

Flege and Davidian (1984) examined the devoicing of word-final singleton voiced stops among 12 speakers each of English, Spanish, Polish, and Chinese. Each subject produced 80 occurrences of the target sounds, and the environment was held constant in that only absolute final position was examined. The results of the study revealed that the native English speakers did not devoice any of the stops; the Polish speakers devoiced 48% of them, the Spanish speakers, 43%, and the Chinese speakers, 30%. In addition, Eckman (1981a, 1981b) found occurrences of devoicing in the English of native speakers of Cantonese and Spanish although no specific rate of devoicing was provided. In another study, Edge (1991) found that both Cantonese and Japanese speakers devoiced word-final obstruents in a number of different tasks; for both groups devoicing occurred much more frequently before a pause or a voiceless obstruent.

In his two studies examining vowel epenthesis before the onsets /st/, /sp/ and /sk/, Carlisle (1991a) found that 47% of the final voiced obstruents before the target onsets were devoiced in the first study and

61% in the second study. Weinberger (1987) found that his four Mandarin subjects devoiced 66% of all word-final voiced obstruents. The frequency of devoicing appeared unrelated to task or to the length of the word-final coda being investigated.

The devoicing of final obstruents has also been found in the L2 of learners whose L1 has no rule of terminal devoicing. In a study of the English production of two native Hungarian speakers, Altenberg and Vago (1983) found that both subjects devoiced some word-final voiced obstruents, even before voiced sounds. A similar finding has been obtained in a study involving native speakers of Farsi, a language that has a voice contrast in word final position (Eckman, 1985). (See chapter 12 for additional discussion of devoicing.)

## ENVIRONMENT

From the very first studies in variation analysis (Labov, 1966, 1969), sociolinguists have recognized the importance of linguistic environment in inducing the frequencies with which the variants of a given variable occur. A careful account of environment has been especially prevalent in the analysis of phonological variables. For example, Wolfram (1969) examined four phonological variables in the English of African Americans living in Detroit. One of the variables was the word-final consonant cluster ending in a stop. All four of the social classes observed deleted the final stop much more frequently before a following word-initial consonant than before a nonconsonant. In the same study, an examination of postvocalic *r* revealed a more complicated influence of environment; *r* was retained most frequently before a vowel in the same word, next most frequently before a vowel across a word boundary, and least frequently before a consonant across a word boundary. These few examples indicate how crucial environment has been in accounting for the patterning of variants, a point recognized by some researchers in L2 acquisition who have lobbied for similar care in analyzing the variability of the interlanguage (Ellis, 1985, 1988; Fasold, 1984).

A number of studies in second language acquisition have examined the influence of linguistic environment in inducing the frequency of variants. In the seminal study in this area, L. Dickerson (1975) examined the production of the variable (z) in English by a group of native Japanese speakers and found that the target variant [z] occurred more frequently before a vowel than before a consonant. In another study of adult Japanese speakers learning English, L. Dickerson and W. Dickerson (1977) examined (r) in prevocalic position and found that the occurrence of the target variant

[r] depended on the height of the following vowel: the lower the vowel, the higher the frequency of the target variant. Gatbonton (1978) examined the production of word-initial (ð) in English by French speakers and found that the target variant [ð] occurred more frequently after a word-final vowel than after any of the four word-final consonantal environments. Finally, Edge (1991) demonstrated that the devoicing of word-final obstruents is related to the following environment. When her Cantonese and Japanese subjects devoiced, the following environment was almost always a voiceless obstruent or a pause.

In another study of Japanese/English interlanguage phonology, W. Dickerson (1976) examined the variable (l) and found an interaction between two environments. The target variant [l] occurred most frequently after silence, less frequently after a vowel in the same word, and least frequently as the second member of a two-member onset. The height of the vowel following the variable also influenced the frequency of the target variant, its presence occurring most frequently before a low vowel and least frequently before a high vowel. These two constraints interacted so that the target variant occurred most frequently in word-initial position before a low vowel and least frequently as the second member of a two-member onset before a high vowel.

Recent research has demonstrated that environment is also a factor in determining the variability of vowel epenthesis. The first evidence that different environments may induce different frequencies of epenthesis came from Tarone's (1980) study examining epenthesis following word-final singleton consonants. An examination of Tarone's raw data, which she provided for the reader, indicates that of the 45 instances of epenthesis after word-final singleton consonants, over 50% occurred before a pause, 40% before a word-initial consonant, and less than 5% before a word-initial vowel.

In four independent studies of native Spanish speakers learning English, Carlisle (1991a, 1991b, in press) found that vowel epenthesis was significantly more frequent after consonants than after vowels before word-initial onsets of the form /sC/ (where C represents any permissible consonant in this type of onset). In the first two studies, Carlisle (1991a) examined the frequency of epenthesis before /st-/, /sp-/, and /sk-/ . In the first study, five subjects modified 74% of the relevant onsets after a consonant, but only 47% of the onsets after a vowel; and in the second study nine subjects modified 76% of the onsets after a consonant and 63% of the onsets after a vowel. In the third study (Carlisle, 1991b), the frequency of epenthesis was calculated before the onsets /sl-/ and /st-/. Eleven subjects modified 34% of the onsets after a consonant and 22% of the onsets after a vowel. Finally, in the fourth study (Carlisle, in press), the production of /sl-/ and /sN-/ onsets by 14 subjects was examined (where sN is the collapsed category of /sn-/ and /sm-/). As in the other studies, epenthesis occurred more frequently after consonants than after vowels, 35% and 25%, respectively.

In all four studies of word-initial vowel epenthesis just reviewed, the differences in the frequency after the consonantal and vocalic environments was significant. Environment, therefore, is a powerful constraint in determining the frequency with which word-initial vowel epenthesis will occur. The strength of the environmental constraint also was displayed in the correlations among the environments before the different onsets; in all cases the correlations were positive and significant, indicating that the rank orders of consonants and vowels were similar before the different onsets. In addition, in all four studies a significantly higher number of subjects adhered to the constraint than violated it. In fact, of the 106 possible cases in the four studies 23 violations occurred.[3] That is, in 23 cases a subject used epenthesis more frequently after a vowel than after a consonant.

In two separate studies, Wolfram (1985, 1989) examined tense marking in English by native speakers of Vietnamese. In both studies, two separate groups were investigated depending on their length of residence (LOR) in the United States; the first group had an LOR of 1–3 years, and the second group 4–7 years. As part of his studies, Wolfram examined the tense marking of regular past tense verbs ending in clusters. In English, if the stem of a regular verb ends in a consonant (with the exception of an alveolar non-continuant), the verb conjugated in the past tense will end in a consonant cluster because the two relevant past tense allomorphs are both consonantal: [t] and [d]. The former allomorph co-occurs with voiceless sounds; the latter with voiced sounds. For example, the stem of the regular verb, *miss*, ends in a voiceless consonant and the past tense form, *missed*, ends in the cluster [-st]. Phonological environment was a crucial constraint in accounting for the unmarking of regular past tense verbs ending in such consonant clusters; the relevant verbs were much more frequently unmarked when they were followed by a consonant than when followed by a nonconsonant. In the first study, subjects with an LOR of 1–3 years left 94.8% of the verbs unmarked before a nonconsonant, but 99.1% before a consonant. Subjects with an LOR of 4–7 years displayed an even greater difference: 60% of the verbs were unmarked before the nonconsonantal environment, but 92.5% were unmarked before the consonantal environment. In the second study, subjects with an LOR of 4–7 years left 75% of the regular verbs unmarked

---

[3] The 106 cases is the number of subjects times the number of onsets examined in the four studies. Thus the two studies of /st/, /sp/, and /sk/ produced 42 cases: (5 subjects × 3 onsets + 9 subjects × 3 onsets); the study of /sl/ and /st/ produced 42 cases as well: (14 subjects × 3 onsets), and the study of /sl/and /sN/ produced 22 cases (11 subjects × 2 onsets).

before a nonconsonant, but 91% were unmarked before a consonant. These findings were consistent with those of other variation analyses using native speakers of English as subjects (Labov, 1969; Wolfram, 1969, 1973; Wolfram & Christian, 1976; Wolfram & Fasold, 1974).

## INTERACTION

Only two studies have examined the interaction between markedness relationships and environments (Carlisle, 1991b; Carlisle, in press). In the first study, Carlisle examined the frequency of vowel epenthesis after word-final consonants and vowels before /sl/ and /st/ onsets, the latter being more marked than the former as it violates the Universal Canonical Syllable Structure (UCSS); as discussed previously, research had found a tendency for onsets and codas that did not abide by the UCSS to be modified more frequently than those that did (Tropf, 1987).

The subjects for the study were 11 native Spanish speakers, and it was hypothesized that their primary means for modifying the onsets would be epenthesis as demonstrated in previous studies (Carlisle, 1988, 1991a). A reading instrument was used to gather data. The environments before the word initial onsets were strictly controlled to confirm previous findings that vowel epenthesis before /sC/ onsets in English by native Spanish speakers occurs significantly more frequently after consonants than after vowels.

The results of this study revealed that vowel epenthesis was the strategy used by the native Spanish speakers to resolve the impermissible onsets in the interlanguage. In addition, the proportion of epenthesis after word-final vowels (.221) was significantly less than the proportion of epenthesis after word-final consonants (.343), a finding that confirmed those of two previous studies of vowel epenthesis before /sC/ onsets (Carlisle, 1991a). The proportion of epenthesis also occurred significantly less frequently before the less marked onset /sl/ (.251) than before the more marked onset /st/ (.360). As demonstrated in Table 10–1, the two sets of constraints interacted in that the highest frequency of epenthesis occurred after word-final consonants before the more marked onset (.408) and least frequently after word-final vowels before the less marked onset (.177).

The second study which examined the possible interaction between structures in a markedness relationship and different environments examined the word-initial onsets /sl/ and /sN/ (where /sN/ is the collapsed category of /sm/ and /sn/) (Carlisle, in press). This study was actually a reanalysis of Carlisle's (1988) data. In the original study the primary purpose was to determine whether vowel epenthesis would occur less frequently after the less marked onset /sl/ than before the more marked

**Table 10–1.** Rank order of epenthesis after consonantal and vocalic environments before more marked and less marked onsets

| | Word-Initial Onsets | |
| --- | --- | --- |
| *Environments* | */sl/ - /st/* | */sl/ - /sN/* |
| *Vowel* | | |
| Before less marked onset | .177 | .226 |
| Before more marked onset | .265 | .282 |
| *Consonant* | | |
| Before less marked onset | .286 | .312 |
| Before more marked onset | .408 | .391 |

*Note:* Rankings based on data found in Carlisle (1991b, in press).

onsets /sm/ and /sn/. Consequently, even though environment was strictly controlled before the different onsets, it was not a variable in the statistical analysis; in the reanalysis it was.

The results of this study were very similar to the one just reviewed for /st/ and /sl/. For environment, the subjects, who were native Spanish speakers, used vowel epenthesis significantly less frequently after a word-final vowel (.254) than after a word-final consonant (.351). In addition, epenthesis occurred significantly less frequently before the less marked onset (.269) than before the more marked onset (.336). As in the previous study (see Table 10–1), the two sets of constraints interacted so that the least amount of epenthesis occurred after a word-final vowel before the less marked onset (.226), and the greatest amount of epenthesis occurred after a word-final consonant before the more marked onset (.391).

The consistency of these studies is striking; in both, epenthesis was less frequent after vowels than consonants and less frequent before the less marked onset than the more marked onset. Another consistency was the relative strength of the two sets of constraints. Most variation analyses that have studied interacting constraints have attempted to determine the relative strength of the constraints through an examination of their rank order (Wolfram & Fasold, 1974). As indicated in Table 10–1, the ranking of the proportion of epenthesis is identical for both studies: The mean proportion of epenthesis was less frequent after vowels before both of the onsets than after consonants before both onsets, indicating that environment was a more powerful factor in inducing epenthesis than was the markedness relationship between the onsets.

A consistent finding from all of Carlisle's studies has been that epenthesis occurs significantly less frequently after vowels than after consonants.

Another way of saying this is that the target variant, in this case non-epenthesis, occurs more frequently after word-final vowels than after word-final consonants. A number of studies in both first language production (Wolfram & Christian, 1976) and second language acquisition (Gatbonton, 1978) have documented that target variants of a word-initial variable seem to occur more frequently after a word-final vowel than after a word-final consonant. An example from first language production comes from Wolfram and Christian's study of Appalachian English. In that dialect, a word-initial voiced interdental fricative is less frequently deleted after a word-final vowel than after a word-final consonant. And in her study of word-initial (ð) in the English of native Francophones, Gatbonton (1978) found that the target variant [ð] occurred more frequently after a word-final open syllable than after a closed syllable. These results and others indicate that word-initial target variants occur more frequently after word-final vowels than after word-final consonants. Carlisle (in press) has proposed a tentative explanation for this pattern: Environments can be in markedness relationships just as variables can, and less marked environments will induce a higher frequency of target variants than will more marked environments.

In their exposition of markedness and the syllable, Kaye and Lowenstamm (1981) noted that open syllables, those with a nonbranching rime, are less marked than are closed syllables, those with a branching rime. Thus, syllables of the form CV and V will be less marked than any closed syllables. In the two studies by Carlisle just reviewed it was observed that epenthesis occurred less frequently after vowels than after consonants; another way of saying this, of course, is that epenthesis occurred less frequently after an open syllable, a less marked syllable, than after a closed syllable, a more marked syllable. As a consequence, the two studies of vowel epenthesis actually examined the influence of two sets of constraints, the two-members of each differing in degree of markedness: Less marked onsets were modified less frequently than were more marked onsets, and epenthesis occurred less frequently after open syllables than it did after closed syllables. As indicated in Table 10–2, in the two studies epenthesis occurred least frequently when the two less marked constraints were in conjunction; and it occurred most frequently when the two more marked constraints were in conjunction. An intermediate frequency of epenthesis occurred when a less marked constraint was in conjunction with a more marked constraint.

It thus appears that less marked environments induce a higher frequency of target variants than do more marked environments. However, great caution should be taken with this proposal because there is already some evidence against it from variation analyses of primary languages. Wolfram and Christian (1976) observed that word-initial unstressed vowels were more frequently deleted after a word-final vowel than after a word-final

**Table 10–2.** The interaction of more and less marked environments with more and less marked onsets

| Environments | Onsets | |
| --- | --- | --- |
| | Less Marked | More Marked |
| Open Syllable | – – | – + |
| Closed Syllable | + – | + + |

*Note:* + = more marked constraint; – = less marked constraint.

consonant. In other words, the target variant appeared more frequently after the more marked environment than after the less marked environment. Consequently, it appears as if the alternation of consonant and vowel across word boundaries is more crucial than the markedness of the environments before the variable. This finding differs dramatically from all the others reviewed in this section, and further investigation obviously is needed on the relationship between word-final environments word-initial variables.

## INSTRUCTIONAL IMPLICATIONS

The research on markedness relationships and the effects of environment provide some interesting pedagogical implications for the instruction of pronunciation. If one of the goals of the the teaching of pronunciation is to first provide students with materials and tasks with which they can be assured of having more success, instructors can arrange many phonological structures in a hierarchy of difficulty. As mentioned previously, less marked structures are easier to acquire than more marked structures. Therefore, instructors could present less marked phonological structures before more marked structures. To use the example of onsets, shorter onsets are less marked than longer onsets, so instructors could proceed by teaching two-member onsets before three-member onsets. However, length of onset is just one type of markedness involving onsets; within each group of onset type, some onsets are more marked than others. For example, two-member onsets that are /s/ initial are in the following markedness relationship: /sl-/ < /sm-/, /sn-/ < /st-/, /sp-/, /sk-/. The two onsets /sm-/ and /sn-/ are more marked than /sl-/ according to implicational markedness relationships (Greenberg, 1965), and the three onsets /st-/, /sp-/, and /sk-/ are more marked than the others because they violate the Universal Canonical Syllable Structures for onsets (Tropf, 1987). After these two-member onsets have been presented in this particular order, three-member onsets could then be presented as they are more marked than the two-member onsets.

Order of markedness relationships would be only part of the overall hierarchy of difficulty, however. As discussed previously, environment is exceptionally important in determining the frequency with which given variants occur. Essentially, the target variant of a given variable is more likely to occur after a vocalic environment than after a consonantal environment. Taken in conjunction with the two-member onsets previously mentioned, the following hierarchy of difficulty for two member onsets obtains:

Vocalic environment with /sl/.

Vocalic environment with /sm/ and /sn/.

Vocalic environment with /st/, /sp/, and /sk/.

Consonantal environment with /sl/.

Consonantal environment with /sm/ and /sn/.

Consonantal environment with /st/, /sp/, and /sk/.

Because environment is a more powerful constraint than is the markedness relationships among the onsets, all onsets are more easily acquired first before the vocalic environment.

## CONCLUSION

Markedness relationships and environment are two of the most crucial factors in structuring interlanguage phonology. The testing hypothesis on the influence of markedness has essentially been that less marked structures are easier to acquire than are more marked structures; another way of saying this, of course, is that less marked structures will be less frequently modified than will more marked structures or that a higher frequency of the target variant will occur for the less marked structure than for the more marked structure. The fairly impressive number of studies examining the relationship between markedness relationships and interlanguage variability have been uniform in their findings: Less marked structures are less frequently modified than are more marked structures.

Environment has also been shown to be an important factor in determining the frequency with which target variants occur; some environments induce a higher frequency of the target variant than do others. An interesting question is whether environments themselves can be in markedness relationships and whether the less marked environment will induce a higher frequency of a target variant than will a more marked environment.

In spite of the obvious importance of both markedness relationships and environment in structuring the interlanguage, very little research has examined their interaction. Studies that have examined variables in markedness relationships generally have not considered the concomitant influence of environment, and the studies that have examined environment dealt with variables that were not in markedness relationships. The few studies that have examined the interaction have concluded that environment is a more powerful constraint than is markedness.

# REFERENCES

Altenberg, E., & Vago, R. (1983). Theoretical implications of an error analysis of second language phonology production. *Language Learning, 33*, 427–448.

Anderson, J. (1987). The markedness differential hypothesis and syllable structure difficulty. In G. Ioup & S. Weinberger (Eds.), *Interlanguage phonology: The acquisition of a second language sound system* (pp. 279–291). Cambridge, MA: Newbury House.

Battistella, E. (1990). *Markedness: The evaluative superstructure of language.* Albany: The State University of New York Press.

Beebe, L. (1977a). The influence of the listener on code-switching. *Language Learning, 27*, 331–339.

Beebe, L. (1977b). Dialect code-switching of bilingual children in their second language. *CUNY Forum, 3*, 141–158.

Beebe, L. (1980). Sociolinguistic variation and style shifting in second language acquisition. *Language Learning, 30*, 433–447.

Benson, B. (1988). Universal preference for the open syllable as an independent process in interlanguage phonology. *Language Learning, 38*, 221–242.

Broselow, E. (1983). Non-obvious transfer: On predicting epenthesis errors. In S. Gass & L. Selinker (Eds.), *Language transfer in language learning* (pp. 269–280). Rowley, MA; Newbury House.

Broselow, E. (1984). An investigation of transfer in second language phonology. *International Review of Applied Linguistics, 22*, 253–269.

Broselow, E., & Finer, D. (1991). Parameter setting in second language phonology and syntax. *Second Language Research, 7*, 35–59.

Cairns, C., & Feinstein, M. (1982). Markedness and the theory of syllable structure. *Linguistic Inquiry, 13*, 193–225.

Carlisle, R. (1988). The effect of markedness on epenthesis in Spanish/English interlanguage phonology. *Issues and Developments in English and Applied Linguistics, 3*, 15–23.

Carlisle, R. (1991a). The influence of environment on vowel epenthesis in Spanish/English interphonology. *Applied Linguistics, 12*, 76–95.

Carlisle, R. (1991b). The influence of syllable structure universals on the variability of interlanguage phonology. In A. D. Volpe (Ed.), *The seventeenth LACUS forum 1990* (pp. 135–145). Lake Bluff, IL: Linguistic Association of Canada and the United States.

Carlisle, R. (in press). Environment and markedness as interacting constraints on vowel epenthesis. In A. James & J. Leather (Eds.), *New sounds 92*. Amsterdam: University of Amsterdam Press.

Clements, G., & Keyser, S. (1983). *CV phonology: A generative theory of the syllable.* Cambridge MA: The MIT Press.

Comrie, B. (1984). Why linguists need language acquirers. In W. Rutherford (Ed.), *Language universals and second language acquisition* (pp. 11–29). Amsterdam: John Benjamins.

Comrie, B. (1989). *Language universals and linguistic typology* (2nd ed.). Chicago: University of Chicago Press.

Comrie, B. (1990). Second language acquisition and language universals research. *Studies in Second Language Acquisition, 12,* 209–218.

Dickerson, L. (1975). The learner's interlanguage as a system of variable rules. *TESOL Quarterly, 9,* 401–407.

Dickerson, L., & Dickerson, W. (1977). Interlanguage phonology: current research and future directions. In S. P. Corder & E. Roulet (Eds.), *Interlanguages and pidgins and their relationship to second language pedagogy* (pp. 18–29). Neufchatel, Switzerland: Libraire Droz.

Dickerson, W. (1976). The psycholinguistic unity of language learning and language change. *Language Learning, 26,* 215–231.

Eckman, F. (1977). Markedness and the contrastive analysis hypothesis. *Language Learning, 27,* 315–330.

Eckman, F. (1981a). On the naturalness of interlanguage phonological rules. *Language Learning, 31,* 195–216.

Eckman, F. (1981b). On predicting phonological difficulty in second language acquisition. *Studies in Second Language Acquisition, 4,* 18–30.

Eckman, F. (1984). Universals, typologies, and interlanguage. In W. E. Rutherford (Ed.), *Language universals and second language acquisition* (pp. 79–105). Amsterdam: John Benjamins.

Eckman, F. (1987). The reduction of word-final consonant clusters in interlanguage. In A. James & J. Leather (Eds.), *Sound patterns in second language acquisition* (pp. 143–162). Providence, RI: Foris Publications.

Eckman, F. (1991). The structural conformity hypothesis and the acquisition of consonant clusters in the interlanguage of ESL learners. *Studies in Second Language Acquisition, 13,* 23–41.

Edge, B. (1991). The production of word-final voiced obstruents in English by L1 speakers of Japanese and Cantonese. *Studies in Second Language Acquisition, 13,* 377–393.

Ellis, R. (1985). Sources of variability in interlanguage. *Applied Linguistics, 6,* 118–131.

Ellis, R. (1988). The effects of linguistic environment on the second language acquisition of grammatical rules. *Applied Linguistics, 9,* 257–274.

Fasold, R. (1984). Variation theory and language learning. In P. Trudgill (Ed.), *Applied sociolinguistics* (pp. 245–261). London: Academic Press.

Flege, J., & Davidian, R. (1984). Transfer and developmental processes in adult foreign language speech production. *Applied Psycholinguistics, 5,* 323–347.

Gatbonton, E. (1978). Patterned phonetic variability in second-language speech: a gradual diffusion model. *Canadian Modern Language Review, 34,* 335–347.

Greenberg, J. (1965). Some generalizations concerning initial and final consonant clusters. *Linguistics, 18,* 5–34.

Hammarberg, B. (1990). Conditions on transfer in phonology. In J. Leather & A. James (Eds.), *New sounds 90: Proceedings of the Amsterdam symposium of the acquisition of second-language speech* (pp. 198–215). Amsterdam: University of Amsterdam.

Harris, J. (1983). *Syllable structure and stress in Spanish: A nonlinear analysis.* Cambridge, MA: The MIT Press.

Hodne, B. (1985). Yet another look at interlanguage phonology: The modification of English syllable structure by native speakers of Polish. *Language Learning, 35,* 404–422.

Hooper, J. (1976). *An introduction to natural generative phonology.* New York: Academic Press.

Ioup, G. (1984). Is there a structural foreign accent? A comparison of syntactic and phonological errors in second language acquisition. *Language Learning, 34,* 1–17.

Kaye, J., & Lowenstamm, J. (1981). *Syllable structure and markedness theory. In Theory of markedness in generative grammar* (pp. 287–315). Pisa, Italy: Scuola Normale Superiore.

Kiparsky, P. (1979). Metrical structure assignment is cyclic. Linguistic Inquiry, 10, 421–441.

Labov, W. (1966). *The social stratification of English in New York City.* Washington, DC: Center for Applied Linguistics.

Labov, W. (1969). Contraction, deletion, and inherent variability of the English copula. *Language, 45,* 715–762.

Ladefoged, P. (1982). *A course in phonetics* (2nd ed). New York: Harcourt Brace Jovanovich.

Major, R. C. (1987). A model for interlanguage phonology. In G. Ioup & S. Weinberger (Eds.), *Interlanguage phonology: The acquisition of a second language sound system* (pp. 101–124). Cambridge, MA: Newbury House.

Moore, F. B., & Marzano, R. J. (1979). Common errors of Spanish speakers learning English. *Research in the Teaching of English, 13,* 161–167 .

Politzer, R. L., & Ramirez, A. G. (1973). An error analysis of the spoken English of Mexican American pupils in a bilingual school and a monolingual school. *Language Learning, 23,* 39–62.

Riney, T. (1990). Age and open syllable preference in interlanguage phonology. In H. Burmeister & P. Rounds (Eds.), *Variability in second language acquisition: Proceedings of the tenth meeting of the second language research forum: (Vol. 2,* pp. 655–666). Eugene: Dept. of Linguistics, University of Oregon.

Sato, C. (1984). Phonological processes in second language acquisition: Another look at interlanguage syllable structure. *Language Learning, 34,* 43–57.

Sato, C. (1985). Task variation in interlanguage phonology. In S. Gass & C. Madden (Eds.), *Input in second language acquisition* (pp. 181–196). Rowley, MA: Newbury House.

Schmidt, R. (1987). Sociolinguistic variation and language transfer in phonology. In G. Ioup & S. Weinberger (Eds.), *Interlanguage phonology: The acquisition of a second language sound system* (pp. 365–377). Cambridge, MA: Newbury House.

Selkirk, E. (1984). On the major class features of syllable theory. In M. Aronoff & R. Oehrle (Eds.), *Language sound structure* (pp. 107–136). Cambridge, MA: MIT Press.

Shockey, L. (1974). Phonetic and phonological properties of connected speech. *Ohio State Working Papers in Linguistics, 17.*

Smith, B. L., & Stoel-Gammon, C. (1983). A longitudinal study of the development of stop consonant production in normal and Down's syndrome children. *Journal of Speech and Hearing Disorders, 48,* 114–119.

Tarone, E. (1980). Some influences on the syllable structure of interlanguage phonology. *International Review of Applied Linguistics, 18,* 139–152.

Tarone, E. (1988). *Variation in interlanguage.* London: Edward Arnold.

Tropf (1987), H. (1987). Sonority as a variability factor in second language phonology. In A. James & J. Leather (Eds.), *Sound patterns in second language acquisition* (pp. 173–191). Providence, RI: Foris Publications.

Vennemann, T. (1988). *Preference laws for syllable structure and the explanation of sound change.* New York: Mouton de Gruyter.

Weinberger, S. (1987). The influence of linguistic context on syllable simplification. In G. Ioup & S. Weinberger (Eds.), *Interlanguage phonology: The acquisition of a second language sound system* (pp. 401–417). Rowley, MA: Newbury House.

Whiteman, M. F. (1981). Dialect influence in writing. In M. F. Whiteman (Ed.), *Writing: The nature, development, and teaching of written communication: Vol. 1. Variation in writing: Linguistic-cultural differences* (pp. 153–166). Hillsdale, NJ: Lawrence Erlbaum.

Wolfram, W. (1969). *A sociolinguistic description of Detroit Negro speech.* Washington, DC: Center for Applied Linguistics.

Wolfram, W. (1973). *Sociolinguistic aspects of assimilation: Puerto Rican English in New York City.* Arlington, VA: Center for Applied Linguistics.

Wolfram, W. (1985). Variability in tense marking: a case for the obvious. *Language Learning, 35,* 229–253.

Wolfram, W. (1989). Systematic variability in second-language tense marking. In M. R. Eisenstein (Ed.), *The dynamic interlanguage* (pp. 187–197). New York: Plenum Press.

Wolfram, W., & Christian, D. (1976). *Appalachian speech.* Arlington, VA: Center for Applied Linguistics.

Wolfram, W., & Fasold, R. (1974). *The study of social dialects in American English.* Englewood Cliffs, NJ: Prentice-Hall.

# CHAPTER 11

*Pronunciation Difficulties in ESL: Coda Consonants in English Interlanguage*

FRED R. ECKMAN, Ph.D.
GREGORY K. IVERSON, Ph.D.

Over the last 15 years or so, the role of universal principles in explaining facts about second language acquisition has been steadily increasing, especially in the area of syntax (Eckman, 1977; Flynn, 1987; Gass, 1979; White, 1989). The use of universals in the description of second language (L2) phonology, however, has been less prominent; and some of the theoretical approaches to second language acquisition that postulate a significant role for universals in explaining L2 syntax have resorted simply to L1 interference as an explanation for the properties of L2 phonology (Dulay & Burt, 1983; Schachter, 1974). Pedagogical approaches to L2 learning (viz. Krashen 1985), in a similar vein, have devoted much in the way of theoretical apparatus to explaining the acquisition of syntax, but offered little discussion of the mastering of pronunciation, stating only that "speaking emerges on its own" after a sufficient amount of acquisition has taken place. Implicit in this lack of attention to L2 phonology is the assumption that learners' pronunciation of the target language (TL) is not a function of higher order principles of grammar, but instead can be explained largely through L1 interference.

The purpose of the present paper is twofold. First, we report new results of a pronunciation interference study that investigated single consonants in the syllable codas of six subjects (two native speakers each of Korean, Japanese, and Cantonese), all of whom were university-level English as a second language (ESL) learners; second, we offer evidence that the explanation for pronunciation difficulties of ESL learners lies both in L1-L2 differences and in general principles of markedness, which are defined, in the cases under consideration here, on extralinear or prosodic structure. Based on our analysis of certain L2 syllable codas and their relative sonority-sensitivity, more specifically, we observed that the acquisition of single-consonant codas follows an increasingly more familiar pattern: The relatively marked coda obstruents of the target language are considerably more troublesome for learners than are TL coda sonorants. This is true, it appears, even when the native language (NL) contains both obstruents and sonorants in the coda, as well as when the NL contains neither of these consonant types in the coda.

The chapter is structured as follows. First, we present a brief description of the phonological framework and the basic principles involved. We then describe our study, report the results, and interpret our findings. Finally, we consider several implications of this study for L2 acquisition theory and pedagogy.

## THE PHONOLOGICAL FRAMEWORK

For the purposes of this chapter, we follow the now common practice of ascribing a rather rich hierarchical representation to sequences of phonological segments, organizing them along various lines into skeletal timing units (Cs and Vs; Clements & Keyser, 1983), weight-bearing units (i.e., moras; Hayes, 1989; Hyman, 1985; Tranel, 1992), and syllables (Selkirk, 1982, 1984, and many other recent sources). The syllable itself we consider to consist of an obligatory nucleus element (usually a vowel or diphthong) preceded by an optional onset constituent containing one or more consonants; the nucleus, in addition, may be followed by another consonantal configuration internal to the syllable, the coda.

Languages are known to vary considerably as to both the number and type of segments they license to occur in each of the syllabic positions of onset, nucleus, and coda, about which we shall have more to say presently. Aside from a few possible exceptions, however, the linear arrangement of syllable-internal segments follows a cross-linguistic

pattern that has come to be known as the Sonority Sequencing Generalization (1), which in turn is based on an acoustic ranking of sound classes
in terms of the now familiar Sonority Hierarchy, the most general
version of which is presented in (2) below.

(1) Sonority Sequencing Generalization (adapted from Selkirk, 1982).
    Sonority values may not increase from the peak to the margins of the
    syllable.

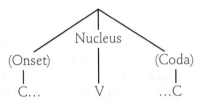

(2) Sonority Hierarchy (Clements, 1990; Selkirk, 1984).

| Major Class | Sonority Index |
|---|---|
| Vowels | 4 |
| Glides | 3 |
| Liquids | 2 |
| Nasals | 1 |
| Obstruents | 0 |

   The Sonority Sequencing Generalization thus places vowels, whose
sonority index is highest, at the peaks of syllables and consonants at the
margins. In a language such as English, which permits more than one
consonant in onsets as well as in codas, the requirement that sonority
values not increase toward the syllable margins sanctions complex
onsets such as obstruent plus liquid, nasal, or glide ("slow," "snow,"
"sway") and codas with the reverse order of consonants ("else," "tense,"
"house"). Even segmentally doubly complex monosyllables like "plump"
or "snort" then are possible because their sonority profiles conform to
the Sonority Sequencing Generalization, whereas the same segments,
when arrayed in a sequence that violates this principle, are not possible
as single syllables (*lpupm, *nsotr, etc.). Under the further, universal
condition that onsets must be maximized, and so are preferred over
codas in cases that would otherwise give rise to indeterminacy of syllabic
affiliation (i.e., CVCV parses as CV.CV rather than CVC.V), multiple
voweled sequences like *complain* will parse into *com.plain* rather than
**co.mplain*. (**Comp.lain* and **compl.ain* would conform to the Sonority

Sequencing Generalization, but these fail to maximize the second syllable's onset.)

Apart from its role in determining the intrasyllabic sequencing of segments, however, the Sonority Hierarchy is involved, at least in part, in the actual selection of segments. Generally speaking, any consonant in a language's inventory of phonemes may be found to occur in (single) onset position, as indeed is the case in English (e.g., "pea," "bee," "tea," "sea," "me," "Lee," "we," . . .) except for the rather marginal word-initial exclusion of the voiced alveopalatal fricative (French *Jacques*) and the much stronger prohibition of the syllable-initial velar nasal (Vietnamese *Nga*), which, if it derives from the nasal plus stop cluster /ng/ in English (Chomsky & Halle 1968), is excluded on more general grounds (no initial /mb/, /nt/, etc.). English is a language which also sanctions any consonant in its inventory (save /h/) in the syllable coda; but several currents in syllable theory today are converging on the idea that consonantally weaker or more sonorant segments are preferred in coda position (Clements, 1990; Goldsmith, 1990; Prince, 1984). In many languages, in fact, nonsonorants may not appear at all in the codas of independent syllables; this is the case in Japanese (just a basically alveolar nasal is permitted), Seylayarese (velar nasal only), Mandarin Chinese (either alveolar or velar nasal, or glide), and Hausa (either glide or liquid); other languages (Spanish, German, English, Cantonese) allow at least some members of both the obstruent and sonorant classes to occur at the end of the syllable; still others (Hawaiian, Maori) disallow any type of consonant syllable finally. There appears to be no language, however, that realizes the fourth distributional possibility, in which at least some obstruents but no sonorant consonants are permitted in codas, as shown in (3) below.

(3) Type of permitted (single) coda-consonant

| Sonorant | + | + | − | − |
|---|---|---|---|---|
| Obstruent | + | − | − | + |
| | English | Mandarin | Maori | *** |

Obstruents in syllable codas are thus typologically "marked" relative to coda sonorants, and so would be expected to show less stability over time (Vennemann, 1988), to evince specific limitations on their freedom of occurrence even in reconstructed languages (Iverson & Salmons, 1992), or to emerge relatively late in the process of native language acquisition (Dinnsen, Chin, Elbert, & Powell, 1990). Within the class of obstruents itself, of course, there are other well-known, typologically based markedness relations: Affricates are marked relative to fricatives, fricatives are marked relative to stops, voiced obstruents are marked relative to voiceless ones, and so on (Eckman, 1977). Hence, in German, the syllable-coda neutralizations of voiced obstruents to voiceless ones (Goldsmith, 1990), or in Korean of fricatives and affricates to stops (Kim-Renaud 1978), are also instantiations of the drive toward unmarked articulation in codas, even though, within the class of zero-sonority obstruents, these mergers obviously cannot be motivated by any markedness considerations that relate to sonority. The focus of investigation in this chapter, however, is on the cross-linguistic property of coda sonority-sensitivity presented in (3), as it relates to L2 acquisition; we test in particular the notion that typological markedness is a reliable predictor of difficulty (Eckman, 1977; Hawkins, 1987) in the interlanguage syllable structure patterns of ESL learners.

Previous studies in this general vein (Broselow & Finer, 1991; Eckman & Iverson, 1993) have considered consonant clusters in syllable onsets, showing that typologically marked TL configurations present greater difficulty (cause more errors, are mastered later) than do less marked structures even though neither type exists in the NL (and so both could be expected to contribute basically equal difficulty). For example, in Korean, no consonant clusters are permitted at all in syllable onsets, yet Koreans learning English are less troubled by stop plus liquid onset clusters ("play," "tray") than they are by fricative plus liquid onsets ("fray," "slay"), a finding which is to be expected, we conclude, in view of the typological markedness or cross-linguistic phonological complexity of fricatives as a class relative to stops. Here, however, we turn our attention to the analysis of sonority preferences among single-segment codas in the interlanguage of adult L2 learners of English. Data were gathered as outlined below.

## THE PRESENT STUDY

### METHODOLOGY

Our study interviewed six subjects, two native speakers each of Japanese, Korean, and Cantonese. All subjects were adults between the ages of 20 and 32, and at the time of the study, all were enrolled in the English as a Second Language (ESL) Intensive Program at the University of Wisconsin-Milwaukee. In addition to language background, the subjects were also selected according to overall target-language proficiency, which, based on their placement in the instructional program, was intermediate or high intermediate.

Each of the subjects took part in at least eight casual conversations, lasting from 5 to 10 minutes each. The conversations dealt with a predetermined topic that required the subjects to discuss some aspect of their lives (such as family or a course of study), to give an opinion about something (American food or studying overseas), or to recount some event or procedure (a close brush with death or how to obtain a visa).

The sessions were carried out in a sound-treated room in which the subject and interviewer were seated across a coffee table. The subject's speech was recorded using a high-quality neck-suspended microphone connected to a tape recorder located in an adjacent room. The tapes were then phonetically transcribed by a research assistant, in a close, phonetic transcription. Random 5-minute portions of speech from each task type (approximately 10% to 15% of each tape) were then independently transcribed by a different transcriber to determine reliability. A point-to-point comparison of the transcriptions yielded 85% agreement, which was considered acceptable.

It should be clear that our protocol was not designed to elicit certain types of words, nor was any attempt made to gather a definite number of words. Our procedure instead was designed to induce the subject to converse casually. Although the topics of the conversations were determined ahead of time, there was no attempt to control the vocabulary used by the subject. The object was simply to "cast out a net" in an attempt to gather as many words as possible containing single-consonant codas. This methodology, we believe, elicited a naturally casual pronunciation of the words in question, a style very closely approaching the vernacular.

## SCORING

In this section we briefly outline our scoring procedure, making two points: (1) we scored only L2 words in which the codas of the underlying representation (UR) contained a single consonant; and (2) we scored the utterances in question only in terms of whether the target consonant was present or absent. Each of these points will be discussed in turn.

The decision to score the subjects' utterances on the basis of the UR has several consequences. The first and most obvious is that we had to determine the UR of any relevant utterance. This was done by attesting alternant phonetic representations. Thus, for example, to score the form [laj] *like* as lacking the obstruent in the coda, we needed to attest the form [lajk], in which the coda consonant appeared. On the basis of these two utterances, we would postulate /lajk/ as the UR in the subject's interlanguage and would consider the target coda as [k]. If we attested only the form [laj] and no alternant was attested, clearly no coda consonant could be established as part of the UR, and the utterance [laj] was not counted as lacking a [k] in the coda. The second consequence of this decision was that we scored only utterances whose UR contained a single-consonant coda. We therefore ignored utterances that contained a superficial single-consonant coda if this resulted from the reduction of an underlying consonant cluster in the coda. For example, if a subject uttered both [tes] and [test] for *taste*, we determined that the UR for these utterances was /test/; because this form contains a cluster in the coda, neither [tes] nor [test] was scored. The rationale for this procedure was that our goal was to determine the relative difficulty of single-consonant codas, and we did not want our results confounded by forms that superficially contained only one consonant in the coda, where that single consonant resulted from a process of reduction.

The second point we wish to make about the scoring is that we considered only whether a target consonant was present or absent in the coda and whether this consonant was final. Consequently, we scored as errors target coda consonants that were absent or occurred before a paragogic vowel. Thus, subjects were scored as producing coda consonants even when the consonant of the L2 utterance and the the consonant of the TL form did not match. For example, if a subject said [wɪf] for [wɪθ] *with*, [bɪk] for [bɪg] big, the subject was given credit for producing a single consonant in the coda. If the subject inserted a final vowel after the target consonant, the utterance was counted as an error.

## RESULTS AND DISCUSSION

The results for each subject are presented individually in Tables 11–1 through 11–6. The subjects' performance is reported for each type of consonant: obstruents, nasals (labial, alveolar, and velar), liquids, and glides. Because we had to allow for the phonetic differences between English /r/ and the [r]-sound in Cantonese, Japanese, or Korean, which is a tongue-tip consonant in complementary distribution with a lateral, we credited a subject with any pronunciation of English /r/ ranging from a flap [r] to [l]. Therefore, the tables do not distinguish between [r] and [l] codas, but consider them together under the rubric of liquids.

Another consideration in reporting the data is the phonological context in which the coda consonant appeared. Because the data were gathered in connected discourse, we distinguished three environments for the codas: whether the following word began with a consonant, whether there was a pause following, or whether the following word began with a vowel. For each type of coda consonant in each of the three environments, we report the total number of targets attempted, the number of errors, and the percentage of error.

In evaluating our overall claim, one final consideration needs to be taken into account, namely, interference from the NL phonology. Other things being equal, our claim will be supported to the extent that subjects evinced better performance (i.e., a lower percentage of error) on codas which are relatively less marked than they did on codas that are relatively more marked. By "other things being equal" we mean, once NL-TL phonological differences have been factored out. Therefore, when we compare coda types, we need to take into account whether the NL phonology interacts with the coda type in question. Consider, for example, an NL such as Korean, which has both obstruent and nasal codas. We predict that, in the interlanguage, obstruent codas should be more difficult than nasal codas by virtue of the relatively marked nature of obstruent codas, even though the NL sanctions codas of both types.

The results reported in Tables 11–1 through 11–6 show that the predictions are, in general, supported. The results for the two Cantonese subjects are reported in Tables 11–1 and 11–2. Both Cantonese subjects encountered more difficulty with obstruent codas than with nasal codas, as shown by the greater percentage of errors. Because obstruent codas are marked relative to nasal codas, this bias in the distribution supports our prediction. Cantonese itself includes both of these coda types, though it allows far fewer varieties of coda obstruents than does English; thus, in Cantonese, the only obstruents permitted in codas are the unreleased, voiceless stops [p], [t], and [k] (in addition to glides and all three nasals). Nonetheless, both Cantonese subjects produced a significant percentage of obstruent coda errors on voiceless stops: 35 out of 104, or 34%, for subject WKS (Table 11–1), and 85 out of 188, or 72%, for subject HCN (Table 11–2). An explanation based simply on NL interference, of course, would not be able to account for errors among TL stops which also are possible in the NL. First language interference does appear to be at play, though, in explaining the reported Cantonese difficulty with coda liquids; as this segment type does not occur in the codas of the NL, it would be expected to be a locus of interlanguage error.

The results for the Korean subjects, shown in Tables 11–3 and 11–4, reveal the same sort of pattern, although the NL syllable structures are somewhat different in this case. Thus, both Korean subjects had more trouble with obstruent codas than they did with nasal codas. This was true even though Korean, like Cantonese, includes both voiceless stops and all three nasals in coda position. For subject YSK, 9% (5 of 58, Table 11–3) of the errors on coda obstruents involved voiceless stops, and for

**Table 11–1.** Coda consonant errors of Subject WKS. Native Language: Cantonese

|        | Obstruent | | | [m] | | | [n] | | | [ŋ] | | | Liquid | | | Glide | | |
|--------|-----|-----|-----|-----|-----|-----|-----|-----|-----|-----|-----|-----|-----|-----|-----|-----|-----|-----|
|        | _C | _## | _V | _C | _## | _V | _C | _## | _V | _C | _## | _V | _C | _## | _V | _C | _## | _V |
| Number | 260 | 119 | 124 | 41 | 13 | 15 | 77 | 23 | 28 | 36 | 12 | 9 | 104 | 31 | 80 | 48 | 15 | 36 |
| Errors | 82 | 10 | 12 | 0 | 0 | 0 | 1 | 0 | 1 | 0 | 1 | 0 | 7 | 0 | 0 | 0 | 0 | 0 |
| % error | 32 | 8 | 10 | 0 | 0 | 0 | 1 | 0 | 4 | 0 | 8 | 0 | 7 | 0 | 0 | 0 | 0 | 0 |

**Table 11–2.** Coda consonant errors of Subject HCN. Native Language: Cantonese

|        | Obstruent | | | [m] | | | [n] | | | [ŋ] | | | Liquid | | | Glide | | |
|--------|-----|-----|-----|-----|-----|-----|-----|-----|-----|-----|-----|-----|-----|-----|-----|-----|-----|-----|
|        | _C | _## | _V | _C | _## | _V | _C | _## | _V | _C | _## | _V | _C | _## | _V | _C | _## | _V |
| Number | 414 | 152 | 225 | 84 | 18 | 32 | 159 | 41 | 57 | 78 | 32 | 33 | 153 | 60 | 59 | 63 | 20 | 48 |
| Errors | 78 | 13 | 27 | 0 | 0 | 0 | 2 | 1 | 1 | 1 | 1 | 1 | 28 | 8 | 14 | 1 | 0 | 0 |
| % error | 16 | 8 | 11 | 0 | 0 | 0 | 1 | 2 | 2 | 1 | 3 | 3 | 18 | 13 | 24 | 2 | 0 | 0 |

**Table 11–3.** Coda consonant errors of Subject YSK. Native Language: Korean

|        | Obstruent | | | [m] | | | [n] | | | [ŋ] | | | Liquid | | | Glide | | |
|--------|-----|-----|-----|-----|-----|-----|-----|-----|-----|-----|-----|-----|-----|-----|-----|-----|-----|-----|
|        | _C | _## | _V | _C | _## | _V | _C | _## | _V | _C | _## | _V | _C | _## | _V | _C | _## | _V |
| Number | 239 | 54 | 163 | 18 | 4 | 10 | 37 | 4 | 18 | 14 | 1 | 13 | 52 | 20 | 49 | 70 | 1 | 13 |
| Errors | 34 | 5 | 19 | 0 | 0 | 0 | 0 | 0 | 0 | 0 | 0 | 0 | 2 | 1 | 5 | 1 | 0 | 0 |
| % error | 14 | 9 | 12 | 0 | 0 | 0 | 0 | 0 | 0 | 0 | 0 | 0 | 4 | 5 | 9 | 1 | 0 | 0 |

**Table 11–4.** Coda consonant errors of Subject JKY. Native Language: Korean

|        | Obstruent | | | [m] | | | [n] | | | [ŋ] | | | Liquid | | | Glide | | |
|--------|-----|-----|-----|-----|-----|-----|-----|-----|-----|-----|-----|-----|-----|-----|-----|-----|-----|-----|
|        | _C | _## | _V | _C | _## | _V | _C | _## | _V | _C | _## | _V | _C | _## | _V | _C | _## | _V |
| Number | 354 | 147 | 139 | 15 | 16 | 9 | 46 | 22 | 13 | 19 | 22 | 9 | 91 | 55 | 26 | 105 | 9 | 54 |
| Errors | 83 | 35 | 11 | 1 | 0 | 0 | 2 | 0 | 0 | 0 | 0 | 1 | 9 | 5 | 8 | 0 | 0 | 0 |
| % error | 23 | 24 | 8 | 6 | 0 | 0 | 4 | 0 | 0 | 0 | 0 | 11 | 4 | 5 | 9 | 0 | 0 | 0 |

JKY, 14% of the obstruent-coda errors (18 of 129, Table 11–4) were in voiceless stops. The overall case for interlanguage sonority sensitivity becomes even stronger when we consider the Korean subjects' production of glides in the coda. Despite the phonological absence of glides in coda position in Korean, English codas with /w/ and /y/ presented far less difficulty than did codas with fricatives or affricates, or even stops. Again, our hypothesis that the relatively marked, low sonority codas should cause more difficulty than the relatively unmarked, high sonority codas was borne out.

However, the situation regarding the liquids is not so easily explained for Korean learners of English. In the case of the Cantonese subjects, we accounted for the difficulty with liquid codas in terms of a basic NL-TL difference. That is, Cantonese allows no liquids in codas, hence a high error rate in their attempted English TL pronunciation is to be expected. Korean, on the other hand, does permit liquids in codas, so the difficulty with these segments reported for our Korean subjects needs to be explained. Thus, we note that in Korean, [r] and [l] are in complementary distribution, with [r] restricted to onsets and [l] to codas (Iverson & Sohn, 1993). The two Korean subjects made the great majority of errors involving liquids on TL words containing [r] in the coda: Subject YSK (Table 11–3) produced eight errors on target liquid codas, all of which involved deleting a final [r] or inserting a paragogic vowel after it; subject JKY (Table 11–4) produced 22 errors on liquid codas, all but one (95%) deleting the [r] or inserting a vowel following it. Only one error involved (deletion of) a final [l]. We conclude that Korean speakers have no difficulty producing instances of syllable-final [l] because the phonology of the NL happens to stipulate lateral articulation for all coda liquids; but coda [r] is troublesome for Korean speakers because the NL also happens to exclude centrally released liquids from coda position.

These results of our Cantonese and Korean subjects' performance on English liquids may be worth further discussion. Although a phonetically lateral liquid ([l]) does occur syllable initially in Cantonese and other varieties of Chinese that do not sanction liquids in coda position, there is no contrast in Cantonese between [l] and a centrally released liquid ([r]). Thus, as in Korean, the feature [lateral] in Cantonese serves no role in the phonology per se, but rather is provided merely "by default" (i.e., allophonically) at the phonetic level. In Cantonese this feature accrues only to syllable-initial liquids, in Korean only to syllable-final liquids; accordingly, lateral pronunciations do not contrast with centrally released liquids in either Cantonese or Korean. But although the free occurrence of phonetically lateral liquids in Korean codas apparently transfers directly to the learner's English interlanguage, the absence of any coda liquids at all in Cantonese means that the phonologically noncontrastive feature [lateral] is also phonetically inaccessible in that position, with the result that coda [l] in the interlanguage of Cantonese speakers is predictably troublesome. In short, then, we explain the behavior of the Cantonese and Korean subjects with respect to obstruent and nasal codas in terms of principles of markedness and sonority differentiation; but we explain their behavior regarding liquids in terms of principles and distributions of the NL phonology. In this sense, language specific principles (e.g., the precluding of liquids from the codas of Cantonese and the transfer of this pattern into the interlanguage) take precedence over cross-linguistic principles (e.g., the predicted greater ease of producing higher sonority over lower sonority codas).

For the Japanese speakers, similarly, English coda liquids present a substantial interference challenge. Neither [l] nor [r] occurs finally in Japanese, and the language makes no contrast between the two sounds elsewhere in the word (Vance, 1987). Not surprisingly, then, Tables 11–5 and 11–6 show that the Japanese subjects made a relatively high percentage of errors on coda liquids. Although nasal segments, as a class, do occur finally in Japanese—alveolar nasals are permitted—there is no contrast in this position with the language's other nasal phoneme, /m/; in addition, the NL velar nasal allophone is restricted to word internal, preconsonantal environments. One of the two Japanese subjects (CH, Table 11–6) was particularly affected by this difference between the NL and the TL, and produced a substantial paragogic error rate in the attempted articulation of

**Table 11–5.** Coda consonant errors of Subject II. Native Language: Japanese

|  | Obstruent | | | [m] | | | [n] | | | [ŋ] | | | Liquid | | | Glide | | |
|---|---|---|---|---|---|---|---|---|---|---|---|---|---|---|---|---|---|---|
|  | _C_ | _##_ | _V_ | _C_ | _##_ | _V_ | _C_ | _##_ | _V_ | _C_ | _##_ | _V_ | _C_ | _##_ | _V_ | _C_ | _##_ | _V_ |
| Number | 279 | 109 | 168 | 48 | 6 | 17 | 52 | 9 | 32 | 36 | 9 | 13 | 97 | 13 | 55 | 145 | 3 | 14 |
| Errors | 26 | 2 | 8 | 0 | 0 | 0 | 1 | 0 | 0 | 0 | 0 | 1 | 17 | 2 | 3 | 0 | 0 | 0 |
| % error | 9 | 2 | 5 | 0 | 0 | 0 | 2 | 0 | 0 | 0 | 0 | 7 | 17 | 15 | 5 | 0 | 0 | 0 |

**Table 11–6.** Coda consonant errors of Subject CH. Native Language: Japanese

|  | Obstruent | | | [m] | | | [n] | | | [ŋ] | | | Liquid | | | Glide | | |
|---|---|---|---|---|---|---|---|---|---|---|---|---|---|---|---|---|---|---|
|  | _C_ | _##_ | _V_ | _C_ | _##_ | _V_ | _C_ | _##_ | _V_ | _C_ | _##_ | _V_ | _C_ | _##_ | _V_ | _C_ | _##_ | _V_ |
| Number | 287 | 111 | 146 | 40 | 8 | 17 | 53 | 18 | 24 | 39 | 7 | 18 | 73 | 21 | 36 | 75 | 9 | 27 |
| Errors | 47 | 27 | 23 | 2 | 0 | 2 | 6 | 1 | 10 | 8 | 3 | 8 | 12 | 8 | 6 | 0 | 0 | 1 |
| % error | 16 | 24 | 16 | 5 | 0 | 12 | 11 | 6 | 42 | 21 | 43 | 44 | 16 | 38 | 16 | 0 | 0 | 4 |

coda labial and velar nasals. The TL glides, however, presented essentially no difficulty, as our syllabic markedness hypothesis predicts. However, obstruents in coda position were somewhat troublesome, although perhaps not as much as expected in comparison to liquids and nasals. One confounding factor is that Japanese speakers have to learn to produce a contrast between liquids in an environment in which no liquids at all occur in their NL. Another factor is that vowels in Japanese typically are phonetically voiceless when between voiceless segments or when phrase-final following a voiceless sound. Such vowels often are hardly audible even to the trained ear, and the probability that some of them escaped the attention of our transcribers may account in part for the unexpectedly low incidence of error recorded among coda obstruents, many of which, of course, are voiceless.

In concluding this section, we note that our explanation of the subjects' performance on English coda consonants includes both language-specific and universal principles, with the former taking precedence over the latter. Using this combination of both principle types to explain the subjects' L2 pronunciations is parallel to to what has been hypothesized in L2 acquisition syntax. Thus, Flynn (1987) and White (1989)—who take the position that UG governs L2 acquistion—postulate that, when the settings of a given parameter of universal grammar (UG) differ in the native and target languages, the NL parameter setting is originally carried over into the early stages of the interlanguage. Subsequently, this parameter must be reset to a parametric value that more closely corresponds to the TL, and is allowed by UG.

To summarize, the relatively marked coda obstruents of English are generally more troublesome for speakers of Cantonese, Korean, and even Japanese than are English coda sonorants. This was true for subjects in the current study despite the fact that two of the NLs studied, Korean and Cantonese, have rather rich coda structures, including both nasals and stops at three places of articulation (along with one liquid in Korean), but excluding low sonority fricatives and affricates (as well as high sonority glides in Korean).

## PEDAGOGICAL IMPLICATIONS

Having shown that second language pronunciation—as has been argued in the literature for L2 syntax—is subject to higher order principles of grammar, we turn now to the topic of the implications that these findings have for teaching pronunciation in the L2 classroom. In this regard, we wish to make three points. First, our results strongly suggest that it is possible to teach pronunciation simply because it is governed by principles. Second, our findings indicate that problems of pro-nunciation in L2 acquisition depend crucially on where the segment occurs in the syllable. In particular, because codas are restricted more than onsets, problems are more likely to occur in the coda than elsewhere. And finally, the mere presence or absence of a type of segment, either in the inventory or in the coda of the NL, is not the best predictor of difficulty. Each of these points will be discussed in turn.

The claim that L2 pronunciation can be affected by instruction may appear at first to be either obvious or naive (or both). However, over the years, much has been said about the systematic nature of L2 syntax, while little, if anything at all, has been generalized about phonology, especially in the realm of pedagogy. Our results suggest that L2 pro-nunciations do not have to be learned by rote or haphazardly, and that there are higher order principles in phonology that impinge on L2 pronunciation, predicting, for example, that L1 obstruent codas are more difficult than sonorant codas.

Moreover, pronunciation problems are as much a function of the position of the segment in the syllable as of segment type. Because codas are more restricted than onsets, two conclusions follow: (1) More problems are to be expected in codas than in onsets, and (2) although mastery of a segment in the coda position generally implies mastery of a segment in the onset position, the converse is not true; namely, mastery of a segment in the onset position generally does not imply mastery of that segment in the coda. This point is well worth underscoring in view of the exercise bias toward onset consonants found in standard pronunciation manuals designed for ESL instruction (e.g., Nilsen & Nilsen, 1973; Prator & Robinett, 1972). Rather than simply focusing equally on initial, medial, and final position in the word, or even with greater emphasis on initials vis-à-vis finals, our findings indicate that the majority effort should be directed toward finals, because it is in codas that NL limitations on consonantal freedom of occurrence are most severe.

Finally, pronunciation problems cannot be predicted simply on the basis of segment inventory comparison between the NL and TL. Our results included cases in which the subjects found one segment type in the coda more difficult than another segment type, even though the NL contained both segment types in the coda; and we also found evidence of the opposite situation (e.g., cases where subjects found no difficulty with glides in the coda despite the fact that the NL [Korean] itself contains no glides in that position). In aggregate, these and similar results indicate that pronunciation difficulties on the part of L2 learners are a function of the same kind of considerations involving typological markedness that have been invoked to explain difficulties in L2 syntax.

## ACKNOWLEDGMENTS

Parts of this paper were presented at the Second Language Acquisition-Foreign Language Learning III Conference held at Purdue University, February 26–28, 1993. We thank members of that audience for their thoughtful comments, especially Yuru Wu for her observations about Chinese and Edith Moravcsik for her discussions with us about the place of markedness in second language acquisition. The first author was supported in part for this work by a grant from the National Science Foundation (No. BNS 8213384), whose contribution is gratefully acknowledged.

## REFERENCES

Broselow, E., & Finer, D. (1991). Parameter setting in second language phonology and syntax. *Second Language Research, 7,* 35–59.

Chomsky, N., & Halle, M. (1968). *The sound pattern of English.* New York: Harper & Row.

Clements, G. N. (1990). The role of the sonority cycle in core syllabification. In J. Kingston & M. Beckman (Eds.), *Papers in laboratory phonology I* (pp. 283–383). Cambridge: Cambridge University Press.

Clements, G. N., & Keyser, S. J. (1983). *CV phonology: A generative theory of the syllable. Linguistic Inquiry* (monograph series, no. 9). Cambridge, MA: MIT Press.

Dinnsen, D., Chin, S., Elbert, M., & Powell, T. (1990). Some constraints on functionally disordered phonologies: phonetic inventories and phonotactics. *Journal of Speech and Hearing Research, 33,* 28–37.

Dulay, H., & Burt, M. (1983). Goofing: An indicator of children's second language learning strategies. In S. Gass & L. Selinker (Eds.), *Language transfer in language learning* (pp. 54–68). Rowley, MA: Newbury House Publishers.

Eckman, F. (1977). Markedness and the contrastive analysis hypothesis. *Language Learning, 27,* 315–330.

Eckman, F., & Iverson, G. (1993). Sonority and markedness among onset clusters in the interlanguage of ESL learners. *Second Language Research, 9,* 234–252.

Flynn, S. (1987). *A parameter setting model of L2 acquisition.* Dordrecht: D. Reidel.

Gass, S. (1979). Language transfer and universal grammatical relations. *Language Learning, 29,* 327–345.

Goldsmith, J. (1990). *Autosegmental and metrical phonology.* Oxford: Basil Blackwell.

Hawkins, J. (1987). Implicational universals as predictors of language acquisition. *Linguistics, 25,* 453–473.

Hayes, B. (1989). Compensatory lengthening in moraic phonology. *Linguistic Inquiry, 20,* 253–306.

Hyman, L. (1985). *A theory of phonological weight.* Dordrecht: Foris.

Iverson, G., & Salmons, J. (1992). The phonology of the Proto-Indo-European root structure constraints. *Lingua, 87,* 293–320.

Iverson, G., & Sohn, H. -S. (1993). Liquid representation in Korean. In Y. -K. Kim-Renaud (Ed.), *Selected papers from the Eighth International Conference on Korean Linguistics*. Stanford, CA: Center for the Study of Language and Information.

Kim-Renaud, Y. -K. (1978). The syllable in Korean phonology. In C. -W. Kim (Ed.), *Papers in Korean linguistics* (pp. 85–98). Columbia, SC: Hornbeam Press.

Krashen, S. (1985). *The input hypothesis*. London: Longman.

Nilsen, D., & Nilsen, A. (1973). *Pronunciation contrasts in English*. New York: Regents.

Prator, C., & Robinett, B. (1972). *Manual of American English pronunciation* (3d ed.). New York: Holt, Rinehart & Winston.

Prince, A. (1984). Phonology with tiers. In M. Aronoff & R. Oehrle (Eds.), *Language sound structure: Studies in phonology presented to Morris Halle by his teacher and students* (pp. 234–244). Cambridge, MA: MIT Press.

Schachter, J. (1974). An error in error analysis. *Language Learning, 24,* 205–214.

Selkirk, E. (1982). The syllable. In H. Van der Hulst & N. Smith, (Eds.), *The structure of phonological representations, Part II* (pp. 337–384). Dordrecht: Foris.

Selkirk, E. (1984). On the major class features and syllable theory. In M. Aronoff & R. Oehrle (Eds.), *Language sound structure: Studies in phonology presented to Morris Halle by his teacher and students* (pp. 107–136). Cambridge, MA: MIT Press.

Tranel, B. (1992). CVC light syllables, geminates, and moraic theory. *Phonology, 8,* 291–302.

Vance, T. (1987). *An introduction to Japanese phonology*. Albany: State University of New York Press.

Vennemann, T. (1988). *Preference laws for syllable structure and the explanation of sound change*. Berlin: Mouton de Gruyter.

White, L. (1989). *Universal grammar and second language acquisition*. Philadelphia: John Benjamins.

# CHAPTER 12

## Final Stop Devoicing in Interlanguage

MEHMET YAVAŞ, PH.D.

Stops occur in all languages of the world and have been tagged as the "optimal" consonants (Jakobson & Halle, 1956; p. 42). Three places of articulation—bilabial, dental/alveolar, velar—are the most popular places for stop sounds (99.1%, 99.7%, and 99.4% respectively in UPSID data.)[1] English has both voiced and voiceless stops in all three places of articulation and reveals the contrasts without any restrictions (e.g., /p, b/ *pit-bit, cap- cab*; /t, d/ *tip-dip, right-ride*; /k, g/ *cap-gap, back-bag*). A similar situation is observed in languages such as Bengali, Hindi, Marathi, Gujarati, and Armenian. However, such patterns are not shared by many languages, as there can be limitations as to the consonants that can occur in final position. Some languages simply do not allow final consonants: Kikuyu, Twi, Swahili. Some other languages allow only sonorants in this position: Japanese, Mandarin, Tamil. Hausa allows final sonorants and rarely, /s/; Portuguese has liquids and /s/ in this position, whereas Spanish limits its final consonants to continuants. However, by far the most common restriction on the final stops is probably the one

[1] UPSID: UCLA Phonological Segment Inventory Database.

that allows only the voiceless stops: German, Basque, Turkish, Bulgarian, Dutch, Finnish, Polish, Russian, Gaelic, Efik, and Zoque. In these languages the voicing contrast in stops is restricted to word-initial and word-medial positions, and the opposition is neutralized in favor of the voiceless member of the pair in final position.

Speakers of languages with systems that do not allow final voiced stops have been shown to have difficulties when they learn English. Eckman's (1977) Markedness Differential Hypothesis (MDH) predicts that English word-final voiced stops (actually relevant for all final voiced obstruents) will be problematic for second language (L2) learners whose native languages (NLs) do not allow such consonants, as these are a marked linguistic feature.

> Those areas of the TL (target language) that are different from the NL and are relatively more marked than in the NL will be difficult. (Eckman, 1985, p. 291)

This, of course, begs the question of "what is marked?" to which Eckman (1985) answered:

> A phenomenon or structure X in some language is relatively more marked than some other phenomenon or structure Y if cross-linguistically the presence of X in a language implies the presence of Y, but the presence of Y does not imply the presence of X. (p. 290)

Dinnsen and Eckman (1975) advanced the typology that categorizes languages in the following implicational relationship: The presence of a voice contrast in obstruents in final position implies a contrast medially, which in turn implies a contrast initially. However, the reverse relationships do not hold. Consequently, the final position is the unmarked position for the voiceless and the marked position for the voiced obstruents.

The difficulties that are experienced by interlanguage learners of English in final voiced obstruents are also in accordance with Eckman's (1991) "Interlanguage Structural Conformity Hypothesis," which states that the universal generalizations that are valid for first languages also hold for interlanguages.[2] Because final devoicing is observed in first language (L1) acquisition studies, it also will be expected in interlanguage

---

[2] As stated by Eckman (1991), Structural Conformity Hypothesis (SCH) is a stronger hypothesis than Markedness Differential Hypothesis (MDH), as the former makes predictions only on the basis of implicational universals whereas the latter, besides universals, considers the differences between the native language and the target language.

phonologies (see the section on the naturalness of final devoicing). Given what has been stated so far, what can we expect of the speakers of languages that do not share the pattern of English when they encounter the final voiced stops of English? For speakers of the languages in the last group mentioned earlier (German, Turkish, Russian, etc.), the situation is more predictable than others: Because these languages allow unmarked voiceless stops in final position, speakers are expected to devoice the marked English targets /b, d, g/ and realize them as [p, t, k], respectively. The situation, however, is not so predictable for the speakers of languages that do not permit any stops in final position (Japanese, Mandarin, Portuguese, etc.). Here, there are three possibilities to examine: deletion of the target, vowel epenthesis after the target, and devoicing of the target. A close look at the literature reveals that all three possibilities are realized in different studies, although it is a truism to say that the last two alternatives—epenthesis and devoicing—are more prevalent (Anderson, 1987; Carlisle, 1991; Eckman 1981a, 1981b, 1985; Edge, 1991; Flege & Davidian, 1984; Flege, McCutcheon, & Smith, 1987; Tarone, 1980; Weinberger, 1987; Yavaş, 1993). Although the native language interference might be a viable explanation for the epenthesis and deletion cases (to avoid having a stop in final position which is not allowed by these languages), it certainly is out of question as an explanation for devoicing. Consequently, final devoicing in the interlanguages of speakers with these language backgrounds provide excellent opportunities to examine this independently motivated (universal) tendency.

In the following pages we will look at final stop devoicing in interlanguages. First we will examine the studies that have dealt with data regarding the devoicing of the target English voiced final stops in the interlanguages of speakers from different languages. Then, we will look at how natural the process is by considering it in different populations. Finally, we will discuss some possible implications for teaching and will suggest possible future work that could enhance our understanding of this topic.

## FINAL DEVOICING IN INTERLANGUGE PHONOLGY

Eckman (1981a) was one of the earliest studies to talk about final devoicing ("terminal devoicing" in his terminology) in interlanguage studies. Examining the data gathered via various tasks such as listening and repeating a list of words, modified cloze reading test, and discussing a riddle, Eckman looked at the target final voiced stops of English in the speech of Spanish and Mandarin speakers. The results revealed that a final devoicing rule is needed for the interlanguages of Spanish speakers. It is quite clear that this rule is not motivated by the native language of these speakers, because Spanish is a language that does not allow any stops (voiced or voiceless) in final position (save the doubtful cases of /d/, e.g., *ciudad*). Likewise, because there is no motivation for such a rule in English, it could not have been learned as a target language rule. From these facts, Eckman concluded that it was an independent rule of interlanguage. He also qualified this rule as a natural rule because it is also found in the grammars of the languages which are acquired as first languages.

Another study that commented on data from interlanguages with final devoicing was Weinberger (1987). Although the primary objective of this study was to investigate the phenomenon of word final syllable simplification in L2 (i.e., deletion,and epenthesis) and not to examine final devoicing, significantly high rates of final devoicing necessitated its mention. Four Mandarin speakers who participated in the study produced isolated words, read short paragraphs, and also told a story from their personal experiences. The results revealed that subjects devoiced two thirds of word-final obstruents.

Flege and Davidian (1984) examined the data from 12 native speakers each of English, Spanish, Mandarin Chinese, and Polish who were asked to produce 10 English test words, all ending in a voiced stop /b, d, g/, both in isolation and at the end of a short carrier phrase.

It is worth noting that these languages differ significantly in terms of their structures for final position. Chinese does not allow any obstruents whereas Spanish allows a limited number of fricatives in this position. Polish has the greatest variety, including voiceless stops, but disallowing voiced stops. Thus, the expectations are that Polish speakers, following their native language, would devoice more than the Spanish and the Chinese speakers.

Flege and Davidian's (1984) results revealed that Polish speakers devoiced most (48.3%) overall, although it is notable that there was a large individual variation (lowest devoicing with 0%, highest voicing with 100%). Spanish speakers' overall frequency for devoicing was quite close to that of Polish speakers (43%), with individual variation ranging from 19 to 71%. The overall score for devoicing by Chinese speakers was 29.5% with 3 to 70% individual variation. None of the stops produced by the English subjects were perceived to have been devoiced.

Although the group scores on devoicing are highest in Polish and lowest in Chinese with Spanish in between, statistically there was no significant difference between any of the non-native speaker groups. The authors pointed out that individual final stop devoicing was not an inevitable consequence of language background. The wide range of variability among individual subjects made any judgment on high or low rates of devoicing specific to a group impossible. Subjects from all three language backgrounds were among the strong devoicers (devoicing English targets more than 50% of the time), as well as among the weak devoicers (devoicing less than 10% of the time). Flege and Davidian, however, were quick to acknowledge that different speakers in their groups could have made different degrees of progress in their English at the time of the experiment, and they cautioned that their results should be interpreted with this in mind.

Edge (1991) stands out as a study that took the environment into consideration in the examination of final devoicing. Her data from seven Japanese, seven Cantonese and four English speakers were collected in three different ways: (1) picture-elicited storytelling, (2) oral reading of a short story, and (3) oral reading of 41 randomly ordered words. The target words contained word-final voiced obstruents. Tokens of word-final voiced obstruents were then classified as target deletion, glottal stop substitution, devoicing, epenthesis, fricativization, and other consonant substitution. They were also tabulated in different environments such as before a pause, before a vowel, before a voiced consonant, and before a voiceless consonant. Across tasks native speakers of English had 11% devoicing, whereas Japanese and Cantonese speakers had 63% and 67%, respectively (current author's calculations).

These were the overall scores; the picture is rather different if just the stops are considered. First, almost all devoicing found in the native speakers' data is related to final fricatives, thus leaving the stops almost free of devoicing.[3] The numbers go down rather dramatically if the same criteria are applied to Japanese and Cantonese speakers, whose percentages for final stop devoicing were 25 and 39% respectively.

Probably the most interesting aspect of Edge's results is the differential effects found for the different environments. The overwhelming majority of the devoicing cases were found "before a pause." The next most favorable environment for devoicing was "before a voiceless consonant," which is followed by "before a voiced consonant." "Before a vowel" was the least favorable environment for devoicing of final stops. Although these results might be expected, this study was the first to explicity show the effects of different environments.

As Edge's study stands out as the first that incorporated the effect of environment, Flege, McCutcheon and Smith (1987) was the first study on interlanguage word-final stops that did not rely on impressionistic data. Some of the earlier studies that dealt with word-final devoicing did

3 Ohala (1983) found that fricatives were more than twice as likely to be voiceless as were stops.

not specify the limits of de/voicing. The difficulties of judgment were expressed at times:

It was sometimes difficult to judge whether final stops were phonetically voiced or voiceless. (Flege and Davidian, 1984, p. 334)

However, Flege and Davidian later claimed that the transcriptions were adequately reliable. Edge (1991) defined the criterion for being voiceless in the following way:

Devoicing includes any instance of *perceptible* (my emphasis) devoicing, as well as the substitution of voiceless for voiced consonants. (p. 383)

It is of course debatable whether "perceptible" is something that would easily be agreed on unanimously.

Although these remarks are not an attempt to invalidate the results of the studies cited, Flege, McCutcheon, and Smith was welcome addition to the studies of word-final devoicing. The authors examined acoustic, temporal, and aerodynamic characteristics of English /p/ and /b/ produced by 32 subjects in word-final position. The subjects were divided in four groups, consisting of English- and Chinese-speaking children and adults (8 each). Speech material consisted of minimally paired CVC words in isolation. Adult Chinese speakers' production of /b/, which was sometimes misidentified as /p/, differed from that of English speakers who sustained closure voicing in /b/ significantly longer. Flege et al. then addressed the question of what determines this ability. To answer this question, the percentages of "delayed" and "bimodal" waveforms prior to the release of labial constriction were calculated for each group. The results revealed that for the English-speaking adults voicing continued 18 ms longer than Chinese-speaking adults in /b/ tokens with delayed and bimodal waveforms than in tokens in which oral pressure increased continuously. This maintanence of longer voicing was attributed to the active enlargement of the supraglottal cavity which was lacking (not acquired) in Chinese speakers.

Another instrumental study, Yavaş (1993), also incorporated different environments in the examination of word-final English stops in the interlanguages of different groups. Unlike Edge (1991), however, who focused on the environment following the word final obstruents, Yavaş, inspired by Plevyak (1982) and Parucci (1983) (see next section), concentrated on the stop itself and the environment preceding the stop. More specifically, the effects of the place of articulation on word-final voiced stops and the height of the vowel preceding these stops were considered. The motivation for the differential effects of place of articulation come from speech aerodynamics.

Factors like cavity size, air pressure, and passive enlargement of the vocal tract are believed to be responsible for different magnitude of devoicing in stops with different places of articulation (Ohala & Riordan, 1979). Specifically, velars are more prone to devoicing than alveolars, and those in turn are more prone to devoicing than bilabials. This is because the larger the supraglottal area is, the better it can accomodate glottal flow for some time before oral pressure exceeds subglottal pressure and stops the vocal cord vibration.

The effect of the height of the preceding vowel, on the other hand, is based on the idea that the production of high vowels creates higher supraglottal pressure (raising the tongue creates more constriction and makes vowels more like obstruents). Consequently, these vowels are more prone to devoicing than non-high vowels (Jaeger, 1978). Their vulnerability to devoicing would be carried over to the following (in this case final) stops, because the increased pressure would still be present at the time of consonantal closure.

To test these hypotheses Yavaş (1993) examined the data from 19 subjects who were speakers of Mandarin Chinese (9), Japanese (5), and Portuguese (5), languages that do not allow any stop (voiced or voiceless) in final position. Subjects read a list of words all ending in voiced stops preceded by vowels of different heights. Data from four native speakers for the same words were also obtained for comparison. Waveform analysis of the recordings examined the voicing of the closure period which begins at the vowel termination and ends by the release of the stop.

Results are shown in Figure 12–1. For non-native speakers, when stops were preceded by high vowels, all pairs of means were significantly different. However, for low vowels, no pair of means was significantly different. Thus, only preceding high vowels affected the voicing of bilabial, alveolar, and velar stops. Subjects revealed more devoicing as the place of articulation of the final stop moved from labial to alveolar and from alveolar to velar. Changing the vowel from low to high did not make a difference for the bilabial stop, but made a significant difference for alveolar and velar stops. Similar tendencies also were observed in the native speakers' production, although the magnitude of devoicing was far less than that of the nonnative speakers.[4]

## NATURALNESS OF FINAL DEVOICING

The tendency for final stop devoicing reported in the studies of interlanguage phonologies just discussed is shared by other populations.

---

[4] As stated by Ladefoged (1982), the "voiced stops" of English are not actually voiced throughout the articulation unless the next sound is also voiced.

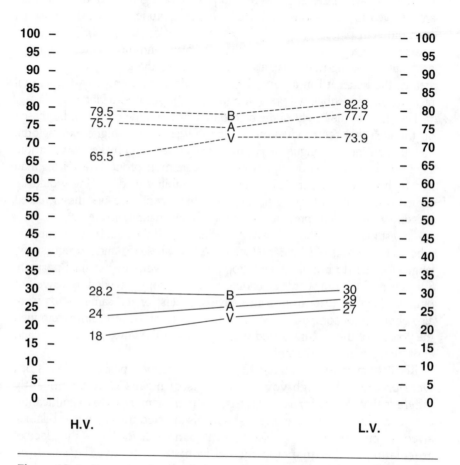

**Figure 12–1.** Percentage (mean of voicing of the target voiced stop with preceeding vowel environment in native (solid line) (*n* = 4) and no-native (dashed line) (*n* = 19) speakers (B = bilabial, H.V. = high vowel, A = alveolar, L.V. = low vowel, V = velar)

Naeser (1970) was one of the earliest to deal with this topic in English-speaking children.[5] Smith (1979), Flege (1982), and Smith and Stoel-Gammon (1983) are other studies that dealt with word-final stop devoicing in children. The process is very common in phonological development and is suppressed by great many children before the age of 4.[6] This, however,

---

[5] Kolarič (1959) and Pačesova (1968), as reported in Locke (1983), reveal examples of this phenomenon in the acquisition of Czech.

[6] In babbled syllables of infants there are more final voiceless stops than voiced stops (MacNeilage, Hutchinson, & Lasater, 1981)

may not be the case in phonologically disordered children, whose devoicing may last much longer (Edwards & Shriberg, 1983; Elbert & Gierut, 1986; Grunwell, 1981, 1985, 1987; Hodson, 1980; Hodson & Paden, 1981; Ingram, 1976; Stoel-Gammon & Dunn, 1985).

It is also not uncommon to find word-final devoicing in stops in adult speech. Smith (1979) and Flege (1982) included adult speakers in their subjects and noted devoicing tendencies similar to those of children.

Although studies mentioned above dealt with final devoicing in stops, the effects of the place of articulation and/or the height of the preceding vowel were not systematically examined.[7] Thus, the following two studies stand out in this respect.

Parucci (1983) investigated two variables—place of articulation of the stop and the effect of the preceeding vowel—with data from eight adult native speakers of English. In an oscilloscopic analysis of 360 CVC syllables where final stops were preceded by vowels of different heights, she measured the duration of consonantal closure and voicing. The results revealed that velar stop /g/ was less voiced than the other phonemically voiced stops, thus (partially) confirming the place of articulation effect in devoicing. As for the effects of different vowel height, this study did not find any difference.

Plevyak (1982) described a similar study in the investigation of final stop devoicing. It included eight 3-year-old children who produced syllables with final stops with different vowels preceding them. The predicted vocalic effects (more devoicing after a high vowel than a low vowel) were observed before /g/ and partially before /d/. The effects of different places of articulation were also confirmed in that /g/ was devoiced more than /b/ and /d/, although this was true only in high vowel environments.

Another piece of evidence which supports the idea that voicelessness of a final stop is sensitive to the height of the preceding vowel is found in Locke's 1983 study where he examined English monosyllabic words that end in bilabial and velar stops which are preceded by each of the 10 vowels.[8] The calculations of the number of voiced and voiceless stops by each of the vowels revealed that, in English, regardless of the height of the preceding vowel, final position was more frequently occupied by voiceless stops than by voiced stops. However, when the preceding vowel was high, the tendency became much stronger.

---

[7] Some studies have dealt with the effects of place of articulation and vowel height in relation to de/voicing, but they did not examine these effects in final position. Schwartz (1972), for example, studied the effects of vowel height in the de/voicing of the previous stops. Zlatin and Koenigsknecht (1976), and Smith (1978) examined the effects of place of articulation in relation to prevoicing of initial stops.

[8] Data from Moser (1969).

As demonstrated by these studies, devoicing of word-final stops is a common process in both first and second language acquisition; the patterns revealed in these studies are also reflected in the structure of languages of the world. All these clearly show that the process of final devoicing is a phonetically motivated universal tendency.

## IMPLICATIONS FOR TEACHING

The findings reported here, if confirmed by more studies of similar nature in interlanguage phonologies, could provide important clues for teaching English as a second/foreign language. To give some specific examples, we can grade the teaching material by practicing first the most favorable combination for producing the target final voiced stops: words with final bilabial stops that are preceded by low vowels. Examples such as *tub, cab, rob*, and so on provide the best opportunities. The next move would necessitate a decision between a combination of bilabial stop preceded by a high vowel and an alveolar stop preceded by a low vowel. In other words, the question is "which dimension (vowel height or place of articulation) carries more weight?" The effects of place of articulation seem much less controversial than the effects of the height of the preceding vowel. This fact suggests that we should proceed with the bilabial stop preceded by a high vowel (e.g., bib). After we finish the bilabials, we would be ready to deal with the next best place of articulation: alveolar. Again we start with the target, together with a low vowel. Words like *bed, bad, red*, and so on would be ideal candidates for this stage. Once the learner has mastered these and similar cases, we would continue with words such as *food* and *kid*, where the target voiced alveolar stop is preceded by high vowels. Finally, the last (and the most difficult) place of articulation, velar, could be worked on in a similar fashion (i.e., first with low vowels: *bag, dog, egg* and then with high vowels: *pig, big*, etc.)

As the reader must have noticed, all the words chosen are monosyllabic CVC items, because this facilitates the success without introducing additional difficulty with regard to the syllabic structure. Once the learner is comfortable with these targets words with more complicated syllabic structures would be added to the training material. These may include items with consonant clusters (e.g., *proud, grab*) and/or items with more syllables.

What we have just described is a step-by-step procedure that requires the complete mastery of each step before moving on to the next. This strategy, however, requires a rather long time which is not desirable. In many situations, we might want to skip certain steps by relying on generalization. In other words, after working with the final stop targets with high vowels we may test the learner with targets involving non-high vowels and see to what extent the abilities acquired with high vowels are carried over to new situations.

All the above, of course, refers to items trained in isolation, which is a necessary component in training but obviously insufficient for our final goal. Because these items will be employed in communicative situations in normal language behavior, the learner needs to acquire the skills in the context of flowing speech. Here, the findings of Edge (1991) provide guidelines. As mentioned earlier, the environment that was most conducive for the correct realization of the final voiced stop targets was "before a vowel." Once the learner is successful in such a context, he or she can move on to the next most favorable environment which is "before a voiced consonant." Only after managing these, would he or she be ready to go on with the remaining two environments "before a voiceless consonant" and "before a pause."

It is also possible, and in fact advisable, to mix the stages of training using both isolated words and words in a context of a following vowel/voiced consonant/voiceless consonant in full sentences. One might want to try, for example, working with second degree difficulty (e.g., alveolar stop preceded by a high vowel in isolation a moderately difficult target in a rather manageable task), while incorporating a less difficult target (e.g. bilabial stop preceded by a non-high vowel) in a somewhat favorable environment (e.g., before a vowel or before a voiced consonant in connected speech) (a less difficult target in a more difficult task).

These remarks are by no means intended to be authoritative statements about the teaching situation. Rather, they should be taken as some thoughts that might be of help for the training of the subjects. Needless to say, an experienced and alert teacher can find better uses of the results of the studies cited above. It is this author's belief, however, that whatever the teaching philosophies and strategies of the teacher are, the research in L2 phonologies may provide valuable data that can be used to enhance learning.

Finally, although the aim of this chapter is not to deal with the difficulties of children in the acquisition of their native language, whatever has been said regarding the training of interlanguage learners also can be applied to therapy for phonologically disordered children. As we have seen, there are many overlapping situations and the same variables are suggested to be responsible for the ease or difficulty in the acquisition of final voiced stops in both L1 and L2 acquisition.

# DIRECTIONS OF FUTURE RESEARCH

Among the indicators of voicing in final consonants, "voicing in closure" was investigated in some of the above mentioned studies. Lisker (1978) suggested that this is a strong indicator for the perception of a voiced stop. Also, Raphael (1981) showed that voicing in closure was used more consistently than any other cue when it was present in a stimulus. He stated that, other things being equal, a decrease in the voiced portion of the final stop led to a decrease in perception. Although this is a strong cue for a stop to be perceived as voiced or voiceless, it is definitely not the only cue. Another often-mentioned dimension for the perception of voicing of stops is the "preceding vowel duration." In English, vowels before voiced consonants may be twice the length of those preceding voiceless consonants. Speakers may devoice their final stops but still be perceived as making the distinction between voiced and voiceless stops by lengthening the vowels before the target voiced stops (Denes, 1955; House & Fairbanks, 1953; Raphael 1972). English-speaking children who devoice final stops lengthen their vowels before the voiced targets (Naeser 1970). The information on "preceding vowel duration" in interlanguage phonology does not reveal any significant lengthening before voiced stops (Elsendorn, 1983; Flege & Port 1981; Mack 1982). This may be due to the native language patterns of the speakers studied, as many languages, unlike English, have small difference in vowel length according to whether the following consonant is voiced or voiceless. There are even some languages that do not show this effect (Flege, 1979; Keating, 1979).[9] However, before we totally dismiss this variable in interlanguage phonology we would like to have a larger database, because speakers of some other languages might have similar vowel lengthening to English and may employ this strategy in learning English. Depending on the degree of lengthening of the vowel before the voiced stop in a particular language, this aspect may be exploited in remedial teaching.

Other cues relevant for the voiced/voiceless distinction have been cited in the literature. These are "closure duration" and/or "release burst" (Hogan & Rozsypal, 1980; Wolf, 1978). Voiceless stops have greater duration than voiced stops, and the release burst for voiceless stops is greater in amplitude and duration and higher in frequency than for voiced stops. The role played by these cues, however, does not seem to be strong, as they are inconsistent and require that the stops be released.

---

[9] It might be thought that vowel duration before the stop is phonetically governed and is proportional to the phonetic "voicedness" of the stop; but as Keating (1984) showed there are several arguments against this account.

All of the above makes it quite clear that further research on these two dimensions, voicing in closure and preceding vowel duration, in interlanguage phonologies could enhance our knowledge on final stop devoicing. Studies that combine different variables could reveal differential effects of each of the contributing factors. For example, new studies can test the place effect together with the effects of the following context: Is final voiced bilabial stop with a following voiceless consonant at the beginning of the next word easier than a velar stop which is followed by a voiced consonant in the next word? The results of such studies would have a direct bearing on how we approach teaching and on how we grade our material.

## CONCLUSION

Final stop devoicing is an independently motivated universal tendency and is observed in interlanguage phonologies as well as first language acquisition (both normal and disordered). This is another instance which shows that interlanguages are natural languages and are subject to universal constraints. Thus, any study contributing to knowledge of the underlying regularities and differential effects of the variables related to this topic should be of great interest to linguists as well as to professionals who deal with language learners' difficulties.

## REFERENCES

Anderson, J. (1987). The markedness differential hypothesis and syllable structure difficulty. In G. Ioup & S. Weinberger (Eds.), *Interlanguage phonology* (pp. 279–291). New York: Newbury House.

Carlisle, R. (1991). The influence of environment on vowel epenthesis in Spanish/English interphonology. *Applied Linguistics, 12,* 76–95.

Denes, P. (1955) Effect of duration on the perception of voicing. *Journal of the Acoustical Society of America, 27,* 761–764.

Dinnsen, D. A., & Eckman, F. R. (1975). A functional explanation of some phonological typologies. In R. Grosman et al. (Eds.), *Functionalism.* Chicago: Chicago Linguistic Society.

Eckman, F. R. (1977). Markedness and the contrastive analysis hypothesis. *Language Learning, 27,* 315–330

Eckman, F. R. (1981a). On the naturalness of interlanguage phonological rules. *Language Learning, 31,* 195–216.

Eckman, F. R. (1981b). On predicting phonological difficulty in second language acquisition. *Studies in Second Language Acquisition, 4,* 18–30.

Eckman, F. R. (1985). Some theoretical and pedagogical implications of the markedness differential hypothesis, *Studies in Second Language Acquisition, 7*, 289–307.

Eckman, F. R. (1991). The structural conformity hypothesis and the acquisition of consonant clusters in the interlanguage of ESL learners. *Studies in Second Language Acquisition, 13*, 23–41.

Edge, B. A. (1991). The production of word-final voiced obstruents in English by L1 speakers of Japanese and Cantonese. *Studies in Second Language Acquisition, 13*, 377–393.

Edwards, M. L., & Shriberg, L. D. (1983). *Phonology: Applications in communicative disorders.* San Diego: College-Hill Press.

Elbert, M., & Gierut, J. (1986). *Handbook of clinical phonology* London: Taylor & Francis.

Elsendoorn, B. A. G. (1983). Quality and quantity in English by Dutchman: Two parameters inducing double Dutch. In M. Van den Broecke, V. van Heuven, & W. Zonneveld (Eds.), *Sound structures, studies for Atonie Cohen* (pp. 53–69) Dordrecht, The Netherlands: Foris.

Flege, J. E. (1979). *Phonetic interference in second language acquisition.* Unpublished doctoral dissertation, Indiana University, Bloomington.

Flege, J. E. (1982). English speakers learn to suppress stop devoicing. In K. Tuite, R. Schneider, & R. Chametzky (Eds.) *Papers from the 18th Regional Meeting of the Chicago Linguistics Society* (pp. 111–122) Chicago: Chicago Linguistics Society.

Flege, J. E., & Davidian, R. D. (1984). Transfer and developmental processes in adult foreign language speech production. *Applied Psycholinguistics, 5*, 323–347.

Flege, J. E., McCutcheon, M. J., & Smith, S. C. (1987). The development of skill in producing word final English stops. *Journal of Acoustical Society of America, 82*(2), 433–447.

Flege, J. E., Port, R. (1981). Cross-language phonetic interference: Arabic to English. *Language and Speech, 24*, 125–146.

Grunwell, P. (1981). *The nature of phonological disability in children.* New York: Academic Press.

Grunwell, P. (1985). *Phonological analysis of child speech.* Windsor, UK: Nfer-Nelson.

Grunwell, P. (1987). *Clinical phonology.* Rockville, MD: Aspen.

Hodson, B. W., (1980). *The assessment of phonological processes.* Danville, IL: Interstate Printers and Publishers.

Hodson, B. W. & Paden, E. P. (1981). Phonological processes which characterize unintelligible and intelligible speech in early childhood. *Journal of Speech and Hearing Disorders, 46*, 369–373.

Hogan, J. T., & Rozsypal, A. J. (1980). Evaluation of vowel duration as a cue for the voicing distinction in the following word-final consonant. *Journal of the Acoustical Society of America, 67*, 1764–1771.

House, A. S., & Fairbanks, G. (1953). The influence of consonant environment upon the secondary acoustical characteristics of vowels. *Journal of the Acoustical Society of America, 25*, 105–113.

Ingram, D. (1976). *Phonological disability in children.* New York: Elsevier.

Jaeger, J. J. (1978). Speech aerodynamics and phonological universals. *Proceedings of the Berkeley Linguistic Society, 4*, 311–329.

Jakobson, R., & M. Halle (1956). *Fundamentals of language.* The Hague: Mouton.

Keating, P. A. (1979). A phonetic study of a voicing contrast in Polish. Unpublished doctoral dissertation, Brown University, Providence, RI.

Keating, P. A. (1984). Phonetic and phonological representation of stop consonant devoicing. *Language 60*(2), 286–319.

Ladefoged, P. (1982). *A course in phonetics*. New York: Hartcourt Brace Jovanovich.

Lisker, L. (1978). On buzzing the English /b/. *Haskins Laboratories Status Report on Speech Research* (No. SR-55/56, pp. 181–188). New Haven, CT: Haskins Laboratories.

Locke, J. L. (1983). *Phonological acquisition and change*. New York: Academic Press.

Mack, M. (1982). Voicing dependent vowel duration in English and French: Monolingual and bilingual production. *Journal of the Acoustical Society of America, 71*, 173–178.

MacNeilage, P., Hutchinson, J., & Lasater, S. (1981). The production of speech: Development and dissolution of motoric and pre-motoric processes. In J. Long & A. Baddaley (Eds.), *Attention and performance* (pp. 189–216). Hillsdale, NJ: Lawrence Erlbaum.

Magnusson, E. (1983). *The phonology of language disordered children: Production, perception and awareness*. Lund, Sweden: CWK Gleerup.

Moser, H. (1969). *One-syllable words*. Columbus, OH: Charles E. Merrill.

Naeser, M. A. (1970). *The American child's acquisition of different vowel duration* (Tech. rep. no. 144). Madison: Wisconsin Research and Development Center for Cognitive Learning.

Ohala, J. J. (1983). The origin of sound patterns in vocal tract constraints. In P. F. MacNeilage (Ed.), *The production of speech* (pp. 189–216). New York: Springer-Verlag.

Ohala, J. J., & Riordan, C. J. (1979). Passive vocal tract enlargement during voiced stops. In J. J. Wolf & D. Klatt (Eds.), *Speech communication papers* (pp. 82–92). New York: Acoustical Society of America.

Parucci, R. (1983). *Effects of vowel height on final stop devoicing*. Unpublished master's thesis, University of Maryland, College Park.

Plevyak, T. (1982) *Vocalic effect on children's final stop devoicing*. Unpublished master's thesis, University of Maryland, College Park.

Raphael L. J. (1972). Preceding vowel duration as a cue to the perception of the voicing characteristic of word final consonants in English. *Journal of the Acoustical Society of America, 51*, 1296–1303.

Raphael, L. J. (1981). Durations and contexts as cues to word final cognate opposition in English. *Phonetica, 38*, 126–147.

Schwartz, M. F. (1972). Bilabial closure durations for /p/ /b/, and /m/ in voiced and whispered vowel environments. *Journal of the Acoustical Society of America, 51*, 2025–2029.

Smith, B. L. (1978). Effects of placement of articulation and vowel environment on "voiced" stop consonant production. *Glossa, 12*(2), 163–175.

Smith, B. L. (1979). A phonetic analysis of consonantal devoicing in children's speech. *Journal of Child Language, 6*, 19–28.

Smith, B. L., & Stoel-Gammon, C. (1983). A longitudinal study of the development of stop consonant production in normal and Down's syndrome children. *Journal of Speech and Hearing Disorders, 48*, 114–119.

Stoel-Gammon, C., & Dunn, C. (1985). *Normal and disordered phonology in children*. Baltimore: University Park Press.

Tarone, E. (1980). Some influences on the syllable structure of interlanguage phonology. *International Review of Applied Linguistics, 18*, 139–152.

Weinberger, S. (1987). The influence of linguistic context on syllable simplification. In G. Ioup & S. Weinberger (Eds.), *Interlanguage phonology* (pp. 401–417). New York: Newbury House.

Wolf, C. G. (1978). Voicing cues in English final stops. *Journal of Phonetics, 6,* 299–309.

Yavaş, M. (1993). The effects of vowel height and place of articulation in interlanguage final stop devoicing. Manuscript submitted for publication.

Zlatin, M. A., & Konigsknecht, R. A. (1976). Development of the voicing contrast: A comparison of voice onset time in stop perception and production. *Journal of Speech and Hearing Research, 19,* 93–111.

# CHAPTER 13

*Functional and Phonetic Constraints on Second Language Phonology*

STEVEN H. WEINBERGER, Ph.D.

Learning the sound system of a language entails more than just learning how to pronounce phonetic elements in words. A learner must not only adequately develop the segmental structure, the syllable structure, and the prosodic structure of a new phonology, the learner also must use linguistic mechanisms to optimize lexical understandability. Language learners must develop a linguistic knowledge that recognizes the listener. This chapter aims to demonstrate that there are two independent types of linguistic knowledge involved in phonological development—a phonetic knowledge and a functional knowledge.

## PHONETIC VERSUS FUNCTIONAL LINGUISTIC KNOWLEDGE

One of the goals of language learners is to produce speech that phonetically approximates the ambient language. This presumably would entail setting the proper articulatory parameters for segments. For instance, the learner would need to accurately determine a set of place and manner features that uniquely define each sound in the language. For example, a speaker must learn facts such as "English contains [–continuant, +velar] sounds ([k], [g]) but does not allow [+continuant, +velar] sounds like [x] and [ɣ]." Moreover, learners are required to have a knowledge of the set of language-specific context-sensitive phonological alternation rules that modify structure. So, among other rules to be learned, English learners must realize that stressed syllable-initial unvoiced stops are aspirated. In addition to segment-structure knowledge, learners also must produce the appropriate syllable structure in the language. They have to be cognizant of the language's possible syllable inventory. This includes developing a knowledge of phonotactics—the constraints on segment clustering. Prosodic knowledge of stress, tone, and intonation is also essential for the language learner. Every native speaker possesses this type of information about his or her language. I will refer to this as a speaker's *phonetic* knowledge. Phonetic knowledge is language-specific and ultimately is governed by an innate capacity of Universal Grammar.

Language learners also are subject to the conflicting requirements of the speaker and the listener. Bever (1981) insightfully commented on this push and pull effect:

> The listener optimally requires that the internal grammatical and semantic relations be explicitly marked in the surface sequence. This would make the perception of the sentence homonymous with the recognition of the surface elements—no further processing would be necessary. The needs of the speaker are the converse of explicitness: The optimal situation for the speaker would be one in which each utterance could consist of a single monosyllabic grunt, which the listener would always interpret correctly. (p. 186)

Humans do not grunt language with guaranteed reception. Speech production is subject to perceptual constraints. In fact, according to Cutler (1987), the demands of the perceptual system operate to constrain many phonological processes such as elision and assimilation—processes that tend to obstruct word recognition for the listener. Similarly, in discussing the etiologies of some phonological processes, Kaye (1989) noted, for instance, that many harmony and stress assignment systems function to delimit the acoustic signal. That is, they provide word or morpheme boundary information to the listener.

This type of knowledge which acts to authorize possible phonological processes I will call *functional* knowledge. Given that a grammar can be conceived of as some sort of noise-reduction device, acting to keep the words and sentences in a language intelligible (Cambell 1982), we may assign this functional knowledge to the grammar domain.[1]

I will show that these two independent types of knowledge— phonetic and functional—interact in interesting ways and can explain the variation that we find between different types of language learners, particularly between first and second language learners.

Many linguists believe that adult language acquisition is quite unlike child language acquisition. This is most evident in adult language learners' consistent failure to attain native proficiency, particularly in the realm of pronunciation. The reason for this failure is believed to be due to the unavailability of an innate linguistic mechanism responsible for the rapid and complete acquisition of a language (Schachter 1988). This innate linguistic mechanism, also known as universal grammar, is available to the language learner during a "critical period" which spans the ages of two to puberty (Lenneberg, 1967). After puberty a language learner rarely can overcome a phonetic foreign accent (Scovel, 1988). Without universal grammar, the reasoning goes, the adult language learner can access only the linguistic knowledge from his or her native language, and therefore we find an abundance of "transfer" errors, where native sounds are substituted for target language sounds. This type of simplistic classical transfer of phonetic elements has tended to reduce adult second language phonological research to a trivial matter for linguistic theory.

I believe that the study of adult second language phonology is very relevant to linguistic theory insofar as it allows us to test the claims about the critical period and universal grammar. I suggest that the critical period con- strains only a subset of linguistic knowledge. It impedes specific phonetic and phonotactic abilities but does not affect some of the more globally functional principles. I will demonstrate the independence of these functional and phonetic abilities by showing that certain adult syllable simplification strategies are fundamentally different from those found in child first language acquisition. These differences will allow us to tease apart and understand the differential development of functional and phonetic knowledge.

## CHILDREN AS GOOD SAMPLES: UNIVERSALS IN FIRST LANGUAGE PHONOLOGY

Most language acquisition researchers assume that first language (L1) acquisition patterns conform more closely to language universals than do

---

[1] See Halle (1979) for another view.

second language (L2) acquisition patterns. Ever since Lenneberg posited the critical period hypothesis (1967), most theoretical linguists have not considered second language acquisition data as a valid source for studying Universal Grammar. L2 acquisition patterns traditionally were believed to be due to transfer and, therefore, quite unlike L1 patterns. In spite of some of the methodological and theoretical problems involved in the comparison of L1 and L2 surface productions however, there have been investigations that certainly contributed to the demotion of the once dominant role of transfer (see White, 1989, on the role of universal grammar in L2 syntax). The degree to which typological universals are reflected in acquisition data is also under review. Gass and Ard (1980) concluded that, with respect to relative clause formation, L2 data correspond more closely to Keenan and Comrie's (1977) typological language universals than do L1 data. The situation in L2 phonology is not so articulated. There are indeed some universal grammar principles that remain accessible in the adult learner. Broselow and Finer (1991), for example, found that L2 grammars are constrained by some version of the Sonority Sequencing Constraint. Nevertheless, real-time phonological development in adult second language is quite different from child first language. Processes found in L1 phonology are not found in L2 phonology.[2] The first language substitution and assimilation processes shown in (1) and (2) below (from Stoel-Gammon & Dunn 1985) generally are found in L1 development regardless of the language being acquired.

(1)  Substitution Processes
    a.  Fronting:
        ship      —>    [sɪp]
        key       —>    [ti]
        make   —>    [met]
    b.  Stopping:
        TV        —>    [tibi]
        nose    —>    [nod]
        that    —>    [dæt]
        juice   —>    [dus]
(2)  Assimilation Processes
    a.  Consonant harmony:
        dog      —>    [gɑg]
        zip       —>    [bɪp]
        boot    —>    [bup]
    b.  Reduplication:
        water   —>    [wawa]

---

[2] Certainly some of these types of processes may be found in L2 phonologies, but they typically are due to transfer from the native language.

noodle   —>   [nunu]
bottle    —>   [baba]

# SYLLABLE STRUCTURE PROCESSES IN LANGUAGE ACQUISITION

## *CHILD FIRST LANGUAGE*

Unlike the child-specific processes in (1) and (2), all language learners, both children and adults, when confronted with syllable structures that are far too complex for their phonetic ability, will modify those structures to make them conform with their present level of phonetic ability. One method of simplifying relatively difficult syllable structure is to delete the offending consonant. This type of syllable simplification is shown in example (3):

(3) Consonant deletion
    target item      produced item
    "seed"            [si]

Another logical possibility is for the language learner to simplify a relatively complex syllable structure by adding a vowel, as demonstrated in (4) below:

(4) Vowel epenthesis
    target item      produced form
    "seed"            [sidə]

Vowel epenthesis is not employed regularly among language learners. In fact, young L1 learners rarely utilize epenthesis; instead, they typically delete consonants to reduce syllable structure. According to the child phonology data reported in Moskowitz (1970), Olmsted (1971), Vihman (1980), and Macken and Ferguson (1983), vowel epenthesis (as in [4]) is extremely rare. These studies have reported abundant rates of consonant deletion, yet none of them registered significant amounts of epenthesis. Moskowitz found only one case in analyzing approximately 200 tokens. Olmsted also found only one case (3.7%), and Vihman found less than 1% of epenthesis out of 660 tokens. In most cases where epenthesis is found (including data from Ross, 1937), the subjects were above 21 months of age. Moreover, both Kornfeld (1971) and Ingram (1976) have reported that in longitudinal studies where a child used deletion and epenthesis to reduce consonant clusters, the deletion strategy always preceded the epenthesis strategy. Some examples of the more common L1 syllable structure modifications are given in (5):

(5)  First Language Syllable Structure Processes
    a.  Cluster reduction:
        bread  —>  [bɛd]
        blue   —>  [bu]
        snow  —>  [no]
    b.  Final consonant deletion:
        dog    —>  [dɑ]
        mouse —>  [maʊ]
        milk   —>  [mɪ]
Stoel-Gammon and Dunn (1985, p. 37–38)

## ADULT SECOND LANGUAGE

Adult second language learners simplify complex syllable structure in a similar fashion, but unlike young children, they tend to use a significant amount of vowel epenthesis, even when there is no identical context-sensitive rule of epenthesis in their native language. Examples of adult L2 syllable modifications are shown in (6):

(6)  L2 syllable structure processes (from Tarone, 1980):
    a.  Cluster reduction
        blanket    —>      [bæŋkətə]   (Portuguese)
        prepares   —>      [pipɛas]    (Cantonese)
    b.  Final consonant deletion
        out   —> [au:]    (Cantonese)
        road  —> [ro:]    (Cantonese)
        school —> [sku:]   (Korean)[3]
    c.  Epenthesis
        class   —> [kəlæs]    (Korean)
        sack   —> [sækə]    (Korean)
        sandwich  —> [sænwɪtʃə] (Cantonese)

As syllable simplification strategies, the operations of vowel epenthesis and consonant deletion both serve the same phonetic function by simplifying syllable structure. And as demonstrated in (3) and (4) above, both consonant deletion and vowel epenthesis convert a CVC syllable into simpler CV syllables. Their respective pronunciations, however, differ with respect to the ease with which a listener can recover the intended underlying form. That is, although deletion results in an unrecoverable derivation, epenthesis tends to preserve the underlying form.

[3] Korean does have a native language consonant deletion rule, but it functions only to simplify tri-consonantal clusters. See Kim (1972) for details.

For example, if we abstract away from external cues, the possible words that could be associated with (5) are limited in comparison to those words that could be associated with the produced form in (6) (see the examples [7] and [8].

(7)  Recoverable derivation
     "seed"  —>    [sidə]   seed, cedar
(8)  Non-recoverable derivation
     "seed"  —>    [si]     seed, seat, seep, seek, seize,
                            siege, . . .

Because the deleted *d* is not recoverable, an underlying contrast is not maintained. Recoverability is being used here as a principle that constrains the amount of ambiguity that results from a linguistic and—in this case—a phonological operation. Recoverable operations such as epenthesis tend to limit ambiguity, whereas nonrecoverable operations such as consonant deletion proliferate lexical ambiguity.

## RECOVERABILITY IN LANGUAGES

Languages tend to preserve underlying contrasts. In fact, Kenstowicz (1981) presented data from Malay to demonstrate that certain phonological rules are constrained by this functional notion. As shown in (9) below, the causative affix *məŋ-* assimilates the point of articulation of a following consonant which will delete if voiceless.

(9)  Malay voiceless consonant deletion

|     | **Active** | **Causative** | **Gloss** |
|-----|-----------|---------------|-----------|
| a.  | adʒoʔ     | məŋadʒuki     | tease     |
| b.  | bayar     | məmbayari     | pay       |
| c.  | daki      | məndaki       | climb     |
| d.  | dʒawap    | məndʒawapi    | answer    |
| e.  | gali      | məŋalii       | dig       |
| f.  | kael      | məŋaili       | fish      |
| g.  | pukol     | məmukoli      | beat      |
| h.  | tules     | mənulisi      | write     |
| i.  | satu      | mənatui       | unite     |
| j.  | sumbu     | məŋumbui      | cause to wick |

The stems that begin with [tʃ] are of special interest. In the given dialect of Malay, this [tʃ] will, like the other voiceless consonants in (9), optionally delete after the causative affix (məŋ) is added. But there are a significant number of words where the [tʃ] will not delete. Some of these are given in (10):

(10) tʃiom      məŋtʃiumi     məɲiumi                        to kiss
     tʃatu      məŋtʃatui     *mənatui     (cf. 9i)   to ration
     tʃumbu     məŋtʃumbui    *məɲumbui    (cf. 9j)   caress

It turns out that in each case where a stem initial [tʃ] fails to delete, there is another stem of exactly the same phonetic shape, except that it begins with [s]. In other words, the rule deleting voiceless consonants after the prefix məŋ- may not apply to [tʃ] where such deletion would lead to homophonous forms.

We have seen how the principle of recoverability can prevent certain phonological rules from operating in a language. Adherence to the principle of recoverability also can affect rule ordering relationships. As an illustration, Kaye (1981) showed how the functional notion of recoverability operates in Ojibwa, an Algonquian language of North America. In Ojibwa, the operation of phonological rules is not necessarily governed by the theory of markedness of rule-ordering relationships but rather by the degree of recoverability that the derivation exhibits. Essentially, grammars are constrained by alternative forces: a constraint against opaque (marked) rule ordering and a constraint against ambiguity. The constraint against ambiguity (recoverability) dominates the opacity constraint when an unacceptable degree of ambiguity results.

Kaye argued that languages do in fact exhibit derivations with marked (counterfeeding or counterbleeding) rule orderings, as long as they result in relatively more recoverable outputs. The evidence from Ojibwa that Kaye presented demonstrates that counterfeeding orders reduce surface ambiguity. Ojibwa possesses the following phonological rules: (a) nasal assimilation, whereby a nasal adopts the place of articulation from the immediately following consonant; and (b) vowel syncope, where an unstressed short vowel is deleted. Given the underlying form /a:naki:/ *although*, two possible rule orderings can result in two possible phonetic outputs (see [11] and [12]).

(11) Counterfeeding rule order
     /a:naki:/      *although*

     ‾‾‾‾‾‾                      nasal assimilation
     a:nki:                      vowel syncope
(12) Feeding rule order
     /a:naki:/      *although*
     a:nki:                      vowel syncope
     a:ŋki:                      nasal assimilation

If nasal assimilation precedes vowel syncope, a marked counterfeeding ordering relationship, we obtain [aːnkiː], as shown in (11). Notice that nasal assimilation did not apply because the syncope rule had not yet deleted the intervening unstressed vowel between /n/ and /k/. The second rule ordering, the unmarked version shown in (12), orders the rules so that the first creates the required environment for the second to operate. So, if nasal assimilation now follows vowel syncope, the intervening unstressed vowel is deleted first, allowing the nasal to be immediately adjacent to the consonant. Nasal assimilation is therefore allowed to take place, and the output [aːŋkiː] is obtained.

Given that Ojibwa has three possible underlying unstressed vowels, /i/, /o/, and /a/, and two underlying nasals, /n/ and /m/, the output from the marked ordering (counterfeeding) [aːnkiː] (in [11]), is three-ways ambiguous, as shown in (13):

(13) Ambiguity resulting from counter-feeding

$$/\text{aːn} \left\{ \begin{array}{c} i \\ o \\ a \end{array} \right\} \text{kiː}/$$

The result of the unmarked rule ordering (feeding) relationship, [aːŋkiː] (in [12]) is seven-ways ambiguous, as shown in (14):

(14) Ambiguity resulting from feeding

$$/\text{aː} \left\{ \begin{array}{c} n \\ m \end{array} \right\} \left\{ \begin{array}{c} i \\ o \\ a \\ \emptyset \end{array} \right\} \text{kiː}/$$

It is because of the principle of recoverability, Kaye argued, that the less ambiguous form [aːnkiː] obtains in Ojibwa. According to Kaye (1981), this notion of recoverability can be viewed as a "global constraint on the degree of ambiguity permitted in a phonology" (p. 471).

## RECOVERABILITY IN DEVELOPING LANGUAGES

This preference for marked rule orderings that abide by the principle of recoverability also can be seen in the developing grammars of child first language acquisition. The phenomenon of "displaced contrast" as described by Smith (1973) is an example of an opaque rule ordering. When Smith's child Amahl was approximately 2;6 years old, he produced the word *puzzle* as [pʌdəl]. During the same point in time he produced the word *puddle* as [pʌgəl]. Based on evidence of this sort, Smith posited two rules, which must be explicitly ordered:

(15)  Amahl's rules
    a. d  —>  g/ _____ əl
    b. z  —>  d/ _____ əl

Kiparsky and Menn (1977) remarked that the rules in (15) represent a counterfeeding order and thus are evidence that children's phonologies contain marked, opaque rule orderings. They suggested that there is no a priori reason to assume that children's grammars should obey rule ordering markedness constraints. I believe that Smith's data show that his child is, in fact, obeying a functional linguistic constraint—that of recoverability.

    Consider the results if the rules were ordered in a more unmarked feeding order, as in (16):

(16)  Feeding order
    a. z  —>d/ _____ əl
    b. d  —>g/ _____ əl

If this feeding order had obtained in Amahl's phonology, the forms for *puzzle* and *puddle* would be merged into one output: [pʌgəl]. I suggest that, in Amahl's system, counterfeeding rule ordering is selected over a feeding order for recoverability purposes. The hypothetical output of (16), [pʌgəl], does not allow a recoverable underlying form. Amahl's opaque rule order is therefore consistent with recoverability.

    Grunwell (1987) also presented evidence that demonstrates counterfeeding orders. A misarticulating child, age 5; 5 had the following pattern. The rules in (17a) (18a) account for the data in (17b) and (18b), respectively.

(17)  word-initial affricatization
    a. t,d —>  tʃ,dʒ/ # _____ V
    b. two    [tʃu]
      tie     [tʃaɪ]
      daddy [dʒadi]
      don't  [dʒoʊnt]
(18)  word-initial fronting
    a. k,g —>  t,d/ # _____ V
    b. cat    [tat]
      cup   [tʌp]
      girl  [dɤl]
      gun  [dʌn]

The rule of word-initial fronting (18a) must be ordered after word-initial affricatization (17a) in a counterfeeding order. If the rules were ordered in a feeding order, [t],[d] and [k],[g] would be neutralized as [tʃ],[dʒ]. Grunwell's 5; 6-year-old subject apparently is preserving the distinction between underlying word-initial alveolar and velar stops.

These examples demonstrate that the principle of recoverability has a strong effect on languages. Languages show a positive predilection toward evolving recoverable derivations (Gussman, 1976; Hankamer, 1973; Kaye, 1981). This principle is formally stated in (19):

(19)  Recoverability Principle
      Recoverable representations take precedence over unrecoverable ones.

## THE INDEPENDENT DEVELOPMENT OF THE RECOVERABILITY PRINCIPLE

I propose that the recoverability principle is one of the components of grammar that matures according to some preset schedule (Borer & Wexler, 1987; Felix, 1984). Moreover, once it is available, it must be triggered by linguistic input. Apparently it is not available to children in the very early stages of phonological development because they regularly violate it.[4] They are creating relatively nonrecoverable, and hence ambiguous forms, when they delete consonants to simplify syllable structure. Faced with their phonetic inability to produce complex syllables, they are opening syllables via consonant deletion rather than by epenthesis. Children are choosing the deletion strategy as the default syllable simplification process because they do not yet possess the recoverability principle.[5]

One consequence of the deletion of consonants in child L1 acquisition is homonymy—the merging of two or more lexical items into one form. Many researchers cite evidence of homonymy at an early stage in phonological acquisition (cf. Ingram, 1975, 1985; Priestly, 1980; Tervoort, 1969; Vihman,

---

[4] Recall that all of the children who exhibited significant amounts of vowel epenthesis were older than 21 months. Recoverability-minded Amahl was also beyond the early stages of phonological development. He was 30 months old.

[5] Because epenthesis creates an extra syllable, one could argue that the child chooses deletion over epenthesis because of the constraint on word length. But this position would fail to account for the fact that many children favor multisyllabic words during the early stages of language acquisition. Schwartz, Leonard, Wilcox, and Folger (1980) and Fee and Ingram (1982) noted that children reduplicate during the time that they are unable to produce final consonants. Branigan (1976) also suggested that the preference for open syllables is more pervasive than any constraint on word length.

1981). And although some children do maintain subtle distinctions (Weismer, Dinnsen, & Elbert, 1981), the level of listener ambiguity remains high.

Although the issue of the degree of homonymy is a controversial one, the presence of some homonymy supports the proposal that the recoverability principle is not fully available to the child's phonology. Only when the recoverability principle comes on line, is the child made aware of the violations in his or her grammar and the need to restructure it to conform with the principle. In other words, the child should dispense with homonymy and begin to use epenthesis to simplify the hard-to-pronounce complex syllables.

But as we have seen, vowel epenthesis is quite rare in young children. This is because the recoverability principle becomes accessible at the same time that the child develops the phonotactic ability to produce complex syllables (like CVC, CVCC, and CCVC). Because the development of the recoverability principle and phonotactic ability are coetaneous in normal children, epenthesis never has the opportunity to surface in the normal child. Instead, the child progresses from a stage of syllable simplification where deletion is used to a stage where no syllable simplification is required. The epenthesis stage typically is passed over (see Figure 13–1).

The reason epenthesis occurs in adult L2 acquisition is the fact that the recoverability principle is accessible while the learner concurrently possesses a low level of phonetic accuracy in the second language. This suggests that phonetic ability and the knowledge of the recoverability principle can develop differentially (see Figure 13–2).


## RECOVERABILITY IN EXCEPTIONAL LANGUAGE

I want to stress that this simultaneous maturation of the recoverability principle and phonotactic skill applies only to normal child L1 learners. If the recoverability principle and phonotactic skill are independent components of a grammar, logically it is possible to have cases where phonotactic skill lags behind recoverability.

Indeed, we can obtain the following logical possibilities, shown below in (20):

(20)  The Independence of Recoverability and Phonotactic Skill

| **Recoverability** | | **Phonotactic skill** |
|---|---|---|
| a. | yes | yes |
| b. | no | yes |
| c. | yes | no |
| d. | no | no |

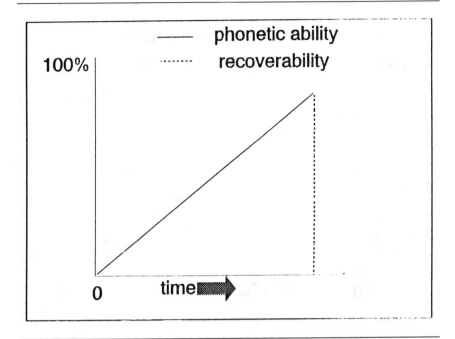

**Figure 13–1.** Child Language: Phonetic knowledge versus recoverability.

The result of (a) is normal adult speech. The result of (b) is unattested. The result of (c) is epenthesis, and the result of (d) is deletion. Certain types of exceptional language evidence can be adduced in support of this possibility.

## PRECOCIOUS LANGUAGE

One example comes from precocious language learners—early talkers who surpass other children of their age in lexicon size, mean length of utterance (MLU), and size of phonetic inventory. It is clear that in many respects these early talkers are linguistically advanced language learners. Stoel-Gammon and Dale (1988) tested 12 of these early talkers at 20 months of age. One of the things their data show is an exceedingly high rate of final vowel epenthesis. Of the 12 subjects, 6 exhibited epenthesis at a mean rate of 30%. We can explain this inordinate use of epenthesis from a differential developmental perspective. Although these children are considered to be linguistically advanced, it is unreasonable to presume that these 20-month-old early talkers have mastered the production of all English syllable types, especially closed syllables.

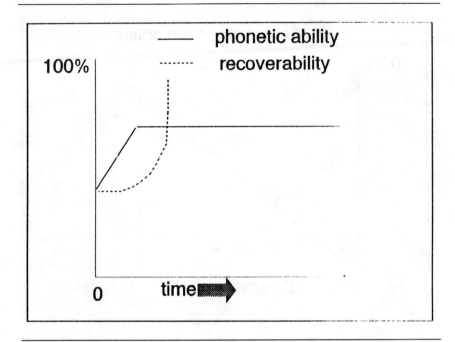

**Figure 13–2.** Adult Second Language: Phonetic knowledge versus Recoverability.

Therefore, phonotactically at least, they may be at roughly the same level as normal children. Indeed, they have not even attained full adult consonant inventories. But because these early talkers are linguistically advanced, we can hypothesize that their grammars require a high level of Recoverability. Accordingly, these children will employ a relatively high degree of vowel epenthesis to simplify syllable structure. For these precocious children then, adult levels of phonotactic skills and recoverability are not attained at the same point in time as in normal children. Rather, the recoverability principle is accessible in precocious talkers well before an adult level of phonetic ability is reached.

## DISORDERED SPEECH

I noted above that normal children simultaneously develop phonotactic skills and the recoverability principle (see Figure 13–1). For precocious talkers, however, the recoverability principle is prematurely available. A theory of the independence of recoverability logically should predict the existence of a population of speakers who contrast with these precocious speakers precisely with respect to the availability of recoverability. That is, we should find child speakers whose grammars demonstrate a protracted absence of the principle of recoverability. There is, of course, such a population. It is the set of child speakers whose speech is identified as functionally inadequate (Leinonen, 1991). These are the children who typically continue to neutralize contrasts in their phonological systems with familiar processes such as consonant deletion, fronting, devoicing, and stopping. According to Leinonen's (1991) calculations for word-final environments, the process of consonant deletion leads to the most severe functional loss. This is because final consonant deletion potentially results in the highest number of homophonous pairs of words in English. Without access to the principle of recoverability, these children are not alerted that their grammar is violating this functional constraint. If they were so internally informed, and if they continued to lack the phonotactic skills necessary for producing closed syllables, then we would expect them to use vowel epenthesis to maintain open syllable structures. This is, of course, the situation that obtains in the precocious population.

Unlike the precocious talkers (who have access to the principle of recoverability but no phonotactic skill), children whose speech is functionally inadequate have not one but two obstacles to surmount: They must somehow develop a functional knowledge (recoverability), and they must acquire adult-like phonotactic abilities.

## APHASIC SPEECH

Syllable simplification in aphasia also can be examined within this knowledge-differential framework. It is not uncommon for victims of aphasia to experience production difficulties with complex syllable structure. Many studies of the phonological systems of pathological speech have reported that patients often simplify final consonants and consonant clusters and, moreover, that these speakers simplify clusters more than single consonants (Blumstein, 1973; Trost & Canter, 1974). Because aphasia can affect different levels of speech processing, we can assume that the linguistic component responsible for recoverability and the phonetic component responsible for syllable structure can be impaired independently. We then can hypothesize that speakers whose aphasia affects only the phonotactic component and leaves the recoverability component intact will use vowel epenthesis for syllable simplification.

Indeed, we do find pathologies where epenthesis is the preferred syllable simplification strategy. Johns and Darley (1970) found that patients suffering from apraxia of speech (an impairment of phonological programming) or dysarthria (a phonetic implementation impairment) used epenthesis at a rate of 18%. They used deletion less than 1% of the time. Béland (1990) also reported that his French aphasic subjects used a significant amount of epenthesis during word repetition and word reading tasks.[6]

By similar reasoning, this modular impairment hypothesis would also predict that both the phonetic and the recoverability components could be affected at the same time. We should then find cases where aphasic subjects use an inordinate amount of consonant deletion and very little epenthesis. This is exactly what Valdois (1990) found in her study of French aphasics.

The fact that Béland (1990) and Valdois (1990) both used French speaking patients and comparable elicitation tasks makes it difficult to explain why one group favored epenthesis and the other preferred deletion. I suggest that the differences are due to the type of aphasia. Béland's subjects included 7 Broca, 10 Wernicke, 6 mixed, and 6 conduction aphasics. Valdois' group consisted of 3 Broca, 2 Wernicke, 3 conduction, and 1 anarthric. Even though both studies apparently included a range of aphasia types, the labels may be misleading due to severity of injury, time of recovery, and so on. Neurolinguists are constantly searching for more precise methods of diagnosis.

If the hypothesis that recoverability and phonotactic ability are independent components of a grammar is correct, then evidence of the differential use of epenthesis and deletion can serve as a useful diagnostic for aphasiology.

## VARIATION IN ADULT SECOND LANGUAGE

Because a predominance of epenthesis would presume that an adult language learner was obeying the recoverability principle, and because this principle is subsumed under a theory of universal grammar, we are led to the conclusion that universal grammar is indeed available, although perhaps to a limited extent, to adult phonological development.

The available data, however, suggest that there is significant variation in the use of deletion and epenthesis by adult L2 learners, even when the subjects tested are all from the same native language background and where there are no analogous native language rules of vowel epenthesis or consonant deletion. For example, Eckman (1981) reported that his Mandarin Chinese subjects employed epenthesis only when they simplified English syllable structure, whereas the Mandarin Chinese subjects tested by Heyer (1986) and Weinberger (1987) used both epenthesis and deletion when simplifying English syllables. The percentages are given in (21):

---

[6] Béland noted that his normal subjects used epenthesis strategies as well, but to a much smaller degree.

(21)  Mandarin Chinese Syllable Simplification

| Student Level | Epenthesis | Deletion | |
|---------------|-----------|----------|------------------|
| Advanced      | 100%      | 0%       | (Eckman, 1981)   |
|               | 71%       | 29%      | (Heyer, 1986)    |
| Intermediate  | 50%       | 50%      | (Weinberger, 1987) |

It has been shown that the testing situation plays a major role in determining the syllable simplification strategy (Edge, 1991; Weinberger, 1987). Context-free tasks (e.g., word list reading) elicit less deletion, whereas context-rich tasks (e.g., paragraph reading) lead to more deletion. This is predicted within the recoverability framework because ambiguity is automatically constrained in context-rich tasks. All of the data reported in (21) were obtained using both context-free and context-rich tests, and the gross second language proficiency levels of the subjects were indicated. I propose that L2 proficiency is related to the epenthesis-deletion differential. Given that phonetic ability (i.e., the skill to pronounce complex syllable structure) does not develop significantly after puberty, adult L2 learners with a more developed knowledge of the target language lexicon will more fully operationalize the recoverability principle. That is, once the adult language learner is aware that ambiguity is a real possibility, he or she should utilize epenthesis significantly more often than deletion. Therefore, all things being equal, advanced learners typically should show a greater degree of epenthesis than nonadvanced learners (see Figure 13–2). This proposal follows from the claim that adult second language phonetic ability is independent of the develop-. ment and triggering of the recoverability principle.

## CONCLUSION

By identifying two distinct types of linguistic knowledge, I have shown that the differences between first and second language phonological processes can be adequately accounted for. The apparent differences in the role that epenthesis plays in first and second language phonology can be explained with the grammatical principle of recoverability. Along with other types of exceptional language data, L2 data provide a way to see through the problem of the apparent lack of epenthesis in the L1 data caused by the coincidence that recoverability and phonotactic ability are simultaneously achieved in the child's phonological development.

It is also implied here that exceptional language phenomena like precocious child speech and some aphasic language are related to proficient L2 language. All three are hypothesized to possess an enhanced functional knowledge, but low phonotactic skill. By contrast, early nonproficient L2 language seems to share a pattern with the disordered speech of children who lack both functional and phonotactic knowledge.

The prevalence of epenthesis in L2 phonological acquisition suggests that a subset of universal grammar is available to second language learners insofar as they have access to the principle of recoverability.

Essentially, what I have shown here is that L2 phonological data can make a valuable contribution to both understanding L1 acquisition and refining and confirming some important constructs of linguistic theory.

# REFERENCES

Béland, R. (1990). Vowel epenthesis in aphasia. In J.-L. Nespoulous & P. Villiard (Eds.), *Morphology, phonology, and aphasia* (pp. 235–252). New York: Springer-Verlag.

Bever, T. (1981). Normal acquisition processes explain the critical period for language learning. In K. C. Diller (Ed.), *Individual differences and universals in language learning aptitude* (pp. 176–198). Rowley, MA: Newbury House.

Blumstein, S. (1973). *A phonological investigation of aphasic speech.* The Hague: Mouton.

Borer, H., & Wexler, K. (1987). The maturation of syntax. In T. Roeper & E. Williams (Eds.), *Parameter setting* (pp. 123–172). Dordecht: Reidel.

Branigan, G. (1976). Syllabic structure and the acquisition of consonants: The great conspiracy in word formation. *Journal of Psycholinguistic Research, 5*, 117–133.

Broselow, E., & Finer, D. (1991). Parameter setting in second language phonology and syntax. *Second Language Research, 7*, 35–59.

Campbell, J. (1982). *Grammatical man.* New York: Simon & Schuster.

Cutler, A. (1987). Speaking for listening. In A. Allport, D. MacKay, W. Prinz, & E. Scheerer (Eds.), *Language perception and production* (pp. 23–40). New York: Academic Press.

Eckman, F. (1981). On the naturalness of interlanguage phonological rules. *Language Learning, 31*, 195–216.

Edge, B. (1991). The production of word-final voiced obstruents in English by speakers of Japanese and Cantonese. *Studies in Second Language Acquisition, 13*, 377–393.

Fee, J., & Ingram, D. (1982). Reduplication as a strategy of phonological development. *Journal of Child Language, 9*, 41–54.

Felix, S. (1984). Maturational aspects of universal grammar. In A. Davies, C. Criper, & A. Howatt (Eds.), *Interlanguage* (pp. 133–161). Edinburgh: Edinburgh University Press.

Gass, S. & Ard, J. (1980). L2 data: Their relevance for language universals. *TESOL Quarterly, 14*, 443–452.

Grunwell, P. (1987). *Clinical phonology.* Baltimore: Williams & Wilkins.

Gussman, E. (1976). Recoverable derivations and phonological change. *Lingua, 40*, 281–303.

Halle, M. (1979). Formal and functional considerations in phonology. In B. Brogyanyi (Ed.), *Current issues in linguistic theory* (pp. 325–341). Amsterdam: John Benjamins.

Hankamer, J. (1973). Unacceptable ambiguity. *Linguistic Inquiry, 4*, 17–68.

Heyer, S. (1986). *English final consonants and the Chinese learner.* Master's thesis, Southern Illinois University, Carbondale.

Ingram, D. (1975). Surface contrast in children's speech. *Journal of Child Language, 2,* 287–292.

Ingram, D. (1976). *Phonological disability in children.* London: Edward Arnold.

Ingram, D. (1985). On children's homonyms. *Journal of Child Language, 12,* 671–680.

Johns, D., & Darley, F. (1970). Phonemic variability in apraxia of speech. *Journal of Speech and Hearing Research, 13,* 556–583.

Kaye, J. (1974). Opacity and recoverability in phonology. *The Canadian Journal of Linguistics, 19,* 134–149.

Kaye, J. (1981). Recoverability, abstractness, and phonotactic constraints. In D. L. Goyvaerts (Ed.), *Phonology in the 1980's* (pp. 469–481). Ghent: Story-Scientia.

Kaye, J. (1989). *Phonology: A cognitive view.* Hillsdale, NJ: Lawrence Erlbaum.

Keenan, E., & Comrie, B. (1977). Noun phrase accessibility and universal grammar. *Linguistic Inquiry, 8,* 63–99.

Kenstowicz, M. (1981). Functional explanations in generative phonology. In D. L. Goyvaerts (Ed.), *Phonology in the 1980's* (pp. 431–444). Ghent: Story Scientia.

Kim, C. (1972). Two phonological notes: A-sharp and B-flat. In M. Brame (Ed.), *Contributions to generative phonology* (pp. 155–170). Austin: University of Texas Press.

Kiparsky, P., & Menn, L. (1977). On the acquisition of phonology. In J. MacNamara (Ed.), *Language learning and thought* (pp. 47–78). New York: Academic Press.

Kornfeld, J. (1971). Theoretical issues in child phonology. *Papers from the Seventh Regional Meeting, Chicago Linguistics Society* (pp. 454–468). Chicago: Chicago Linguistics Society.

Leinonen, E. (1991). Functional considerations in phonological assessment of child speech. In M. Yavas (Ed.), *Phonological disorders in children* (pp. 121–141). London: Routledge.

Lenneberg, E. (1967). *Biological foundations of language.* New York: John Wiley.

Macken, M., & Ferguson, C. (1983). Cognitive aspects of phonological development: Model, evidence, and issues. In K. Nelson (Ed.), *Children's language* (Vol. 4, pp. 255–282). Hillsdale, NJ: Lawrence Erlbaum.

Moskowitz, A. (1970). The two-year-old stage in the acquisition of English phonology. *Language, 46,* 426–441.

Olmsted, D. (1971). *Out of the mouth of babes.* The Hague: Mouton.

Priestly, T. (1980). Homonymy in child phonology. *Journal of Child Language, 7,* 413–427.

Ross, A. (1937). An example of vowel-harmony in a young child. *Modern Language Notes, 52,* 508–509.

Schachter, J. (1988). Second language acquisition and its relationship to universal grammar. *Applied Linguistics, 9,* 219–235.

Schwartz, R., Leonard, L., Wilcox, M, & Folger, M. (1980). Again and again: Reduplication in child phonology. *Journal of Child Language, 7,* 75–87.

Scovel, T. (1988). *A time to speak.* New York: Newbury House.

Smith, N. (1973). *The acquisition of phonology.* Cambridge: Cambridge University Press.

Stoel-Gammon, C., & Dale, P. (1988). *Aspects of phonological development of linguistically precocious children.* Paper presented at the Midwest Child Phonology Conference, Champaign, IL.

Stoel-Gammon, C., & Dunn, C. (1985). *Normal and disordered phonology in children.* Baltimore: University Park Press.

Tarone, E. (1980). Some influences on the syllable structure of interlanguage phonology. *IRAL, 18,* 139–152.

Tervoort, B. (1969). Developmental word-homonymy in beginning child-language. *Lingua, 23,* 233–240.

Trost, J., & Canter, G. (1974). Apraxia of speech in patients with Broca's aphasia: A study of phoneme production accuracy and error patterns. *Brain and Language, 1,* 63–79.

Valdois, S. (1990). Internal structure of two consonant clusters. In J.-L. Nespoulous & P. Villiard (Eds.), *Morphology, phonology, and aphasia* (pp. 253–269). New York: Springer-Verlag.

Vihman, M. (1980). Sound change and child language. In E. Traugott, R. Labrum, & S. Shepherd (Eds.), *Papers from the Fourth International Conference on Historical Linguistics* (pp. 303–320). Amsterdam: John Benjamins.

Vihman, M. (1981). Phonology and the development of the lexicon: Evidence from children's errors. *Journal of Child Language, 8,* 239–264.

Weinberger, S. (1987). The influence of linguistic context on syllable simplification. In G. Ioup & S. Weinberger (Eds.), *Interlanguage phonology* (pp. 401–417). Rowley, MA: Newbury House.

Weismer, G., Dinnsen, D., & Elbert, M. (1981). A study of the voicing distinction associated with omitted word-final stops. *Journal of Speech and Hearing Disorders, 46,* 320–328.

White, L. (1989). *Universal grammar and second language acquisition.* Amsterdam: John Benjamins.

# Index